The World-Famous
ALASKA HIGHWAY

A Guide to the Alcan & Other
Wilderness Roads of the North
2nd Edition

Tricia Brown

Alaska Northwest Books®
Anchorage • Portland

*F*or Jennifer, the homesick Alaskan

Text and photographs © 2005 Tricia Brown

The World-Famous Alaska Highway provides many safety tips about weather and travel, but good decision making and sound judgment are the responsibility of the individual. Neither the publisher nor the author assumes any liability for injury that may arise from the use of this book.

Second printing 2006

Library of Congress Cataloging-in-Publication Data
Brown, Tricia.
  The world-famous Alaska Highway : a guide to the Alcan & other wilderness roads of the north / Tricia Brown.— 2nd ed.
     p. cm.
  Includes bibliographical references and index.
  ISBN 0-88240-602-7 (softbound)
 1. Alaska Highway—Guidebooks. 2. Automobile travel—Northwest, Canadian—Guidebooks.
3. Automobile travel—Alaska Highway—Guidebooks. 4. Wilderness areas—Northwest, Canadian—Guidebooks. 5. Wilderness areas—Alaska—Guidebooks. 6. Northwest, Canadian—Guidebooks.
7. Alaska—Guidebooks. I. Title.
  F1060.92.B79 2005
  917.9804'52—dc22   2004025353

Cover image: Along the Canadian Rockies, stone sheep often come near the road for natural mineral licks.

Alaska Northwest Books®
An imprint of Graphic Arts Center Publishing Co.
P.O. Box 10306
Portland, OR 97296-0306
503-226-2402 • www.gacpc.com

President: Charles M. Hopkins
General Manager: Douglas A. Pfeiffer
Associate Publisher, Alaska Northwest Books®: Sara Juday
Editorial Staff: Timothy W. Frew, Kathy Howard, Jean Bond-Slaughter
Editor: Don Graydon
Production Staff: Richard L. Owsiany, Susan Dupere
Cover Design: Elizabeth Watson
Interior Design: Michelle Taverniti; Jean Andrews

Acknowledgments

*T*hank you, Perry, who always pulls over without waiting for a please. Special thanks to Bob Calderone and the rest of the folks at Cruise America, who helped make our travels exceptionally comfortable, and thank you, Marlene Blessing, for inviting me to hit the road again. To all the counter people at all of the visitor centers throughout the Northland, the museum volunteers, the friendly clerks in gift shops, the coach drivers, the railroad dining car servers, the concierge staff, the tour reservation operators—you do a great service to your state or province. Your love for the place you live is contagious. Continue to share it with enthusiasm, knowing that for most people, this is a one-and-only trip of a lifetime.

Unimproved portions of the Alaska Highway are becoming more rare, but do expect construction.

Crossing into Alaska usually involves a stop for picture taking at this magnificent sign.

The lure of gold brought thousands of stampeders to the Northland in the late 1800s.

A longtime Yukon wood-carver, "Scully" Gordon uses burl wood to create distinctive sculptures, bowls, benches, you-name-it. The burls are the result of fungus in the wood.

Contents

Introduction: The Road to Hell? 9

1 Getting Ready 12

2 What You Need to Know, A to Z 23

3 History of the Alcan: The Soldiers' Road 38

4 The Eastern Route: Through Alberta to Dawson Creek, B.C., and Mile 0 43

5 The Western Route: Through British Columbia to Dawson Creek, B.C., and Mile 0 87

6 The Alaska Highway 119

7 Western Canada's Northbound Byways 169

8 Alaska's State Highways 183

9 Alaska Marine Highway System 269

Further Reading 271

Alaska Highway Distance Charts 273

Index 275

About the Author 288

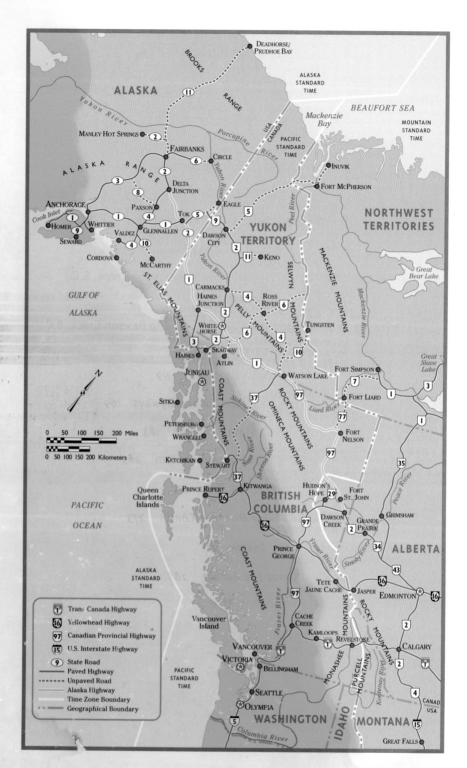

The Road to Hell?

*Winding in
and winding out
fills my mind
with serious doubt,
as to whether the lout
who planned this route,
was going to hell
or coming out.*

Along the Alaska Highway, you may see those frank words on paper place mats, wall hangings, bumper stickers, and T-shirts. Another favorite is, "I Drove the Alcan . . . and Survived!" The messages echo from earlier days of driving North America's best-known wilderness road. Labeled the Alcan during its construction through Canada and Alaska's backcountry, the Alaska Highway began as a World War II supply line from the continental United States to its far-off territory. At war's end,

after the road opened to the public, the civilian world learned what the military already knew: This two-lane gravel road was a beast, known for its twists, miry stretches, and burdensome length, and yet it wound through extraordinary scenery that dared you to take your eyes off the road.

After decades of improvements, the route has matured into a destination unto itself, and those who travel its length never forget the journey.

The "before" shot of our home-made trailer, back in 1978.

Yet another stop for more repair work. With all that mud, it was hard to tell there was a trailer under there. We slept in the back of the Blazer.

Now past its 60th birthday, the Alaska Highway has been surveyed, straightened, graded, rerouted, paved, and populated in places, but it remains a wild thing that's only somewhat tamed. This route through some of the most uncivilized parts of the continent still embodies the romance and challenge that adventure travelers seek. For some, it's not the getting to Alaska that matters anymore—although Alaska is a lifetime dream for many—it's having done the road. That's why the souvenirs sell so well—just driving the highway places you in the "I did it!" club.

Going to hell or coming out? Looking back more than 25 years, I remember asking myself that question. On my first trip up the Alaska Highway, most of the road was unpaved, dangerously gooey in the rain and dust-choked in the sun. More miles were crooked than straight, and washboard had developed on nearly every turn. A person could get seasick hundreds of miles from the ocean. I remember dark thoughts drumming through my head one day as I kicked 3 inches of muck off our bumper while my then-husband shinnied under the trailer to see about a broken axle. Our two toddlers were crying, their play having turned to fight. We had stopped asking ourselves if we were doing the right thing, and were on a tight-lipped march to our finish line in Fairbanks.

A new life in the Last Frontier awaited there, 4,000 miles from our home in northern Illinois. Modern pioneers in a 1978 Chevrolet Blazer, we towed a little trailer intended for snowmobiles, not the hulking plywood box that carried all of our worldly goods. I had painted a colorful emancipation proclamation on the side: "Alaskabound." It looked like a clown car. The trailer generated lots of goodwill, waves, and blessings. But somehow Alaskabound didn't look so jaunty when it was propped up at a weird angle along the road. Turns out the thing was so weighty that tire blowouts were a daily occurrence. We stocked up on spares in every town we came across, knowing we'd be changing tires as often as we changed our socks. Our total came to 12 flats. A broken trailer tongue and the busted axle topped off the tally, and repairs slowed us by days. We crept along with help from good people along the way and discovered the meaning of northern hospitality. Meanwhile, we solemnly drank in mountainscapes that we flatlanders had seen only in books and movies. Did we know what we were getting into when we left? No. We were young and blessed with excessive hope.

During two decades in Alaska, I drove every highway on its limited state road system. I've picnicked above the Arctic Circle, trundled down the sole road into Denali National Park, and retraced the pioneering route of the Valdez-to-Fairbanks Trail, now the Richardson Highway. In one 10-year span, I put nearly 200,000 miles on my vehicle—all of them Alaska miles. But I never drove the Alaska Highway again. Oh, friends and relatives made the trip up without incident, arriving with glowing reports of moose and bear sightings, serene lakeside campgrounds, and awesome scenery. "The road's great!" they proclaimed. "It's almost completely paved now. You wouldn't recognize it." But I had vowed long ago, like a fist-shaking Scarlett O'Hara of the North: As God is my witness, I shall never drive that road again!

I laughed when I was asked to write this book, then found myself breaking my own promise. But I had to do it, to see for myself what the Alaska Highway has become. Maybe it's the same urge for that firsthand experience that has you captivated, too, and you feel you must go. With the assistance of some great folks at Cruise America, my husband and I loaded our things into one of their Tioga motor homes, and we headed out, learning as much about land cruising as we did about the people and places along the highway. In two subsequent update trips, traveling with and without pets, we enlarged our experiences and watched the road further evolve into the remarkably safe and comfortable route that it is today.

In this book, I'll introduce you to roadside history, geography, Native cultures, and recreational opportunities in Alberta, British Columbia, the Yukon, and Alaska, covering miles well beyond the Alaska Highway itself. I've included details about attractions, restaurants, hotels, and campgrounds. You'll also meet some of the colorful characters who make the northland so memorable, and get tips from road warriors we met along the way. I hope this guide enhances your travels. We had a ball, and you will, too.

Remember this, though: The Alcan, with all of its history, romance, and wonder, is not just about driving. It's a passageway to places you've only dreamed about: the stomping grounds of the gold rush stampeders and pioneers. Land that's steeped in centuries of Native culture. Crystalline streams, jade-colored lakes, wild animals, snowy mountain peaks, and spruce forests. You'll meet new friends who are on the same journey, and those who live along the way. The beauty will linger in your mind well beyond the boundaries of your trip, indelible pictures that you'll carry yet lack words to express. You, too, will find that until you've experienced the Alaska Highway for yourself, it's kind of hard to explain it. Welcome to the club.

Chapter 1

Getting Ready

*P*LANNING FOR MONTHS, traveling for weeks, remembering for a lifetime. Those are the pleasures of a road trip to the Far North. On the road to Alaska, you'll wend through farms and prairies and vast acres of pristine forest; you'll climb the Canadian Rockies and breach the continental divide. You will head for the Yukon, a place-name that still rings with the promise of gold, as it did a century ago during the Klondike gold rush. And you'll view the famous Yukon River, so broad and unspoiled. The road leads farther north, into Alaska, where you'll explore a state highway system that measured to scale against this landscape, is nothing more than a dozen pieces of thread thrown against a fabulous, multicolored king-size quilt.

How to prepare for such an unparalleled adventure? Any experienced traveler knows the importance of researching a place before embarking on a trip. Next in line is packing smart. Not too much, not too little. This chapter outlines in detail how to get ready for weeks on the road.

Your Travel Timeline

Time is the issue that separates the two types of highway travelers: those who just want to get to a place, and those who know that the journey can be as enjoyable as the destination. The first and best rule of thumb is: Take your time. This is not a race. Stop for ice cream. Read the historical signs. Try not to think about making good time. Most of all, be mindful that posted speed limits are not suggestions but law.

The laws of physics aren't flexible either. Some Alaskans (mostly male, for some reason) claim special bragging rights to having made their personal best time in covering the Alaska Highway. "Why, we went from Seattle to Fairbanks in 72 hours. 'Course, we never stopped. We traded off on driving." This is no great achievement, but rather an expression of recklessness, not only for themselves and their passengers, but also for others on the road. The Alaska Highway as yet is no superhighway.

What to Pack

The old joke you've probably heard in your own hometown is true here as well: If you don't like this weather, just wait a few minutes. That's particularly true in the northland during the summer months. So be ready with a little of everything, and if it turns chilly, put it all on!

Whether you travel by motor home or motorcycle, a successful trip requires careful planning.

The length of the Alaska Highway crosses several climate zones through Canada, with microclimates within them. In Alaska, it's no different. It can be 55°F at Mount McKinley while it's 80°F in Fairbanks, just 2 hours away.

Beauty salons or barbershops are easy to find in most towns. Make an appointment, or walk in. Usually it's not a problem. Pharmacies likewise are not difficult to find.

The benefits of the midnight sun are many, including the growth of unnaturally large cabbages and squash, and excessive energy in human beings. But for those who have trouble getting to sleep in the daylight, bring along a sleep mask.

Following is a packing checklist to help you get started. You decide how many of each item to bring, remembering that there will be no shortage of self-service laundries, so less is better.

Clothing

Underwear
Short-sleeved shirt
Long-sleeved shirt
Lightweight pants or shorts
Pants for chilly weather
Hooded sweatshirt or sweater
Windbreaker
Raincoat
Bathing suit
Towel
Jacket with zip-in lining for extra
   warmth
Comfortable walking shoes
   (soft soles for grip in slippery places)
Dress clothes (just in case)
Dress shoes
Socks and stockings
Slippers
Lightweight gloves
Knit hat or baseball cap

Other Items

Sunglasses
Toiletries
Hair dryer
Curling iron
Prescription drugs and refill
   prescriptions
Mosquito repellent
Identification
Emergency medical information
Contact numbers
First-aid kit
Plastic grocery bag
Zip-closure plastic bags
Film, tapes, and batteries for
   your cameras
One or two bottles of water
Your pet's health certificate
   (for border crossings)
Cash
Bank card/ATM card

What Not to Bring

Although I'm suggesting one set of "nice" clothes might be a good idea—in the "just in case" department, leave your fanciest clothes and jewelry at home. Alaska and the Canadian north are places where informality reigns. Although you can dress up for a night on the town if you like, at any given event or restaurant you'll find people in all kinds of clothes, from cocktail dresses to jeans. Men, pack a jacket and tie if you plan to dine at a four-star restaurant in Calgary, Edmonton, or Anchorage. Ladies, a simple dress will do.

Don't bring guns. Unless you're headed into the backcountry on your own, you won't need one, and unless you know how to use it, you're probably more dangerous to yourself than that charging grizzly bear is. Hire a guide to take you backcountry hiking or fishing; he or she will likely carry a protective weapon. Canada is explicit and firm about the transport of firearms across its borders (see the section on Guns/Ammo in Chapter 2, "What You Need to Know, A to Z").

Don't bring extra luggage for bulky or weighty souvenirs. You can have anything shipped home, from a chainsaw carving of a brown bear to a new parka, a hunk of jade, a piece of etched baleen, even your children's book collection—one for every child and grandchild in the family! Don't weigh yourself down. Insure the expensive stuff and ship it. I vote for mailing home all the paper you pick up at visitor centers, too—brochures, travel magazines, postcards, note cards, everything. It's so much better to travel light.

Preparing Your Vehicle

Make sure your vehicle is at its best before you leave home. If you're not mechanically oriented, take it to your mechanic for a once-over, or use this checklist to ensure that you don't overlook any of the automotive essentials:

Tires in good condition	Belts/seals/hoses
Spare tire, fully inflated	Brakes/bearings
Jack, and knowledge of how to use it	Exhaust system
Tune-up	Windshield wipers
Oil change	Air-conditioning (yes, it may be needed)
Fluids	Radiator

Also, carry the following emergency equipment:

First-aid kit	Pencil and paper
Tow cable	Bottles of drinking water
Toolbox	Paper towels
Road flares/reflectors	Nylon rope
Flashlight and fresh batteries	Squeegee (for muddy windows)
Jumper cable	Spare headlight
Matches in a sealed container, like a	Gas can
film canister	Cell phone (even though it may not
Candles	work in some remote regions)

If you're a U.S. resident, check with your insurance company about claims from within Canada and what will be provided for you in case you need assistance. Read

Milton and Dee Roberts of Connecticut met Californians Dave and Evelyn Singleton in the Dawson Creek visitor center parking lot. Dave had asked Milton about his grill protector. The answer: he'd customized it from one of those screens you use to keep the dog in the back of the car.

your policy and understand it well, then ride on that security. Don't worry. Accidents are not commonplace. If you're a member of an auto club, familiarize yourself with their procedures in case of an emergency. Keep your membership number handy.

Windshields are sometimes nicked or chipped by flying gravel. If you're concerned about your windshield, headlights, or paint job, consider attaching a screen to your vehicle's front end for extra protection.

There was a day when long-distance travelers carried many gallons of extra gas. That's really not necessary anymore, unless you're on Alaska's Dalton Highway or one of Canada's more remote unpaved roads that have not yet developed routine road-side services. Throughout the length of the Alcan and along most of Alaska's state highways, you'll find gas stations at regular intervals. An informal rule of thumb: Never let the tank get below the halfway mark. Top it off before you leave a community.

Traveling by RV

Like many people who drive the Alaska Highway, my uncle and aunt, Gerald and Lillian Stinson, bought a camper upon retirement and set out for their new life as Alaskan snowbirds. They leave Alaska and head south to Michigan about the time that the folks in Michigan are pointing toward Arizona. Christmas is spent in Florida, then it's back to the Midwest for spring, then on to Alaska for the summer. I guess they've driven the Alaska Highway 30 times or more. (Actually, they should be writing this book, not me.) They're so accustomed to preparing for travel that they can pack up their camper and be ready for the road in a matter of hours, without making notes. They have a system, and it works. It's figuring out the system that can be painful.

Everyone who has ever spent a weekend or more in an RV knows the practice of living in a moving motel has its pluses and minuses. It's wonderful to have everything in its place, to unpack only one time, to fix a meal when you're hungry, and to slip between familiar sheets at night. But other matters must be considered, such as: Who is driving and who is navigating? Can he/she be trusted with the task? Did you remember to put the stairs up? Could you at least get your feet out of the way when I'm carrying a hot dish? Like naughty children thrown together in a room to have it out and then get along, traveling companions usually work these things out, and comfortable patterns emerge.

If you're already a regular RV traveler, you'll have shortcuts and camping methods of your own, and likely have traded ideas with others in campgrounds across the country. That's another great thing about RV travel—making new friends and comparing notes about travel experiences and opportunities.

We learned that some people lighten their load by keeping the freshwater tank empty. They bring bottled water for cooking and drinking, and hook up only occasionally for dishwashing and showers (or use the shower house). Others believe that carrying the extra weight is less of a problem than finding a campsite with full hookups.

RV campgrounds with full hookups are not always available, so empty your gray water and sewer tanks every day or two, and keep the fresh water topped off in case you decide to switch to the generator and take hot showers. Often, just electricity is available. Hot showers are commonly available at campgrounds that don't offer full hookups. Pull-throughs, those campsites that allow RVers to pull in at one end and go out the other, may be at a premium late in the day, so consider settling in before dinner.

"Dry camping" is a common option, and not a bad one if there's a shortage of space. That can be the case in June, July, and early August. The more spontaneous types don't mind driving into the unknown of "where shall we stay tonight?" Others prefer a smartly choreographed itinerary with reservations in place, from one end of the country to the other, before leaving home. That doesn't leave much room for the winds of chance, but offers a lot of security. You'll find lists of campgrounds, some of which accept reservations, in the chapters that follow. And don't forget that, even in Alaska, superstores like Wal-Mart have an open-parking-lot policy for wandering folks like you. This is not recommended for the best camping experience, but it sure works for a middle-of-the-night, sleepy-driver situation—not to mention that you can stock up before you head out again.

Own or Rent? Packing the RV is dependent upon your travel timeline and on whether you own the RV or are renting. Owners normally keep a second set of everything in their campers, road-trip ready. RV renters can arrange one-way or round-trip packages. Everything you need for the kitchen is available for an extra fee.

One-way travelers can bring along the basics with an eye toward shipping it all back home or throwing it in an extra suitcase for the homeward flight.

My husband, Perry, and I chose a rental RV with Cruise America, a company with offices all over the United States and Canada. Painted in its distinctive colors and logo, our vehicle was a rolling billboard for the company's 800 number, and we waved whenever we saw others like us on the road. Check the Yellow Pages for your choice of company, or look in your local newspaper's classified section for private owners who will rent their recreational vehicles. It's extremely important to pay close attention or even take notes when the RV company representative or owner is explaining how everything works.

Recommended packing for the extra-light traveler: For each person, bring one dish, one cup, one glass, one bowl, one set of silverware, two bath towels, a washcloth, and a hand towel. Linens should include one set of sheets, two blankets and pillows, and two dishtowels and dishcloths. For the kitchen, find a small screw-top container for dish soap rather than bringing the full-size bottle. Buy disposable salt-and-pepper containers and pack minimal other spices. Bring two sizes of cooking pots and lids, one pan and lid, spatula, large plastic spoon, slotted spoon, ladle, and manual can opener. Bring along a broom and, if you can, a small, electric-powered Dirt Devil (especially good for dog fur on upholstery). I threw in a sample-size piece of left-over carpet as a doormat—you really do need one, so buy one if you have to. Buy chemicals for the toilet; bring soap, shampoo, and other basic toiletries.

We decided to premeasure laundry soap into plastic bags so we wouldn't have to deal with a big carton. I also preground my coffee beans and left my coffeepot at home, figuring that I'd just pour hot water through a one-cup filter holder (which I then forgot). I improvised by cutting holes in the bottom of a plastic margarine container, and felt immensely clever.

It really did feel like playing in a dollhouse. Within a day or two, it was easy to make a meal, wash the dishes, sweep up, and be ready to roll in record time. The routine took on its own familiarity even though we were far from home.

If you're like us, at the end of each day you will be road-weary and yearning for a quiet place, so keep a wary eye out for the location of a busy road or railroad tracks before you choose a campsite. We cruised the campgrounds to check out the party sites before we picked the one farthest away. In most cases, however, people were extremely respectful of each other, and the noise level went down around 10 P.M. Parents with children likewise were understanding of those who are not accustomed to noisy play, and they made sure the kids were in tow by evening.

At the end of the day, we walked, read, and played cards, and I sewed while he studied maps and made notes. I created a travel journal and kept track of our daily mileage, too, and I urge you to use a travel journal for your own notes and remembrances. It's also a great place to write down information about the photographs you took that day. What seems indelible in your mind today will become blurred without notes, believe me.

A Kenai Peninsula fisherman tries his luck. If you don't have appropriate fishing gear, you can pick it up in Alaska, or hire a guide.

All in all, traveling by RV was extremely satisfying—it allowed the security of familiar surroundings as we entered the larger picture of a world to explore together.

Cameras

Oh, the photos that were never taken because the battery died at that moment! Or you ran out of film. Alas, it could have been a *National Geographic* cover. So be forewarned and pack plenty of film and an extra camera battery. Even if you have a rechargeable battery for your video camera, think about bringing backup. You won't always have access to power for recharging, and after all, this is your trip of a lifetime.

Driving on unpaved roads poses a dust concern, so keep your electronics in their tote bags unless you're shooting pictures.

Winter travelers need to consider the effect of static electricity on film that's rewinding. If your photos come back with white veins on the negatives, you're a victim. If you rewind by hand, go slowly. If your camera is auto rewind, consider saving that last shot for indoors, in a room with higher humidity. Here's the test: If you can scoot your feet across the carpet and shake hands without shocking somebody, you'll be all right.

A few shooting tips: First and foremost, don't harass the wildlife. That means don't creep up too close for their comfort and your safety. The best wildlife photographers choose a spot and wait for their shot. If you don't have time for that, then buy a bigger lens, or risk a ticket from an Alaska Fish and Wildlife Protection officer.

Secondly, watch for groups of vehicles that have pulled over. That's a sure sign that something big and hairy, or feathery, or furry, is near the edge of the road and

THE WORLD-FAMOUS ALASKA HIGHWAY

will be the subject of many vacation photographs. Pull off the road completely and stop your vehicle before you begin shooting. Alaskans have seen it a million times—people standing in the middle of the road with their cameras stuck to their faces and no clue that an oncoming Winnebago is about to make a significant impact on their lives.

Videographers, remember to spend a few seconds shooting pictures of identifying signs to help establish where you are. Or while you're taping, have a traveling companion read from a travel guide, brochure, or informational sign as you capture the scene. It's better than relying on memory later.

And one more tip for good measure: Don't forget the people in your trip. Shots of beautiful scenery and wildlife are important vacation remembrances, but 10 or 20 years from now, or more, it will be the photos of the people with you, and the people you meet along the way, that will cause you to ooh and aah.

Strategy for Medical Needs

The greatest disruption on a vacation is getting sick. Worse still is not having the medicine you need to feel better. So bring along the basics, and make sure your prescription medications have been filled just before you leave. Ask for a refill slip from your doctor if you expect to be gone for long.

Make a see-through zipper bag your first-aid kit. For its contents, buy travel-size containers to keep it from becoming unwieldy. Drop in your vitamins, adhesive bandages of various sizes, first-aid ointment, aspirin or other pain reliever, alcohol swabs, hydrogen peroxide, an Ace bandage, muscle ache ointment, cotton balls, a few safety pins, hand sanitizer, cold-medicine tablets, chewable tablets for indigestion, and throat lozenges, along with prescription drugs that you don't normally carry with you. You might keep your prescriptions for refills in the first-aid kit, too.

In your purse or wallet, along with your identification and insurance card, carry a written statement of any medical conditions, allergies or other health alerts, and medicines that you're currently taking. List the name and number of your family doctor and of the person to call in case of an emergency.

Driving in Winter

Winter driving is possible, and some people actually prefer it, claiming that the road is better with fewer vehicles in front of them and a good layer of compacted snow under them. But extra care must be taken to pack smart. I remember the winter my father and brother slid off the road on a lonely stretch near the Alaska-Canada border. It was −40°F. They bundled up, then Dad built a fire and climbed back up to the road to flag down help, which happily did arrive before either of them suffered frostbite. They had packed emergency gear such as extra warm clothes, sleeping bags, and matches. Even though the car was totaled, in the end they were merely banged up, but it easily could have gone another way had they not been prepared.

It's a good idea to equip your vehicle with these extras:

Studded snow tires or chains	Shovel
Ice scraper/brush	Blanket or sleeping bag
Nonperishable snack foods	Extra parka, snow pants, warm boots,
Heavy-duty extension cord	mitts
(see next paragraph)	Chemical-pack hand-warmers
Sandbag or kitty litter, for extra	CB radio (if you want an extra measure
traction should you become stuck	of security)

The farther north you drive, the colder it gets. So before you leave home, ask your mechanic to use 5-30W motor oil in your car. And have the shop install an engine-block heater or, at the least, an oil-pan heater, so the oil will not become so thick that you can't turn the engine over. With either heater under the hood, you will end up with a short, three-pronged electric cord sticking out of the grill. Buy a 15- to 20-foot heavy-duty extension cord so you can access power when you turn the car off for 2 or more hours, or when you park it for the night. Many hard-core northerners loosely loop this extension cord from their side mirrors, so it's always handy.

In the Far North, outdoor electric outlets are common; in Fairbanks or Dawson City, you'll see them at the heads of parking spaces in public lots. Ask about where to plug in when you check in at your motel. If you haven't plugged in all night, do so an hour or so before you plan to leave. Plugging in at 10°F or colder is a good idea. It means less wear and tear on your engine and less drain on your battery, not to mention a reassuring sound when the engine turns over effortlessly. And the sooner the engine heats up, the sooner you'll have warm air coming out of your interior blower.

Another trick among winter drivers of the north has to do with a quick-and-cheap addition to your front end: a large piece of corrugated cardboard. Wedge the flattened piece between your grill and radiator to prevent super-cold air from passing through the radiator. The engine will get warm and stay warm much faster, and in the end, your interior heater will be much more effective.

Remember that winter days in the north are extremely short. You'll be driving in dim light or darkness, even if you limit your driving time to daytime, so working headlights are especially important. Snowstorms can surprise you, too, so check your radio dial and ask the locals about the forecast when you stop, or request a number to call for recorded messages on road conditions.

Sharing the road with tractor-trailers can be a challenge, because they tend to kick up a blinding snow shower, so back off rather than pass them. Vision is critical, so make sure your windshield wipers are in good shape. Use common sense for safe snow driving: Bring down your speed a notch, never jam on the brakes, and as your driver's ed teacher told you, steer in the direction of the slide.

And, at the risk of nagging, we'll say it again: Take your time.

This is a no-no. Don't leave your vehicle and approach a wild animal. Not only is it stressful for the animal, it could be dangerous for both of you.

Chapter 2

What You Need to Know, A to Z

*A*LASKA-SPEAK. English is spoken in Canada and the United States, but occasionally a regional term can trip you up. Here's a quick list of words in the Alaskan vocabulary:

Outside. Anywhere not in Alaska

Cheechako. A greenhorn, a newcomer

Wanigan. Lean-to, usually in add-a-room style attached to a cabin

Carhartts. Brand of warm, durable clothing commonly worn in winter; the Alaska tuxedo

Bunny boots. Large, usually white, rubber boots with a built-in vapor barrier for extra insulation; boomed in use during construction of the trans-Alaska oil pipeline during the 1970s; still very popular

Breakup. Spring season when ice breaks up and moves out from the rivers

Termination dust. First snow that dusts the mountaintops; signals the termination of summer

Kuspuk. Brightly colored tunic dress with flounce worn by Native Alaskan women

Native Alaskan. Person of ancient heritage—Eskimo, Indian, or Aleut descent

native Alaskan. Person of any race who was born and raised in Alaska

Sourdough. An old-timer, a pioneer Alaskan

Rondy. Anchorage Fur Rendezvous, the biggest winter carnival in the country

PFD check. Portion of interest dividends and capital gains on state's oil revenues; annual payment mailed by the state to every eligible resident. In 2004, the amount was $919.84 per person.

Alaska State Troopers

Not every town on the Alaska road system has its own police force. Alaska State Troopers enforce the law along the miles and miles of highway. Dialing 911 remains the universal call for help throughout the state, and Trooper posts may be found in the following communities along the highways: Anchorage, Cantwell, Coldfoot, Cordova, Cooper Landing, Delta Junction, Fairbanks, Girdwood, Glennallen, Homer, Nenana, Ninilchik, Northway, Palmer, Seward, Soldotna, Talkeetna, Tok, and Valdez.

The Municipality of Anchorage extends from the Knik River Bridge on the Glenn Highway to the town of Girdwood on the Seward Highway, and a host of police officers patrols the highways in this vast area, with support from the Alaska State Troopers.

Other road-system cities with their own police force include Wasilla, Palmer, Valdez, Homer, Soldotna, Kenai, Seward, and Fairbanks. In the remote, off-road villages, law enforcement is handled by a VPSO, a Village Public Safety Officer. State Troopers fly into villages when a VPSO needs assistance.

Alaska Fish and Wildlife Protection officers serve in a special branch of the State Troopers. Even though they are sworn to enforce fish-and-game laws, they can and will issue traffic tickets and pursue other criminal activity.

Alaska has no counties, so there are no sheriffs or deputies.

Alcoholic Beverages

Alcohol is not sold in grocery stores in Alaska, and liquor stores will not sell to individuals younger than 21. Drinking-and-driving laws are tough, so stop for the night before you crack open that beer. Some Alaska villages are dry; some are damp. Just to be sure, don't fly into a village with alcohol in your suitcase.

U.S. citizens who are 19 or older may transport duty-free alcoholic beverages over the U.S.–Canada border in these quantities: 40 ounces (1.182 liters) of liquor or wine, or 24 containers, at 12 ounces (355 milliliters) each, of beer or ale.

Border Crossings

Citizens of the U.S. or Canada should have photo identification, proof of citizenship, and vehicle registration ready as your approach the border. While a valid passport is not necessary to pass between the United States and Canada, it serves efficiently as both ID and proof of citizenship; otherwise, a driver's license with a birth certificate or voter's registration card will work.

For visitors from the U.S. who were not born in the U.S., Canadian authorities will ask for a Certificate of Naturalization, a "Green Card," and perhaps a visa, depending on one's country of citizenship. No photocopies will be accepted.

Most crossings are fairly routine. You will be asked a dozen questions or more, and allowed to continue on your journey.

Occasionally, officials ask permission to look around inside a car or camper. Every so often, even after answering all questions honestly, a driver may be detained further as officials make a more thorough inspection of the vehicle or its contents. (Also see the following entries in this chapter: Alcoholic Beverages; Duty-free Shopping; Guns/Ammo; Pets; Plants.)

Campgrounds

Among those who love to camp, you'll find the spectrum of tastes and comfort zones. Some folks take their home with them on vacation in the form of a recreational vehicle—and their rolling accommodations include power, water, microwave, stove, refrigerator, toilet, shower, stereo, and VCR. At the other end of the scale are the tent campers, who sleep with a thin layer of waterproof material separating them from raw nature. No matter what the style, great numbers of mobile travelers have discovered the joys of camping.

As you travel throughout the north, you'll find plentiful options among campgrounds, and good signage to help direct you. In the chapters that follow, we've included directions and contact information for campgrounds along the way. Operated privately or by government agencies, campground offerings range from a simple opening in the forest with a picnic table and fire ring, to places equipped with extras such as cable, a swimming pool, golf course, horseshoe pits, playgrounds, swimming beach, boat dock, and, almost as important as hot showers to some campers, access to a computer modem.

RV travelers will be most interested in whether a campground offers full hookups, meaning power, water, and sewer service. In a partial hookup, power and water are usually available, but sewer service is not. In most cases, however, a dump station (or sani-station, as it's often called in Canada) is available for emptying gray water and sewerage. Also note that campgrounds in Canada will refer to sites as serviced or unserviced, indicating whether hookups are available.

In Alaska it is legal (but not much fun) to park for the night on a road wayside where the parking area is fully off the road. Nowhere in Alaska or Canada is it legal to dump sewerage or gray water anywhere except in designated dump stations.

For provincial parks, you can pay in person at the campground fee station after you've chosen your site. In British Columbia, provincial campground reservations are available by calling 1-800-689-9025, or visit *www.discovercamping.ca.* Yukon travelers may prepurchase daily territorial campground permits at retail outlets along the highway, visitor reception centers, lodges, fuel stations, and at all Environment Yukon offices. The Alaska state campgrounds do not accept reservations. Charge cards are accepted in most privately owned campgrounds. Checks are rarely accepted.

Canada-speak

Engaged in conversation with a Canadian, you could swear you were from the same country until an unusual treatment of a familiar word pops up: "I'm in the PRO-cess of moving," "Let's check the SHED-yule," or "Tell me a-BOOT your problem." Here are some tips to aid interpretation:

Eh? This nonword peppers the ends of many sentences. It is not a question, but rather a charming way to end a statement with an invitation for the other person to speak next . . . or it's just a regional speech pattern that means nothing whatsoever.

First Nations people. Descendants of the ancient Native groups who first made this region their home

Gold dredges. Floating gold PRO-cessing ships that sorted out nuggets from rock and soil before depositing the tailings back on the ground

Loonie. The $1 coin imprinted with the image of a loon

The Russian River Ferry on Alaska's Kenai Peninsula gets brisk business when the reds are in. Powered by the stream's current, the ferry moves anglers to the opposite bank and back.

Mounties. Royal Canadian Mounted Police, or RCMP

Pumpjack. Slow-moving oil pumps that draw oil out of the ground and into a pipeline or storage tank; often seen in rolling fields

Stampede. The "rush" in gold rushes of a century ago, when men and women stampeded from one gold discovery to the next. Or the term for a regional rodeo event, as in the Calgary Stampede.

the Yukon. Use the territory's name without the "the" and you've just revealed that you're not from around these parts. That, and you keep getting your quarters mixed up with Loonies.

Toonie. The $2 coin, worth two Loonies

YOOP. Yukon Order of the Pioneers

Cell Phone Service

The farther north you go, the less likely you'll have continuous cell phone service, although areas surrounding major urban centers usually pose no problem. The best advice is to mentally prepare yourself for that reality, and don't let the number of bars on your phone dictate whether you're going to have a good day. You can get yourself a calling card, if you don't already have one, and use a pay phone.

Children

Due to the increase in child abduction by noncustodial parents, travel agencies and airlines are suggesting that you always travel with paperwork that documents your right to travel with minor children. The same is true for border crossings between the United States and Canada. Carry birth certificates for the children and, if you're divorced, your proof-of-custody papers. For noncustodial parents or grandparents, ask the child's custodial parent to sign and notarize a permission slip for that child to travel with you, stating where you plan to go and the dates you will be traveling.

Daylight Hours

The farther north you travel in summer, the more daylight you will encounter, especially during the days surrounding June 20 or 21, the summer solstice. Fairbanks basks in 22 hours of daylight during its Solstice Celebration, which includes a Midnight Sun Baseball Game that begins at 10:30 P.M. without artificial lights. Farther south, in Anchorage, the longest day provides a mere 19.5 hours of daylight, enough to make bedtimes a challenge for adults and children alike.

Throughout the Yukon, northern British Columbia, northern Alberta, and Alaska, short growing seasons are supplemented by these long, long hours of sunlight, resulting in fabulous floral displays, grain crops, and certain vegetables that grow to gigantic proportions. Look for giant cabbages mixed in with border plants in many northern gardens.

On the other side of the calendar, December 20 or 21 is winter solstice, when darkness is at its peak after eating away at hours of daylight for months. In Fairbanks, the sun may rise and set before office workers get a chance to look out the window, rising at about 11 A.M. and setting just 3 hours later. In Dawson City, Yukon, daylight on winter solstice is 4.5 hours; in Whitehorse, the shortest day is 5.5 hours.

Duty-free Shopping

If the value of your purchases does not exceed $400, residents of the United States who travel in Canada for more than 48 hours and less than 30 days may bring home personal or household merchandise without paying U.S. duty and tax. The $400 figure applies for each member in your party. To avoid delays at the border crossing, keep receipts and purchases handy.

Fishing

A fishing license is required in all provinces and in Alaska, but it is easy to obtain one through most sporting goods stores or other businesses.

Alberta. Sportfishing licenses are available at Natural Resource Services offices, most tackle shops and sporting goods stores, campgrounds, and many department stores. No license is required for children 14 and younger. You may pick up the current *Alberta Guide to Sportfishing Regulations* when you purchase your license. For more information on licensing requirements and costs, contact Alberta Natural Resources, Fish and Wildlife Division, 14515 122nd Avenue, Edmonton, Alberta T5L 2W4. Call 780-427-3574 or visit the Web site at *www3.gov.ab.ca/srd/fw/*.

British Columbia. You'll have to buy separate licenses for saltwater and fresh-water fishing in British Columbia. You can pick them up at government agency offices, sporting goods stores, and many other retailers. Other specific licenses are required in all national parks and may be obtained at park headquarters. Call BC Fisheries in Victoria for general inquiries at 250-387-4573 or read the fresh-water fishing regulations on the Ministry of the Water, Land, and Air Protection Web site at *wlapwww.gov.bc.ca/fw/fish/recreational.html*. For tidal water or saltwater regulations, the federal Department of Fisheries and Oceans' Web site is at *www.dfo-mpo.gc.ca.*

Yukon Territory. Licenses are available at most sporting goods stores or convenience stories. Barbless hooks are required for angling on all Yukon waters. Salmon fishing is permitted throughout the territory, with restrictions. Pick up the Recreational Fishing Regulations Summary when you obtain your license, but be aware that short-notice closures can occur. Before you go fishing, check with the Department of Fisheries and Oceans at 867-393-6722. For salmon fishing, you must have both the Yukon Angling License and a Salmon Conservation Catch Card. As soon as you catch a salmon, record necessary details on your catch card. If you are fishing in Kluane, Ivvavik, or Vuntut National Parks, a separate National Park Fishing License is required. For more information about sportfishing regulations and fees, browse *www.environmentyukon.gov.yk.ca/yukonfishing.*

Beginning in January 2005, the governments of Alaska and Yukon Territory began observing a "good neighbor" policy that's beneficial to their sportfishing citizens. Those residents who are licensed in their home state or province may purchase a similar license at the resident rate should they cross the border to fish.

Alaska. Sportfishing licenses are required for anyone 16 and older. A nonresident license costs $10 for a single day, up to $100 for a calendar year. Anglers fishing for king salmon can expect to double those fees to cover the cost of a "king stamp." Licenses and fishing regs are available at most sporting goods stores and grocery stores. To arrange a license in advance, or for more information, write the Alaska Department of Fish & Game, Division of Sport Fish headquarters at P.O. Box 25526, Juneau, AK 99802-5526. Call 907-465-4180 or visit the Web site at *www.sf.adfg.state.ak.us/statewide/sf_home.cfm.* To speed up the process, you may choose to apply for your license and purchase your king salmon stamp online.

Fuel

In Canada, gasoline is measured by the liter, which equals about a quarter of a U.S. gallon, so there are roughly 4 liters per gallon. To convert exactly, multiply the number of liters by 0.2642 to find the number of U.S. gallons. (See the section on Metric Conversion, in this chapter.)

You may see an unusual fuel pump at some stations: Propane-powered vehicles are becoming more common in western Canada.

Guns/Ammo

Canada has strict regulations regarding entry of firearms into the country. And below the federal level, individual provinces have varying regulations, so be sure to get all the facts before you pack.

At the border, you will be asked to declare any firearms. No joking on this matter. If your memory fails you, your firearms will be seized, and you may be fined. Sport or recreational-use firearms are admissible, and hunters may carry up to 200 rounds of ammunition. Before entry to any of Canada's national parks, rifles and shotguns must be broken down or in their cases. U.S. Customs suggests that U.S. residents register their guns at the border so that officials can match up the list on the return trip. Don't plan to add to your collection while you're on the trip, however. Only licensed gun dealers may import firearms. When you cross back into the United States, officials will want to ensure that the same guns are in your possession as when you entered Canada.

What is prohibited? The stuff of Rambo, James Bond, and Jackie Chan: fully automatic rifles and machine guns, silencers, excessive rounds of ammunition, sawed-off shotguns or rifles, automatic switchblades, tear gas, Mace, and some martial arts weapons. Revolvers and pistols also are prohibited. If you have questions, call the Canadian Firearms Center, 1-800-731-4000 (from the U.S. only) or 1-506-624-5380 (from other countries), or visit the center's Web site at *www.cfc-ccaf.gc.ca.*

Hunting
Licenses and permits are required in individual provinces and in Alaska. No hunting is allowed in national parks.

Alberta. Licensing and permits are dependent upon the species, season, location, and other variables. You must be 12 to obtain a license. For more information, contact the Fish and Wildlife Division, Great West Life Building, 9920 108 Street, Edmonton, Alberta, Canada T5K 2M4. Call 780-944-0313 or visit the Web site at *www3.gov.ab.ca/srd/fw/hunting/laf.html.*

British Columbia. A hunting license as well as a species license is required for all resident and nonresident hunters. For Ministry of Water, Land, and Air Protection hunting regulations or license information, contact the Fish and Wildlife Recreation and Allocation Branch, P.O. Box 9363, Victoria, British Columbia, Canada V8W 9M2. Call 250-387-9589. A synopsis of the hunting and trapping regulations is available online at *wlapwww.gov.bc.ca/fw/wild/synopsis.htm.*

Yukon Territory. To hunt for big game in the Yukon, you are required to arrange for a licensed guide. A waiting period is required for licensing, so plan ahead. For more information on local guides, browse *www.yukonoutfitters.net/default.asp.* Hunting regulations are available through any Environment Yukon office, or by writing the Department of Environment, Government of Yukon, P.O. Box 2703, Whitehorse, Yukon, Canada Y1A 2C6. Call 867-667-5652 or fax 867-393-6213. More information is available online at *www.environmentyukon.gov.yk.ca/hunting/index.shtml.*

Alaska. U.S. citizens who are not residents of Alaska may obtain a nonresident hunting license for $85, or a combination hunting/sportfishing license for $185. Either is good for the calendar year in which it is purchased. Fees vary for nonresident aliens. An additional fee will be charged for a tag, with a fee amount that is dependent upon the species that you're hunting. Licensed, nonresident hunters seeking a brown/grizzly bear, Dall sheep, or mountain goat must hunt with a licensed guide or with a resident family member who is 19 or older. A federal migratory bird-hunting stamp must be obtained for duck hunting. For more details on fees, seasons, and management units, contact the Alaska Department of Fish and Game, P.O. Box 25526, Juneau, AK 99802 or call 907-465-4100. Online hunting information is available at *www.wildlife.alaska.gov/hunt_trap/hunt_home.cfm*. You may purchase your license and big game tags online at *www.admin.adfg.state.ak.us/license*.

Insurance

Health insurance. All legal residents of Canada are part of a national health care system that's paid for through taxes and administered by each province. U.S. citizens who need to see a doctor or visit a clinic while traveling in Canada should expect to pay for services up front. You'll have to file for reimbursement from your insurer later. Check with your insurer regarding extended coverage while you travel, and what kind of help is available in case of an emergency that requires an ambulance or medevac services.

Vehicle insurance. Check before you leave home. You may need supplemental insurance for the trip. Make sure you understand how to file a claim if an accident occurs while you are driving in Canada. Carry proof of coverage with you at all times.

Lodging

Noncampers love the daily comfort of a clean, spacious bed, a hot shower, and cable television—and, if they're feeling especially wild, room service. In the following chapters, a list of hotels, motels, and lodges, along with contact information, follows each community profile. The amenities listed for each property will help you estimate the price range and whether the lodging is suitable for your party. More than ever, people are traveling with pets, and more hotels and motels can accommodate them today, so be sure to ask when making a reservation.

As you travel north, fewer places advertise that they are air-conditioned, and more advertise their "winter plug-ins," parking places where winter travelers can plug in a vehicle that's equipped with an engine-block heater. Contact numbers for local bed-and-breakfast associations also are included in some listings.

Certain hotels in the United States and Canada display their Diamond Rating, awarded by the American Automobile Association or the Canadian Automobile Association. Ratings go from One Diamond for an establishment considered good, to Five Diamonds for a top-ranking luxury property with outstanding amenities. Also look for those businesses that have received a star rating in the Canada Select program, which rates cleanliness and maintenance standards, from one star for "good" to five stars for "exceptional."

Reservations are not always necessary, but it's best to call at least a day or two ahead anyway. Note that in some cases, toll-free numbers are operational only within the province or state, or only within Canada. If you hear that annoying message "Your call cannot be completed as dialed," it means you are outside the toll-free service area that was purchased by that business. Web sites are included where available.

Metric Conversion

Canada uses the metric system of measurement, while the U.S. system prevails on the other side of the border. A Canadian speed limit of 90 kilometers per hour is roughly equivalent to 55 miles per hour. Most speedometers are equipped with a dual scale. After several days in Canada, U.S. residents usually become accustomed to the unfamiliar and make the conversion to kilometers easily.

Here's a tip: Use your speedometer as a scale to translate distances accurately. A kilometer is roughly six-tenths (0.6) of a mile; a mile is roughly 1.6 kilometers. Here are a few sample conversions, all approximate:

Kilometers		Miles
1	=	0.6
100	=	60
150	=	90
200	=	120
300	=	180

To convert precisely between U.S. and metric measurements, use the following chart:

U.S. / Metric Conversion

From	Multiply by	To get
miles	1.6093	kilometers
kilometers	0.6214	miles
feet	0.3048	meters
meters	3.2808	feet
U.S. gallons	3.7853	liters
liters	0.2642	U.S. gallons
imperial gallons	4.5460	liters
liters	0.2201	imperial gallons
pounds	0.4536	kilograms
kilograms	2.2046	pounds

Money

Visit your bank before you leave home to exchange pocket money into Canadian dollars. They'll inform you of the latest exchange rate, which fluctuates almost daily. Generally you'll get more bang for the U.S. buck in Canada. Also, Canadian businesses are savvy about calculating the exchange, and often will do so as a courtesy if you have only U.S. dollars. Vending machines and telephones will see U.S. quarters and Canadian quarters as the same denomination.

Traveler's checks (or cheques in Canada) are always a safe way to go, but you'll get the change in Canadian, and may end up with odd dollars and cents in your pocket when you reenter the United States. If you don't want to carry around large quantities of Canadian cash, use your credit card for purchases and meals. Your bank will make the conversion to U.S. dollars on your billing statement. ATMs, or cash machines, may be found in most towns, and likewise your bank will make the conversion in your account. Be prepared to pay an ATM fee.

Also, get ready to carry your dollars in a coin purse or pocket. Canada's favorite nonpaper currency is the Loonie, a $1 coin imprinted with a loon. The $2 coin, worth two Loonies, is a Toonie.

In Alaska most businesses accept Canadian coins, except for the Loonie or Toonie. Visit the bank or currency exchange to trade the Canadian dollar coins and currency.

Mosquitoes

Alaskans like to joke that the mosquito is the Alaska state bird. After you see their unusually large size you may stop laughing and start running. Their cousins in Canada are just as big and persistent. They won't kill you, but they can make your outdoor experience an unhappy one.

Many a sourdough can recount stories of caribou herds incited to stampede because of mosquitoes, or backcountry hikers who jumped in a lake to escape. In fact, the term "gone caribou" often applies to people who, lacking spray-on repellent, begin hollering, waving their arms, and running to get away. Bring mosquito repellent and use it liberally.

Sporting goods stores and catalogs offer hats equipped with mosquito netting to cover your face and neck. Hikers sometimes invest in a full suit of mosquito netting to wear over shorts and a T-shirt, rather than covering up and overheating in long sleeves and pants.

Here's a tip for those who jump in the car to escape a swarm of mosquitoes: No doubt many of them will follow you into the car. Rather than swat at them as you drive, open the windows and speed up to blow them out.

The gnat-size biting insects known as no-see-ums are a greater concern to backcountry travelers, as they can creep under cuffs and into tight places. Sometimes, swarms of no-see-ums can become so thick that, without a headnet, you cannot avoid breathing them in.

Pets

The most important piece of luggage for your dog or cat is a leash. Bring it along and use it. Campgrounds are pet friendly, as are some hotels and motels (call ahead), but all of them require use of a leash outdoors.

Nearly all rest stops have pet areas. Bring a rubber glove or plastic bags and pick up after your pet's daily constitutional. Plastic newspaper wrappers work great.

Take your dog or cat to a licensed veterinarian a week or less before you leave home, and obtain a signed health certificate showing a rabies vaccination within the last 36 months. Keep its health certificate handy for international border crossings. The collar tag will not be enough proof.

Make sure that your pet's prescription drugs are adequate for the number of days you'll be gone. Keep your hometown veterinarian's number close by in case an advisory call is needed.

Postage

If you are traveling in Canada and sending mail to a U.S. address, expect to pay 80 cents (Canadian) for a stamp on mail weighing up to 30 grams (about an ounce), and 98 cents for postage on 30-50 grams. If your postcard or letter weighs up to 30 grams and is going to an international address, it will need $1.40 (Canadian) in postage.

Restaurants

The restaurant listings in the chapters that follow include a mix of casual family dining establishments, take-out or fast-food restaurants, ethnic dining choices, and fine dining restaurants.

Because chefs of the northland pride themselves on their regional foods, we suggest you take advantage of northern specialties on the menu. In British Columbia, the Yukon, and Alaska, you may sample seafood entrees such as wild Pacific salmon (far superior in flavor and texture to farmed fish), king crab, shrimp, or scallops. Or try reindeer or buffalo for the first time. You're certain to discover new favorites or find a new spin on an old one.

Road Manners

Good manners know no international boundaries, so when you're driving the Alaska Highway, or any of the highways in this guide, give the other guy the benefit of the doubt, and don't drive like you're on the Beltway. Do not ride his bumper; do not pass in anger, or on a double yellow; and remember that RV drivers go only as fast as safety will allow. They know their vehicle limits.

Especially important for RV drivers: Alaska law states that if you are driving under the speed limit, and there are at least five vehicles behind you, you must pull over at the next available opportunity or you may be ticketed. Should you pass by a wild animal on or near the road, flash your headlights to warn oncoming drivers to be on alert.

Keep your headlights on. Use your turn signals. Pass on the left. Smile and wave to the flagger. And have a good trip.

Royal Canadian Mounted Police

Originally established in 1873 as the North-West Mounted Police, the officers of the RCMP, or Mounties, bear the burden of the romantic image created in movies and books about their daring deeds. During the 1898 gold rush to the Canadian Klondike, the North-West Mounted Police brought order to Dawson City and to the border crossings at the Chilkoot and White Passes, demanding that stampeders carry a year's worth of supplies with them.

The Mounties are easily recognized in their dress uniforms of classic red tunics, sharply creased hats, and leather boots. Their daily work uniforms are much more mundane, as is the nature of most of their work. Like law enforcement everywhere, it's not all that romantic.

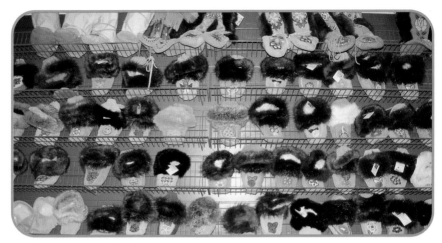

The Yukon Trapper's Association operates a store in Whitehorse, offering snowshoes, moosehide slippers, and tanned furs. Call the Customs office before you get to the border. It may not be legal to transport certain purchases across the border.

Born to be wild? A cushy ride in a motor home sure beats a hard back porch. Allow plenty of breaks to stretch your pet's legs—and yours.

This Cook Inlet, Alaska, halibut ran 211 pounds and cost me in medical bills for tendonitis! Better to catch a "chicken," a smaller fish in the manageable 15- to 30-pound range. Photo courtesy Joel Doner.

Time Zones

Most of Alaska is in the Alaska Time Zone, one hour behind Yukon Territory and British Columbia (Pacific Time Zone), which is one hour behind Alberta (Mountain Time Zone). So if it is noon in Anchorage, Alaska, it is 1 P.M. in Whitehorse, Yukon; also 1 P.M. in Prince George, British Columbia; and 2 P.M. in Calgary, Alberta. Daylight saving time applies to all of these time zones. They "spring ahead" one hour in April to daylight saving time, then "fall behind" one hour in October to standard time.

Weather

In Canada, temperature is measured on the Celsius scale, and precipitation is measured in millimeters. Values below have been converted to Fahrenheit and inches.

To convert between U.S. and Canadian measurements, use these formulas:

Fahrenheit to Celsius:
Subtract 32 from the Fahrenheit temperature. Multiply by 5 and divide by 9.

Celsius to Fahrenheit:
Multiply Celsius temperature by 9. Divide by 5. Add 32.

1 mm = .0394 inch   1 inch = 25.38 mm

Weather Chart

ALASKA	Temperatures °F		
Community	January Mean Low	July Mean High	Annual Precip./Inches
Anchorage	6	65	15
Denali Park	−8	43	15
Eagle	−13	73	11
Fairbanks	−21	72	10
Haines	18	67	47
Homer	15	61	24
Juneau	16	64	52
Ketchikan	29	65	156
Prudhoe Bay	−22	45	5
Seward	18	63	66
Skagway	19	67	28
YUKON TERRITORY	Temperatures °F		
Burwash Landing	−9.2	54.5	11
Dawson City	−30.5	72	12
Watson Lake	−12.3	58.8	16
Whitehorse	−1.7	57.2	11

ALBERTA

Community	January Mean Low	July Mean High	Annual Precip./Inches
Calgary	14.7	61.5	16
Edmonton	6.4	60.8	18
Grande Prairie	4.3	60.8	18
Lethbridge	16.9	65.1	16

BRITISH COLUMBIA

Abbotsford	36	62.8	62
Dawson Creek	5.2	59.2	19
Fort Nelson	−7.6	62.1	18
Lytton	27.9	70.5	17
Prince George	14.2	59.5	24

Wheelchair Access

Never before have so many travel opportunities opened for vacationers who rely on wheelchairs for mobility or for seniors who need a little extra help as they travel. Throughout Alaska and western Canada, you will find many hotels and motels equipped with access ramps, nonslip flooring, grab bars in the tub and shower, bath boards, and easy-open doors. Visitors with vision loss will be pleased to find large-print information cards, and phones with extra-large numbers; those with a hearing loss may reserve a room with a phone that amplifies sound.

Throughout western Canada, watch for the Access Canada logo in hotel and motel windows. These member businesses have geared a number of their rooms with physical access in mind. For more information on Access Canada and which businesses are participating, contact the following tourism offices.

Alberta: Alberta Hotel & Lodging Association, 5241 Calgary Trail, Edmonton, Alberta T6H 5G8. Call 780-436-6112 or visit *www.explorealberta.com.*

British Columbia: Tourism British Columbia, Box 9830, 1803 Douglas Street, Victoria, B.C. V8W 9W5. Call 1-800-435-5622 or browse *www.HelloBC.com.*

Yukon: Yukon Tourism and Culture, P.O. Box 2703, Whitehorse, Yukon Y1A 2C6. Call 1-800-661-0494 or visit *www.touryukon.com.*

In Alaska, businesses are tuning in to the needs of visitors who require wheelchair access. State parks and recreation areas are often equipped with wheelchair-accessible rest rooms, plus wide, paved surfaces for trails into the woods. Even some of the best fishing holes have been reserved for anglers in wheelchairs. For details, check with the Alaska Division of Tourism, Box 110804, Juneau, AK 99802-5526. Contact the division at 907-465-4100 or at *www.travelalaska.com* or by visiting the state of Alaska's Web site at *www.state.ak.us.*

Wildlife

You cannot pretend that you are driving back in the Lower 48. Every so often, the path of a plodding moose intersects the highway, and the person in the navigator's seat scrambles to grab the camera as you slow the vehicle and pull over in haste. The panic stop will happen again for a band of Dall sheep, for a caribou, a fox, a ptarmigan. It's hard to think clearly when the adrenaline is rushing through your veins, but stay aware of traffic ahead and behind you, and pull completely onto the shoulder before you stop.

What a rare and thrilling opportunity to observe a world that remains so unchanged in the 21st century. But please be mindful of a few basic rules:

Please don't feed the wildlife. Keep a respectful distance, knowing that powerful creatures such as bison or moose may panic and harm you. In the far north, animal life is plentiful, and there are no protective bars between you and the wild things.

A few years ago, a Fairbanks woman driving on Chena Hot Springs Road came car hood to kneecaps with a bull moose standing in the middle of the road. She had slowed and stopped, but the moose didn't appear to be in a hurry. He stayed put. She honked her horn. He snorted. She honked again. He lowered his head and did significant damage to her car's front end before he shuffled off in a huff. The moral of the story is: Don't harass the animals. For roadside wildlife sightings—and you're likely to experience several—it's best to stay in the car. But don't creep closer, honk, or yell. From the comfort of your vehicle, enjoy the vision before you, up close and in focus, with your binoculars or camera equipped with a telephoto lens.

If you are involved in an accident with a big animal, immediately contact the local authorities. A charity will be contacted to field-dress the moose, caribou, or bison, and the meat will be donated to needy families.

Full-day or half-day cruises on the ocean afford the opportunity to see marine mammals in spectacular settings. They are well worth the cost, and often include lunch. Several day-cruise operators have ticket offices in downtown Anchorage, and some provide shuttle transportation to their vessels in a community south of the city, such as Seward, Whittier, or Homer. If you spend any time along the Inside Passage, you'll be treated to views of otters, eagles, plentiful bird life, and occasionally a whale.

Chapter 3

History of the Alcan: The Soldiers' Road

*P*ROTECTING America's northernmost possession was a matter of national security in the early 1940s, and the task became especially critical after the Japanese bombed Pearl Harbor in December 1941. Alaska then became a potential enemy target. Without a land route between the Lower 48 states and Alaska, the U.S. military outposts in Fairbanks, Anchorage, and elsewhere in the territory were virtually stranded, dependent on supply deliveries by water and air, and vulnerable to attack.

In 1942, Ladd Air Field in Fairbanks became especially strategic to the Allies' defense plan. Ladd was the final U.S. destination for warplanes that were flown along the Northwest Staging Route from the continental United States to Fairbanks. Small airstrips along the way constituted a dot-to-dot route through the Canadian wilderness. Along this line, Lend-Lease Program pilots—many of them women, who were not allowed to fly in combat—ferried aircraft for delivery to Russian pilots waiting in Fairbanks. These pilots then continued the journey over the Bering Sea to Russia. All told, nearly 8,000 fighters, bombers, and cargo planes were flown along the Northwest Staging Route.

Clearly a road was needed, and in fact it had been considered as early as 1905, when Major Constantine of the North-West Mounted Police was charged to build a road to the Klondike but was later recalled from that effort. In the late 1920s and early 1930s, other proposed routes

A new addition to the sights at Mile 0 is this sculpture of a road surveyor.

A Lone Road Through the Wilderness

At Watson Lake, the Alaska Highway Interpretive Centre includes a mini-museum on the building of the highway.

Alaska Highway Facts

Length of historic route to Fairbanks: 1,523 miles (2,451 km)

U.S. troops used in construction: 11,000

Civilian workers: 16,000

Pieces of heavy equipment: 7,000

Bridges constructed: 133

Culverts installed: 8,000+

Highest mountain pass: Summit, 4,250 feet, at Historic Mile 392

Cost: $140 million

Began: March 1942

Completed: October 1942

Officially opened: November 20, 1942, at Soldiers Summit, Mile 1061

Time: 8 months, 12 days

Opened to the public: 1948

Beginning, Mile 0: Dawson Creek, British Columbia

Official end: Delta Junction, Alaska, Mile 1422

Unofficial end: Fairbanks, Alaska, Historic Mile 1523

During 50 years of road improvements, Fairbanks was shortened by 35 miles were examined and discarded. World War II was catalyst enough, and in March 1942, Canada and the United States came to terms on building the military road then known as the Alcan. Canada allowed rights-of-way and provided construction materials, while the U.S. military provided the manpower. It was agreed that the Canadian portion of the road would be turned over to Canada at the war's end.

When troop trains began pulling into Dawson Creek, B.C., a quiet hamlet boomed from a population of 600 to more than 10,000 by late March 1942.

Diaries recorded by the men who built the road portray an existence just as life-threatening as it might have been in battle. In the preliminary stage, workers felled trees to create a corduroy road, and the first bridges floated on pontoons. At Charlie Lake, three American soldiers drowned while crossing the lake on a pontoon barge.

That winter, the piercing cold was the enemy, along with the crude, temporary accommodations, bad food, and backbreaking, seven-days-a-week labor. Heavy equipment was sucked into the miry shoulders and sometimes abandoned. In below-zero temperatures, the big machines were kept running 24 hours a day, as they might not start again if allowed to cool. Trucks and bulldozers were pulled out of seemingly bottomless mud holes, and troop morale sagged with little contact from the outside world. In the summer, mosquitoes, no-see-ums, and black flies tortured the work crews.

Just as the American military had feared, Japan attacked and landed troops on U.S. soil in June 1942, briefly invading Alaska's Aleutian Islands at Kiska and Attu, and further heightening the sense of need for the road's completion. An ensuing battle at Kiska killed soldiers on both sides before Japanese troops retreated under cover of fog. Several Native Alaskans were taken from Attu to Japan as prisoners of war.

On September 25, 1942, the 35th Regiment of the U.S. Army Corps of Engineers, working from the south, met the soldiers of the 340th Regiment, working from the north, at a place named by the soldiers themselves: Contact Creek. The final link occurred a month later in Beaver Creek, Yukon Territory, when members of the 97th Engineers met the 18th Engineers and opened the road for military convoys to pass.

A photograph from that day shows two nose-to-nose bulldozers and two weary soldiers—one African-American, one white—shaking hands and smiling broadly for the camera. The official opening, along with a formal ribbon-cutting ceremony, came on a bitterly cold day—November 20, 1942—at what is now called Soldiers Summit at Kluane Lake, Mile 1061. Members of the Royal Canadian Mounted Police suffered in their dress uniforms at –35°F.

The Alcan would not be opened to civilian traffic until 1948, well after the war, and it remained a difficult journey suitable only for jeeps and specially equipped vehicles for many years.

The Canadian Army took over jurisdiction of the Canadian portion of the road in 1946 and continued maintenance until 1964, when that responsibility was handed to the Federal Department of Public Works. Since 1971 the Yukon Department of Highways and Public Works has been in charge of the portion that passes through the Yukon Territory.

With the 50th anniversary celebration of the Alaska Highway in 1992, commemorative license plates were issued for those who drove the route. In preparation for the anniversary year, paved but damaged sections of the highway were repaired, and unpaved stretches were widened and improved. In the following ten-plus years, road crews have continued to work at upgrades in targeted sections, and today the only unpaved stretches are those that are undergoing a second round of stripping and repaving or widening. Vestiges of the old road are occasionally visible, especially where engineers have abandoned the wildly curvy route and blasted a straighter line through rocky barriers that confounded the hurried roadbuilders of the 1940s.

Tourism associations on both sides of the border joined forces to erect "historic mileposts"—which in most cases do not match current milepost or kilometer-post numbers. That's because the highway is now shorter than it used to be, thanks to all of the straightening and rerouting improvements of the last six decades.

Significant historic sites include construction camps, airstrips of the Northwest Staging Route, the memorably steep Suicide Hill, memorial sites for those who lost their lives, and boundary lines marking responsibility of various contractors. The Alaska Highway Interpretive Centre at Watson Lake, Yukon Territory, at Mile 613, offers exhibits on the building of the Alcan including historic documents, photos, and displays of life in the work camps.

In 1996 the emergency wartime road that was built with remarkable speed received special recognition for the wonder that it is. The Alaska Highway was named an International Historical Engineering Landmark, joining the Eiffel Tower and the Panama Canal among the world's construction marvels.

Alcan roadbuilders battled deep mud that mired bulldozers as well as supply trucks.
PHOTO COURTESY U.S. ARMY CORPS OF ENGINEERS.

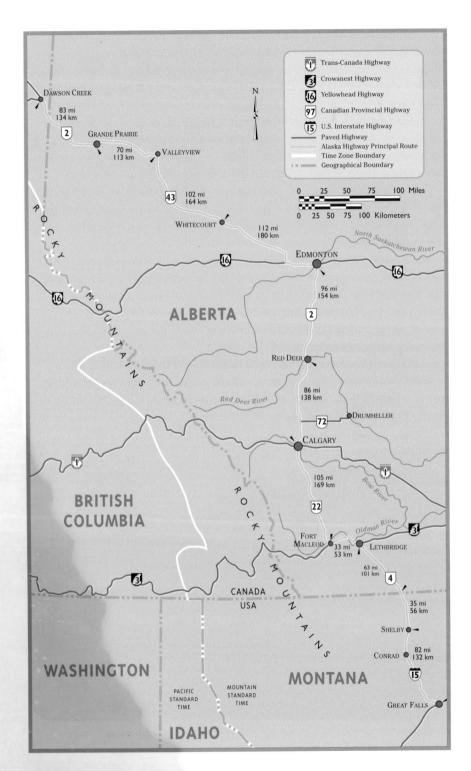

Trans-Canada Highway
Crowsnest Highway
Yellowhead Highway
Canadian Provincial Highway
U.S. Interstate Highway
Paved Highway
Alaska Highway Principal Route
Time Zone Boundary
Geographical Boundary

0 25 50 75 100 Miles
0 25 50 75 100 Kilometers

N

DAWSON CREEK
83 mi
134 km
GRANDE PRAIRIE
70 mi
113 km
VALLEYVIEW
102 mi
164 km
WHITECOURT
112 mi
180 km
North Saskatchewan River
EDMONTON
96 mi
154 km
ALBERTA
RED DEER
86 mi
138 km
Red Deer River
DRUMHELLER
CALGARY
105 mi
169 km
Bow River
ROCKY MOUNTAINS
BRITISH COLUMBIA
FORT MACLEOD
33 mi
53 km
LETHBRIDGE
Oldman River
63 mi
101 km
CANADA
USA
35 mi
56 km
SHELBY
CONRAD
82 mi
132 km
WASHINGTON
PACIFIC STANDARD TIME
MOUNTAIN STANDARD TIME
MONTANA
GREAT FALLS
IDAHO

Chapter 4

The Eastern Route: Through Alberta to Dawson Creek, B.C., and Mile 0

*I*F YOU FIND BEAUTY in serene fields, pasturelands, and unbroken views, then you will cherish the drive north through Montana, across the border, and into Alberta. Far from boring, this is a landscape that is settling to the soul—farms and fields, horses and cattle, and well-used barns. Looking out the side window, your gaze may be met by a cow looking back. Fertile farmland rolls away in gentle, undulating waves beneath a bright sky. In late August, farmers may be seen baling hay, and huge, golden rolls are strewn about the fields in broad symmetry. In small towns, grain elevators are clustered next to the railroad tracks. The pace is nice and easy.

And yet this corridor into Alberta no more represents the entire province than the Chilkoot Pass represents all of Alaska. Depending on where you spend most of your time, your definition of Alberta may be drawn from the stark badlands surrounding Drumheller, from the stunning mountain vistas of Waterton Lakes National Park, from the cityscapes of Edmonton and Calgary, or from the raw, mountainous wilderness of the far north.

Within the past 200 years, across the desertlike landscape of southern Alberta, the Plains Indians once roamed freely and hunted wild game such as buffalo, pronghorn antelope, and coyotes. Here and farther north, these people of the First Nations lived an untrammeled

Southern Alberta is a mix of farmlands and badlands.

existence until the arrival of explorers, traders, cowboys, law officers, and government representatives bearing treaties. The stories of the Natives—or at least a portion of them—are told today in culturally important places such as Head-Smashed-In Buffalo Jump, Fort Whoop-Up, Indian Battle Park, and Calgary's Heritage Park, and in smaller interpretive sites throughout the province. In western Canada, as in other regions of North America, aboriginal people groups are reawakening to some of their lost practices, and regaining tribal pride through dance, song, storytelling, and art.

More recent settlers of southern and central Alberta came to farm, work in the forests, or draw oil and natural gas from beneath the ground. Today farming is flourishing with the aid of modern irrigation practices, and oil, timber, and tourism also feed the province's healthy economy. As you motor through, you'll see livestock sharing some fields with working oil pumpjacks. In "fields" of their own, dense forests are grown for the purpose of cutting, just like wheat and hay—but harvest seasons are decades, not months, apart. Roadside signs show the date when a particular forest was last logged and replanted. In mill towns, visitors are invited in to see the latest manufacturing processes.

Tourism is a burgeoning industry as well, growing in leaps after the Alaska Highway was opened, when travelers were more apt to discover the attractions of Alberta during their long-distance journey. Its diverse wildlife, topography, and climate make this province more than just a place to pass through, but rather a place to count among your travel destinations.

To learn more about what to see and do in Alberta, travel information is available at 1-800-ALBERTA (within North America) or at *www.travelalberta.com*. Hotel and motel information is available at 780-436-6112 or *www.explorealberta.com*. And if you're interested in staying in bed-and-breakfast accommodations, visit the Alberta Bed & Breakfast Association Web site at *www.bbalberta.com*. If you're traveling with a pet, ask the manager of the B&B or hotel as to whether pets are accepted.

Alberta at a Glance

Size: *255,287 square miles or 661,190 square km*

Population: *3,146,066*

Capital: *Edmonton*

Tourism: *Travel Alberta, 1-800-252-3782 or www.travelalberta.com*

Lodging: *Alberta Hotel & Lodging Association, 780-435-6112 or www.explorealberta.com*

Fishing and Hunting: *Alberta Natural Resources, 780-427-3574 or www3.gov.ab.ca/srd/fw/*

Canada Customs, Alberta South: *204-983-3500 (outside Canada) or www.ccra-adre.ge.ca*

Montana–Alberta Border

To Lethbridge, Alberta: 63 miles (101 km)
To Dawson Creek, B.C.: 750 miles (1,200 km)

Before you leave Montana, top off the fuel tank in Shelby. The price there will be lower than any other you'll encounter throughout western Canada. Driving north, the terrain will be familiar in Alberta. Like northern Montana, it is virtually treeless, with grainfields sweeping away from the roadsides. The road is generally straight and wide, with little changing except the occasional rise and fall. Oil pumpjacks are sometimes visible here, too, where a minor oil field lies beneath the farmland.

On the Montana side of the international border, the speed limit is 75 mph (120 kmh). Once you cross the border and start up Alberta Highway 4, no place will be higher than 110—more often it's 100. If you encounter a stretch of road construction, the speed limit may drop to between 50 and 80 kmh (30 to 50 mph).

The border crossing is a cluster of buildings in the middle of nowhere, and open 24 hours a day. On the Montana side, the place-name is **Sweetgrass,** a name it shares with the Sweetgrass Hills, a low mountain range on the eastern horizon. **Coutts** is the Canadian border town. Northbound travelers will stop at U.S. Customs and Immigration to answer a few questions, then continue to Canadian Customs and Immigration. Between them, you'll see a duty-free shop. The shop may be more attractive to southbound U.S. citizens as the place for "last chance" shopping. Here you can purchase Canadian goods with Canadian funds on Canadian soil, with savings on liquor, tobacco, perfume, souvenirs, toys, T-shirts, and caps. (See the section on Border Crossings in Chapter 2, "What You Need to Know, A to Z.")

Road Notes

Like northern Montana, southern Alberta enjoys a semiarid climate, with so much sunshine that farmers rely heavily on irrigation. Above the more level farms, the foothills are wrinkled and dimpled, treeless except for occasional clusters in the distance.

At **Milk River,** 13 miles (21 km) north of the border, you'll find a small, reasonably priced public campground with 34 sites, about half of which have full and partial hookup. Dry camping is available.

Farther up the road in the heart of town, multiple grain elevators alongside the railroad tracks are cleverly painted to look like milk cartons. Expect to see little else but farm country on both sides of the road all the way to Lethbridge—irrigated fields and grain elevators, ranging from the classic wooden buildings to new shiny metal structures.

Just north of Milk River, you can take a tour of ancient petroglyphs by turning east for 26 miles (42 km) on Route 501 and following the signs to **Writing-on-Stone Provincial Park.** This archaeological preserve features huge sandstone outcrops with petroglyphs and pictographs inscribed by the Shoshoni and Blackfoot Indians.

The border crossing at Coutts.

No unguided tours are permitted; however, free guided tours are available throughout the summer. For more information, call 403-647-2364.

Devil's Coulee Dinosaur Egg Interpretive Centre is located in Warner, about 12 miles (19 km) north of Milk River. In the early 1990s, scientists discovered the world's largest dinosaur nesting site in this incredible land formation. A guided hike allows visitors to view the excavation site, including intact embryos. Work continues here as paleontologists search for more clues to this area's prehistory dating from 230 to 65 million years ago. Admission is charged. For more information, call 403-642-2118.

Lethbridge

From the border: 65 miles (105 km)
To Fort Macleod: 35 miles (56 km)

A lovely settlement along the Oldman River, Lethbridge offers the attractions of a big city in a little package. All services and facilities are available in this city of nearly 73,000, from top-rated golfing to a natural history center, art galleries, a theater, beautifully landscaped gardens, and a university and archives. Shopping malls, vast retail outlets, and little shops provide plenty of shopping opportunities. Dine in style or eat on the run, choosing from among dozens of cafés, restaurants, and fast-food establishments.

The **Chinook Country Tourist Association** operates a visitor center near the junction of Highway 4 and Highway 5 (Mayor Magrath Drive). Call 1-800-661-1222 for information. A second center is at Scenic Drive and 3rd Avenue South, near Indian Battle Park.

Among the premier attractions in Lethbridge is its beautiful **High Level Bridge**, the longest and highest steel viaduct railroad bridge in the world. It spans the Oldman River Valley and soars above the site of a historic trading post. Here at

Indian Battle Park, the last of the intertribal battles of North America took place, between the Cree and Blackfoot Indians. Besides picnic areas and playgrounds, the park features walking trails.

Also beneath the High Level Bridge is **Fort Whoop-Up Interpretive Centre,** a great place to learn about the city's beginnings. With its log construction, old-time displays, and friendly gift shop, historic Fort Whoop-Up today seems like a tame tourism stop. Although this is a replica of the original, don't forget that log walls such as these have seen passion, fury, and acts of utter lawlessness.

Established in 1869 by two American fur traders, Fort Whoop-Up was once a critical post for whiskey runners. At that time, trade in buffalo robes flourished between Montana

Fort Whoop-Up in Lethbridge flourished as a whiskey-running stop until the North-West Mounted Police arrived to stop the illegal activity.

and Alberta. Payment with guns or illegal alcohol was commonplace, and powerful men took advantage of those who were addicted to the drink—trappers and pioneers, as well as members of local tribes.

With the arrival of the North-West Mounted Police in 1874, the lawlessness was contained, but the name stuck. A sign in northern Montana—the southern end of the whiskey trail—offered this explanation for the unusual name: "Origin of the name Whoop-Up is possibly from a conversation by a trader on the whiskey-for-furs trade route. Upon his return to Fort Benton, Johny LaMotte was asked 'How's business?' His reply, 'Aw, they're just whoopin' 'er up!'" See more at *www.fortwhoopup.com.*

For outdoor enthusiasts, the **Helen Schuler Coulee Centre** is an urban nature retreat that includes interpretive programs and touchable displays, as well as self-guided trails through the coulees and cottonwood forests on a 200-acre reserve. Watch for great-horned owls, deer, and porcupines that make their homes in the reserve. The city offers numerous other hiking and biking opportunities, too, especially around **Henderson Lake Park.**

Check with the visitor center to see what's happening at the **Lethbridge & District Exhibition Park** at 3401 Parkside Drive, east of Henderson Lake. Over the year, close to a million visitors will roam the 67-acre grounds during events such as horse races, agricultural fairs, and the popular **Whoop-Up Days,** held in early August, highlighting professional rodeo events. If you're in town on a weekend, come down for the Farmers' Market, held every Saturday from May through November. To plan ahead, check *www.lethbridgeexhibition.com*.

Sir Alexander Galt Museum & Archives is located in what was once the Galt Hospital, overlooking the Oldman River Valley at the west end of 5th Street off Scenic Drive. Galt was founder of North Western Coal and Navigation Co. Displays and interactive programs teach about the history of Lethbridge, the settling of southern Alberta, and the area's first people. Browse *www.galtmuseum.com*.

Golfers will be thrilled to play at the championship course of **Paradise Canyon Golf Resort,** rated among Alberta's top seven golf courses by *Canada's Golf Course Ranking Magazine* and one of the best in North America by *Golf Digest.* See *www.paradisegolfresort.com*. Another option is a round at the **Henderson Lake Golf Course** *(www.hendersonlakegolfclub.com)*, at 2721 South Parkside Drive S., in the heart of the city.

The annual **Alberta Airshow** is one of western Canada's best, according to *Canadian Aviation News.* Scheduled for early August at the Lethbridge Airport, the show features military and civilian aircraft in flying demonstrations, while ground displays invite visitors for a closer look. For details, call 403-380-4245.

For more information about Lethbridge, call the Chinook Country Tourist Association at 1-800-661-1222, browse its Web site at *www.chinookcountry.com*, or visit the Lethbridge Convention & Visitors Bureau page at *www.lethbridgecvb.com*.

Nikka Yuko Japanese Garden

The walkway to the entrance of Nikka Yuko Japanese Garden offers a clue to the visual treasures on the other side of the gates. The garden is located off Mayor Magrath Drive in Henderson Lake Park. Don't enter this garden expecting a rush of floral sights and scents. A true Japanese garden offers quietude and the opportunity for meditation, not overstimulation of the senses. In these 4 acres, you will appreciate the beauty in simplicity.

At the center, an authentically built Japanese house—shoes off at the door, please—is surrounded by carefully groomed walkways, pruned trees, and paths that have been meticulously landscaped. Nothing is out of place, not even the rocks in the pond, or the pebbles along its shore specially chosen for their size and shape, then laid in an overlapping design. Everything about this controlled landscape reflects the Japanese desire to express an understanding of humanity's place in the environment.

Kimono-clad women of Japanese heritage guide the way and explain cultural practices, as well as relate how this lovely place came to be. Admission is charged. For more information, call 403-328-3511. ●

Go West to Canada's Crown Jewel

*Consider a side trip to **Waterton Lakes National Park**, which lies about 75 miles (120 km) south and west of Lethbridge on Route 5, or the same distance traveling due west from Milk River on Highways 501 and 5. This area is rich with biological diversity and is extraordinarily beautiful, marked by vast lakes, waterfalls cascading from mountain peaks, and streams full of fish. The park's southern boundary lies adjacent to **Glacier National Park** in Montana. Like Waterton Lakes, Glacier National Park is a natural beauty worthy of exploration. Of course the two national parks are part of a single landscape onto which political boundaries have been applied—and that was only yesterday in geologic time. Indeed, billion-year-old rocks have been identified in this glacier-carved region.*

In 1932 Waterton Lakes National Park and Glacier National Park were together designated as the first International Peace Park, commemorating the friendship between the countries and their commitment to shared resource management. The combined national parks are included on a list of modern-day wonders of the world as a UNESCO World Heritage Site. Both parks offer backcountry hiking, camping, horseback riding, rafting, biking, and other recreation. For more information on Waterton Lakes National Park, call 403-859-2224. For more on Glacier National Park: 406-888-7800 or www.nps.gov/glac.

Lodging

Best Western Heidelberg Inn
1303 Mayor Magrath Drive
1-800-791-8488 or 403-329-0555
66 air-conditioned rooms with cable TV
and modem jacks. Fitness room, sauna.
Three-Diamond rating, AAA/CAA.
Pub, liquor store, restaurant.

Chinook Motel
1245 Mayor Magrath Drive
1-800-791-8488 or 403-329-0555
20 air-conditioned rooms, telephones,
cable TV, modem jacks.

Comfort Inn
3226 Fairway Plaza Road South
1-866-554-4110 or 403-320-8874
www.choicehotels.ca/cn424
58 units, cable TV, high-speed Internet,
fridge/microwave. Pool, hot tub,
exercise room. Free continental
breakfast, coffee. Family rates.

Days Inn Lethbridge
100 3rd Avenue South
1-800-DAYS INN or 403-327-6000
www.daysinn.ca
91 units including nonsmoking rooms.
Cable TV, movies, exercise room,
whirlpool. Free continental breakfast,
coffee. Winter plug-ins, coin laundry.

Econo Lodge
1030 Mayor Magrath Drive
1-800-561-9815 or 403-328-6636
56 air-conditioned units, modem jacks,
cable TV with free movies. Family rates.
Discount at adjacent restaurant.

Econo Lodge and Suites
1124 Mayor Magrath Drive
403-328-5591
www.choicehotels.ca
44 air-conditioned units with fridges,
cable TV. Vehicle plug-ins. Adjacent to
restaurant/lounge.

Holiday Inn Express Hotel & Suites
120 Stafford Drive South
1-866-494-9292 or 403-394-9292
www.hiexpress.com
102 air-conditioned units with
    fridges, high-speed Internet, cable TV.
    Exercise room. Family rates, vehicle
    plug-ins.

Howard Johnson Express Inn
1026 Mayor Magrath Drive
1-800-597-1114 or 403-327-4576
www.hojo.com
37 air-conditioned units with fridges,
    hair dryers, iron and board, modem
    jacks, cable TV. Bridal suites available.
    Pool, vehicle plug-ins, free continental
    breakfast.

Lethbridge Lodge Hotel
320 Scenic Drive
1-800-661-1232 or 403-328-1123
www.lethbridgelodge.com
Full-service hotel with 190 rooms around
    tropical courtyard, indoor pool, hot
    tub, fitness facility. Two restaurants,
    lounge, downtown location. Free
    shuttle service.

Lethbridge Village Inn Travelodge
207 4th Avenue South
1-800-416-0305 or 403-327-2104
www.travelodge.com
32 units with fridges, hair dryers, modem
    jacks, cable TV. Family rates.

Parkside Inn
1009 Mayor Magrath Drive South
1-800-240-1471 or 403-328-2366
www.telusplanet.net/public/parkside/
65 air-conditioned rooms. Cable TV,
    room service, laundry service,
    whirlpool, exercise room, sundeck.
    Lounge with live entertainment.
    Adjacent to Henderson Lake
    Golf Course and Nikka Yuko
    Japanese Garden.

Sandman Hotel Lethbridge
421 Mayor Magrath Drive
1-800-266-4660 or 403-328-1111
www.sandmanhotels.com
139 air-conditioned rooms, with
    nonsmoking available. Cable TV and
    movies. Executive floors, exercise room.
    Restaurant, room service, lounge, hair
    salon, vehicle plug-ins.

South Country Inn
2225 Mayor Magrath Drive South
1-888-653-2615 or 403-380-6677
www.southcountryinn.ca
50 air-conditioned units, family suites,
    cable TV. Hot tub, exercise room.
    Vehicle plug-ins, free continental
    breakfast.

Super 8 Lodge
2210 7th Avenue South
1-800-661-8091 or 403-329-0100
www.super8.com
91 air-conditioned units, some nonsmoking,
    modem jacks. Movies, laundry. Close to
    Japanese gardens. Vehicle plug-ins.

Thriftlodge
1142 Mayor Magrath Drive
1-800-708-8638 or 403-328-4436
56 air-conditioned rooms, with
    refrigerators, fax jacks, VCRs, cable TV,
    and movies. Nonsmoking available.

Travelodge Hotel & Convention Centre
526 Mayor Magrath Drive
1-877-327-5701 or 403-327-5701
www.travelodge.com
102 air-conditioned units, refrigerators, iron
    and board, laundry, modem jacks. Room
    service, sports bar. Indoor pool, hot tub,
    exercise room. Vehicle plug-ins.

Campgrounds
Bridgeview RV Resort
1501 2nd Avenue West
    (0.3 miles west of Oldman River)
403-381-2357
174 sites, 30- to 50-amp service,
    70 pull-throughs, full and partial
    hookups, Internet. Laundry, heated
    pool. Restaurant.

Henderson Lake Campground
3419 Parkside Drive South
(next to Henderson Lake Park)
403-328-5452
100 sites with full or partial hookups.
Showers, laundry, rest rooms.
Grocery store, canoeing.
Shopping and dining nearby.
Next to golf course.

Restaurants
*Also note in the Lodging list that most
major hotels include restaurants and
lounges.*

Bully's Sports & Entertainment Centre
3401 Parkside Drive South
403-380-1900

Casino Lethbridge
1251 3 Ave. South
403-381-9467
Fully licensed dining room, lounge.

Coco Pazzo
1254 3rd Avenue South
403-329-8979
Italian specialties, wood-fired pizza oven.

Dionysios Restaurant
635 13th Street North
403-320-6554
www.dionysios.ca
Greek food, East Indian, pastas,
steaks, ribs.

Douro's Pizza and Steak House
2433 Fairway Plaza Road South
403-327-3067
Restaurant and sports lounge—
full menu.

Earl's Restaurant
203 13th Street South
403-320-7677
Family dining.

Guesthouse Restaurant
A-110 W.T. Hill Blvd.—Highway 3
403-394-9333
Full-service family restaurant featuring
European dishes.

JB's Restaurant
1303 Mayor Magrath Drive South,
in Best Western Heidelberg Inn
403-329-0555
Three meals a day, homemade pies.

La Bella Notte
402 2 Avenue South in Old Firehall No. 1
403-320-0533
Italian dining in the historic Firehall.

Lighthouse Japanese Restaurant
1346 Mayor Magrath Drive South
403-328-4828
Full Japanese restaurant menu.

Luigi's Pizza & Steak House
306 - 13 Street North
403-327-2766

Ric's Grill
200 - 103 Mayor Magrath Drive South
403-317-7427
In the former Lethbridge Water Tower

Ricky's All Day Grill
2420 Fairway Plaza Road
403-327-3263
Belgian waffles, sandwiches, salads, ribs.

Shanghai Chop Suey
610 3rd Avenue South
403-327-3552

Smitty's Restaurant
2053 Mayor Magrath Drive
403-320-7950
Family restaurant; can accommodate
up to 30 in the lounge for business
breakfast meetings.

Sven Ericksen's Restaurant
1715 Mayor Magrath Drive South
403-328-7756
Family, group dining, Sunday brunch, senior
rates, family nights, special events.

**Tom's House of Pizza & The Forgotten
Lounge**
105 12th Street South
403-329-8889
Pizza and lounge, family dining.

Road Notes

Driving west from Lethbridge on Highway 3, and then north from Fort Macleod on Highway 2, you won't see a lot of rest stops. So plan your stops around these bigger towns instead.

The prairies of southern Alberta are windy. The prevailing wind tousles the crops on either side of the road, and it takes only a little imagination to see the surface of the grainfields as sea waves or a living thing that ripples with movement. Lift your eyes and enjoy this far-reaching, big-sky country.

About 18 miles (29 km) west of Lethbridge, you'll enter the Oldman River Valley. Note where the river has created coulees: treeless valleys beneath high ridges. To the west, the Canadian Rockies are visible.

The Fort Macleod Chamber of Commerce hosts a **Tourism Information Centre** accessible from either side of the divided highway on the south end of town. In Fort Macleod, at the junction of Highways 3 and 2, you'll take Highway 2 north.

FORT MACLEOD

From Lethbridge: 33 miles (53 km)
To Calgary: 105 miles (169 km)

This charming city of 3,100 people is centrally located on the crossroads of Highways 2 and 3. One of Alberta's oldest communities, Fort Macleod (muh-CLOUD) was founded in 1874 by the North-West Mounted Police when the patrol established a post on the Oldman River. Today the downtown historic district includes more than 30 historic and architecturally significant buildings dating from 1880 to 1920. Guided or self-guided walking tours are fun, and shopping is plentiful.

Among those buildings is the **Museum of the North-West Mounted Police**, at 219 25th Street, a replica of the original fort that depicts pioneer and Native life in the late 1800s. Summer visitors will enjoy the fort's Mounted Patrol Musical Ride, with red-uniformed riders executing parade dressage, four times a day in July and August. Admission is charged. Their Web site is *www.nwmpmuseum.com*.

Other buildings include the **Fort Macleod Empress Theatre**, 235 Col. Macleod Boulevard, which opened in 1912 and is still in operation. It is Canada's oldest continually operating theater west of Winnipeg. Ask about Eddy, the resident ghost. The theater is located on what is known as the Red Coat Trail, across from the mounted-police museum.

The province government operates a campground on the Oldman River, north of town on Highway 2 near the bridge (see list of campgrounds), and a wildlife reserve adjacent to the Oldman River offers hiking, biking, birding, and fishing. The reserve habitat supports deer, many species of birds, and beavers. Spend a few hours berry picking for local varieties such as Saskatoon, chokecherry, and buffalo.

A side trip to the municipality of **Crowsnest Pass**—56 miles (91 km) west of Fort Macleod on Highway 3—brings you to several attractions. A nearby interpretive center provides a slide show, self-guided walks, and programs that recall the **Frank Slide**, the 1903 disaster that wiped out half the town of Frank as it dumped 90 million tons of rock. Nearby Leitch Collieries features the ruins of a powerhouse, mine manager's residence, coke ovens, and other signs of earlier life in this coal-mining valley. An admission fee is charged. For more information: 403-562-7388 or *www.frankslide.com.*

Elsewhere in Crowsnest Pass, you may go underground for a tour of the **Bellevue Mine**. Throughout the guided tour, each visitor wears a hard hat equipped with a miner's lamp. You will descend through about 330 feet (100 m) of the main rock tunnel and into 660 feet (200 m) of the coal seam. Admission is charged. Call 403-564-4700.

At the **Peigan Reserve**, west of Fort Macleod off Highway 3, you can learn about early Native culture of this area. The reserve includes the **Oldman River Cultural Centre**, with artifacts, historical photos, and resources on the history and language of the Peigan people. Open weekdays. Call 403-965-3939.

The **Piikani Lodge Interpretive Centre** on the reserve invites visitors to join interpretive hikes and special events, such as the Peigan Nation Annual Celebration and Powwow held in August. Call 403-965-4000 for details.

Head-Smashed-In Buffalo Jump is an architectural beauty set into the side of a bluff.

Head-Smashed-In Buffalo Jump

For centuries, the buffalo hunters of the Plains Indians counted on this region's topography to help them kill their prey. Incited to stampede, a portion of the herd would follow the natural contours of the land along a route that gradually narrowed until the animals encountered an escarpment, 37 feet high and 1,000 feet long. The buffalo would fall headlong to their deaths, and the waiting party at the bottom of the cliff would immediately set to work on the meat and hides. Only the bones were left behind to disintegrate with time.

The Plains Indians hunted buffalo this way for more than 6,000 years. At the first arrival of Europeans, there were an estimated 16 million bison on the North American plains. By 1879 they were virtually extinct due to hunting by non-Natives.

Head-Smashed-In is the site of the largest and best-preserved buffalo jump on the continent. Most jumps were disturbed prior to World War II because they held centuries of bones, which are high in phosphorous, a necessary ingredient for munitions, explosives, and gunpowder. Through these hurried and haphazard excavations, most archaeological sites of the Plains Indians were destroyed.

To reach Head-Smashed-In, turn off from Highway 2 about 4.5 miles (7.2 km) north of Fort Macleod. Then take Route 785 west for 10 miles (16 km) to the RV parking area.

A seven-story interpretive center built into the cliffside is open year-round. Displays include a diorama with full-size mounted buffalo, films explaining the traditional hunt, a restaurant, and a gift store. Visitors can handle objects such as a stone club, an arrow, a buffalo robe, tools made from bone, a hide scraper, and a flint knife. Native interpreters are on duty to add to the store of information. A wheelchair-accessible trail leads to the buffalo jump along the edge of the escarpment.

In the museum, the treatment of Natives at the hands of non-Natives is presented without anger: The objects and documents are allowed to tell the tragic stories. Artifacts include a payment book from 1890 listing names of reservation residents and what they were paid annually. Men, women, boys, and girls were paid differently, amounts ranging from $1 to $7. Also on display is a book of passes to leave the reservation, which required the signature of a Department of Indian Affairs agent. Each person's name seems to hold a story: One Owl; Rises with the Sun; No Account Woman.

The name Head-Smashed-In comes from the story of a young man, many years ago, who hid beneath the escarpment during a buffalo hunt and died from a skull fracture.

Westerly winds are nearly constant at Head-Smashed-In, blowing 314 days of the year, sometimes with almost hurricane force. Wear a scarf or a secure hat and clothes that you can button up or zip shut. Bring your sunglasses, too. For more information, call 403-553-2731, or visit the center's Web site at www.head-smashed-in.com.

Lodging

D.J. Motel
416 Main Street
403-553-4011
www.djmotel.com
14 air-conditioned units, some
nonsmoking. Cable TV and movies,
data ports, barbecue area.

Fort Motel
451 24th Street
403-553-3606
14 air-conditioned units, with cable and
satellite TV. Nonsmoking, kitchenettes,
rooms with data ports available. Free
coffee, free local calls.

Heritage House Motel
140 Col. Macleod Trail West End
403-553-2777
12 units, some with air-conditioning.
Cable TV, coffee, family plan.
No phones in room. Senior rates.

Kozy Motel
433 24th Street
403-553-3115
13 air-conditioned units, some
family cabins. Cable TV, movies,
phones, refrigerators, modem
jacks, barbecue area.

Red Coat Inn
359 Main Street
403-553-4434
www.redcoatinn.com
28 units, most air-conditioned,
fridges, microwaves. Cable TV,
free movies, barbecue area, senior
and family rates.

Sunset Motel
104 Highway 3 West
1-888-554-2784 or 403-553-4448
22 air-conditioned units. Refrigerators, free
coffee. Fax-ready telephones, cable TV
and movies, winter plug-ins. Gift shop,
free continental breakfast. Adjacent to
self-service laundry. Two-Diamond
rating, AAA.

Campgrounds

Buffalo Plains RV Park & Campground
7.5 miles (12 km) west of Fort Macleod,
via Route 785
403-553-2592
23 sites with views of foothills and
mountains, full and partial hookups.
Tenting area, firewood, community
fire pit. Showers, laundry, rest rooms,
dump station. Playground.

Daisy May Campground
On Lyndon Road
403-553-2455
120 sites, with full and partial hookups.
Laundry, camp kitchen. Heated pool,
game room, mini-golf. Near golf course.
Open May–October.

Granview RV Park
Off Highway 2 north,
.5 mile east on Highway 519
Near Head-Smashed-In Buffalo Jump
1-888-788-2222 or 403-687-3830
Spacious sites, full or partial hookups,
pull-throughs, fire pits, showers,
laundry. Swimming, fishing. Close
to golf course, attractions.

Oldman River Provincial Recreation Area
0.3 miles (0.5 km) northwest of Fort
Macleod on Highway 2
403-627-3765
40 sites on Pincher Creek. Sheltered
picnic areas, dump station, fishing,
canoe access.

Restaurants

Aunty Lynda's Dining Room
One-half block from Fort Museum
403-553-2655
Family dining featuring steaks, seafood,
pasta, soups, salad

Scarlet & Gold Inn
2373 7th Avenue
403-553-3337
Steaks, seafood, Sunday brunch
specialties.

Road Notes

This semiarid region seems like a Hollywood Western backlot. There is little shade from the sun, the soil is dry and rocky, and hot wind snaps your clothing when you step outside. It's easy to imagine that this place was once thick with buffalo, and you can picture nomadic Indian tribes setting up seasonal hunting camps as they traveled and hunted.

Just ahead is a UNESCO World Heritage Site called Head-Smashed-In Buffalo Jump, where the hunting practices of the Plains Indians, as well as their cultural history, is presented in a beautiful interpretive center. (See sidebar.)

As you continue driving north, the road divides **Claresholm**, a town of about 3,500 people. The Claresholm Museum and visitor information is found in an elegant old sandstone railroad station at 5126 Railway Avenue. You can also visit the town's original 1903 schoolhouse and a nearby log cabin dating from 1902. Other local offerings include bowling, billiards, motels, auto repair, a car dealer, and a grocery store. Call 403-625-3131. Camping with a dump station and playground is available in the town's Centennial Park.

About 25 miles (40 km) beyond Claresholm, you'll enter the historic village of **Nanton**, where antiques are taken seriously. Downtown Nanton shops hold uncountable treasures, crafts, and collectibles, plus the town's old blacksmith shop, the Willow Creek Forge. Also downtown: a tearoom, restaurants, and auto repair and gas services. Aircraft buffs will enjoy a stop at the Nanton Lancaster Society Air Museum on Highway 2 South. Open daily May to October. Weekends in off-season.

Driving north of Nanton, we encountered our first roadside wildlife: a buffalo herd grazing in the roadside grass. Numbering about a dozen, they didn't seem to mind the traffic or the idea of having their picture taken by a woman hanging out of an RV window. Remember, that's the best advice—stay in your vehicle, and if you want close-ups, get a longer lens. But don't risk your safety or harass the wildlife by approaching on foot.

What this part of Alberta lacks in topographic beauty (as compared to more spectacular, mountainous regions), it makes up for in the openness of sky, in the phenomenal shades of blue from delicate to rich, velvety hues—and the natural artistry in the clouds, in their streaks, layers, balls, and fingers in tones from gray to bleach white. It's a pleasure to just gaze at the heavens.

About 163 miles (262 km) north of the Canadian border, you'll see the turn onto Highway 23 West for **High River**, population 6,900. Architects, geologists, and historians alike will enjoy touring High River's sandstone buildings. You can also take a guided tour of local murals. Each summer the city hosts championship chuckwagon racing and a favorite local event, the Little Britches Rodeo. For more information, call the Chamber of Commerce at 403-652-3336. This is the last stop before Calgary, 37 miles (59 km) to the north.

CALGARY

From Fort Macleod: 105 miles (169 km)
To Red Deer: 86 miles (138 km) (not on map)
To Edmonton: 181 miles (291 km)

At the confluence of the Bow and Elbow Rivers, with the purple Rocky Mountains to the west, Calgary is a marvelous place to work and play.

Populated by 905,000 people, this town is experiencing a growth spurt, but it hasn't forgotten its roots in the Wild West. It is that unusual contrast of wilderness and metropolis, cowboys and businessmen, a rodeo among the skyscrapers, that makes Calgary such a popular destination. Throughout western Canada, this city has gained a winning reputation for its restaurants, shopping, museums, festivals, art, music, and flowers. And in the world of professional rodeo throughout North America, it is famed for its main event, the Calgary Stampede.

In the summer of 1875, when an expedition of North-West Mounted Police arrived to establish a fort here, the place very nearly was named Fort Brisebois. Inspector Ephraim Brisebois, an unpopular leader of the troop, intended to name the new fort for himself. Instead, Col. James Macleod, a Scotsman, suggested the name Fort Calgary in remembrance of his ancestral castle on the island of Skye. His choice prevailed.

The presence of white settlers was troubling and unwelcome to the local Niitsitapi, which means "real people" in the Blackfoot language. More than a century of resistance had already passed in bloody and destructive warfare. In 1877 the tribes of the Blackfoot Confederacy signed an important peace agreement, called Treaty 7, that designated boundaries for Native land reserves. Representing the North-West Mounted Police for the Queen of Great Britain and Ireland was James Macleod. Timing was important to the government, which planned to build a transcountry railway across aboriginal land by 1881.

Southern Alberta's Blackfoot Confederacy tribes—Blood, Peigan, Siksika, and Stoney—continue to practice traditions handed down from generation to generation. Learn more about the First Nations people at the **Tsuu T'ina Culture Museum**, 3700 Anderson Road. The museum features artifacts from Edmonton's Provincial Museum and from area residents whose ancestors traded with aboriginal people. For more information, call 403-238-2677.

Calgary's Olympic Park continues to draw athletes and fans from all over the world.

The Calgary Exhibition and Stampede, held in mid-July each year, fills the town with rodeo fans, cowboys, and cowgirls who come for some of the hottest competition in North America. Events include saddle bronco-riding, bull-riding, chuckwagon races, bareback riding, wild cow-milking events, and wild horse races. Rodeo clowns, parades, agriculture exhibitions, square dancing, a midway, and lots of food fill out the 10-day celebration. For details, call 403-269-9822 or visit *www.calgarystampede.com.*

Calgary was the host city for the 1988 Winter Olympic Games, and the ski jump, bobsled run, and slopes became familiar sites to television viewers, who can now ski the same slopes at Canada Olympic Park. In fact, you may even meet one of tomorrow's Olympic champions among the many skiers who train here year-round. You can share the slopes, the 295-foot ski jump, and the bobsled run from November through March. In summer, you'll spy young, daring mountain bikers who ride the ski lift with their bikes hooked on the side of their chairs. They virtually fly back down on two wheels.

The Olympic Hall of Fame and Museum in the park honors the stars of Olympic history. Bobsled and ski jump simulators make the experience real, and exhibits teach about developments in snow sports through decades. Admission is charged. For more information, call 403-247-5452 or visit *www.coda.ab.ca.*

Wondering where to take the kiddies? Let 'em run wild at Calaway Park, the largest outdoor amusement park in Western Canada, with rides, mini-golf, and live musical productions for the whole family. It's located 6 miles (10 km) west of Calgary on Highway 1. Call 403-240-3822 or browse *www.calawaypark.com.*

Fort Calgary Historic Park, at 950 9th Avenue SE, is a reconstruction of the original 1875 fort on a 40-acre site at the confluence of the Bow and Elbow Rivers. Interpreters share the stories of the early settlers and of this site. For information, call 403-290-1875 or see *www.fortcalgary.com.*

Even if you were just an average student in science, you'll reawaken a sense of discovery during a visit to the Calgary Science Centre. Hands-on, discovery-oriented exhibits make science fun again. Enter a world of adventure in the Discovery Dome theater, a surround-your-senses journey. The center is located at 701 11th Street SW. Call 403-221-3700 for more information or see *www.calgaryscience.ca.*

Glenbow Museum, Art Gallery, Library and Archives, at 130 9th Avenue SE, has something of interest for everyone, from excellent displays on cultural and military history to a mineralogy exhibit that includes one of the oldest rocks on the planet. The art gallery shows off its collection of block prints, early watercolors, and Inuit sculpture. For information, call 403-268-4100 or visit *www.glenbow.org.*

Calgary Zoo Botanical Garden & Prehistoric Park is not just for the kids. This world-class zoo features more than 900 animals, including some rare and endangered species, and a tropical aviary. Walk among spectacular, life-size replicas of dinosaurs in a vast park that's a re-creation of their surroundings. It's all found on St. George's Island in the middle of the Bow River. Open year-round. Call the zoo at 403-232-9300 or visit *www.calgaryzoo.ab.ca.*

Bird lovers can explore the **Inglewood Bird Sanctuary,** at 2425 9th Avenue SE, an attraction that features more than 250 species of birds and some mammals. Natural history programs for families introduce children to these natural wonders. Admission is free and they're open year-round. Call 403-269-6688 or browse *www.gov.calgary.ab.ca.* And another indoor, free-of-charge, family-oriented natural wonder is **Devonian Gardens,** with waterfalls, flowers, walkways, fountains, artwork, and playground. You'll find it at 317 7th Avenue SW, 4th floor. Call 403-221-4274 or go to *www.calgary.ca/parks.*

Just twenty-five minutes from downtown, golfers will find **The Links of GlenEagles** at 100 GlenEagles Drive, in Cochrane. This 18-hole course is the "Home of the PGA Tour," and a challenge for any level. Call 403-932-1100 or go to *www.gleneaglesgolf.com.* In Calgary itself, stop by the **McKenzie Meadows Golf Club,** a championship, 18-hole public course with power- and pull-carts, pro shop, restaurant, lounge, and patio. Call 403-253-7473 or visit *www.mckenziemeadows.com.*

If you're up for outdoor adventure, there are plenty of options: motor sports, world-class fly-fishing, photo safaris, hunting, horseback riding, rafting, hiking, and mountain biking. For more details on anything Calgary has to offer, call 1-800-661-1678 or 403-263-8510. Visit their Web site at *www.tourismcalgary.com.*

Lodging
For information on local bed-and-break-fasts, call the B&B Association of Calgary: 403-277-0023 or visit www.bbcalgary.com.

Best Western Port O' Call Inn
1935 McKnight Boulevard NE
1-800-661-1161 or 403-291-4600
www.bestwesternportocall.com
201 rooms, nonsmoking floors, movies, laundry service. Indoor pool, whirlpool, fitness center. Restaurant and two lounges. Free shuttle service.

Best Western Suites Downtown
1330 8th Street SW
1-800-981-2555 or 403-228-6900
www.bestwesternsuitescalgary.com
123 suites with kitchens, cable TV, laundry, fitness center, sauna. Three-Diamond rating, AAA. Close to downtown attractions and Stampede grounds.

Best Western Village Park Inn
1804 Crowchild Trail NW
1-888-774-7716 or 403-289-0241
www.villageparkinn.com
160 units in full-service hotel. Cable TV, hair dryers, free movies, ATM, business center, PC friendly, voicemail, laundry.

Budgetlodge
4420 16th Avenue NW
1-800-661-3772 or 403-288-7115
72 air-conditioned rooms, some nonsmoking. Cable TV, free coffee. Kids 11 and younger free in parents' room.

Calgary Marriott Hotel
110 9th Avenue SE
1-800-896-6878 or 403-266-7331
www.calgarymarriott.com
384 air-conditioned rooms, nonsmoking floors, cable TV, valet parking, gift shop. Room service, roll-in showers, modem jacks.

Coast Plaza Hotel
1316 33rd Street NE
Off Highway 1 at 36th Street
1-800-661-1464 or 403-248-8888
www.calgaryplaza.com
248 rooms, cable TV, movies, voice mail, modem jacks, coffee. Indoor pool, sauna, whirlpool. Restaurant, lounge, gift shop. Free shuttle.

A historic train, oil rig, antique farm equipment, and other working remnants of Alberta's past are housed in Heritage Park.

Take a Walk Through History

Experience time travel as you stroll the grounds of **Heritage Park**, Canada's largest living-history village, set in a 66-acre park at 1900 Heritage Drive SW. One section features an 1860s fur-trading post. Another is reminiscent of an 1880s pre-railway pioneer settlement; another is a street of businesses and residences set in about 1910. You are free to mill in and out of the buildings, relax in the grassy areas, or travel on a steam railway, a riverboat, or an antique carnival ride.

Antique machinery is well oiled and working at the old wooden oil rig. Elsewhere, the village blacksmith is hard at work, but willing to share his knowledge with visitors. A schoolmarm invites you into the old one-room school. Other costumed interpreters reenact a suffragette march, a wedding, a shootout. Children play on the antique carnival rides while parents read about their histories.

Take a ride on the riverboat SS Moxie as it cruises the adjacent reservoir. Peek into every room in the circa-1904 Burnside Ranch House, and wander through the Hudson's Bay Company fort and Indian village across the way. Buy goodies at the bakery, see how a printing press worked, step inside the historic church, savor an ice cream cone in the heat of the day.

It's a lot of walking, but you can pick up a ride on the train or a horse-drawn buggy. Plan your time well and make a day of it. If you arrive between 9 A.M. and 10 A.M. and pay full admission price, you are entitled to the free Western buffet-style breakfast served in the Wainwright Hotel. Parking may be some distance from the park entrance, but you can hop on an antique trolley to shorten the ride. For more information, contact 403-268-8500 or browse www.heritagepark.ca.

Comfort Inn & Suites—Motel Village
2369 Banff Trail NW
1-800-228-5150 or 403-289-2581
www.comfortinncalgary.com
82 units, nonsmoking floors available,
  cable TV, hair dryers, high-speed
  Internet service. Two-story waterslide.
  Free continental breakfast.

Delta Bow Valley Inn
209 4th Avenue SE
1-800-268-1133 or 403-266-1980
www.deltabowvalley.com
398 rooms in landmark facility,
  nonsmoking floors. Cable TV,
  exercise facilities, gift shop.

Econo Lodge—Banff Trail
2231 Banff Trail NW
1-800-917-7779 or 403-289-1921
www.econolodgecalgary.com
62 rooms, cable TV, free movies, hair
  dryers, irons and boards, high-speed
  Internet access. Swimming pool,
  whirlpool, hot tub.

Econo Lodge—Motel Village
2440 16th Avenue NW
1-800-917-7779 or 403-289-2561
56 rooms and kitchenettes, modem
  jacks, laundry. Fitness center,
  pool, free movies. Restaurant,
  free continental breakfast.

Econo Lodge West
10117 West Valley Road SW
403-288-4436
50 units next to Olympic Park, cable TV,
  exercise room, hot tub, laundry, modem
  jacks. Indoor pool, steam/sauna.

Elbow River Inn & Casino
1919 Macleod Trail SE
1-800-661-1463 or 403-269-6771
www.elbowrivercasino.com
75 rooms, cable TV, room service.
  Restaurant with outdoor patio,
  cocktail lounge, casino. On the
  Elbow River, opposite Calgary
  Stampede grounds.

Fairmont Palliser
133 9th Avenue SW
1-800-441-1414 or 403-262-1234
www.fairmont.com
405 rooms in historic downtown landmark,
  full-service hotel, cable TV, health club,
  hot tub, modem jacks, covered parking.
  Room, service, saltwater pool.

Four Points Sheraton Calgary West
8220 Bow Ridge Crescent NW
1-877-288-4441 or 403-288-4441
www.fourpointscalgarywest.com
118 units, suites with fireplaces and
  Jacuzzis available, cable TV, fridges,
  hair dryers, high-speed Internet
  service, microwaves. Gift shop, covered
  parking, room service. Indoor pool
  and water slide.

Greenwood Inn
3515 26th Street NE
1-888-233-6730 or 403-250-8855
www.greenwoodinn.ca/calgary
213 units, full-service hotel. Cable TV,
  nonsmoking floors, laundry and
  room service. Indoor pool, whirlpool,
  steam room, gift shop. Restaurant,
  lounge. Rated 3 Diamond, AAA. Close
  to airport.

Hampton Inn & Suites—Calgary University
2231 Banff Trial NW
1-888-432-6777 or 403-289-9800
www.hamptoncalgary.com
96 units, cable TV, free movies,
  fridges, microwaves, hair dryers,
  free high-speed/wireless Internet
  access. Exercise facility, hot tub, gift
  shop. Water slide, deluxe continental
  breakfast, shuttle.

Holiday Inn Downtown
119 12th Avenue SW
1-800-661-9378 or 403-266-4611
www.holidayinn-calgary.com
188 rooms, cable TV, movies, year-round
  outdoor pool. Restaurant, room service,
  lounge, café. Downtown, close to
  attractions and shopping.

The Pointe Inn
1808 19th Street NE
1-800-661-8164 or 403-291-4681
www.pointeinn.com
151 units, cable TV, fridges, high-speed
    Internet access, laundry. Room service,

Quality Inn
2359 Banff Trail NW, off Highway 1
1-800-661-4667 or 403-289-1973
105 rooms. Indoor pool, whirlpool,
    sauna, steam room. Lounge, poolside
    restaurant. High-speed wireless
    and 24-hour business center. Free
    continental breakfast.

Ramada Limited
2363 Banff Trail NW
1-800-272-6232 or 403-289-5571
www.ramada.com
70 units, close to university, cable TV, free
    movies, hair dryers, irons and boards,
    laundry, modem jacks. Hot tub. Free
    continental breakfast.

Sandman Hotel Calgary Airport
25 Hopewell Way NE
1-866-285-7263 or 403-219-2475
www.sandmanhotels.com
177 rooms and suites, cable TV, fridges,
    hair dryers, PC friendly. Health club/spa,
    hot tub. Free shuttle service. Moxie's
    Classic Grill, room service.

Sandman Hotel Downtown
888 7th Avenue SW
1-800-726-3626 or 403-237-8626
www.sandmanhotels.com
301 rooms, cable TV, movies, voice mail.
    Indoor pool, whirlpool, sauna, fitness
    center. Moxie's Grill & M Bar Lounge,
    room service.

Sheraton Cavalier Hotel
2620 32nd Avenue SE
1-800-325-3535 or 403-291-0107
www.sheraton-calgary.com
306 units in full-service hotel. Cable TV,
    hair dryers, hot tub, high-speed
    Internet access, Concierge, room
    service, sports bar. Indoor waterpark.
    Shuttle service.

**Travelodge Hotel Calgary
    International Airport**
2750 Sunridge Blvd. NE
1-800-578-7878 or 403-291-1260
www.the.travelodge.com/calgary09752
203 rooms 10 minutes from airport.
    Cable TV, hair dryers, room service.
    Free shuttle service, vehicle plug-ins.

The Westin Calgary
320 4th Avenue SW
1-800-937-8461 or 403-266-1611
525 deluxe air-conditioned rooms in
    full-service hotel. Cable TV, high-speed
    Internet, business center, gift shop.
    Pool, whirlpool, exercise facility.
    Senior discount. Downtown location.

Campgrounds
Back Acres RV
8515 36th Street NE
403-273-5289
300 grassy sites for dry-camping RVers
    within Calgary city limits. Reservations
    recommended.

Calaway RV Park and Campground
6 miles (10 km) west of Calgary on Highway 1
403-249-7372
108 sites in country setting, full and partial
    hookups. Showers, laundry, dump
    station. Grocery store. Walking distance
    to amusement park.

Calgary West KOA
Highway 1 southside near Olympic Park
1-800-562-0842 or 403-288-0411
More than 300 sites, with and without
    hookup. Showers, laundry, flush toilets,
    dump station. Picnic grounds, outdoor
    pool, mini-golf, store. Wheelchair
    access. Downtown shuttle.

Camp 'N RV Park
Near Chestermere Lake
1-888-899-2267 or 403-273-5122
140 sites with full and partial hookups,
    tenting. Firepits, picnic tables, Internet
    access. Lake nearby. Shuttle during
    Calgary Stampede.

Mountain View Farm Camping
2 miles (3 km) east of Calgary on Highway 1
403-293-6640 or 403-285-0326
www.calgarycamping.com
160 sites with and without hookup. 15- and
    30-amp service. Propane, showers,
    rest room, campfire pits, shelter.
    Mini-mart. Playground, petting zoo,
    fish pond, mini-golf. Tours available
    by coach or van. Open year-round.
    Reservations recommended.

South of Calgary:
Country Lane RV Park
On Highway 2, 4 miles east of Okotoks
403-995-2330
www.countrylanerv.com
300 treed sites, paved roads, gates security.
    Clubhouse, showers, store, lounge,
    kitchen, library, Internet. Fitness area,
    games room. Newer playground. Wheel-
    chair access. Reservations recommended.

Nature's Hideaway Campground
DeWinton, on Highwood River
403-938-8185
www.natureshideaway.com
Tent and RV campsites. Fishing, swimming,
    playground, free showers.

Pine Creek RV Campground
DeWinton, south of Calgary
403-256-3002
99 sites with 30- and 50-amp service in
    country setting, picnic tables, showers,
    lounge, billiards, covered pavilion,
    laundry, wheelchair access, store.
    Reservations recommended.

Restaurants
Ben Venuto's
118 8th Avenue SW
403-770-0600
Italian dining in historic Tribune Block.
    Patio, live entertainment.

Brava Bistro
723 17th Avenue SW
403-228-1854
www.bravabistro.com
Modern Mediterranean. Honored in
    Calgary Magazine.

Brewsters Brewing Company & Restaurant
101 Barclay Parade SW
403-225-1767
www.brewstersbrewingco.com
Pizza, burgers, entrees, premium beers
    brewed on site.

Buon Giorno Ristorante Italiano
823 17th Avenue SW
403-244-5522
Northern Italian cuisine. Fireplace, private
    dining area.

Buzzards Cowboy Cuisine
140 10th Avenue SW
403-264-6959
www.cowboycuisine.com
Cowboy restaurant featuring beef.

The Calgary Tower
101 9th Avenue
403-266-7171
Above downtown Calgary, a revolving
    restaurant with a 360-degree view
    of city and mountains.

Catch Oyster Bar & Seafood Restaurant
100 Stephen Avenue
403-206-0000
www.creativeri.com
Oyster bar, dining room, skyline view.

Ceili's Irish Pub & Restaurant
125,513 8th Avenue SW
www.ceilis.com
Irish pub sprawling over four
    floors with theme décor.
    Lunch and dinner.

Centini Restaurant & Lounge
160 8th Avenue
403-269-0600
Italian/Continental European cuisine,
    extensive wine selection.

Ed's Restaurant
202 17th Avenue
403-262-3500
www.edsrestaurant.com
Alberta beef, pasta, seafood. Six dining
    rooms in 1911 house.

The Elephant & Castle Restaurant & Pub
100 751 3rd Street SW
403-265-3555
www.elephantcastle.com
British fare, fish and chips a specialty.

Fionn MacCool's Irish Pub
255 Barclay Parade SW
403-517-6699
Traditional Irish and Canadian cuisine.
    Live Celtic entertainment.

Il Giardino Ristorante
344 17th Avenue SW
403-541-0088
Traditional Italian cuisine. Pasta, veal,
    seafood, chicken, beef, lamb.

Japanese Village Restaurant
302 4th Avenue SW
403-262-2738
Teppan-grill dining, tableside cooking.
    Steak, chicken, seafood.

LaCaille Restaurant
100 LaCaille Place
403-262-5554
Casual eatery, two fireplaces, view of Bow
    River, more than 250 wines.

La Chaumiere Restarant
139 17th Avenue SW
403-228-5690
French cuisine featuring rack of lamb,
    grilled tuna, extensive wine list.

The Living Room
514 17th Avenue SW
403-228-9830
Oysters, seafood, Alberta beef, cheese and
    chocolate fondues.

Mother Tucker's Food Experience
345 10th Avenue SW
403-262-5541
Famed salad bar. Prime rib, steaks, ribs,
    children's menu. Sunday brunch.

Oh! Canada Restaurant & Bar Inc.
815 7th Avenue SW, Nexen Tower
403-266-1551
www.ohcanadarestaurant.com
Seasonal and regional features, food and
    drink from across Canada.

The Ranche
15979 Bow Bottom Trail SE
403-225-3939
www.theranche.com
Seafood, game specialties.
    Served in historic mansion.

River Café
Prince's Island Park
403-261-7670
www.river-café.com
Canadian fare, wood-fired cuisine. Organic,
    locally grown ingredients. Park setting.

Rouge
1240 8 th Avenue SE
403-531-2767
www.rougecalgary.com
French cuisine in former home of A. E. Cross.
Seafood, game, beef, lamb.

Teatro
200 8th Avenue SE
403-290-1012
www.teatro-rest.com
Italian-inspired regional cuisine.
    Wood-burning oven, extensive
    wine selection.

Road Notes

Highway 2 between Calgary and Edmonton follows the route of a century-old trail. In the mid-1880s, entrepreneur John Dickson established several "stopping houses" along this rude trail. When he abandoned the southernmost stopping house, a neighboring homesteader, Johnston Stevenson, claimed the site and building and reopened it. Their names were merged as "Dickson-Stevenson Stopping House" for the roadhouse that served travelers for decades.

Although that building no longer stands, motorists can still pull over near its original site for rest and refreshment at the modern **Dickson-Stevenson Stopping House,** located about 24 miles (38 km) north of Calgary on Highway 2. The rest stop offers snacks, fast food, visitor information, and historical plaques about the Old Calgary Trail. The first automobile journey over the decaying trail between Calgary and Edmonton took place in 1906.

A distinct line exists between city and farmland as you travel north out of Calgary. Clearly, controlled growth is under way as subdivision homes are tightly clustered in the middle distance, while cows graze alongside the road. The speed limit is 110 kmh on this six-lane highway. It's easy driving on a flat landscape. You can see a rain-shower coming for miles before the first drop hits the windshield.

As you continue north, dairy cattle become more and more a part of the land-scape, and the road is no longer a superhighway. The land begins to roll in low hills, and more sections are wooded. Here and there, you'll see evidence of the oil industry with solitary pumpjacks at work in fields and pastures.

Red Deer

From Calgary: 86 miles (139 km)
To Ponoka: 35 miles (56 km)
To Edmonton: 96 miles (154 km)

Roughly halfway between Calgary and Edmonton, Red Deer is the government seat for a county of the same name. A city of 60,000, it offers full services for travelers, from automotive repair to major shopping areas, entertainment, lodging, campgrounds, and an abundance of restaurants.

Red Deer takes pride in its area parklands, which range from swimming beaches and wooded trails, to an equestrian facility, golf courses, and (surprisingly) a ski area amid these low, rolling hills. The Red Deer River cuts a canyon through the fertile farms and parklands, and flows through the center of town.

Heritage Ranch on Highway 2 north of 32nd Street is a gateway to the Waskasoo Park system, which lies at the heart of Red Deer. A visitor center at the ranch includes knowledgeable staff, a gift shop, and a café. From here, you can walk, skate, or cycle the vast corridor of river valley nature trails. Within the park you'll find picnic areas, playgrounds, and fishing ponds. There are pony rides for the kids, too. Admission is free. Call 1-800-215-8946 or 403-346-0180.

The **Kerry Wood Nature Centre** hosts nature walks and canoe tours, as well as presentations for children. An exhibit gallery, theater, and bookstore are on site at 6300 45th Avenue. Admission is free. Call 403-346-2010.

You can wander through the original James Bower homestead on a lovely 10-acre site bordering Piper Creek. The homestead is at the **Sunnybrook Farm Museum** and **Agriculture Interpretive Centre**, which offers a relaxing as well as informative tour and a look back at the pioneering ways of running a farm.

Another county jewel is **Sylvan Lake**, 10 miles (16 km) west of Red Deer on Highway 11, which has been developed for holiday fun since 1901. Each summer the lake is dotted with fishermen and water-skiers, boaters, and windsurfers. Even parasailers can be seen flying overhead. Its sandy beaches are perfect for family fun, and playing on the Wild Rapids water slides will consume a whole day before you know it. Nearby are several private campgrounds and the Sylvan Lake Provincial Park.

Red Deer is proud of its Collicutt Centre, with a wave pool, water park, water-slide, ice arena, climbing walls, and much more. Located south of 32nd Street on 30th Avenue, it's a terrific place for families. Other indoor and outdoor pools can be found throughout town. And be sure to investigate Red Deer's historical treasures as well. For more information about Red Deer events and attractions, call 1-800-215-8946 or 403-346-0180, or visit the city's Web site at *www.tourismreddeer.net*.

Lodging

Black Night Inn
2929 Gaetz Avenue
1-800-661-8793 or 403-343-6666
98 deluxe rooms, suites, cable TV, high-speed Internet, fridges, ATM. Whirlpool, indoor/ outdoor pool, spa. Restaurant, lounge.

Capri Hotel & Convention Centre
3310 50th Avenue
1-800-662-7197 or 403-346-2091
www.capricentre.com
219 air-conditioned rooms in full-service hotel. Cable TV, movies, modem jacks, hair dryers, irons and boards. Exercise room, hair salon, gift shop, business center. Winter plug-ins.

Holiday Inn 67 Street
6500 67th Street
1-800-661-4961 or 403-342-6567
www.hi67.com
97 units in full-service hotel. Cable TV, games, fridges, modem jacks, hair dryers, high-speed Internet. Roll-in shower, health spa, room service. Sports bar, business center.

Holiday Inn Express—Red Deer
2803 50th Avenue
1-800-223-1993 or 403-343-2112
92 air-conditioned rooms, family suites, hair dryers, microwaves, irons. Cable TV, laundry, high-speed Internet, coffee. Indoor atrium with saltwater pool. Free continental breakfast.

North Hill Inn
7150 Gaetz Avenue
1-800-662-7152 or 403-343-8800
www.northhillinn.com
117 rooms, including 40 executive rooms. Cable TV, hair dryers, irons, modem jacks. Hot tub, nightly entertainment.

Red Deer Lodge Hotel & Conference Centre
4311 49th Avenue
1-800-661-1657 or 403-346-8841
www.reddeerlodge.net
233 deluxe rooms, air-conditioning, phones, coffee. Hair salon, exercise room, indoor pool, whirlpool, restaurants.

Rest E-Z Inn
37557 Highway 2 South
1-800-424-9454 or 403-343-8444
www.restezinn.com
76 units, cable TV, movies, free local calls, barbecue area, laundry. Vehicle plug-ins. Free continental breakfast.

Sandman Hotel Red Deer
2818 Gaetz Avenue
1-800-SANDMAN or 403-343-7400
www.sandmanhotels.com
142 rooms, cable TV, hair dryers,
   irons, modem jacks. Exercise
   rooms, restaurant.

Service Plus Inns & Suites
6853 66th Street
1-888-875-4667 or 403-342-4445
www.serviceplus.svh.com
92 units, fridges, hair dryers, modem
   jacks, free local calls. Small pets okay
   in smoking rooms. Exercise room.

Stanford Inn—Red Deer
4707 Ross Street
1-877-347-5551 or 403-347-5551
www.stanfordinn.net
62 air-conditioned rooms, hair dryers,
   irons and boards, cable TV, ATM.
   Family restaurant, bar and grill.
   Downtown.

Super 8 Motel Red Deer
7474 50th Avenue
1-877-488-2288
www.super8.com
72 units, cable TV, modem jacks. Free
   local calls, winter plug-ins.

Travelodge
2807 Gaetz Avenue
1-800-578-7878 or 403-346-2011
www.travelodge.com
136 air-conditioned rooms,
   kitchenettes and nonsmoking
   available, cable TV. Modem access,
   self-service laundry. Indoor pool,
   whirlpool. Restaurant.

Area Campgrounds
Red Deer:
Crooked Tree RV Park & Campground
Highway 2 to 11A West, to 275 North
403-314-9577
50 sites with power, water, showers,
   play area, dump station, wood.
   Near golf.

Lions Campground
4723 Riverside Drive, east of 49th Avenue
403-342-8183
89 sites with full hookups, 38 with partial.
   Dump station, wheelchair access,
   showers. Playground, bike trails.

Westerner Campground
4847D 19th Street,
   from Highway 2, take 2A exit
403-352-8801
www.westernercampground.com
99 sites with full or partial hookups,
   41 pull-throughs. Pool, biking and
   hiking trails. 30- and 50-amp service,
   laundry, showers. Close to shopping
   and dining.

Red Deer Area:
A-Soo-Wuh-Um Campground
West off Highway 2 on Route 592 for
   6.5 miles (10.5 km)
403-886-2001
45 campsites for tents or RVs, free showers,
   sani-dump, firewood. Boat launch,
   fishing, playground.

Aspen Beach Provincial Park
On Gull Lake, 17 km west of Lacombe
   on Highway 12
403-784-4066
306 private, treed sites for dry-
   camping or tents; 288 additional
   sites for pull-throughs, full and
   partial hookups.

DeGraff's Camp Resort
On Gull Lake, 9.4 km north of Highway 12,
   or 11 km south of Highway 53
403-782-2193
98 sites with full and partial hookups.
   Family fun: fishing, swimming,
   horse rides, wading pools,
   trampolines, mini-golf, games.
   Boat launch, laundry, showers,
   wheelchair accessible.

Green Acres
On Pine Lake, east on Highway 42,
    then south to #816
1-888-999-4833 or 403-886-4833
450 sites with full or partial hookups.
    15-, 30-, and 50-amp sites.
    Heated swimming pool,
    playgrounds, boat rentals,
    marina, coffee shop, store,
    near golf. Security patrols.

Leisure Campgrounds & Cabins
Highway 42,
    north end of Pine Lake
403-886-4705
www.leisurecampgrounds.com
380 sites and 10 cabins. Sandy
    beaches, fishing boats and
    watercraft rentals, arcade,
    café, groceries, fishing tackle.

Michener Park Campground
5429 53rd Street,
    west end of Lacombe
403-782-1250
www.town.lacombe.ab.ca
57 sites, pull-throughs available.
    Showers, fire pits, free firewood,
    picnic tables, day use area.
    Across from golf.

Restaurants

Dino's Family Restaurant
4617 Gaetz Avenue
403-347-5585
Italian and western cuisine,
    pizza, pasta.

Dragon City Café
2325 50th Avenue, #157
403-340-3388
Weekday lunch buffet, weekend brunch
    and evening buffet.

East Side Mario's
2004 50th Avenue
403-342-2279
A taste of New York's "Little Italy," pasta,
    pizza, salad, New York sandwiches.

The Keg Steakhouse & Bar
6365 50th Avenue
403-309-5499
Steak, prime rib, seafood, pasta.

Lakewood Golf Course & RV Park
Breakfast specialty; burgers, pizza.

Mohave Grill
6608 Orr Drive
403-340-3453
Southwest cuisine.

Montana's Cookhouse
195, 2004 Gaetz Avenue
403-352-0030
Country cooking.

Red Deer Chinese Buffet Restaurant
5320 50th Avenue, #35 in Village Mall
403-342-5555
Szechwan and Cantonese cuisine.

Sylvan Lake Golf & Country Club
5331 Lakeshore Drive
403-887-6695
Bogie's Restaurant features casual dining;
    Eagle's Nest for fine dining.

Tony Roma's
5250 22nd Street
403-358-3223
Ribs, chicken, pasta, seafood entrees.

White Spot
6701 Gaetz Avenue
403-358-6092
Breakfast, lunch, dinner.

Road Notes

We recommend a side trip through Devon on your way to Edmonton. Just before the town of Leduc, turn west on Highway 39, then north on Highway 60 to visit the Leduc No. 1 Historic Site, birthplace of Alberta's oil industry. Here the first major oil find was made on February 13, 1947. A 174-foot (53-m) replica of the original oil derrick stands beside an information center. Other tools of the trade and interpretive signs may be viewed in outdoor and indoor exhibits.

Visit the **Devonian Botanic Garden,** operated by the University of Alberta, on Highway 60 about 3 miles (5 km) north of Devon. Various gardens roll over its 80 acres, including the popular Kurimoto Japanese Garden. You can walk among the butterflies in the Butterfly House and on trails through forest and wetlands. Orchid lovers will find their own house of orchids. There's a gift shop and picnic area, too, and plenty of parking for RV travelers.

Another worthwhile stop, about 40 miles (65 km) before Edmonton, is **Westaskiwin,** a town that truly values history. Collectors will enjoy exploring the many antique shops and restored historical buildings, while the motorheads in the family will linger with the historical cars, tractors, and airplanes in the Reynolds-Alberta Museum collection. This is not your average museum approach to gazing at displays. Visitors may ride in the cockpit of a plane, or go for a joyride in an antique car. The museum celebrating the "Spirit of the Machine" also houses a café and gift shop. Call 1-800-661-4726 or 780-361-1351. Browse their Web site at *www.reynoldsalbertamuseum.com.*

EDMONTON

From Calgary: 181 miles (291 km)
To Whitecourt: 112 miles (180 km)

Edmonton is an old city by western standards. It dates back to 1795, when the Hudson's Bay Company established Edmonton House, a trading post along the mighty North Saskatchewan River. Here, local Cree and Blackfoot Indians traded furs for goods. After a century of growth, it was an incorporated city of 700 people.

Edmonton is Canada's fifth-largest city and a hub for shopping, dining, and cultural events.

Another century passed to find Edmonton a city of polish and sophistication sprouting in the midst of fields, reminiscent of the Emerald City in *The Wizard of Oz*. The area population today: 666,000. And in 2004, Edmonton celebrated a century as an incorporated city.

This is Alberta's capital city, Canada's second-largest metropolitan area west of Toronto, and the fifth-largest city in Canada. Edmonton also is home to West Edmonton Mall, the largest shopping mall in the world (see accompanying sidebar).

Edmonton is known as the **Oil Capital of Canada**. Edmonton Tourism cites this amazing statistic: The amount of crude oil processed in metropolitan Edmonton each day is enough to change the oil of every car in Canada.

The dollars from oil have been poured into the culture and comfort of the citizenry. The city has two dozen art and history museums and more than a dozen theater companies (more per capita than any other city in Canada). Rain or shine, downtown pedestrians can freely move about in elevated, enclosed walkways or through underground and street-level "pedways."

There are 46 golf courses in Metro Edmonton and another 27 in the area, hundreds of shops, dozens of hotels, and more than 2,000 dining establishments. If you want to spend money and feel like you're getting something for it, this is the place to visit. And by the way, Alberta has no provincial sales tax.

Edmonton is a city that loves to play—every month, it seems, the city hosts a festival, rodeo, carnival, anniversary, or other celebration, earning it yet another title: Canada's Festival City. See *www.festivalcity.ca*. These celebrations of music, theater, history, horsemanship, and home can be found in every season, among them: Canadian National Competition Powwow (late May), Northern Alberta International Children's Festival (early June); River City Shakespeare Festival (late June through late July); Canada Day Celebrations (July 1); Klondike Days (late July); Edmonton Heritage Festival (early August); Labatt Blues Festival (late August); Dragon Boat Festival (late August); Enbridge Symphony Under the Sky Festival and Canadian Country Music Week (early September); Global Visions Film Festival (early November); and Canadian Finals Rodeo (mid-November).

For stunning beauty, albeit manmade, visit the **Great Divide Waterfall** on the High Level Bridge. Built to honor Alberta's 75th anniversary, the waterfall is 24 feet higher than Niagara Falls.

The **Provincial Museum of Alberta** is one of Canada's most popular museums, featuring exhibits on a broad range of subjects, from the province's aboriginal people to dinosaurs, geology, insects, Ice Age mammals, and more. Admission is charged. Call 780-453-9100 or visit *www.pma.edmonton.ab.ca*.

Fort Edmonton Park, at Fox and Whitemud Drives, is a 158-acre living-history park, the country's largest, with 60 period buildings to explore. Walk through time at the 1846 fort, or down streets from 1885, 1905, and 1920. Watch a blacksmith or an old-fashioned rope-maker at work. Catch a ride on a stagecoach or the steam train. This is a great place to teach kids about history while they're having fun. You'll find plenty of gift shops and restaurants. For more information, call 780-496-8787 or visit the Web site *www.gov.edmonton.ab.ca/fort.*

A futuristic building at 142nd and 112th Avenues houses the **Odyssium,** Edmonton's space and science museum with five interactive galleries. Inside, kids and adults alike will enjoy observation and hands-on science—from helping to solve a crime with forensic science, to learning more about wildfires, the weather, and other natural phenomena. Features include a planetarium, laser shows, mock Challenger missions, and an IMAX theater. Call 780-451-3344 or visit *www.odyssium.com.*

Church Street (officially 96th Street) is listed in *Ripley's Believe It or Not* for the 16 churches you'll find in one small section. Another local "oddity," although it's not listed in Ripley's, is Edmonton's prized four-story-high cowboy boot at **Western Boot Factory,** 10007 167th Street. This city also claims the distinction of having the longest stretch of urban park in Canada: the North Saskatchewan River Valley park system.

The **Alberta Legislature Building,** at 10800 97th Avenue, is an architectural wonder built in 1912 on the site of Fort Edmonton. An interpretive center follows the building's history and provincial politics. Guided tours are available daily. Call for scheduled times at 780-427-7362 or visit the Web site at *www.assembly.ab.ca.*

Take a cruise on the *Edmonton Queen* riverboat, which offers daily cruises through the river valley. Board at Rafter's Landing, on the south side of the river. Dinner cruises with Dixieland entertainment are available, too. Call 780-424-2628 or see *www.edmontonqueen.com.*

For more information on local events and attractions, call **Edmonton Tourism** at 1-800-463-4667 or 780-496-8400 or visit their Web site: *www.edmonton.com.*

Lodging

Alberta Place Suite Hotel
10049 103rd Street
1-800-661-3982 or 780-423-1565
www.albertaplace.com
85 units, cal TV, modem jacks, fridges, microwaves, high-speed Internet, laundry. Exercise room, indoor pool. Pets welcome.

Algonquin Motor Lodge
10401 Mayfield Road
780-489-401
64 units, some with air-conditioning. Cable TV, free coffee, hot tub. Close to restaurants, tourist attractions.

Best Western City Centre
11310 109th Street
1-800-666-5026 or 780-479-2042
www.bestwestern.com
109 air-conditioned rooms, indoor pool, whirlpool, laundry, modem jacks. ATM, restaurant, lounge. Close to shopping.

Best Western Westwood Inn
18035 Stony Plain Road
1-800-557-4767 or 780-483-7770
169 air-conditioned rooms, cable TV, movies, laundry service. Indoor pool, sauna, whirlpool, steam room, squash court. Restaurant, lounge.

Canterra Suites Executive Hotel

11010 Jasper Avenue
1-877-421-1212 or 780-421-1212
www.canterrasuites.com
44 apartments, 1-3 bedrooms, cable TV,
free movies. Fridges, microwaves,
washer/dryer, free Internet, hair
dryers, irons and boards. Close
to shopping.

Chateau Louis Hotel

11727 Kingsway
1-800-661-9843 or 780-452-7770
140 rooms, suites, family rooms, cable TV,
hair dryers, irons, modem jacks, roll-in
shower. Business center, 24-hour room
service, restaurant, lounge.

Coast Edmonton Plaza Hotel

10155 105th Street
780-423-4811
www.coasthotels.com
299 deluxe rooms, suites, cable TV, laundry
service. Exercise room, indoor pool.
Lounge, family restaurant. Downtown,
close to business and government.

Coast Terrace Inn Edmonton South

4440 Gateway Blvd.
1-888-837-7223 or 780-437-6010
www.coastterraceinn.com
234 spacious rooms with amenities.
Fitness and racquet club, indoor
saltwater pool, sauna, steam rooms.
Restaurant, lounge, pub. Between
airport and downtown.

Comfort Inn & Suites (Downtown)

10425 100th Avenue
1-888-384-6835 or 780-423-5611
102 air-conditioned rooms, modem
jacks. Indoor pool, sauna,
whirlpool. Lounge, restaurant.
Free continental breakfast.

Comfort Inn (West Edmonton)

17610 100th Avenue West
1-800-228-5150 or 780-484-4415
www.choicehotels.ca/cn234
100 rooms, cable TV, movies, PC friendly,
hair dryers, irons, restaurant. Close to
West Edmonton Mall.

Continental Inn & Suites

16625 Stony Plain Road
1-888-484-9660 or 780-484-7751
www.continentalinn.ca
100 units with amenities, cable TV, free
movies, modem jacks, laundry. Dining,
lounge, coffee shop, room service.

Crowne Plaza Chateau Lacombe

10111 Bellamy Hill
1-800-661-8801 or 780-428-6611
www.chateaulacombe.com
307 deluxe rooms, suites, in 24-story hotel.
Gift shop, revolving restaurant, café,
two lounges, baby-sitting. Close
to shopping, entertainment. Airport
shuttle.

Days Inn Downtown Edmonton

10041 106th Street
1-800-267-2191 or 780-423-1925
www.daysinn.com
71 units, cable TV, hair dryers, modem jacks,
ATM. Covered parking, room service.
Airport shuttle.

Days Inn and Suites West Edmonton

10010 179A Street
1-866-441-1441 or 780-444-4440
www.daysinnwestedmonton.com
108 units in new hotel with free high-speed
Internet, cable TV, games, free movies.
Exercise room, saltwater pool, business
center, laundry. Room service.

Delta Edmonton Centre Suite Hotel

10222 102nd Street
1-800-268-1133 or 780-429-3900
www.deltaedmontoncentre.com
169 deluxe suites and rooms. High-speed
Internet, business center, baby-sitting.
Whirlpool, sauna, restaurant, lounge.
In City Centre Shopping Complex.

Edmonton House Suite Hotel

10205 100th Avenue
1-888-962-2522 or 780-420-4000
303 four-room suites with kitchens,
balconies, high-speed Internet.
Indoor pool, exercise and game
rooms. Store, restaurant, lounge.
Airport shuttle.

Dino-riffic Drumheller

If you have an extra day in your travel schedule, take a side trip to Alberta's Badlands and the city of **Drumheller**, 83 miles (134 km) east of Crossfield and Highway 2, via Highway 72. Experience a dramatic change in scenery, as the land around you changes from farms and field to twisting canyonlands, rocks walls, and hoodoos. You can't miss the wonderful dinosaur sculptures on nearly every corner of the town, and a true giant presides over the grounds of the visitor center. He's many stories high, and after climbing many stairs inside, visitors can peek out through his dino-teeth.

The town is named for American businessman Sam Drumheller, who in 1911 launched the area's first coal-mining operation. Now his name is synonymous not with coal, but with dinosaurs. Just outside town, follow the Dinosaur Trail on a 33-mile (53-km) loop from the north side of the river off Highway 9 into the Valley of the Dinosaurs.

Along the way, in Midland Provincial Park, you'll find the **Royal Tyrrell Museum of Paleontology**. In 1884 Joseph Burr Tyrrell found a fossil of a dinosaur nearly as large as the famed tyrannosaur; he named the find Albertosaurus. His discovery launched even more digging as other paleontologists arrived to launch their own excavations. The museum features more than two dozen complete dinosaur skeletons, along with finds of other prehistory creatures. Little is left to the imagination in the walk-through diorama-style exhibits. It's as if you were entering the days of the dinosaurs. Admission is charged. Call 1-800-440-4240 or 403-823-7707. ●

Billed as the world's largest dinosaur, this monster towers over the Drumheller visitor information center. Climb the stairs inside and grab the view from its open jaws.

Edmonton Inn
11830 Kingsway Avenue
1-800-661-7264 or 780-454-9521
www.edmontoninn.com
115 units, cable TV, games, laundry,
modem jacks. ATM, business
center. Exercise room, gift shop,
hair salon, hot tub. Sports bar.
Close to airport, mall.

Executive Royal Inn West Edmonton
10010 178th Street
1-800-661-4879 or 780-484-6000
www.executivehotels.net
236 units, cable TV, games, high-speed
Internet. ATM, business center,
executive wing. Room service.
Gift shop.

Fairmont Hotel Macdonald
10065 100th Street
1-800-441-1414 or 780-424-5181
www.fairmont.com
198 units in downtown four-diamond
hotel. Cable TV, modem jacks, hair
dryers, high-speed Internet. Exercise
room, hot tub, business center.
Saltwater pool.

**Fantasyland Hotel at
West Edmonton Mall**
17700 87th Avenue
1-800-737-3783 or 780-444-3000
www.fantasylandhotel.com
355 units with 11 theme rooms, cable TV,
high-speed Internet, fridges,
hair dryers. Health club/spa, hair
salon, vehicle plug-ins. Adjacent to
World Waterpark.

Greenwood Inn
4485 Gateway Blvd. (Highway 2)
1-888-233-6730 or 780-431-1100
224 rooms in southside hotel. Cable TV,
movies, laundry service. Indoor pool,
whirlpool, steam room, exercise room.
Gift shop, restaurant.

Hilton Garden Inn West Edmonton
17610 Stony Plain Road
780-443-2233
www.westedmonton.hiltongardeninn.com
160 units, cable TV, free movies, modem
jacks, fridges, hair dryers, irons and
boards. Exercise room, hot tub, sports
bar, room service.

Holiday Inn Express Downtown
10010 104th Street
1-800-877-4656 or 780-2450
140 air-conditioned rooms, cable TV,
balconies. Laundry facilities, room
service. Indoor pool, whirlpool, sauna,
hair salon. Restaurant, lounge.

Inn on 7th
10001 107th Street
1-800-661-7327 or 780-429-2861
www.innon7th.com
172 units, cable TV, wireless high-speed
Internet, modem jacks. Free local calls.
Room service

Mayfield Inn & Suites
16615 109th Avenue
1-800-661-9804 or 780-484-0821
www.mayfieldinnedmonton.com
327 units, cable TV, games, high-speed
Internet. ATM, health club/spa, lounge
with live music/entertainment, saltwater
room, room service. Shuttle to West
Edmonton Mall.

Ramada Inn & Conference Centre
11834 Kingsway Avenue
1-888-747-4114 or 780-454-5454
www.ramadaedmonton.com
316 units, cable TV, games, hair dryers,
irons, laundry, high-speed Internet.
Hair salon, gift shop, sports bar,
room service.

Ramada Inn & Waterpark
5359 Calgary Trail
1-800-661-9030 or 780-434-3431
www.the.ramada.com/edmonton07838
123 rooms, nonsmoking floor, cable TV,
movies, laundry service. Two giant
water slides, pool, exercise room, hot
tub. Restaurant, lounge.

Rosslyn Inn & Suites
13620 97th Street
1-877-785-7005 or 780-476-6241
*www.albertadirectory.com/edmonton/
    rosslyn*
92 units, some wheelchair accessible,
    cable TV, free movies, high-speed
    Internet, hair dryers, irons, laundry.
    ATM, exercise room, roll-in shower.
    Restaurant, close to shopping.

The Sutton Place Hotel Edmonton
10235 101st Street
1-866-378-8866 or 780-428-7111
www.suttonplace.com
313 deluxe units, cable TV. ATM,
    hair salon, health club, spa, pool,
    hot tub.

Thornton Court Hotel
1 Thornton Court
1-877-588-9988 or 780-429-9999
www.thorntoncourt.com
200 units overlooking river valley.
    Cable TV, games, hair dryers,
    high-speed Internet, fridges,
    irons. Fitness center, business
    center, covered parking.
    Room service.

Travelodge Edmonton South
10320 45th Avenue South
1-800-578-7878 or 780-436-9770
www.the.travelodge.com/edmonton09761
219 rooms with cable TV, movies, hair
    dryers, room service. Indoor pool,
    whirlpool. Restaurant. Close to
    shopping, dining, nightclubs.

Westin Edmonton
10135 100th Street
1-800-228-3000 or 780-426-3636
www.westin.com/edmonton
413 deluxe units, cable TV, free movies,
    fridges, hair dryers, irons and
    boards, PC friendly. Exercise
    room, hot tub. Business center,
    baby-sitting.

Campgrounds
Edmonton:
Glowing Embers Travel Centre & RV Park
2 miles (3.2 km) west of Edmonton
    on Highways 16A and 60
780-962-8100
268 full-service sites. Internet access,
    RV wash, laundry, washrooms,
    store. Close to West Edmonton
    Mall. Reservations accepted.

Rainbow Valley Campground
Whitemud Park off 122nd Street,
    south of Whitemud Freeway
1-888-434-3991 or 780-434-5531
88 sites, with and without power; tent
    camping. Showers, washrooms,
    laundry, dump station. Store,
    playground, nature trails.

Shakers Acres
21530 103rd Avenue (off Highway 16A)
780-447-3564
165 sites with full or partial hookups,
    showers, laundry, groceries,
    public phone.

Area Campgrounds
Devon:
Lions Campground
20 miles (32 km) southwest of Edmonton
520 Haven Avenue
780-987-4777
180 sites with and without full hookups;
    tent camping. Rest rooms, fire pits.
    Playgrounds, baseball diamond,
    horseshoe pits. Adjacent to Devon
    Golf & Country Club.

Leduc:
Lions Campground
20 miles (32 km) south of Edmonton
50th Street South,
    then east on Rollyview Road
780-986-1882
55 sites with full hookups, tent area.
    Washroom, phone, dump station.
    Heated picnic shelter. Reservations
    accepted.

Sherwood Park:
Half Moon Lake Resort
16 miles (25.5 km) east of Edmonton
via 23rd Avenue
780-922-3045
www.halfmoonlakeresort.com
196 sites, with and without power.
Hayrides, ponies, horseback
rides, petting zoo, wading
pool, lake, playground, trout
pond, mini-golf, boat rentals.
Reservations accepted.

Sherwood Forest Campground & RV Park
23242 Highway 14
780-467-3329
40 sites, with and without power.
Café. Adjacent to golf course and
bird sanctuary.

Spring Lake:
Spring Lake Resort & RV Park
499 Lakeside Drive, 30 minutes west of
Edmonton off Highway 16A
780-963-3993
160 sites with full and partial hookups
or dry-camping. Dump station,
swimming, trout fishing, concession, picnic area. Boat and log
cabin rentals.

Stony Plain:
Allan Beach Resort Campground & RV Park
20 miles (31 km) west of Edmonton,
Highway 43 to Range Road 13
780-963-6362
174 sites with full and partial hookups,
showers, playground, laundry.

Restaurants
Blue Iguana Grill
11304 104th Avenue
780-424-7222
Multiple media mentions for excellence
in food and wine.

The Copper Pot Restaurant
101, 9707 110th Street
780-452-7800
www.copperpot.ca
Specializing in Canadian fare.

The Creperie
10220 103rd Street
780-420-6656
French country, crêpes.

Da-de-o New Orleans Diner & Bar
10548A 82nd Avenue
780-433-0930
Favorites from New Orleans in
1950s-style setting. Fried chicken,
ribs, po' boys.

Doan's Restaurant
Downtown: 10130 107th Street
780-424-3034
Southside: 7909 104th Street
780-434-4448
Vietnamese cuisine.

East Bound Eatery & Sushi Bar
11248 104th Avenue
780-428-2448
Sushi, steak, seafood.

Hardware Grill
9698 Jasper Avenue
780-423-0969
www.hardwaregrill.com
Canadian cuisine.

Haweli
10220 103rd Street, downtown
780-721-8100
Authentic Indian cuisine.

Hy's Steakloft
10013 101A Avenue
780-424-4444
www.hyssteakhouse.com
Specializing in Alberta beef for more
than 40 years.

Japanese Village
10126 100th Street
780-422-6083
Sushi, steak, seafood.

The King and I
8208 107th Street
780-433-2222
Thai cuisine.

Mirabelle
9929 109th Street
780-429-3055
Continental cuisine, steak, seafood, pasta.
Free underground parking after 5 P.M.

New Asian Village
10143 Saskatchewan Drive
780-433-3804
East Indian dining. Top honors among
Canada's ethnic restaurants.

Road Notes

To leave Edmonton, take 16A West toward Spruce Grove and Stony Plain and connect with Highway 43 north. You'll stay on Route 43 all the way across northern Alberta as it wends north and west.

A series of small towns along Route 43 forms a dot-to-dot line between Edmonton and Whitecourt. Services and facilities such as gas stations, self-service laundries, restaurants, motels, and campgrounds are available all along this stretch.

(A few miles past Stony Plain is the junction for the westbound Yellowhead Highway 16. For more information, see the section on the Yellowhead-Cassiar Highways in Chapter 7, "Western Canada's Northbound Byways.")

WHITECOURT

From Edmonton: 91 miles (147 km)
To Valleyview: 102 miles (164 km)
To Grande Prairie: 175 miles (282 km)

The confluence of the Athabasca and McLeod Rivers, two major transportation routes, seemed a natural place for a settlement to spring up in rich, forested land. A family-operated sawmill was established here in 1922 and has since grown into a major employer, along with two other timber-related companies. Forestry, oil and gas, sand and gravel, and tourism keep Whitecourt's people happy and hard at work. The proof lies in the statistics: Less than 3 percent of the population of 8,200 is unemployed, and nearly half of all adults are involved in some form of volunteerism.

The **Whitecourt Tourist Information Centre** is open 7 days a week in summer, and offers directions and advice as well as plenty of printed material. Choices for local recreation include horseback riding, boating, fishing, shopping, or visiting a guest ranch. Watch for moose, deer, and elk in this area. Less visible are black and brown bears.

Golfers are invited to try their hand at the par-72 **Graham Acre Golf and Country Club**. There's something to satisfy every level of expertise, from practice on the putting green and driving range to the challenging 18-hole course itself. Refreshments and snacks are available in the clubhouse.

To prepare for a fishing adventure, call the Fish and Wildlife office in downtown Whitecourt at 780-778-7112 for license and season information. Go after walleye, northern pike, rainbows, and grayling. Another option is to hire a guide at operations such as **Eagle River Outfitting**, at 780-778-3251, which offers half-day and full-day services or drop-off fishing, wilderness camping, and float fishing trips over several days. With a guide, you can expect to pay close to $100 for half a day or about $170 for a full day per person.

The forest products industry has a standing invitation for visitors to tour local state-of-the-art sawmills and fiberboard and pulp plants. For a program of industrial tours, stop by the Chamber of Commerce office on Highway 43 by the traffic lights.

For more information on Whitecourt, visit the city's Web site at *www.town. whitecourt.ab.ca.*

Lodging

Alaska Highway Motel
3511 Highway Street
1-800-778-4156 or 780-778-4156
36 units with balconies, cable TV, fridges, modem jacks, free coffee.

Green Gables Inn
3527 Highway Street
1-800-779-4537 or 780-778-4537
www.telusplanet.net/public/ggables
49 units, kitchenettes, some nonsmoking. Cable TV with movie channel, free continental breakfast. Restaurant.

Quality Inn Whitecourt
5420 47th Avenue,
just off Highway 43 North
1-800-265-9660 or 780-778-5477
74 air-conditioned rooms, suites. Executive rooms with fax/modem outlets. Cable TV, sauna, hot tub, exercise facility. 24-hour café, restaurant; dining overlooks McLeod River. Children under 18 stay free.

Ramada Limited Whitecourt
3325 Caxton Street
1-866-706-3366 or 780-706-3349
www.ramada.com
50 units including executive suites with Jacuzzis. Cable TV, free movies, free local calls, fridges. Exercise room, hot tub, laundry, free newspaper.

The Ritz Café & Motor Inn
Highway 43 North
1-800-639-6765
www.ritzmotorinn.com
63 units, cable TV, free movies, fridges, free coffee, modem jacks. Winter plug-ins, restaurant.

Travelodge Hotel Whitecourt
5003 50th Street
1-888-778-2216 or 780-778-2216
74 air-conditioned rooms, suites, nonsmoking available. Cable TV and movie channel, fax/modem outlets, hot tub, room service. Lounge, family restaurant.

Campgrounds

Alaska Highway Motel & RV Park
3511 Highway Street
780-778-4156
22 campsites. Showers, rest rooms, dump station. Sheltered picnic sites.

Camp in Town RV Park
Downtown Whitecourt
780-706-5050
Year-round camping with full and partial hookups, pull-throughs. Washrooms, showers, laundry.

Carson-Pegasus Provincial Park
16 miles (25 km) north of Whitecourt on
    Highway 43; follow signs
780-778-2664
182 sites with partial hookup; group
    camping, firewood. Showers,
    laundry, tap water, dump station.
    Store. Beach, swimming, fishing,
    wheelchair-accessible fishing area,
    horseshoe pits.

Eagle River Wilderness Adventure
10 minutes south of Whitecourt
    on Highway 32
780-778-3251
27 sites with 15-amp service,
    pull-throughs, cabins. Fishing,
    tubing, canoe rentals, firepits,
    swimming area.

Sagitawah RV Park
Just northwest of town on Highway 43
780-778-3734
88 sites, some with full hookups,
    pull-throughs. Free showers;
    laundry, fire pits. Store, propane
    sales, RV parts and service.
    Playground, mini-golf, movie rentals.
    Senior discount.

Whitecourt Lions Club Campground
1 mile (1.5 km) east of Whitecourt on
    Highway 43
780-778-6782
70 sites, some pull-throughs, water,
    firewood, showers, laundry
    facility, dump station. Lots of trees,
    playground, horseshoe pits.
    Senior discount.

Shopping with a Map

The **West Edmonton Mall** sprawls over a 110-acre site, featuring 800 stores and services, an ice arena, thrill rides, kiddie rides, a water park, and aquariums. Located at 87th Avenue and 107th Street, it's not hard to find. Roadside signs will lead the way. And once you're inside, you'll pick up a map to figure your way from there. Wear your walking shoes, and be sure to bring your swimsuit, ice skates, and maybe your bowling ball.

This remarkable indoor megamall—billed as the largest shopping and entertainment center in the world—includes more than 110 restaurants, plus lots of attractions that could serve as parks all by themselves. Kids in Edmonton have no excuse for saying, "There's nothing to do!" More likely it's, "There's too much to do!"

The mall includes **Galaxyland Amusement Park,** with 24 rides and attractions; **World Waterpark,** with slides, a wave pool, and kiddie water play; the **Deep Sea Adventure,** with submarine rides, performing dolphins, and a full-size replica of the Columbus ship Santa Maria; **Professor Wem's Adventure Golf,** a miniature course; and the **Ice Palace,** an ice rink that's occasionally used by the Edmonton Oilers hockey team. Dining and entertainment options include **Planet Hollywood, Red's, Hard Rock Café,** and **Jubilations Live Dinner Theatre.**

For more information, call 780-444-52000 or visit www.westedmontonmall.com.

Restaurants

A & W
Hilltop on Highway 43
780-778-6611
Burgers, fries, shakes, root beer
specialties.

Boston Pizza
3836 Kepler Street,
  Highway 43 SW
780-778-2500
Family dining, pizza, pasta,
  sandwiches.

Ernie O's Restaurant & Pub
Next to the Guest House Inn
780-778-8600
Steaks, seafood.

Green Gables Inn Restaurant
Highway 43
780-778-3142
Lunch and dinner, steaks, seafood, ribs,
  prime rib, salad bar.

KG's Sandwich Bar
4912 50th Avenue
780-778-5286
Fresh-baked cinnamon buns,
  homemade soups.

Mountain Pizza & Steakhouse
3823 Highway Street
780-778-3600
Pizza, steaks, Italian food, ribs, chicken,
  soups, salad.

Road Notes

Between Whitecourt and Grande Prairie are 172 miles (277 km) of increasingly striking vistas as the route leads toward the foothills of the Canadian Rockies and away from populated areas. The Athabasca River, then the Little Smoky River, may be seen along the road as you continue north and west on Highway 43.

Fifty miles (80.5 km) past Whitecourt is **Fox Creek**, the seat of the area's oil-and-gas exploration efforts. Lodging, meals, laundry facilities, and gas stations may be found in this community. A few miles farther still is the tiny town of Little Smoky.

Just before you enter **Valleyview**, a roadside visitor information center and rest stop offers picnic tables, water, and a dump station for RV travelers. You can make a phone call, mail a letter, and buy souvenirs here, too.

Valleyview calls itself the Portal to the Peace Country, a region through which the mighty Peace River flows. Originally a transportation route for trappers, explorers, and traders, the river today is famed for its outdoor recreation opportunities. When you reach Valleyview, you have traveled 214 miles (344.5 km) from Edmonton. Grande Prairie, the next large community on the Alaska Highway, lies 70 miles (112.5 km) ahead, via Highway 43.

Eleven miles (17.5 km) past Valleyview, we followed the signs to **Williamson Provincial Park** for our next overnight stay. Located on Sturgeon Lake, Williamson Park is a forested campground, which lends a sense of privacy to each campsite. The park offers 60 sites, with full or partial hookups, or tent camping. There are showers, a dump station, and a public phone. The nearby lake is an easy place to launch a boat to fish for perch, pickerel, northern pike, or whitefish.

Other camping also is available on this stretch of Highway 43 that leads to Grande Prairie. Watch for private and provincial campground signs.

GRANDE PRAIRIE

From Whitecourt: 175 miles (282 km)
To Dawson Creek: 75 miles (121 km)

Grande Prairie, at the junction of Highways 43 and 40, is the regional center for northwest Alberta and northeast British Columbia, with an economy that's based on agriculture, forestry, oil, and gas. The city symbol is the trumpeter swan, and these elegant white birds are frequently seen on local lakes. As you enter the city, stay on the Highway 43 bypass and watch for the blue-and-white question-mark signs that lead the way to the impressive cedar-and-pine-constructed **Visitor Information Centre 2000**, with rest rooms, free literature about Grand Prairie and other towns in the region, and helpful travel counselors at the counter.

Centre 2000 overlooks **Muskoseepi Park** and the **Bear Creek Reservoir**. Nearby is the **Rotary Park Campground** along the reservoir (see list of campgrounds). The fraternal organization also offers free bus tours of the city and county every Monday, Tuesday, and Thursday evening during summer months, leaving Centre 2000 at 7 P.M.

RV travelers will appreciate the city's free sani-dump and fresh water at the old visitor information log cabin, located about five minutes south of Centre 2000 on 106th Street. And a fully accredited medical facility, the **Queen Elizabeth II Hospital,** is located at 98th Street and 105th Avenue.

This region was home to First Nations people for centuries. The first white arrivals were fur traders, who came on the scene in 1771. The town's name is credited to Father Emile Grouard, who first viewed this vast, treeless area around Lake Saskatoon in the mid-1800s and called it *la grande prairie*. The first settlement here was established in 1911. Today more than 40,000 people live in a city that has prospered since its founding. Another 210,00 live in the surrounding region, with Grande Prairie as a hub.

At the information center, ask for directions to **Kleskun Hills,** east of town, where you can view fossilized marine life and dinosaur remains in an area that was once a river delta. Or visit the **Crystal Lake Waterfowl Refuge** for birding, walking along nature trails, or just soaking up the sunshine. Call 780-538-0451 for details.

Another local natural treasure is **Muskoseepi Park,** which covers about 1,000 acres in Bear Creek Valley. The park pavilion is the stage for outdoor concerts and festivals. Recreation includes camping, golf, hiking, wildlife-watching, and lawn bowling. The park also invites swimming, boating, fishing, and other water sports.

In this wonderful park you'll find the **Grande Prairie Museum,** which features exhibits on dinosaurs, aboriginal tribes, explorers, trappers, traders, missionaries, and pioneer families. Early-day buildings, churches, and bridges moved here from their original sites tell the story of the city's beginnings. The museum is wheelchair accessible and open year-round. Another place to enjoy a portion of the museum's collection is on the lower level of Centre 2000, where its Heritage Discovery Centre exhibits capture the imagination of travelers at the visitor center. Call 780-532-5482.

To learn more about northern Alberta's forestry industry, visit the pulp mill, sawmill, and forests of **Weyerhaeuser Canada**, which offers public tours all summer. Call 780-539-8255 for a reservation. And tours through the **Canfor Lumber Mill** are available by booking a day in advance at 780-538-7756.

And don't miss the **Grande Prairie Stompede**, featuring broncos, bulls, ponies, and chuckwagon races, a town tradition since 1977. Festivities include a giant midway, entertainment, and all the professional rodeo you can handle. Call 780-532-4646 or browse *www.gpstompede.com*.

Lodging

Best Western Grand Prairie Hotel & Suites
10745 117th Avenue
1-866-852-2378 or 780-402-2378
www.bestwestern.com
100 units, some theme rooms. Cable TV, high-speed Internet, fridges, microwaves, hair dryers, free newspaper, modem jacks. Roll-in shower, swimming pool, tanning salon, room service. Free shuttle.

Grande Prairie Inn
11633 Clairmont Road
1-800-661-6529 or 780-532-5221
202 deluxe air-conditioned rooms in full-service hotel. Whirlpool, sauna, indoor pool. Gift shop, restaurant, piano bar lounge, nightclub. Three-Diamond rating, AAA. Next to major shopping mall.

Holiday Inn Grande Prairie Hotel & Suites
9816 107th Street
1-800-465-4329 or 780-402-6886
www.holiday-inn.com
146 units in large convention facility, cable TV, high-speed Internet, free local calls. Health club/spa, hair salon, room service, free shuttle service.

Quality Hotel & Conference Centre Grand Prairie
11201 100th Avenue
1-800-661-7954 or 780-539-6000
www.qualityhotelgrandprairie.com
102 air-conditioned rooms, executive suites, kitchenettes, nonsmoking rooms available. Cable TV, free breakfast, exercise room, gift shop. Shuttle service.

Sandman Hotel Grande Prairie
9805 100th Street
1-800-726-3626 or 780-513-5555
www.sandmanhotels.com
136 air-conditioned rooms, executive suites, nonsmoking available. Cable TV, fax/modem outlets, in-room movies and games. Fitness facilities, pool, hot tub, whirlpools. 24-hour Denny's restaurant.

Service Plus Inns & Suites
10810 107A Avenue
1-888-875-4667 or 780-538-3900
www.serviceplus-svh.com
123 deluxe air-conditioned rooms. Cable TV, movies, laundry service, continental breakfast. Indoor pool, waterslide, hot tub. Exercise room, restaurant, lounge. Shuttle service.

Stanford Inn
11401 100th Avenue
1-800-661-8160 or 780-539-5678
www.stanfordinn.net
204 rooms, nonsmoking available.
In-room movies and coffee,
computer jacks, high-speed
Internet. Family restaurant.

Super 8 Motel
10050 116th Avenue
1-888-888-9488 or 780-532-8288
www.super8.com
103 air-conditioned rooms, suites,
kitchenettes; nonsmoking floors
available. Laundry, free continental
breakfast and newspaper. Pool with
water slide, exercise room.

Trumpeter Hotel & Meeting Centre
12102 100th Avenue
1-800-661-9435 or 780-539-5561
www.trumpeterhotel.com
118 air-conditioned rooms, suites,
nonsmoking available. Modem
jacks, in-room coffee, cable TV.
Exercise room, hot tub. Casual
fine dining.

Western Budget Motel
13825 100th Street
780-538-3366
www.westernbudgetmotel.com
101 units, cable TV, free movies,
fireplaces, modem jacks,
fridges. Exercise room, hot tub.

The city symbol of Grand Prairie, the swan, is sometimes visible on local lakes.

Campgrounds

Camp Tamarack RV Park
5 miles (8 km) south of Grande Prairie on Highway 40
1-877-532-9998 or 780-532-9998
www.camptamarackrv.com
87 sites with power and water, most with pull-throughs, plentiful trees. Private showers, laundry, rest rooms, dump station. Satellite and cable hookups, fax machine, Internet access. Store, RV supplies, RV pressure-wash.

Country Roads RV Park
2.5 miles (4 km)
west of Highways 43 and 2 junction
780-532-6323
www.countryroadsrvpark.com
65 sites with full hookups, some pull-throughs; tent sites. 15-, 30-, and 50-amp sites. Showers, laundry, washrooms, fire pits, lots of trees. Fish pond, playgrounds. Close to golf.

Grande Prairie Rotary Park
On Highway 43 bypass
780-532-1137
59 sites with full and partial hookups. Firewood, shelter, laundry, phone. No reservations.

Saskatoon Island Provincial Park
13 miles (21 km) west of Grande Prairie and 2.5 miles (4 km) north of Highway 43
780-766-3485
96 sites with partial hookups; group camping and day-use area. Dump station, store. Beach, swimming, playground, wheelchair access.

Stompede Campground & RV Park
6.5 km south of Holiday Inn on Highway 407, 4.5 km east to Evergreen Park
780-532-4568
82 sites with full and partial hookups. 15- and 30-amp service. Equestrian trails, stabling. Archery range, batting cage, close to golf. Laundry, free firewood, phone, fire pits.

Wee Links Golf & Campground
9209 95th Avenue, south end of city
780-538-4501
23 sites with 30-amp service. Water, phone, fire pits, concession. 9-hole par 3 golf course and driving range.

Restaurants

Barcelona Steakhouse & Bar
9816 107th Street
780-532-4201
Steaks, chops, seafood.

Earl's
9825 100th Street, downtown
780-538-3275
Canadian-certified Angus steaks.

East Side Mario's
10622 99th Avenue
780-513-8900
New-York-style Italian food, pizza, pasta, sandwiches.

Egan McSwiggin's Irish Ale House & Pub
11920 100th Street
780-402-7090
Traditional Irish fare and brews.

Ricky's All-Day Grill
10030 116th Avenue, next to Super 8 Motel
780-831-7425
Family dining.

Sorrentino's Bistro-Bar
10745 117th Avenue, across from Centre 2000
780-814-7171
Italian cuisine.

Road Notes

Eighty-three miles (134 km) ahead is Dawson Creek. Don't let a finish-line mentality stop you from enjoying the hospitality offered by small towns between Grande Prairie and Dawson Creek, however. Wembley, Beaverlodge, Tupper, and Pouce Coupe are towns of varying size and distinct personalities. This region is steeped in pioneering history, so be sure to take in small-town attractions such as the South Peace Centennial Museum, just east of Beaverlodge, where antique farm equipment has been restored to working order. Also, Pouce Coupe is proud of its museum in the old railroad station, which houses artifacts tracing this community's beginnings as a trading post in 1908.

These roadside communities also offer fuel, meals, and lodging. Multiple camping opportunities lie along this stretch of the road, from small municipal campgrounds to provincial parks. Watch for the signs.

As you near Dawson Creek and enter British Columbia, be sure to set your clocks back one hour to reflect the Pacific Time Zone. If you follow the Alaska Highway through British Columbia and the Yukon Territory, you won't have to change the time again until you cross the Alaska–Yukon border.

DAWSON CREEK, British Columbia

From Grande Prairie: 83 miles (134 km)
From the Montana border: 750 miles (1,200 km)
To the Alaska border: 1,190 miles (1,915 km)
To Fairbanks: 1,488 miles (2,395 km)

Symbolically, Dawson Creek is the end of this road, and the beginning of another. You have arrived at Mile 0 of the famed Alaska Highway, and a new leg of your adventure is about to begin. For a complete description of Dawson Creek and its services, facilities, and attractions, see Chapter 6, "The Alaska Highway."

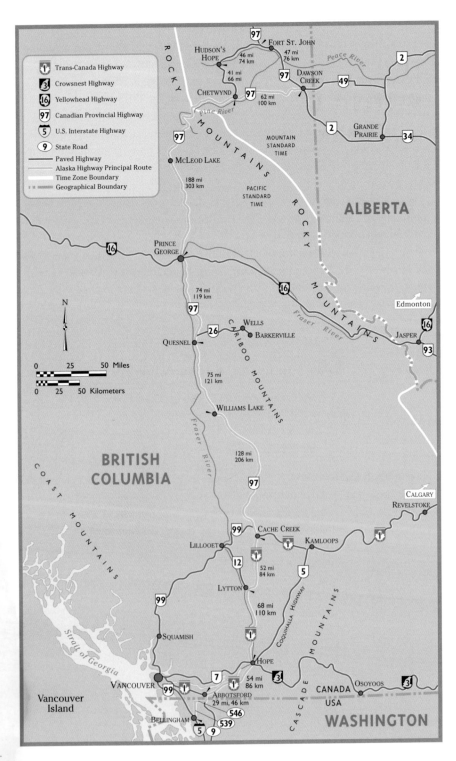

Trans-Canada Highway
Crowsnest Highway
Yellowhead Highway
Canadian Provincial Highway
U.S. Interstate Highway
State Road
Paved Highway
Alaska Highway Principal Route
Time Zone Boundary
Geographical Boundary

ROCKY MOUNTAINS

97 FORT ST. JOHN
HUDSON'S HOPE
46 mi 74 km
47 mi 76 km
Peace River
2
41 mi 66 mi
97 DAWSON CREEK
49
CHETWYND
97
62 mi 100 km
2
GRANDE PRAIRIE
34
97
MOUNTAIN STANDARD TIME
MCLEOD LAKE
188 mi 303 km
PACIFIC STANDARD TIME
ALBERTA
ROCKY

16 PRINCE GEORGE
74 mi 119 km
16
Edmonton
97
WELLS
MOUNTAINS
Fraser River
JASPER 16
26 BARKERVILLE
QUESNEL
CARIBOO MOUNTAINS
93
75 mi 121 km
WILLIAMS LAKE
Fraser River
128 mi 206 km
97
CALGARY
REVELSTOKE

N

0   25   50 Miles
0   25   50 Kilometers

BRITISH COLUMBIA
COAST MOUNTAINS
99 CACHE CREEK
KAMLOOPS
1
LILLOOET
1
12
52 mi 84 km
5
LYTTON
68 mi 110 km
COQUIHALLA HIGHWAY
1
SQUAMISH
99
Strait of Georgia
1
HOPE
54 mi 86 km
3
CASCADE MOUNTAINS
OSOYOOS 3
VANCOUVER
99 1
7
ABBOTSFORD
29 mi, 46 km
CANADA
USA
Vancouver Island
546
BELLINGHAM
5 9
539
WASHINGTON

Chapter 5

The Western Route: Through British Columbia to Dawson Creek, B.C., and Mile 0

*B*EAUTIFUL BRITISH COLUMBIA. If natural beauty were measured on a scale of 1 to 10, British Columbia would easily break out the top, like an overheated thermometer. This is an exceptionally beautiful province, from south to north, west to east.

Motoring along the northbound highways that lead to Dawson Creek, you will see for yourself the fascinating juxtaposition of the cultivated and uncivilized: orderly farms and untamed rivers, formal street grids beneath a tumble of mountains, logging trucks rumbling by tearooms.

In British Columbia, evidence of British, French, and American influence is present. This region also is rich in ancient culture that should not be overlooked in your travels. In museum exhibits and in daily practice, the First Nations people demonstrate the continuation of centuries-old traditions.

Be sure to stop at the wonderful culture-based attractions offered by

Minter Gardens in Chilliwack features 32 acres of themed gardens, topiary, water gardens, and rest stops.

British Columbia at a Glance

Size: 365,900 square miles or 947,680 square km

Population: 4,095,500

Capital: Victoria

Tourism, Lodging: 1-800-HELLOBC or www.hellobc.com

Provincial and National Park Camping: 1-800-689-9025 or www.discovercamping.ca

Sportfishing: wlapwww.gov.bc.ca

Hunting: www.gov.bc.ca/wlap

Canada Customs: 204-983-3500 (outside Canada) or www.ccra-adrc.gc.ca

members of various Native American groups. Learn about life in this country before contact with Europeans, along with customs and traditions in dance, art, and storytelling that continue today.

This traditional homeland of Canada's first people remains rich in resources such as big game, fish, birds, and small furbearers. As you drive, take care to watch for wildlife-viewing opportunities. We saw caribou, stone sheep, bison, eagles, hawks and other birds, plus numerous species of fish during our trip. In the case of big game on the road, keep your eyes open for safety's sake, as well as for photographic opportunities.

Canada's southwestern province also can boast of its magnificent coastline, the Fraser and other wild rivers, fruitful farmlands, mountain lakes, glaciers and ice fields, and the longest stretch of the Canadian Rockies. Victoria and Vancouver, its major cities in the southwestern part of the province, rival many in Europe for cultural attraction and architectural wonder. Fertile farms in the south feed British Columbia and contribute to the province's export economy. Farther north, the historic Cariboo Country holds stories of a gold rush that lingered well past that of the Klondike.

As you travel toward Cache Creek, the landscape turns drier and rockier, and the scent of sagebrush and juniper lingers in the air, bringing with it a sense of the Old West. Indeed, Canada's Old West holds as much wonderful and bizarre history as that of the United States, with ranchers, cowboys, miners, outlaws, and the women who loved them. You can visit historic Hat Creek Ranch or Barkerville to learn more about the Cariboo Wagon Road and the stagecoach line that once connected the western towns.

Like elsewhere in western Canada, the northernmost reaches are the rough-and-ready regions, where timber, oil, and natural gas take economic precedence over farming. This is not surprising, considering that the number of frost-free days shrinks with every northbound step in latitude, and the soil tends toward spotty sections of permafrost. As you drive, you'll also see incredible evidence of mankind's ability to harness energy through building dams and extracting oil and gas.

WASHINGTON–BRITISH COLUMBIA BORDER

To Chilliwack, B.C.: 27 miles (43 km)
To Dawson Creek, B.C.: 705 miles (1,134 km)

To begin your northward journey through British Columbia, you will likely be starting out on north-south U.S. Interstate 5 in western Washington. Take I-5 north from Seattle to Bellingham, the southernmost port city on the Alaska Marine Highway System. (See Appendix 1 for more information on ferry routes.)

At Bellingham, I-5 connects with northbound Route 539. Take Exit 256A and stay on this road to the junction with Highway 546 to Sumas. From the I-5 turn-off to the international border it's about 25 miles (40 km). (See the section on Border Crossings in Chapter 2, "What You Need to Know, A to Z.")

On the U.S. side, the border town is Sumas, Washington; on the Canada side, it's Huntington, B.C. The border crossing is open 24 hours a day.

Road Notes

Heading north from the border, stay on Highway 11 for 4.5 miles (7 km) to **Abbotsford,** a community famous for its abundant raspberry, blueberry, and strawberry crops. Pick your own at area farms, and join the Berry Blitz festival in June and July for a taste of desserts and berry entrees. An International Airshow in mid-August features flying stunts by Canadian and international pilots, plus ground displays of fixed-wing, military, warbirds, homebuilt, and civilian planes. Call 604-852-8511 or see *www.abbotsfordairshow.com.*

The mechanically oriented member of the family will enjoy a tour of the **Barrowtown Pump Station,** 10 miles (16 km) east of Abbotsford off Trans-Canada Highway 1, where since 1923, pumps have drained what once was Sumas Lake, opening up 30,000 acres of land for farming. Call in advance for a tour: 604-823-4678.

To learn more about Abbotsford-area attractions, visit the Chamber of Commerce at 2478 McCallum Road or call 604-859-9651. Another tourism information Web site is *www.tourismabbotsford.com.*

From Abbotsford, follow Highway 1 east for 17 miles (27 km) to Chilliwack.

CHILLIWACK

From the border: 27 miles (43 km)
To Hope: 27 miles (43 km)

The **Fraser River Valley** is a suitable setting for a painting, with snowcapped peaks as a backdrop to widespread farms and a pretty city. This is a place for folks who appreciate life in a rural setting with the convenience of a nearby metropolis. Vancouver is just an hour's travel to the west.

Home to 60,186 people, Chilliwack prides itself on its recreational opportunities as well as its agriculture-based economy. Water is the tie that binds—the Fraser River, Chilliwack River, and Cultus, Chilliwack, and Harrison Lakes are playgrounds for locals and visitors.

Generous water sources, along with southern B.C.'s temperate climate and good soil, have made agriculture king here. In local fields, you'll find flowers, grain, corn and other vegetables, herbs, pumpkins, and, like the northwest United States, apples. Among growers with an open-door policy is **The Apple Farm**, which produces 25 varieties of apples. A guided tour of the orchards and apple tastings are available by reservation. For a farm guide, visit the **Chilliwack Visitor Information Centre**, 44150 Luckakuck Way, or call 1-800-567-9535 or 604-858-8121.

If golf is your game, you'll find more than 10 courses within a half hour from downtown Chilliwack. Among them is a full range of challenge up to world-championship level, and in southern B.C.'s mild temperatures, you can easily golf into late autumn.

At **Minter Gardens**, paths wend through, under, and around 32 acres of perfectly groomed hillsides that look as if an artist has applied color to the foliage in sweeps of paint, not plantings. Eleven themed gardens feature creative topiary, water gardens, and serene rest stops. Allow at least 2 hours to walk the paths among the gardens, aviary, and bonsai display. It's right off Highway 1 at Exit 135. Call 1-888-MINTERS or visit *www.mintergardens.com.*

Grab a taste of cultural history at any of several museums in the area. At the **Sto:lo Native Interpretive Centre and Longhouse,** you can learn about the aboriginal people who lived in this region long before Chilliwack's 1908 incorporation. At the **Chilliwack Museum,** objects and artifacts help tell the story of this community's beginnings and the diverse people who have lived in this valley. Rated one of the top 10 museums in British Columbia by *Westworld Magazine,* the Chilliwack Museum is located at 45820 Spadina Avenue, in a 1912 structure that was the former city hall. Call 604-795-5210.

In mid-May, Chilliwack hosts the **Country Living Festival,** a celebration of its agricultural roots. The three-week event includes agricultural exhibitions, horse races, a parade, arts and crafts displays, and concerts.

For family fun, look just east of Chilliwack, where **Bridal Falls** offers a dinosaur theme park, golfing, water slides, and bumper boats. Campsites for tents or RVs are nearby. To reach the Trans-Canada Water Slides and these other neighboring attractions, take Exit 135 on Highway 1 east. Call 1-888-883-8852 or 604-794-7455.

Or check out the **Cultus Lake** area, where either the provincial park or resort accommodations offer more fun for all members of the family. On the water: canoeing, kayaking, and fishing. On land: hiking, horseback riding, biking, and walking trails. Or in the resort park, enjoy the water slides and go-carts, come rain or shine. Access to Cultus Lake is via Exit 119B south. Call 604-858-7241 or browse *www.cultus.com.*

For more information, contact Tourism Chilliwack at 1-800-567-9535, 604-858-8121, or *www.tourismchilliwack.com.*

Lodging

Best Western Rainbow Country Inn
43971 Industrial Way
1-800-665-1030 or 604-795-3828
www.rainbowcountryinn.com
74 air-conditioned rooms. Laundry,
coffee, sauna, whirlpool. Indoor
pool, family restaurant, coffee shop,
lounge. Golf packages available.

Comfort Inn
45405 Luckakuck Way
1-800-228-5150 or 604-858-0636
www.choicehotels.ca/cn235
83 air-conditioned rooms, nonsmoking
available. Cable TV, dataports,
hair dryers, irons and boards.
Continental breakfast available.
Restaurants, shopping, golf nearby.
Kids 18 and younger stay free with
parent or grandparent.

Days Inn—Chilliwack
8583 Young Road S.
1-800-559-3022 or 604-792-1955
www.daysinn.ca
29 air-conditioned units. Cable TV,
fridges, microwaves, dataport.
Complimentary coffee, breakfast,
newspaper.

Parkwood Lodge
8600 Young Street
1-877-793-1234 or 604-795-9155
30 deluxe air-conditioned rooms,
some kitchenettes, cable TV, coffee.
Heated outdoor swimming pool,
playground. Close to restaurants,
shopping.

Rainbow Motor Inn
45620 Yale Road
1-800-834-5547 or 604-792-6412
www.rainbowmotorinn.com
40 air-conditioned rooms, efficiencies,
free local calls, movies, laundry.
Adjacent to restaurants, garden.
Senior discount.

Rhombus Hotels & Resorts
Downtown Chilliwack
45920 1st Avenue
1-800-520-7555 or 604-795-4788
www.rhombushotels.com
110 air-conditioned rooms with mountain
views. Coffee, sauna, whirlpool,
restaurant, lounge, fitness center, pool,
hot tub. Downtown location.

Royal Hotel
45886 Wellington Avenue
1-888-434-3388 or 604-792-1210
www.valleyimall.com/royal
35 units in circa 1908 inn, private baths,
cable, air-conditioning. Honeymoon
suite with jacuzzi. Full breakfast
included. Restaurant.

Traders Inn Motor Hotel
45944 Yale Road
1-888-792-9839 or 604-792-0061
www.tradersinn.bc.ca
32 air-conditioned rooms, cable TV,
movies. Internet access. Whirlpool,
sauna, exercise room. Near shopping,
restaurants, library. Senior discount.

Travelodge Chilliwack
45466 Yale Road
1-800-566-2511 or 604-792-4240
www.travelodgechilliwack.com
82 air-conditioned units, some kitchenettes.
Cable TV, in-room coffee. Indoor pool,
jacuzzi, laundry, arcade, restaurant.

Campgrounds

Bridal Falls Camperland
53730 Bridal Falls Road; Highway 1, Exit 135
604-794-7361
www.holidaytrailsresorts.com
175 sites for high-quality resort camping
with amenities: pool, hot tubs,
clubhouse, restaurant. Near dining,
attractions, golf, entertainment.

Chilliwack Campsite & RV Park
50850 Hack Brown Road; Highway 1, Exit 129
604-794-7800
51 sites with full hookups, some pull-throughs.
Treed wilderness setting. Showers, cable,
laundry, store. Near golf course.

Cottonwood Meadows RV Country Club
44280 Luckakuck Way
604-824-7275
109 level sites with full hookups,
    pull-throughs, cable hookup,
    security gate. Free showers,
    clubhouse, steam room.
    Close to services.

Orchard Trailer Park
46289 Yale Road E.;
    Highway 1, Exit 119A
604-795-7634
20 sites three blocks east of
    downtown, off highway,
    treed sites, full hookups,
    pull-throughs, showers,
    cable, laundry.

Sunnyside Campground
3405 Columbia Valley Highway;
    Highway 1, Exit 119.
604-858-5253
www.cultuslake.bc.ca
245 campsites. Showers, rest
    rooms, firewood. Boat launch,
    fishing, canoeing, hiking,
    go-carts, water slide, beaches.
    Restaurants.

Vetter River Campground
5215 Giesbrecht Road;
    West from Hope, Exit 119A
604-823-6012
www.cultuslake.bc.ca
196 sites, full hookups, pull-
    throughs, showers, sani-station,
    laundry. Group sites, playground,
    horseshoe pits.

Restaurants
Dakota's Restaurant
45850 Yale Road, #200
604-795-2215
Angus Beef, prime rib, ribs,
    seafood. Bar, two patios,
    private dining room.

Garden Court Restaurant
43971 Industrial Way, in Best Western
    Rainbow Country Inn
1-800-665-1030 or 604-795-3828
Continental menu featuring aged steaks,
    seafood. Live entertainment on
    weekends. Sunday brunch buffet.

La Mansione Ristorante
46290 Yale Road East
604-792-8910
Steak and seafood; historic setting in nearly
    century-old mansion decorated with
    collectibles and fine art.

Mill Street Café
9381 Mill Street
604-795-4640
Casual fine dining. Organic and whole
    foods, Old-world wines.

The Pantry
45610 Yale Road West
604-792-2110
Family dining, breakfast all day. Seniors'
    and children's menus.

Rhombus Hotels and Resorts
Downtown Chilliwack
45920 1st Avenue
604-795-4848
Casual fine dining and lounge in
    full-service resort hotel.

Wellington Cottage Tearoom
45775 Wellington Avenue
604-795-4848
Reservations recommended for tea in a
    Victorian cottage. Light lunch, home
    baking, gift shop.

White Spot Restaurant
45373 Luckakuck Way
604-858-0602
Well-known B.C. restaurant serves
    breakfast, lunch, dinner. Burgers, pasta,
    steak, chicken.

Road Notes

Wouldn't a nice soak in a mineral hot springs do the trick right now? If you're willing to follow that urge, just past Chilliwack take Exit 135 to Highway 9 and east to Highway 7.

Harrison Hot Springs is a lovely resort village in the mountains, and only about a half hour away from Chilliwack. Fewer than 1,000 people live here on the shores of Harrison Lake, but water enthusiasts come from miles around for boating, wind-surfing, swimming, or camping. Each September, sand sculptors and their fans arrive for the World Championship Sand Sculpture Competition on the beaches of the lake. Their amazing creations remain on display for a full month. The hot springs itself is a rare treat, with water coming out of the ground so hot that it must be cooled to 105°F. The public pool is open year-round. For more information, call 604-796-3425.

If you go, retrace your route back to Highway 1 for the best, fastest access to Hope.

Hope

From Chilliwack: 27 miles (43 km)
To Lytton: 68 miles (110 km)

This charming community at the confluence of the Fraser and Coquihalla Rivers is home to 6,184 people. Hope seems surrounded by mountains as well as by rivers, and its beautiful natural setting has made it a vacation destination as well as the site for two major motion picture productions: *First Blood,* starring Sylvester Stallone as John Rambo, and *Shoot to Kill,* starring Sidney Poitier and Kirstie Alley. The area and its temperate climate attract a unique variety of coastal and interior birds, so birders often arrive hoping to add to their life lists.

For all the possibilities of how Hope was named, there is no agreement. One of our favorites was attributed to old-time gold miners who wintered here between lousy mining seasons: "They lived in Hope and finally died in despair."

This little city vies with Chetwynd, B.C., as Chainsaw Sculpture Capital of British Columbia. Hope's grassy, treed downtown park features the chainsaw artistry of a local sculptor named Pete Ryan. In 1991, when a few of the giant old trees in **Memorial Park** began to die, Ryan made a proposal. Rather than raze the trees, he asked the city to leave 12-foot stumps. From them he has carved detailed works of art depicting miners, burros, rams, and, best of all, bears. Today you can see two dozen or more of his works in the park and in other venues around town.

In 1981 Hollywood transformed Hope into a movie set for its filming of *First Blood* at sites all over town. A hundred locals were cast as extras, and for a while, actors Sylvester Stallone and Brian Dennehy were small-town regulars. Just outside the visitor center, a full-size wooden cutout of Stallone (minus the face), in warfare gear and muscles, allows visitors to photograph each other in good humor.

East of town, in the **Coquihalla Canyon Provincial Recreation Area,** five tunnels were cut through solid granite for the now-abandoned Kettle Valley Railway, built from 1911 to 1916. Because the chief engineer was a Shakespeare fan, he used Shakespearean names on railroad bridges, waysides, and this grouping of five tunnels: the Othello-Quintette Tunnels.

Hiking trails for all levels of fitness can be found throughout the area, and the **Hope Visitor Information Centre** has detailed maps of local trails, plus maps of nearby Manning and Skagit Valley Provincial Parks. Members of the Hope Volunteer Search & Rescue have prepared trip itineraries for you to fill out and leave at the visitor center, in case of an emergency. Visitor center maps include walking tours to Pete Ryan's sculptures and to locations where *First Blood* was filmed.

The helpful people at the center will tell you about local activities and attractions and answer questions about highway conditions and weather, as well as direct you to lodging and restaurants. The center is at 919 Water Avenue, along Highway 1. Call 604-869-2021, or browse *www.destinationhopeandbeyond.com.*

Lodging

Alpine Motel
505 Old Hope–Princeton Way
1-877-869-9931 or 604-869-9931
14 air-conditioned, ground-level rooms,
  kitchenettes. Free coffee, fridges.
  At-door parking.

Beautiful Lake of the Woods Resort
22805 Trans Canada Highway 1
1-888-508-2211 or 604-869-9211
www.lakewoods-resortmotel.com
17 units, lake views, cable TV, fridges,
  free coffee. Canoe rental, fishing,
  swimming, hiking, playground.
  Senior discount.

Best Continental Motel
860 Fraser Avenue
604-869-9726
13 air-conditioned units, cable TV,
  free movies, fridges, free coffee.
  Near shopping, bus depot.
  Senior discount.

City Centre Motel
455 Wallace Street
604-869-5411
16 air-conditioned rooms, cable TV,
  fridges, in-room coffee/tea, movies.
  Senior discount. Close to park, grocery.

Colonial "900" Motel
900 Old Hope–Princeton Way
604-869-5223
16 air-conditioned, nonsmoking
  rooms with mountain views.
  Cable TV, fridges, free coffee,
  landscaped grounds. Adjacent
  to restaurant.

Coquihalla Motel
724 Hope Princeton Highway
604-869-3572
15 recently renovated units in quiet
  setting, air-conditioned 1-, 2-,
  or 3-bedroom suites, some
  with kitchens. Cable TV, movies,
  free coffee.

Holiday Motel & RV Resort
63950 Old Yale Road
604-869-5352
www.holiday-motel.com
20 cabins and kitchenettes with 1 or
  2 bedrooms in quiet neighborhood.
  Outdoor heated pool, playground.
  Near restaurant, pub.

Inn Towne Motel
510 Trans Canada Highway 1
1-800-663-2612 or 604-869-7276
www.inntowne-motel.com
16 air-conditioned rooms, deluxe
 suites, kitchenettes, nonsmoking
 available. Laundry, indoor pool,
 whirlpool, sauna, garden patio.
 Close to attractions.

Lucky Strike Motel
504 Old Hope–Princeton Way
604-869-5715
www.luckystrikemotel.com
14 air-conditioned units, cable TV,
 movies, mountain views, landscaped
 grounds. Near restaurant, shopping.
 Senior discount.

The Maple Leaf Motor Inn
377 Old Hope–Princeton Way
1-888-530-1995 or 604-869-7107
38 recently renovated rooms,
 kitchenettes, cable TV, movies.
 Indoor pool, whirlpool, sauna.
 Dining, coffee shop.

Quality Inn
350 Old Hope–Princeton Way
1-800-424-6423 or 604-869-9951
25 air-conditioned rooms, 24-hour
 movies, sports, news. Free continental
 breakfast. Indoor hot tub, pool,
 sauna. Three-Diamond rating, AAA.
 Walk to downtown.

Red Roof Inn
477 Trans Canada Highway 1
604-869-2446
27 air-conditioned units, some
 nonsmoking. Cable TV, indoor
 spa, whirlpool. Mountain views,
 restaurant, indoor swim spa,
 whirlpool.

Royal Lodge Motel
580 Old Hope–Princeton Way
604-869-5358
21 air-conditioned units, some
 connecting. Movie and sports
 channels, in-room coffee.

A Shakespeare fan and railroad builder blasted five tunnels through solid rock near Hope. Today the route is a hiking path through what are collectively known as the Othello-Quinette Tunnels.

Skagit Motor Inn
655 3rd Avenue
1-888-869-5228 or 604-869-5220
www.skagit-motor-inn.com
30 air-conditioned rooms at ground
floor in wooded setting. Cable TV,
free movies, Continental breakfast,
pool, whirlpool, spa. Mountain views,
close to downtown. Near restaurants.
Senior discount.

Slumber Lodge
250 Fort Street
1-800-757-7766 or 604-869-5666
34 air-conditioned rooms, suites. Downtown location. Indoor swimming pool,
sauna, restaurant.

Swiss Chalets Motel
456 Trans Canada Highway 1
1-800-663-4673 or 604-869-9020
www.swisschaletsmotel.com
26 air-conditioned rooms, family chalets,
kitchenettes, fireplaces. Cable TV,
in-room coffee. Near Fraser River.

Windsor Motel
778 3rd Avenue
1-888-588-9944 or 604-869-9944
www.bcwindsormotel.com
24 air-conditioned rooms in downtown
setting. Family units, kitchenettes,
nonsmoking available. Cable TV,
in-room coffee, senior discount.

Campgrounds
Coquihalla Campground
800 Kawkawa Lake Road
1-888-869-7118 or 604-869-7119
Full or partial hookups, riverfront sites,
24-hour security. Laundry, dump
station, store. Recreation area,
playground. Video games, covered
picnic area. Senior discount.

Holiday Motel & RV Resort
63950 Old Yale Road
604-869-5352
www.holiday-motel.com
20 sites with full hookups, cable,
heated outdoor pool. Near
restaurant, pub.

Hope Valley Campground
62280 Flood Hope Road; Highway 1, Exit 168
604-869-9857
130 sites with full or partial hookups,
pull-throughs, tent sites. Showers,
laundry, rest rooms. Store, ice, gift
shop. Game room, swimming pool,
playground.

Othello Tunnels Campground & RV Park
67851 Othello Road; Highway 5, Exit 183
604-869-9448
www.othellotunnels.com
40 sites with full and partial hookups, tent
sites, firepits. Laundry, free showers,
barbecue area, rainbow trout fishing
pond. Store, playground. Near Othello
Quinette Tunnels.

Telte Yet Campsite
600 Water Avenue
604-869-9481
29 full hookup sites, tent camping.
Showers, laundry, dump station.
Group rates. Acres of trees along Fraser
River. Walking distance to Hope.

Whistlestop RV—Tent Park
59440 St. Elmo Road; Highway 1, Exit 160
1-877-869-5132 or 604-869-5132
39 sites, full and partial hookups, tent
sites, fire pits. Wheelchair access. Free
showers; laundry, dump station. Store,
playground, grass and shade.

Wild Rose Campground & RV Park
62030 Flood Hope Road; Highway 1,
Exit 165 or 168
604-869-9842
www.wildrosecamp.com
68 sites with full and partial hookups.
15 and 30 amp. Cable TV, Internet,
showers, laundry, dump station.
Discount for Good Sam, KOA,
CAA/AAA, seniors.

Restaurants
Blue Moose Coffee House
322 Wallace Street
604-869-0729
Sandwiches, soups, espresso, desserts,
high-speed wireless Internet.

Darrell's Place Family Restaurant
241 Wallace Street
604-869-3708
Quality family dining.

Grammy's Greek Taverna
904 Old Hope Princeton Way,
    next to Colonial 900 Motel
604-869-7141
Greek food, steaks, pizza, pasta.

Home Restaurant
665 Old Hope Princeton
605-869-5558
Home-cooked food, baked goods,
    family dining.

Hope Drive-in & Restaurant
590 Hope Princeton Way
604-869-5380
Family owned since 1962,
    seating for 100.

Kibo Japanese Restaurant
267 King Street
604-869-7317
Teriyaki, ribs, tempura, and more.

Kim Chi Japanese & Korean Restaurant
821A 6th Avenue
604-869-0070

Little Tokyo Japanese Restaurant
359 Wallace Street
604-869-5628
Sushi, sashimi, teriyaki, tempura,
    Canadian cuisine.

Rolly's Restaurant
888 Fraser Avenue
604-869-7448
Breakfast all day, casual dining.

Sharon's Deli & Lunch Bar
340A Wallace Street
604-869-3354
Daily luncheon menus, sandwiches, salads,
    hard ice cream.

Road Notes

Fourteen miles (23 km) north of Hope, you'll come upon **Yale**, a historic village site along the gold rush trail. In its advantageous position at the southern entrance of the Fraser Canyon, Yale was the site for paddlewheelers to unload cargo that would continue its journey on the Cariboo Wagon Road, more commonly known as the Cariboo Trail. The Cariboo gold rush was still going strong by 1863, when the **Church of St. John the Divine** was constructed. It is now the oldest church on the B.C. mainland, and designated a B.C. Heritage Site. As you take a tour of the town, peek inside the church and get an eyeful of its magnificently carved pump organ. Visit the pioneer cemetery with its unique grave markers. Arrange a rafting trip or try gold panning by calling 604-863-2324 or browse *www.heritage.gov.bc.ca/yale/yale.htm*.

The Fraser Canyon is postcard beautiful from one end to the other. Just past the first of several tunnels in this section of road, note the historical marker at a pullout to the east. This explains more about the Cariboo Trail and the difficulty of transportation during that mid-1800s gold rush.

Farther north, about 33 miles (53 km) from Hope on Highway 1, you will encounter the natural wonder called **Hells Gate**, a tight narrowing in the canyon through which the Fraser River pours at great speed. From the edge, looking down, the water is fast and fearful, and it's no wonder the name stuck. **Hells Gate Airtram** offers a scary look at the river from above. For a fee, you can ride the tram across the

For a fee, you can ride the Hell's Gate Airtram over Fraser Canyon.

canyon while descending 502 feet. On the opposite side, a pleasant, tourist-oriented boardwalk village has been built into the cliff. And for the intrepid, a suspension bridge lets you walk back over the river and enjoy an unadulterated view of the swirling current beneath your feet. Enjoy a meal at the **Salmon House Restaurant,** or buy some food and eat at a picnic table in the sun. Watch an interpretive film, spend some cash in the gift shop, and load up on fudge at the candy store. Informative signs add to the enjoyment. We were amazed to learn that nearly 2 million salmon swim up the Fraser River each summer. For more information, call 604-867-9277 or visit *www.hellsgatetram.com.*

Two campgrounds operate within the 10 miles (16 km) north of Hells Gate. **Canyon Alpine RV Park & Campground** offers 31 sites, with full hookups and pull-throughs, fire pits, washrooms, and showers. The facility is close to a restaurant, store, phone, and self-service laundry. For information, call 604-867-9734. **Anderson Creek Campground** is alongside the Fraser and Anderson Rivers in a 30-acre setting with lots of trees. They offer full and partial hookups, showers, and a sani-dump. Call 1-604-867-9089.

LYTTON

From Hope: 68 miles (110 km)
To Cache Creek: 52 miles (84 km)

Situated at the confluence of the **Thompson River** and the mighty **Fraser River** (Canada's third largest), Lytton is the place to park and play—a river-rafter's dream. Looking down at the rivers' confluence from above, you can see a distinct edge where the clear, blue Thompson blends into the cloudy gray of the Fraser. A third, the **Nahatlatch River**, is smaller and steeper, offering dramatic class 4 and class 5 rafting.

As the whitewater rafting capital of British Columbia, Lytton offers plentiful choices for outfitters. You can go with a group, hire a guide for your own group, or rent what you need to go on your own. You can't miss rafting company signs all along this stretch of road. Among them is **Kumsheen Raft Adventures**, which has been leading power and paddle rafting trips on area rivers for more than 30 years. Call 250-455-2296 or visit the Web site at *www.kumsheen.com.* The **Reo Rafting Resort** specializes in trips on the Nahatlatch. Call 1-800-736-7238 or see *www.reorafting.com.*

Laying rail through Fraser Canyon proved a challenge for the railroad builders of the last century.

This meeting place of the rivers has been a gathering spot for centuries, as evidenced in ancient pictographs and rock paintings. First Nations people chose the spot for its abundance of wildlife, water, and trees for food and building material. You can visit a reconstruction of a traditional pit house in **Lion's Heritage Park**. These semi-underground homes were used for winter quarters by local Natives up to about a century ago. During the annual Lytton Days, you can learn more about First Nations culture through art, dance, and storytelling. Native arts and crafts, including soapstone carvings, baskets, and beaded leather, can be purchased in Lytton. Call 250-455-2146 for more information.

After prospector Billy Barker discovered gold in 1862, more than 100,000 people joined the ensuing rush and swarmed into British Columbia to mine for gold, traveling the famed Cariboo Wagon Road to reach the goldfields. As a stop along the way, Lytton thrived as a place for the stampeders to outfit themselves.

In 1881 intrepid railway builders arrived to cut a rail bed into the sides of this canyon. The Canadian Pacific Railway and the Canadian National Railway continue to move freight and passengers on this route that parallels the river and the road through Fraser Canyon.

This area is still rich with wildlife. Along the backroads and hiking trails, you may see elk, bighorn sheep, deer, eagles, and ospreys. Hidden from sight are the more human-shy animals: coyotes, bears, cougars, bobcats, and lynx.

The city was named for Sir Edward Bulwer-Lytton, whose writing is familiar to almost everybody. Drawing a blank? He's the one who penned the famous introductory phrase "It was a dark and stormy night."

Lytton is also Canada's "hot spot" with a recorded high of 111°F.

For more information on the area, stop by the Lytton Visitor Information Centre, open year-round at 400 Fraser Street. Call 250-455-2523 or visit *www.lytton.ca.*

Road Notes

In the 52 scenic miles (84 km) between Lytton and Cache Creek, you'll find two provincial parks and several private campgrounds.

Just 5 miles (8 km) beyond Lytton is **Skihist Provincial Park**, with 58 campsites, a picnic area, rest rooms, and an RV dump station. Another 12 miles (19 km) later, the less-developed **Goldpan Provincial Park** lies to the west, with 14 sites along the river. You can go fishing or put your canoe in the water here.

Along the way, pay attention to the historic buildings and opportunities to stop for coffee, pie, or a meal, and learn more about the area's gold rush history. Less than 10 miles (16 km) south of Cache Creek, the oldest roadhouse in British Columbia is still in business, as it has been since 1862. The **Ashcroft Manor & Tea House** offers rooms, meals, campground (with pull-through sites for RVers), jade gifts, and an invitation to walk the grounds and visit the historic outbuildings. For more information, call 250-453-9983.

You Want Coffee with That Jellyroll?

Sedimentary geologists and other earth scientists will appreciate an unusual attraction in the heart of downtown Lytton. Across from Lytton's **Visitor Information Centre**, at 400 Fraser Avenue, is the tiny **Caboose Park**, where a retired Canadian National Railway caboose is parked alongside a picnic table and grassy area. But it's the thing on the exterior wall of an adjacent building that makes scientists and curiosity seekers walk closer and squint. The "thing" is called the **Lytton Jellyroll**, a cast of a geological formation that was discovered south of the village. The unusual structure is a rolled layer of silt encased in coarse sands and gravel. Scientists believe it was created from 11,000 to 25,000 years ago during an event in the last glaciation period. That makes it very young by geological standards. But it is the size of the formation that makes it special. Normally a find such as this would be measured in inches, not feet. Erected by the Lytton and District Chamber of Commerce, this detailed replication of the real thing could fool an amateur.

Seven miles (11 km) south of Cache Creek is the **Eagle Motorplex**, a drag-racing facility sanctioned by the National Hot Rod Association. Racers come from around the world to race and show their cars.

During Cache Creek's mid-June **Graffiti Days**, restored vehicles are paraded and parked for a show-and-shine celebration. Festivities include a dance, barbecue, and racing at the motorplex.

CACHE CREEK

From Lytton: 52 miles (84 km)
From Hope: 120 miles (193 km)
To Williams Lake: 128 miles (206 km)

Set in a semiarid region of low, rolling hills, Cache Creek is home to a scant 1,115 people who live at the confluence of the Bonaparte River and Cache Creek. Here, too, is the junction of Trans-Canada Highway 1 with Highway 97.

The scent of sage wafts through the air on hot, summer days, and at the town's main intersection, a wooden gold miner stands, arms extended, to welcome you to this frontier town that was built on the backs of gold miners.

These days there's less gold mining than there is cattle ranching and ginseng growing. That's the crop beneath the acres and acres of elevated black cloth that protects the delicate plants. Farmers also grow wheat in irrigated fields.

A sculpture of a miner and his tools welcomes visitors to Cache Creek at the junction of Highway 98 and the Trans-Canada Highway 1.

Cache Creek services include lodging, restaurants, grocery stores, a post office, and a golf course. Most visitors are passing through on their vacations. But 150 years ago, this town was overrun with miners and people who wanted to trade gold for goods and services.

As a major point on the Cariboo Wagon Road, Cache Creek grew quickly. After the rush, some mining continued, along with farming, logging, and cattle ranching. Tourism helps keep Cache Creek cooking, too.

Just north of town, an 1860 landmark along the Cariboo Wagon Road is the historic **Hat Creek Ranch**, at the intersection of Highways 97 and 99. This 320-acre ranch was once an important roadhouse stop for horse-drawn wagons along the B.C. Express Stage Line (also known as the BX) that led to Barkerville and beyond. More than 20 buildings dating from 1863 to 1915 may be found on the grounds. Step back in time and explore the Victorian-style rooms of the main house, visit the BX Barn, watch the blacksmith at work, and view a First Nations pit house. You can also take a horse-drawn ride on the famous Cariboo Wagon Road and follow the footsteps of the gold miners. For more information, contact the Cache Creek Tourist/Visitor Information folks. Their booth at the junction of Highways 97 and 99 is open May 15 through September 30. Phone 1-800-782-0922 or 250-457-9722, or browse their Web site at *www.hatcreekranch.com.*

Lodging

Best Value Inn Desert Motel
1069 Trans-Canada Highway South
1-800-663-0212 or 250-457-6226
www.bestvalueinn.com
43 air-conditioned units, kitchenettes.
Cable TV and in-room coffee. Grass
courtyard with outdoor pool. Winter
plug-ins. In town center, close to shops
and restaurants.

Bonaparte Motel
1395 Cariboo Highway 97 North
1-888-922-1333 or 250-457-9693
24 air-conditioned rooms and kitchenettes
with refrigerators, cable TV, fax service.
Outdoor pool, indoor whirlpool. Close
to restaurants and golf.

Desert Motel
On Highway 1
1-800-663-0212
Clean, comfortable accommodations
in a Best Value Inn.

The Good Knight Inn
827 Trans-Canada Highway
1-800-736-5588 or 250-457-9500
20 deluxe rooms with cable TV and movies,
data phones, e-mail. Whirlpools,
continental breakfast, picnic area.

The Oasis Hotel
250-457-6232
Full hotel facilities, banquet room, lounge,
restaurant.

Robbie's Motel
1067 Todd Road
1-866-327-6221 or 250-457-6221
18 air-conditioned units at ground
level, cable TV, movies, fridges,
microwaves, free coffee. Near
restaurants, shopping, golf.

Sage Hills Motel
1390 Cariboo Highway 97 North
1-888-649-9494 or 250-457-6451
www.bcinfonet.com
18 air-conditioned units, cable TV,
in-room coffee. Pool with slide
and shower, grassy courtyard.
Senior discount.

Green and Gold

Outside **Cariboo Jade & Gifts** in Cache Creek, B.C., at 1093 Todd Road, you'll see a massive boulder made of jade, an obviously valuable piece of inventory that just sits out on the sidewalk. Managers Ben Roy and Bill Elliott don't worry too much about shoplifting. It would take a D-9 Caterpillar to walk away with that boulder.

Inside, these two brothers-in-law manage the business traffic that the boulder generates, like a billboard that says, "Come inside." While we were there, a busload of French-speaking travelers from eastern Canada arrived and filled every aisle of the modest shop.

In the back of the shop, behind a glass partition, Ben cuts British Columbia jade on special rock saws to accommodate its extreme hardness. Bill's specialty is working in gold. Together they create jewelry and other specialty pieces. British Columbia jade is nearly as prized as gold. Four times harder than marble, this jade is difficult to cut and finish into sculpture and jewelry. For more information on B.C. jade, call 250-457-9566. ●

Sandman Inn Cache Creek
Intersection of Highways 1 and 97
1-800-726-3626 or 250-457-6284
www.sandmanhotels.com
35 air-conditioned units, cable TV,
    in-room coffee. Restaurant.
    Senior discount.

Sundowner Motel
1085 Trans-Canada Highway
1-877-507-2887 or 250-457-6216
18 air-conditioned units, cable TV, movies,
    kitchens, fridges, microwaves. Near
    restaurants, golf.

Tumbleweed Motel
1221 Quartz Road
1-800-667-1501 or 250-457-6522
25 deluxe air-conditioned rooms in
    parklike setting, cable TV, free movies,
    picnic area. Near restaurants, golf.

Campgrounds
Brookside Campsite
0.6 miles (1 km) east of Cache Creek
    on Highway 1
250-457-6633
Pull-through sites, tent sites, free showers,
    heated pool. Playground, arcade, store.
    Adjacent to golf course.

Evergreen Fishing Resort
1820 Loon lake Road
250-459-2372
www.evergreenfishingresort.ca
Furnished lakeside log cabins, tenting
    campsites, full and partial hookups,
    store, laundry. Boat rentals, moorage.

Historic Hat Creek Ranch
Junction of Highways 99 and 97
1-800-782-0922 or 250-457-9722
www.hatcreekranch.com
8 campsites with electrical hookups
    only. Flush toilets, hot showers. Near
    historical roadhouse, Shuswap village,
    restaurant, gift shop. Also available,
    4 sleeping units.

Restaurants
A&W
Highway 97 North,
    at Copper Canyon Chevron
250-457-9668
Burgers, root beer, chicken, and more.

BB's Bar & Grill
In the Oasis Hotel
250-457-5232
Canadian fare, entertainment.

Manie's
Oasis Plaza
250-457-9999
Pizza and pasta, dine in or take out.

Sandman Inn Family Restaurant
Junction of Highways 1 and 97
250-457-9330
Pasta, steaks, Greek dishes, coffee shop,
    dining room, cocktail lounge.

Wander Inn Restaurant
Junction of Highways 1 and 97
250-45-6511
Sterling Silver AAA Steaks, Cantonese food,
    coffee shop, dining room, cocktail lounge.

Road Notes
From Cache Creek to the towns of 100 Mile House and 150 Mile House, the highway continues to follow the historic route of the Cariboo Wagon Road. The numbers used in the names of these towns and of other sites along this way are a measurement of their distance from Lillooet, which was Mile 0 on the mid-1880s Cariboo route. 100 Mile House today is a lumber town that also claims the title of International Nordic Ski Capital. It hosts the Cariboo Marathon each February, attracting skiers from around the world. Learn more about this district, its history, natural history, as well as local dining and lodging at the South Cariboo Visitor Info Centre, 422 Highway 97 in 100 Mile House. Call 1-877-511-5353 or 250-395-5353 or see *www.tourism.100mile.com.*

WILLIAMS LAKE

From Cache Creek: 128 miles (206 km)
To Quesnel: 75 miles (121 km)
To Prince George: 149 miles (240 km)

During construction of the Cariboo Wagon Road, a Williams Lake landowner would not lend money to road builders, so the trail bypassed the town, instead routing through 150 Mile House. That decision nearly killed the town's economy, putting it off the major transportation route for the thousands of people moving in and out of the goldfields.

Williams Lake was nearly abandoned, except for two business partners, William Pinchbeck and William Lyne, who built a lumber mill, grist mill, and a farm. But their real income earner was the sale of home-brewed whiskey. You might assume that this town took its name from the two Williams, but it is attributed to the local Shuswap Chief William.

By the 1940s, twenty years after the railway arrived, this was a ranching town that had grown into the largest cattle-shipping center in British Columbia. Today about 12,000 people call Williams Lake home and nearly 40,000 people live in the area, called "The Hub of the Cariboo." Ranching remains an important part of the economy.

Williams Lake is the Old West in action, and at no time of the year is there more action than during the **Williams Lake Stampede**, the first week of July: the town's population doubles with 13,000 spectators. This family event includes chuckwagon races, barn dances, a rodeo, and mountain horse races. A parade and midway are part of the fun, too. Camping is available right next to the Stampede grounds. For more information, call 1-800-71RODEO or 250-392-6585. The **Museum of the Cariboo Chilcotin** is a full-fledged rodeo museum that is entrusted with the story of the Williams Lake Stampede, which dates back to 1919, and the history of this region, the Cariboo Chilcotin.

The **Xats'ull Heritage Village** is an excellent place to learn about the region's first people. Hear the stories and view the village site, artifacts, petroglyphs, and a sweat lodge. For more information call 250-989-2323.

Williams Lake—the actual lake itself—lies along a major flyway for migrating waterfowl. **Scout Island Nature Centre**, at the west end of the lake, offers bird-watching opportunities along a corridor of trails. Between the Fraser River and the lake, you can see sandstone hoodoos—mushroom-shaped formations still standing after the forces of erosion removed the rock all around them.

The **Williams Lake Visitor Information Centre**, at 1148 Broadway South, is open year-round, and they can help you with such things as lining up a stay at a guest ranch or arranging for some horseback riding. Golfers can choose between two courses, and there's mini-golf for the kids. For more information on Williams Lake and the surrounding district, call 250-392-5025 or browse *www.bcadventure.com/wlcc.*

Lodging

Drummond Lodge Motel
1405 Highway 98 South
1-800-667-4555 or 250-392-5334
www.drummondlodge.com
23 air-conditioned units, kitchenettes, nonsmoking units available. Movie and sports channels, high-speed Internet, in-room coffee, continental breakfast, laundry facilities. Overlooking lake.

Fraser Inn
285 Donald Road
1-800-452-6789 or 250-398-7055
www.fraserinn.com
75 air-conditioned units, cable TV, movies, room service. Gift shop, whirlpool, sauna, free passes to Gold's Gym. Restaurant, lounge, patio.

Overlander Hotel
1118 Lakeview Crescent
1-800-663-6898 or 250-392-3321
www.overlanderhotel.com
57 air-conditioned units in full-service hotel. Fitness facilities, tour packages. Restaurant, pub. Downtown location, near shopping. Senior discount.

Sandman Inn & Suites Williams Lake
664 Oliver Street
1-800-726-3626 or 250-392-6557
www.sandmanhotels.com
90 air-conditioned units, executive suites, kitchenettes. Cable TV, laundry, room service, sauna, pub. Near shopping, adjacent to 24-hour restaurant.

Springhouse Trails Ranch
3061 Dog Creek Road
250-392-4780
www.springhousetrails.com
20 units available May-September. Kitchenettes, some with fireplaces. Meals, lounge. Horseback riding.

Super 8 Motel (Williams Lake)
1712 Broadway Avenue South
1-800-800-8000 or 250-398-8884
53 air-conditioned units, nonsmoking available. Cable TV, whirlpool, complimentary breakfast.

Valleyview Motel
1523 Highway 97 South
250-392-4655
20 sleeping and housekeeping units with mountain and lake views. Cable TV, free coffee, near restaurant. Senior discount.

Campgrounds

Big Bar Provincial Park
281 1st Avenue
250-398-4414
www.elp.gov.bc.ca/bcparks
Full and partial hookups, pull-throughs.

Springhouse Trails Ranch
3061 Dog Creek Road
250-392-4780
www.springhousetrails.com
12 RV full-hookup sites, showers, washrooms. Horseback riding.

Williams Lake Stampede Campground
850 South Mackenzie Street
250-398-6718
www.williamslakestampede.com
69 sites with full or partial hookups, phone, cable hookup. Tent sites, free firewood. Showers, rest rooms. Four blocks to downtown.

Restaurants

Fraser Inn
285 Donald Road
1-800-452-6789 or 250-398-7055
Outdoor seating available, lounge.

The Hearth Restaurant
99 South 3rd Avenue
250-398-6831
Sandwiches, soups, salads.

Locked in a Time Warp

Actors in costume make the past come alive again in Barkerville.

For a worthwhile side trip, take the Highway 26 turnoff just beyond Quesnel and follow it for 51 miles (82 km) east to Barkerville, where the gold-rush past comes alive again.

Founded in 1862, **Barkerville** first sprang to life when Billy Barker discovered gold in Williams Creek. Now more than 125 heritage buildings and displays on the original town site celebrate the past. Costumed interpreters remain in character as they answer questions and carry on conversation, moving about the streets of the mining town.

Museum displays about mining and about Barkerville and its namesake are in the main building through which you access Barkerville—which is kind of like a Hollywood back-lot, except that these buildings are real. And at each one, you learn about its former resident or business owner. Street performances add to the feeling that this was once a busy town of miners, Chinese immigrants, churchmen, and partygoers. Two cemeteries hold the remains of former residents. A stagecoach driver invites passengers to ride to the other end of the town. Guided tours begin at regular intervals.

We were pelted by a hailstorm while visiting Barkerville, and people rushed into the saloon, candy store, general store, or museum building. Others huddled beneath building overhangs until the storm passed. This was in August—an indicator of this place's elevation of about 4,200 feet (1,280 m) above sea level. Museum docents explained that snow comes early in these mountains. The mining was hard work; the living was just as hard.

For more information, call BC Heritage at 250-994-3332 or visit the agency's Web site at www.heritage.gov.bc.ca. ●

Joey's Grill
177 Yorston Street
250-398-8727
Pasta, steak, chicken.

Rendezvous Restaurant
240B Oliver Street
250-398-8312
Family dining, full menu.

The Overlander
1118 Lakeview Crescent
1-800-663-6898 or 250-392-3321
Downtown restaurant, adjacent to hotel.

Savala's Steakhouse
36 North 3rd Avenue
250-398-8246
Steaks, seafood, pasta.

Road Notes

Seventy-five miles (120 km) north of Williams Lake is Quesnel, which, like many area towns, boomed during the Cariboo gold rush of the early 1860s. Today this town of more than 11,000 people is supported by lumber, pulp, and plywood manufacturing, cattle ranching, mining, and, of course, tourism. All travelers' services may be found here, from shopping, lodging, and dining to assistance in planning your trip. Learn more about Quesnel's history, which really began long before the gold rush, at the **Quesnel Museum** in the Visitor Info Centre, in downtown Quesnel on Highway 97. Observe the city's illustrated history of more than a century in photos, and see Mandy, the famed "haunted doll" in their collection.

In mid-July, Quesnel celebrates Billy Barker's discovery of gold with **Barker Days**, four days of river races, dances, games, concerts, and contests for pie eaters and watermelon-seed spitters. A midway multiplies the family fun. An amateur rodeo draws big crowds to Alex Fraser Park. Learn more at *www.pgonline.com/billybarkerdays*.

West of Quesnel the **Blackwater River** flows almost 200 miles (322 km) from the Coast Mountains to the Fraser River. Its pristine waters attract fly fishers, canoeists, and kayakers. The Alexander Mackenzie Heritage Trail parallels the river; in 1793, Mackenzie followed this Native trading trail to the Pacific Ocean.

Heading north toward Prince George, you will be within range of some excellent lake fishing for rainbow and brook trout, char, burbot, and more. There are about 1,600 lakes within a 100-mile radius of Prince George. Contact Tourism Prince George at 1-800-668-7646 or 250-562-3700 for a free fishing guide and info on licensing.

Ten Mile Lake Provincial Park, 7 miles (11 km) north of Quesnel, offers 141 campsites with water, showers, rest rooms, and an RV dump station. For recreation there's a playground, a swimming beach on the lake, and a boat launch, as well as nature trails for walking and wildlife viewing. Watch for several private campgrounds just south of Prince George, too.

PRINCE GEORGE

From Quesnel: 74 miles (119 km)
To Chetwynd: 188 miles (303 km)
To Dawson Creek: 250 miles (402 km)

Here in what is known as the Lakes and Rivers District, Prince George is looked on as the capital of northern British Columbia. It is home to 72,406 people who understand and enjoy the natural treasure that's around them and the city they helped to create.

Just minutes from downtown in any direction, you'll find some form of outdoor recreation: walking, fishing, swimming, boating, backpacking. The local lakes and streams are thick with trout, salmon, burbot, Dolly Varden, char—for a fly fisher, this is world-class water. And there's no shortage of campgrounds, provincial and private. Hunkering in the distance is **Mount Robson,** highest peak in the Canadian Rockies, inviting those who prefer a lot of challenge in their outdoor adventure.

In winter, visitors and residents head out for downhill skiing, cross-country skiing, hockey, ice skating, even dogsledding. Snow typically begins in November and stays on the ground into late March.

The driving force behind the Prince George economy is the pulp and forest industry. **Northwood Inc.** offers scheduled tours of its pulp mill, sawmill, and plywood mills. Call Tourism Prince George to arrange a tour: 250-562-3700 or browse *www.tourismpg.com.*

This is a frontier city at its roots, yet it "cleans up real nice" with its own brand of polish. Just as you finish a half-day trail ride, Prince George's nightlife offerings will revitalize you with concerts, art galleries, theater openings, or an evening of jazz. The city claims several resident theater groups, a symphony orchestra, and many dance troupes. The **Two Rivers Art Gallery,** with pieces by local, regional, and national artists, can be found in the downtown Civic Complex. And the **Prince George Playhouse** was renovated and expanded for an ever-growing audience.

Also downtown, the **Centennial Fountain** at 7th Avenue and Dominion Street depicts the early history of Prince George in mosaic tile, from life among the First Nations people to the arrival of explorers, settlers, the railway, and forward into 20th-century life.

Along the banks of the Fraser River, at the end of 20th Avenue, **Fort George Park** is a favorite among more than 120 parks in the city limits. Come down to the river to picnic, and follow the Heritage Trail that links this park with several others. Inside the park, you'll find the **Fraser-Fort George Regional Museum,** with natural and cultural history exhibits and a small-gauge steam engine that offers rides for children. A hands-on science gallery, **The Exploration Place,** accelerates learning by touching.

Nearby, stop at the **Prince George Railway and Forestry Museum,** an outdoor repository for antique or merely retired railcars, engines, and more. There's even a

The Prince George Railway and Forestry Museum features retired vehicles, railway cars, cabooses, and track.

full-size train depot here, faithfully moved piece by piece from a spot along the British Columbia Railway between Quesnel and Prince George. Steam locomotives, cranes, sleeping cars, cabooses, even logging and agricultural machinery are part of the walk-about display.

Summer visitors are welcome to attend a **First Nations powwow** at Cottonwood Park, at the confluence of the Fraser and Nechako Rivers, where you can watch the dancing and shop for Native-made crafts. Each July the work of Native artists is featured at the **Northern British Columbia Native Arts & Crafts Trade Show**, held in the Convention Center. For more information, call 250-567-5795.

A **Prince George visitor center** lies at the junction of Yellowhead Highway 16 and Highway 97. Just outside is an unmistakable greeting from a three-story "log man" whose friendly wave welcomes you to town. A second visitor center, the office of Tourism Prince George, is centrally located downtown at the corner of Victoria Street and Patricia Boulevard.

(For more on Yellowhead Highway 16, see Chapter 7, "Western Canada's Northbound Byways." If you're heading to Dawson Creek, however, you will continue your journey north on Highway 97.)

For more information on the city's attractions and events, contact Tourism Prince George at 1-800-668-7646 or 250-562-3700 or *www.tourismpg.bc.ca.*

Lodging

97 Motor Inn
2713 Spruce Street
250-452-6010
17 units in newer inn, kitchenettes, cable, movies. Close to restaurants, shopping.

Best Western City Centre
910 Victoria Street
1-888-679-6699 or 250-563-1267
53 air-conditioned units in downtown location. Free local calls, cable TV, indoor pool, sauna, fitness room, laundry. Restaurant. Next to Civic Centre. Senior discount.

Bon Voyage Motor Inn
4222 Highway 16 West
1-888-611-3872 or 250-964-2333
96 air-conditioned units, kitchenettes, suites. Cable TV, free coffee. Gift shop, restaurant, RV parking, winter plug-ins. Adjacent to gas, diesel station, car wash. Winter plug-ins.

Brother's Inn Motel
2270 Hart Highway
1-866-562-1789 or 250-562-1789
20 air-conditioned rooms, suites, kitchenettes. Cable TV, adjacent to restaurant and pub. Near golf course. Senior discount.

Camelot Court Motel
1600 Central Street
1-800-668-3361 or 250-453-0661
www.camelot.prince-george.com
69 air-conditioned units, cable TV, movies, restaurant, indoor pool. Near malls. Senior discount.

Carmel Motor Inn
1502 Highway 97
1-800-665-4484 or 250-564-6339
90 air-conditioned sleeping and kitchen units. Cable TV, movies, restaurant, RV parking. Gift shop, adjacent to diesel station, car wash.

Coast Inn of the North
770 Brunswick Street
1-800-663-1144 or 250-563-0121
www.coasthotels.com
153 air-conditioned deluxe units. Three restaurants, pool, sauna, gym, lounge. Senior discount.

Downtown Motel
650 Dominion Street
250-563-9241
43 air-conditioned rooms, cable TV, movies. Winter plug-ins. Close to Civic Centre and pool. Senior discount.

Economy Inn
1915 3rd Avenue
1-888-566-6333 or 250-563-7106
www.economyinn.ca
30 air-conditioned rooms, kitchenettes, dataports. Cable TV, in-room coffee. Whirlpool, exercise room. Winter plug-ins. Near restaurants, shopping.

Esther's Inn
1151 Commercial Drive
1-800-663-6844 or 250-562-4131
www.esthersinn.com
122 air-conditioned rooms. Whirlpools, sauna, exercise club, pool with water slides. Dining room, lounge. Close to attractions, shopping.

Prince George's history is played out in mosaics at the Centennial Fountain.

Grama's Inn
901 Central Street
1-877-563-7174 or 250-563-7174
www.esthersinn.com/gramas
60 air-conditioned rooms, hospitality
room. Guests may use facilities of
sister hotel, Esther's Inn: pool,
whirlpool, exercise club.

PG Hi-Way Motel
1737 20th Avenue
1-888-557-4557
www.princegeorge.com/pghiway/
45 budget and deluxe rooms, kitchenettes.
Winter plug-ins. Near restaurants,
laundry, shopping.

Queensway Court Motel
1515 Queensway Street
250-452-5068
22 air-conditioned sleeping units, cable TV,
laundry. Near downtown.

Ramada Hotel Downtown Prince George
444 George Street
1-800-830-8833 or 250-563-0055
www.ramadaprincegeorge.com
193 air-conditioned units and executive
suites in downtown location.
Cable TV, movies, indoor pool,
sauna, whirlpool. Dining, pub,
casino, gift shop. Airport shuttle.

Red Cedar Inn
4581 Highway 16 West
250-964-4427
20 housekeeping units, cable TV, phones,
laundry. Close to shopping.

Sandman Inn & Suites Prince George
1650 Central Street
1-800-726-3626 or 250-563-8131
www.sandmanhotels.com
144 units, from 1- and 2-bedroom
suites to kitchenettes. Free in-room
coffee, indoor pool, sauna,
24-hour restaurant, room service.
Senior discount.

Travelodge Goldcap
1458 7th Avenue
1-800-663-8239 or 250-563-0666
77 air-conditioned units in downtown
location. Cable TV and movie channel.
Laundry, beauty salon, sauna. Family
restaurant, lounge. Close to Civic Centre.

Campgrounds

Bednesti Lake Resort
Mile 33 Highway 16 West
250-441-3500
7 sleeping units and 40 campsites with
full or partial hookups, some pull-
throughs, satellite TV, flush toilets,
showers, laundry, picnic area,
playground. Dining, café, lounge.
Swimming, boating, boat launch,
convenience store. Fuel, propane.

Bee Lazee RV Park, Campground &
Honey Farm
15910 Highway 97, 9 miles (15 km) south of
Prince George
250-963-7263
49 sites with full hookups, pull-throughs,
tent camping. Free showers; laundry,
washrooms, car and RV wash.
Playground, heated pool.

Blue Spruce RV Park and Campground
3 miles (5 km) west on Highway 16 from
intersection with Highway 97
250-964-7272
128 sites with full hookups, pull-throughs,
cable TV, tent camping, cabins.
Showers, laundry, store. Heated pool,
mini-golf, playground, sani-station.
Near golf, gas, shopping.

Hartway RV Park
7729 Kelly Road South, 6 miles (9 km) north
of Prince George on Highway 97
250-962-8848
40 landscaped sites with full and
partial hookups, pull-throughs, free
cable TV. Free showers, self-service
laundry, gift shop, near restaurants
and shopping.

Red Cedar Inn & RV Park
4581 Highway 16 West
250-964-4427
40 full and partial hookup sites with
sani-station. Close to shopping.

Sintich RV Park
7817 Highway 97 South, 3 miles (5 km)
south of Prince George on Highway 97
250-963-9862
50 spacious landscaped lots for adult
campers, pull-throughs, power, cable
TV. Free showers; laundry. Near store
and gas station.

Stone Creek RV Park & Campground
31605 Highway 97 South
250-330-4321
15 sites in quiet, landscaped park on the
Fraser River. Hookups, showers, lounge.
Walking trails, fishing.

Restaurants

Cariboo Steak & Seafood Restaurant
1165 5th Avenue
250-564-1220

Checkers' Lunch Box
4722 Continental Way
250-960-1180

China Sail Restaurant
4288 5th Avenue
250-564-2828
Chinese dining, buffets.

China Taste Restaurant
3601 Massey Drive
250-564-1283
Chinese cuisine.

De Dutch Pannekoek House
101-910 Victoria Street
250-563-2946
www.dedutch.com
Continental dining.

Earl's Place
1440 Central Street E.
250-562-1527

Esther's
1151 Commercial Drive
250-562-4131
Restaurant, coffee garden in hotel.

Golden Place
1645 3rd Avenue
250-564-3811

The Great Escape Restaurant
7740 St. Patrick Avenue
250-566-4565

JJ's Pub & Restaurant
1970 Ospika Blvd.
250-562-0001

Joey's Only Seafood & Tennessee Jacks
892 Central Street E.
250-562-4444

**Kelly O'Bryans Neighbourhood
Restaurant**
1375 2nd Avenue
250-563-8999

Moxie's Classic Grill
1804 Central Street E.
250-564-4700
Burgers, pasta, daily entrees

Red Robin
101-1600 15th Avenue
250-614-0800
Burgers, chicken, ribs.

Ric's Grill
547 George Street
250-614-9096
Burgers, chicken, seafood.

Suzuran Japanese Restaurant
1667 15th Avenue
250-564-0114
Japanese cuisine.

Temptations Restaurant
409 George Street
250-563-7109

Dam Drive

On the map, the **Hudson's Hope Loop** road—Highway 29 running north from Chetwynd—looks like a great way to shave off time and miles from your Alaska Highway trip. Don't be fooled by the two-dimensional aspects of the map. The 87-mile route will lead you through some beautiful country, but it is a narrow, winding affair that's best left to the sports-car set. And besides, if you take this cutoff, you'll miss Dawson Creek completely, along with the fun of seeing your way around the Mile 0 city.

But do make a side trip along Hudson's Hope Loop to enjoy the countryside and visit two massive dams across the Peace River: the Peace River Dam and the W.A.C. Bennett Dam. See the dams, and then come back to Chetwynd

Parts of British Columbia are suitable for shooting a Hollywood Western.

so you can launch your Alaska Highway adventure at Dawson Creek.

Along Hudson's Hope Loop, the landscape changes from pasture to aspen forest to wheat fields in a broad river valley. The narrow road is patchy at times, and elevation changes can be rather steep, so you may just decide to pass on this side trip if you're driving a big rig.

Dinosaur footprints are part of an outside display at **W.A.C. Bennett Dam**. The dam itself is 600 feet (183 m) tall and 1.25 miles (2 km) long, creating Williston Lake, a 230-mile-long (370-km) reservoir that's the 10th largest in the world. In the modern visitor center theater, a film shows historical footage of the river before the dam's construction, and explains why it was built here and how it all came together. Hands-on science experiments demonstrate how much energy is needed to light a bulb. Take a tour of the underground powerhouse. Parking is plentiful, and there are excellent views and photo opportunities.

Farther along the loop road is **Peace Canyon Dam**. While this is the more modest of the two dams, the visitor center here includes museum dioramas that depict early life for settlers in this area. Just inside the front door are full-size replicas of dinosaurs that once roamed the region. An upper deck allows a generous view of the dam and the valley. ●

Chetwynd has so many chainsaw sculptures around town that it claims the title of "Chainsaw Sculpture Capital of the World."

CHETWYND

From Prince George: 188 miles (303 km)
To Dawson Creek: 62 miles (100 km)

Whereas the town of Hope seems content with claiming the title of Chainsaw Sculpture Capital of British Columbia, Chetwynd is more ambitious—seeing itself as the Chainsaw Sculpture Capital of the World. Chetwynd is proud of the 45 sculptures you'll see around town, beginning with the welcome sign that features a family of curious bears. Stop at the **Chetwynd Visitor Information Centre** along Highway 97 to pick up a driving map that shows where the sculptures are on display: at the **Chainsaw Sculpture Park** and at businesses around town.

Chetwynd lies in coal and timber country in Little Prairie Valley. In fact, the early-day fur traders originally called it Little Prairie. The name Chetwynd honors Ralph Chetwynd, a government minister who helped bring the Pacific Great Eastern Railway to town. Many of Chetwynd's 3,200 people are employed at the sawmill, the coal mine, or the two dams up Hudson's Hope Loop. If you want to learn more about mining and forestry, industrial tours are available. Check at the visitor center for reservations.

Take a walk along any of the extensive trails in the Chetwynd Greenspace Trail System. They range from a 5-minute walk to an hour or more on trails varying from rustic to improved. A popular route is the Old Baldy Hiking Trail, which offers excellent views of the valley, along with plenty of places to rest. The Community Forest features interpretive walking and hiking trails, a tree registry, and a demonstration forest, along with picnic areas in forested settings.

Take the kids for a few hours of water fun at the Chetwynd Leisure Wave Pool, one of the best in the area, located at 46th Street and the North Access Road off Highway 97. Other local recreation includes your choice of two nine-hole golf courses, mountain biking, and terrific fishing. You can obtain your mandatory fishing license and all the tackle you need at Lonestar Sporting Goods. Call 250-788-1250.

For more information on any Chetwynd activities and events, call the Chetwynd Visitor Information Centre at 250-788-1943 or *www.gochetwynd.com.*

Lodging

Chetwynd Court Motel
5104 North Access Road
250-788-2271
17 rooms, kitchenettes, cable TV, laundry facilities, wheelchair access, pets allowed. Restaurant.

High Country Inn
5000 North Access Road
250-788-9980
32 air-conditioned rooms, pets allowed, coach parking. Dining. Cold beer and wine store.

Pine Cone Motor Inn
5224 53rd Avenue
1-800-663-8082 or 250-788-3311
54 air-conditioned units, including kitchenettes. Cable TV. Pets allowed. Coffee shop, dining room.

Stagecoach Inn
5413 South Access Road
1-800-663-2744 or 250-788-9666
55 air-conditioned rooms, kitchenettes, nonsmoking available, wheelchair access. Cable TV, sauna, whirlpool, laundry. Winter plug-ins. Pets on approval. Restaurant.

The Swiss Inn
4812 North Access Road
250-788-2566
Quality, comfortable accommodations. CAA Diamond rated. On-site restaurant.

Campgrounds

Caron Creek RV Park
On Highway 97, 10 miles (16 km) west of Chetwynd
250-788-2522
40 sites with full and partial hookups, pull-throughs on gravel and grass. Free showers; washrooms. Senior discount.

Westwind RV Park
On 53rd Avenue, 2 miles (3 km) north past junction of Highways 97 and 29
250-788-2190
50 pull-through sites with full hookups. Showers, laundry, rest rooms, dump station. Grassy sites, tent sites, picnic tables, fire pit area, playground.

Restaurants

High Country Inn
5000 North Access Road
Adjacent to Chetwynd Court Motel
250-788-2271
Dining, cocktails.

Kentucky Fried Chicken
4800 North Access Road
250-788-9866
The fast-food favorite in chicken.

Murray's Pub
4613 47th Avenue
250-788-9594
Appetizers, meals, cocktails.

Subway
5300 North Access Road
250-788-7824
Hot and cold subs, salads.

Stagecoach Inn
5413 South Access Road
250-788-9665
Dining with views of Sunkunka Valley.

The Swiss Inn Restaurant
4812 North Access Road
250-788-2566
Steaks, pizza, European cuisine.

*D*AWSON CREEK, BRITISH COLUMBIA

From Chetwynd: 62 miles (100 km)
From the Washington border: 705 miles (1,134 km)
To the Alaska border: 1,190 miles (1,915 km)
To Fairbanks: 1,488 miles (2,395 km)

Symbolically, Dawson Creek is the end of this road, and the beginning of another. You have arrived at Mile 0 of the famed Alaska Highway, and a new leg of your adventure is about to begin.

For a complete description of Dawson Creek and its services, facilities, and attractions, see Chapter 6, "The Alaska Highway."

A group of travelers poses at the "World Famous" sign in Dawson Creek to capture the official start of their Alcan experience.

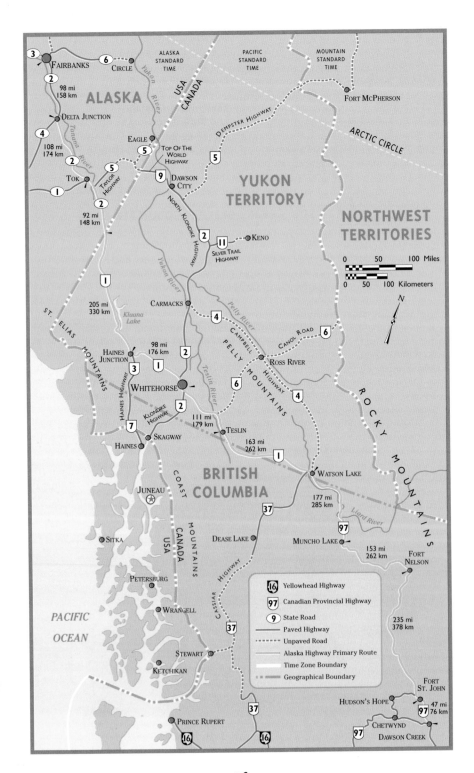

FAIRBANKS 6 CIRCLE

ALASKA STANDARD TIME

PACIFIC STANDARD TIME

MOUNTAIN STANDARD TIME

FORT McPHERSON

98 mi
158 km ALASKA

DELTA JUNCTION

DEMPSTER HIGHWAY

ARCTIC CIRCLE

108 mi
174 km

EAGLE 5 TOP OF THE WORLD HIGHWAY 5

TOK TAYLOR HIGHWAY

5 9 DAWSON CITY

YUKON TERRITORY

NORTHWEST TERRITORIES

92 mi
148 km

NORTH KLONDIKE HIGHWAY 2 11 KENO

SILVER TRAIL HIGHWAY

0   50   100 Miles

0   50   100 Kilometers

N

205 mi
330 km CARMACKS

Kluane Lake

Pelly River

St. Elias Mountains

98 mi
176 km 2

HAINES JUNCTION 3 1

CAMPBELL HIGHWAY

CANOL ROAD 6

PELLY MOUNTAINS

ROSS RIVER

WHITEHORSE

Teslin River 6 4

KLONDIKE HIGHWAY 2

7 SKAGWAY

111 mi
179 km TESLIN

HAINES

HAINES HIGHWAY

163 mi
262 km 1

WATSON LAKE

ROCKY MOUNTAINS

JUNEAU

BRITISH COLUMBIA

177 mi
285 km

37

97

Liard River

SITKA

COAST MOUNTAINS

DEASE LAKE

MUNCHO LAKE

153 mi
262 km FORT NELSON

CANADA
USA

PETERSBURG

CASSIAR HIGHWAY

WRANGELL

37

PACIFIC

OCEAN

STEWART

KETCHIKAN

16 Yellowhead Highway
97 Canadian Provincial Highway
9 State Road
—— Paved Highway
•••• Unpaved Road
—— Alaska Highway Primary Route
—— Time Zone Boundary
—•—• Geographical Boundary

235 mi
378 km

FORT ST. JOHN

HUDSON'S HOPE

47 mi
76 km 97

37 CHETWYND
97 DAWSON CREEK

PRINCE RUPERT

16

16

Chapter 6

The Alaska Highway

WHETHER you arrive in Dawson Creek, B.C., via the Alberta route or the British Columbia route, you are now about to begin a driving experience of a lifetime. After traveling hundreds of miles to get to this starting line, most people about to embark on the Alaska Highway shed any lingering road weariness in Dawson Creek. Instead, they are revived by a sense of excitement and anticipation.

However, don't expect the adventure part to begin immediately, for the road really doesn't change for many more miles. It's still paved and easy to navigate and is basically a continuation of what you've been seeing for a long distance already.

Until you sense the wonder of place that gradually unfolds as you travel north, the start of this adventure is more of a mindset. It's the knowledge that you are following in the footsteps of those intrepid workers who laid

Jim and Frieda Applebury of Missouri were leading a convoy of camping couples up the highway when we met. Their badges read "Wagonmaster" and "Mrs. Wagonmaster." This was Jim's fourteenth trip up the highway.

the groundwork for this highway more than five decades ago—and in the winter, no less—pushing a route through forests and along mountains, skirting jewel-colored lakes, battling the quagmire of newly exposed permafrost, to complete one of the world's great road-building projects. Carry those images with you as you travel, and be sure to stop at the historic mileposts to learn more about this incredible road north.

DAWSON CREEK, British Columbia

Mile 0 of the Alaska Highway
To Fort St. John: 47 miles (76 km)
To the Alaska border: 1,190 miles (1,915 km)
To Fairbanks: 1,488 miles (2,395 km)

Tucked into the far northeast corner of British Columbia, little Dawson Creek gained international attention in March 1942 when thousands of U.S. troops "invaded" to begin construction of the Alaska Highway from the south end of the route. For a brief time, Dawson Creek was overpopulated, straining its transportation grid, local accommodations, and food services, and filling its streets with GIs. The boom was short-lived, however.

Dawson Creek, B.C., and Dawson City, Yukon, farther north, were both named for **George Mercer Dawson**, a geologist who surveyed these parts of Canada in 1879. His work paved the way for settlement and development in both Dawsons. Incorporated as a city in 1958, Dawson Creek remains a small town with fewer than 12,000 residents.

At the city limits, near Dawson Creek Airport, stands a welcome sign declaring **Mile Zero City, Where the Adventure Begins!** And at the traffic circle in Dawson Creek that connects Highway 2 to Highway 97, you'll spot the oft-photographed sign proclaiming: **You Are Now Entering the World Famous Alaska Highway.**

Another not-to-be-missed landmark, the **Mile 0 Milepost**, is in an unfortunate place—dead center in the busy intersection of 10th Street and 102nd Avenue—making posed photos a dangerous proposition. Atop the monument, sign-makers have painted the number of miles from Dawson Creek to Fort St. John (48), Fort Nelson (300), Whitehorse (918), and Fairbanks (1,523). The numbers no longer match the actual driving distance, because the road has been straightened (and shortened) since it was first constructed. At that time, Canada used miles to measure distance. The country has since switched to the metric system, and kilometer posts have replaced mileposts along the highway.

Just beyond the traffic circle connecting Highways 2 and 97 stands another landmark, a huge, wooden grain elevator that was relocated to this place in the **Northern Alberta Railway Park** (NAR Park). Today it houses a gift shop and art gallery, and features a spiral ramp, making access to the exhibits easy for everybody. The building of the Alaska Highway is portrayed in historical photos. On Saturdays, come down to the **Farmers Market** on the park grounds for the freshest vegetables and fruits and for crafts and sweets. Get your picture taken at the "World Famous" sign at the Mile 0 cairn, and note the newest addition to the Dawson Creek experience: at the center of the nearby traffic circle is a unique metal sculpture depicting a surveyor. When I asked about him in the visitor center, I was told, "Some say it's [George Mercer] Dawson himself, since he was a surveyor; others say it's a U.S. soldier surveyor because of his hat; some say it's a Canadian surveyor." She told me where to ask about the artist's intent, but I wasn't in a hurry to get the answer. I liked the idea that this surveyor could be whoever you wanted him to be.

On any given summer day, the NAR Park lot is filled with RVs from all over the U.S. and Canada—a true cross section of the North American camping world. These are people who are always ready for conversation and to compare travel notes, and new friendships have been forged here.

From the NAR Park lot, it's a little hard to see the entrance to the **Dawson Creek Visitor Information Centre** at 900 Alaska Avenue. Just follow the brick footpath past the railcar to the renovated railway station that's now a combination visitor center/museum. Tens of thousands visit the center each year to get answers, pick up free brochures, freshen up, and buy books and souvenirs that mark this memorable trip. With a free copy of the self-guided *Historic Walking Tour,* you'll stroll by the buildings that were standing when the American soldiers arrived in March of 1942. A downtown mural project enhances the beauty and history of the downtown core.

This town of 10,074 people supports a wide-ranging community of farming families. Agriculture and tourism are the leading economic drivers. If you're visiting during early August, be sure to make it to the **Dawson Creek Exhibition & Stampede**, which includes farming exhibits, horse shows, handicrafts, a food fair, and a rodeo. And for the fright of your life, watch the professional chuckwagon drivers' race. The **Mile Zero Park** (oddly enough, located at Mile 1 of the Alaska Highway) includes the **Walter Wright Pioneer Village** and some beautiful botanical treats, shops, and a restaurant.

In Dawson Creek there is no shortage of restaurants, hotels, campgrounds, bakeries, car and RV washes—anything you need for resting up or stocking up before beginning your journey up the Alaska Highway. For more information on the area's attractions and services, call 1-866-645-3022 or 250-782-9595. View the Web site at *www.tourismdawsoncreek.com.*

Lodging

Alaska Hotel
10213 10th Street
250-782-7998
www.alaskahotel.com
12 units, old-world decor. Restaurant, entertainment.

Cedar Lodge Motel
801 110th Avenue
250-782-8531
42 units, with kitchenettes, refrigerators, cable TV, laundry. Across from mall.

The George Dawson Inn
11705 8th Street
1-800-663-2745 or 250-782-9151
80 well-appointed, air-conditioned rooms, executive suites, cable TV. Coffee shop, lounge, dining room, fitness center. Small pets. Senior rates.

Inn on the Creek
10600 8th Avenue South
1-888-782-8136 or 250-782-8136
www.innonthecreekbc.ca
48 deluxe air-conditioned rooms and kitchenettes. Fridges, microwaves, family restaurant. Adjacent to mall, close to attractions.

The Lodge Motor Inn & Café
1317 Alaska Avenue
1-800-935-3336 or 250-782-4837
www.lodgemotorinn.com
40 modern, air-conditioned rooms, cable
TV, free local calls. Dining. Centrally
located, near mall. Family plan.

Northwinds Lodge
623 103rd Avenue
1-800-665-1759 or 250-782-9181
20 air-conditioned units; kitchenettes.
Cable TV, fridges, free coffee, winter
plug-ins.

Peace Villa Motel
1641 Alaska Avenue
1-800-782-8175 or 250-782-8175
46 air-conditioned rooms, movies, laundry,
office services, sauna. Senior discount.
Near golf course and restaurants.

Ramada Limited Dawson Creek
1748 Alaska Avenue
1-800-663-2749 or 250-782-8595
www.the.ramada.com/dawson_creek13099
41 units on one level, fridges, coffee, irons
and boards, cable TV, high-speed wireless. Free deluxe continental breakfast.
Close to restaurants, downtown, and
tourist information. Two pet rooms.

Super 8 Motel (Dawson Creek)
1440 Alaska Avenue
1-888-482-8884 or 250-782-8899
www.super8.com
48 air-conditioned units, cable TV, high-
speed Internet, fridges, coffee, hair
dryers, irons. Laundry, fitness passes.
Award winner for clean and friendly.

Campgrounds
Alahart RV Park
Junction of Highway 97 and Alaska Highway
250-782-4702
www.alahartrvpark.com
Full hookups, pull-throughs, tent
camping. Free showers, self-service
laundry, dump station, free ice.
Windshield repair. Close to downtown, next to restaurant.

Mile O RV & Campground
Mile 1.5, next to Rotary Lake and
Walter Wright Pioneer Village
250-782-2590
Partial hookups, pull-throughs, shady
sites. Free showers; laundry, dump
station, Mile 1 Café.

Northern Lights RV Park
On Highway 97 South, just west of junction
with Highway 97 North
1-888-414-9433 or 250-782-9433
55 sites, spacious pull-throughs, full and
partial hookups. Free satellite TV,
modem hookup, free showers, self-
service laundry, washrooms. RV wash;
full service for Alaska Highway preparation. Gift shop, trout-fishing pond.
Large groups welcome.

Tubby's RV Park
1913 Hart Highway (Highway 97 South)
250-782-2584
97 full-hookup sites, pull-throughs, tenting.
Free showers, self-service laundry, rest
rooms, dump station. Car and RV wash,
auto services. Internet access. Near
swimming pool and Pioneer Village.

Restaurants
The Alaska Café & Pub
Near Mile O milepost
250-782-7040
www.alaskahotel.com
Private dining and meeting rooms.
Caravans welcome.

Caruso's
1025 Alaska Avenue
250-782-4938
Steak, seafood, pasta.

China Kitchen
10600 8th Avenue
250-782-1596
Chinese favorites, full menu or
take-out.

An old grain elevator has been transformed into an art and photo gallery near the Dawson Creek Visitor Centre.

Dawson Co-Op Cafeteria
11300 8th Street
250-782-4858
Full menu and take-out.

Dawson Creek Diner & Deli
10221 10th Street
250-782-1182
Burgers, sandwiches, pizza.

Dawson Creek Golf & Country Club
Highway 97 North
250-782-5156
Breakfast, lunch, dinner, views.
    Reservations.

Lily's Dining Room
11705 8th Street,
    in the George Dawson Inn
250-782-9151
Full menu, fine dining.

Ma's Stopping Place
11705 8th Street,
    in the George Dawson Inn
250-782-9151
Coffee shop featuring down-home
    breakfasts, lunches, dinners.

Mr. Mike's West Coast Grill
1501 Alaska Avenue
250-782-1577
Full menu or take-out. Patio seating.
    Reservations accepted.

Panago Pizza
10508 8th Street
250-310-0001
Pizza, wings, salads.

Smitty's Family Restaurant
11300 8th Street
250-782-5442
Family dining, seniors' and children's menus.

Road Notes

The price of gas in Dawson Creek is typically higher than in the smaller towns to the south. And after Dawson Creek, the farther north you go, the more you pay.

As you drive north toward Fort St. John, notice the pumpjacks in the fields. These mechanisms draw the oil out of the ground and into a pipeline or a storage tank. Most of the oil and gas is sold to markets in Canada and the United States.

Get sweeter than honey just south of Fort St. John at **The Honey Place**, which boasts the world's largest glass beehive. You can learn about bee behavior and what makes quality honey. Get your honey here, or pollen, or other souvenirs. It's on the west side of the road, about 5 miles (8 km) before Fort St. John. Call 250-785-4808.

*F*ORT ST. JOHN

From Dawson Creek: 47 miles (76 km)
To Fort Nelson: 235 miles (378 km)

Fort St. John calls itself The Energetic City, with a nod to the industries that power the city's economy: natural gas and oil extraction, hydroelectric power, forestry, agriculture, and tourism. This city of 16,034 people is the oldest non-Native settlement on the British Columbia mainland. Another 30,000 people live throughout the North Peace region, where the Peace River snakes through a broad, green valley. These rural residents and First Nations communities look to Fort St. John as a regional hub for business and services. The city offers shopping, dining, and cultural attractions such as live theater, dance, and music at the **North Peace Culture Centre,** 10015 100th Avenue. Call 250-785-1992. And it's a pet-friendly town—your traveling pets are welcome in nearly every hotel, motel, or lodge in Fort St. John.

As the main town of the North Peace region, Fort St. John lies within a diverse landscape, from rolling farmlands and valleys to canyons carved by rivers. The staff at the Visitor Information Centre, open year-round at 9923 96th Avenue, will help you plan an outdoor adventure. Call 250-785-3033 or 250-785-6037 or browse the Web site at *www.fortstjohnchamber.com.* The center offers a list of local guides and outfitters and their specialties. Think about a day of hiking on **Fish Creek Community Forest** trails, golfing on one of the three nearby courses, swimming, horseback riding, or fishing for walleye or northern pike in **Charlie Lake.** And golfers may choose from four excellent courses within easy driving distance from town.

Check with the folks at **Backcountry,** 10040 100th Avenue, for mandatory fishing licensing as well as outdoor clothing and gear. The folks there can book a guide for you, too. Call 250-785-1461. In Charlie Lake, stop by the General Store at Mile 52 Alaska Highway, or call 250-787-0655.

The **North Peace Leisure Pool** complex, at 9505 100th Street, is a modern addition to the recreational possibilities in Fort St. John. Outside is a free splash park, perfect for kids on hot, sunny days. Inside you'll find a six-lane lap pool, wave pool, rapids channel, water slide, and a kiddie pool. Relax in the steam room or sauna and the road miles will melt away. Call 250-785-8178.

The annual **Fort St. John air show,** held in late July, includes flying by the Canadian Forces Snowbirds, Skyhawks, Warbirds, and Air Combat Canada. This flying spectacle attracts thousands each year.

Exhibits at the **North Peace Museum** reflect on the region's First Nations roots, its settlement by fur traders, and its development into the regional power that it is today. Back in 1942, Fort St. John was the unofficial starting line for the builders of the Alaska Highway. A gravel road already existed between Dawson Creek and this outlying community, and that road was incorporated into the route. Six thousand troops descended on what was then a town of 200 people. You'll find the museum at the foot of the landmark oil derrick at 9323 100th Street. Call 250-787-0430.

Just north of town, you can turn west to access Highway 29, **Hudson's Hope Loop**, from the north end. This road leads to some beautiful driving country, but the road does get narrow and patchy in places. Steep grades and switchbacks are not advisable for oversize RVs. Two dams along this loop road are major area attractions, as is Hudson's Hope Museum. For more information, see the section on the town of Chetwynd in Chapter 5, "The Western Route."

Lodging

Alexander Mackenzie Inn
9223 100th Street
1-800-663-8313 or 250-785-8364
www.mackenzieinn.com
126 air-conditioned rooms, kitchenettes.
Cable TV, ATM, laundry, wheelchair access. Restaurant, lounge, nightclub. Close to shopping.

Best Western Coachman Inn
8540 Alaska Road
1-888-388-9408 or 250-787-0651
70 deluxe rooms, nonsmoking and pet rooms available. Cable TV, sauna, whirlpool, fitness room.

Blue Belle Motel
9705 Alaska Road,
Mile 47 of the Alaska Highway
1-866-833-2121 or 250-785-2613
40 air-conditioned units in newer motel, kitchenettes, fridges, microwaves, cable TV. Free coffee, laundry, barbecues.

Cedar Lodge Motor Inn
9824 99th Avenue
250-785-8107
47 air-conditioned units, some kitchenettes. Fridges, microwaves, cable TV. Winter plug-ins.

Esta Villa
9603 Alaska Road
250-785-6777
Air-conditioned rooms and kitchenettes, cable TV, microwaves, fridges, free coffee. Plug-ins. No pets.

Fort St. John Motor Inn
10707 102nd Street
1-888-988-8846 or 250-787-0411
www.fortstjohnmotorinn.com
96 air-conditioned rooms, cable TV, free local calls, fridges, laundry, winter plug-ins. Quiet surroundings.

Four Seasons Motor Inn
9810 100th Street
1-800-523-6677 or 250-785-6647
www.fourseasons.wo.to
60 air-conditioned rooms, kitchenettes, cable TV, high-speed Internet, winter plug-ins. Close to shopping, restaurants. Senior discount.

Northwoods Inn
10627 Alaska Road
250-787-1616
Comfortable air-conditioned rooms, cable TV. Dining, coffee shop, lounge, pub, entertainment.

Quality Inn Northern Grand
9830 100th Avenue
1-888-663-8312 or 250-787-0521
www.qualityinnnortherngrand.com
125 units in full-service hotel, suites, cable
TV. Fitness facility, swimming pool,
sauna, whirlpool. Restaurant, lounge,
pub. Downtown location.

Ramada Limited Fort St. John
10103 98th Avenue
1-888-346-7711 or 250-787-0779
www.ramada.com
73 deluxe rooms, suites, kitchenettes,
fridges, microwaves, irons and
boards. Cable TV, high-speed Internet,
voice mail, guest laundry. Fitness
facility, winter plug-ins. Free airport
shuttle. Restaurant, free passes to
Leisure Pool.

Campgrounds
Rotary RV Park
6 miles (9.5 km) north of Fort
St. John
250-785-1700
40 sites with full or partial hookup, pull-
throughs. 30-amp service, showers,
laundry, dump station. Boat dock on
Charlie Lake. Next to nature reserve.

Sourdough Pete's RV Park
7704 Alaska Road, Mile 45 Alaska Highway
250-785-7664
94 sites, full and partial hookups, long
pull-throughs. Tent camping, flush
toilets, laundry, showers, sani-dump.
Next to family amusement park.

*The province manages two easy-access
parks north of Fort St. John. For more
information, contact the Parks District
Office in Fort St. John at 250-787-3407.
The parks are:*

Beatton Lake Provincial Park
2 miles (3 km) north, then 5 miles (8 km)
east of Fort St. John
37 RV and tent sites, with Charlie Lake
access. Swimming, playground, fishing,
boat launch.

Charlie Lake Provincial Park
7 miles (11 km) north of Fort St. John
58 sites with picnic tables,
outhouses, dump station.
Playground, short hiking trail
to Charlie Lake.

Restaurants
Apple Betty's
10108 101st Avenue
250-787-2585
Lunch and early buffet for families.

Charlie Lake General Store
Mile 50.6 Alaska Highway
Charlie Lake
250-787-0655
Take-out chicken and ribs.

Irene's Tiny Café
10608 100 th Avenue
250-787-7147
Breakfast and lunch specialties.

Mings Kitchen
9005 100th Avenue
250-787-1177
Lunch, dinner buffet, eat in or
take out.

Northern Lights Restaurant
9823 100th Avenue
250-787-9085
Greek and Western cuisine.

Plaza Diner
8111 100th Avenue
250-787-9292
Affordable choices for lunch and dinner.

White Spot
9839 100 h Avenue
250-261-6961
Breakfast, lunch, dinner. Lounge.

*Also stop by major local hotels, which
feature full lunch and dinner menus in
their dining rooms.*

Road Notes

Certain mileposts you may see at roadside represent the distance from Dawson Creek on the original Alaska Highway—they show the Historical Miles. Many were erected in 1992, the road's 50th-anniversary year, as a way to provide markers with historical information about the significance of various places. These mileposts do not take into account the road improvements and shortening that have taken place over the years. Many towns and businesses have refused to give up their former addresses when the road was shortened, so they now refer to themselves as being at Historic Milepost such-and-such, further muddying the question of just exactly where you are. And as British Columbia and the Yukon work on the road, milepost markers are often missing. So if you are following the numbers closely and your math is coming out funny—it's not you. The next major city, Fort Nelson, is 235 miles (378 km) down the road. That's the longest segment of the Alaska Highway without a town of 1,000 residents or more. Nonetheless, on this wilderness drive you'll find the occasional roadhouse, gas station, restaurant, or campground tucked in quaint little places along the way, so don't worry about heading into the unknown. Services are available at these locations with their Historic Milepost addresses:

Shepherd's Inn (Mile 72), Wonowon (Mile 101–102), Pink Mountain (Mile 143–147), Sikanni Chief (Mile 162), Buckinghorse (Mile 175), and Prophet River (Mile 233). Plus, there's so much beauty to behold: This country is crisscrossed with rivers, and the Rocky Mountains to the west will keep you company. Use extra caution as you approach Sikanni Chief, as there's a 9 percent grade with a 50 km/hr speed corner as you descend this dangerous hill— really tough if you're pulling a big rig. Note the remains of the original wooden bridge crossing this stream. During road construction, as temporary bridges were replaced with permanent spans in 1943, this was the first bridge to be replaced. The historic structure was burned by an arsonist in 1992.

Also through this stretch, you'll come across a couple of historical stops on the **Northwest Staging**

Beyond Dawson Creek, we spotted a lone cycler on the Alaska Highway.

Route, the series of airstrips that were used during World War II to deliver supplies and Lend-Lease Program airplanes to Fairbanks. From there, Russian pilots ferried the planes over the Bering Sea. One such historical site is at Mile 146 (236.5 km), the Sikanni Chief flight strip on the east side of the road. This was the southernmost end of the Northwest Staging Route. Another abandoned airstrip can be seen near Mile 217 (349 km), where a side road crosses the old airstrip. As you drive, you'll notice segments of the original road that have been abandoned to the weeds through the years as the route has been straightened (and shortened).

The **Muskwa Bridge** at Mile 281 (452 km), just a couple of miles before Fort Nelson, is the lowest point on the Alaska Highway, at an elevation of only 1,000 feet (305 m).

While driving the road for the second edition of this book, we traveled in early June and saw single black bears on four separate occasions before we reached Fort Nelson. The bears were feeding at the forest edge, well away from the roadside, but clearly visible. They were intently munching on the new grasses of spring, and while they kept a wary eye on slow-moving vehicles with cameras, they didn't instantly scramble away. Again, we stayed in the camper and took pictures from a distance.

*F*ORT NELSON

From Fort St. John: 235 miles (378 km)
To Muncho Lake: 153 miles (246 km)
To Watson Lake: 330 miles (531 km)

Fort Nelson boasts that it has the longest main street in the world: the Alaska Highway. And the city's address is Historical Mile 300 (483 km)—a reference to the town's distance from Dawson Creek on the original Alaska Highway. (Road realignment now puts Fort Nelson just 282 miles from Dawson Creek.)

Established in 1805 as a fur trading post, this community in the northeast corner of British Columbia was named for Admiral Horatio Nelson, famed for the Battle of Trafalgar. About 4,100 people live in this town near the convergence of four rivers: the Muskwa, Prophet, Sikanni, and Fort Nelson. The extraction of natural resources fuels the local economy, with diverse industries represented on the city's snowflake-shaped emblem: gas and oil, mining, lumber, wildlife, agriculture, tourism, and trapping.

Like other small towns of the north, the emphasis is on opportunity and friendliness. Each Monday through Thursday in June and July, travelers are invited to stop by the **Phoenix Theatre** in the town square for a free welcome-visitor slide show presentation at 6:45 P.M. For information: 250-774-2956. Visitors are free to use computers at the **public library** on the town square to check their e-mail accounts on any service that does not require long-distance dialing. For more information, call 250-774-6777. This town is a good place to restock the RV with groceries and other necessities.

At the **Fort Nelson information center,** located inside the recreation center at Mile 284 Alaska Highway, help yourself to a free cup of coffee and learn about things to see and do in the Northern Rockies. The center's number is 250-774-6400; check out their Web site at *www.northernrockies.org.* Cash machines and U.S. currency exchanges are available at banks along the frontage road of the highway.

For the flavor of the past, visit the **Fort Nelson Heritage Museum,** in a log cabin across from the information center. The museum features a mounted white moose in its display of local wildlife, and film footage taken during the building of the Alaska Highway can be seen in the museum's Muskwa Theatre. On the grounds are several historical buildings that have been recovered and moved here, as well as a vintage car collection. Browse through the trapper's log cabin, gift shop, and an old-time general store. Call 250-774-3536.

Golfers can play a nine-hole, par-35 course with grass greens at **Poplar Hills Golf and Country Club,** just outside town. Take advantage of the midnight sun and play from dawn to dusk in summers. Call 250-774-3862.

Winter visitors will marvel at the northern lights in these parts. Aurora borealis displays above Fort Nelson draw scientists who observe and record the events. The northern lights can occur year-round, but are easiest to see during the winter months.

Lodging

The BlueBell Inn
Mile 300 Alaska Highway
1-800-663-5267 or 250-774-6961
58 air-conditioned rooms, kitchenettes. ATM, cable TV, self-service laundry, store, winter plug-ins. Restaurant, fuel station. Senior rates.

Fort Nelson Hotel
5110 50th Avenue North
1-800-663-5225 or 250-774-6971
135 air-conditioned rooms, kitchenettes. Cable TV, gift shop, indoor pool, saunas. Dining room, cocktail lounge, entertainment and dancing.

Ramada Limited Fort Nelson
5035 51st Avenue
1-866-774-2844 or 250-774-2844
41 units, some kitchenettes in central downtown location. Cable TV, coffee, irons and boards, free Internet access. Free continental breakfast, hot tubs. Winter plug-ins.

Travelodge Fort Nelson
4711 50th Avenue South
250-774-3911
www.travelodge.com
69 air-conditioned rooms, plus laundry service, office services, winter plug-ins. Sauna, whirlpool. Small pets welcome. Restaurant, dining room, lounge with TV and fireplace. Free airport shuttle.

Woodlands Inn
3995 50th Avenue South
1-866-966-3466 or 250-774-6669
www.woodlandsinn.bc.ca
131 spacious, air-conditioned rooms, suites, kitchenettes. Cable TV, dataports, coin-operated laundry, steam bath, hot tub, fitness room. Restaurant, sports lounge. Free shuttle.

Campgrounds
The BlueBell Inn
Mile 300 Alaska Highway
1-800-663-5267 or 250-774-6961
42 full-service sites, laundry, fuel, store, ice, ATM. Sleeping rooms also available. Restaurant.

Husky 5th Wheel Campground
5 miles (8 km) south of downtown
    Fort Nelson on Alaska Highway
250-774-7270
55 RV sites with full hookups, some
    pull-throughs, 14 tent sites. Showers,
    laundry, store, fuel, restaurant. Cable TV,
    Internet access. Llama viewing.

Westend RV Campground
On Alaska Highway,
    next to Heritage Museum
250-774-2340
160 sites with full and partial hookups,
    pull-throughs, grassy tent sites, free
    firewood. Showers, laundry, cable TV,
    dump station. Gift shop, free car wash,
    RV supplies and wash. Walking distance
    to local attractions. Auto services, tours.

*The province manages two easy-access
parks west of Fort Nelson. For more
information, contact the Parks District
Office in Fort St. John at 250-787-3407.
The parks are:*

Testa River Regional Park
48 miles (77 km) west of Fort Nelson,
    then south for 1 mile (1.5 km)
25 campsites, tenting area, firewood,
    outhouses, water, wheelchair access.

115 Creek Provincial Campsite
57.5 miles (92.5 km) west of Fort Nelson
8 campsites, water, picnic tables, garbage
    barrels. Fishing nearby in 115 Creek and
    MacDonald Creek.

Restaurants
Coachhouse Restaurant
4711 50th Avenue North
250-774-3929
Full-menu dining room.

Dan's Neighborhood Pub
4204 50th Avenue North
250-774-3929
Full menu, daily lunch specials.

Dixie Lee Chicken
5011 50th Avenue South
250-774-6226
Hamburgers, chicken, fish and chips,
    ice cream.

Fort Pizza
5148 Laird Street
250-774-2405
Pizza, fast food, ice cream.

Fort Restaurant
5100 50th Avenue North
250-774-7840
Lunch and dinner, family dining.

P&T Restaurant
4103 50th Avenue South
250-774-6244
Family dining, full menu.

Pizzarama Pizzaria
12 Landmark Plaza
250-774-7100
Eat-in or take-out pizza.

Subway
4904 50th Avenue North
250-774-SUBS
Hot and cold deli sandwiches.

*Also stop by major local hotels, which
feature full lunch and dinner menus in
their dining rooms.*

Road Notes

Over the years, we've seen fewer mileposts and kilometer posts along the road, mainly because they aren't always replaced after road maintenance. Again, be aware that the mileposts won't necessarily jibe with mileage showing on your odometer.

Mileage and kilometer figures used in this text are based on the actual current number of road miles from Dawson Creek.

Thirty-four miles (54.5 km) past Fort Nelson, at the summit of 3,500-foot (1,067-km) **Steamboat Mountain**, you'll gain spectacular views of the Muskwa River Valley and the Rocky Mountains. Looking at the shape of Steamboat Mountain, you'll see how it got its name.

Another 8 miles (13 km) along, you'll catch the first views of a classic Indian profile in the high, craggy rocks. Stop for a photo at the turnout in another mile. Drive another couple of miles to Teetering Rock viewpoint, another turnout with litter barrel and trailheads.

The highest point on the Alaska Highway (4,250 feet) occurs at **Summit**, 90 miles (145 km) from Fort Nelson.

One more note on wildlife, which seemed especially abundant on this early June trip of ours. Since early June is still spring in the Northland (after all, you may still find snow and ice at the river's edge), we were not surprised to see the carcasses of three dead moose at various spots along the road. They'd likely died during the snowy months and have only been revealed at breakup. I've already mentioned the four black bears we saw before Fort Nelson. In the miles to come, we would see another five black bears, a dozen stone sheep, a red-tailed hawk, a gigantic bull bison, and what appeared to be a recently killed caribou, probably hit by a vehicle. All this without opening the door to the camper. The signs that advise watching out for wildlife are serious, and especially useful when animals such as stone sheep come right down to the shoulder of the road to sample the natural mineral licks.

Heading toward Muncho Lake, you'll view several rivers, but the most beautiful must be the Toad River, which parallels the road for many miles. It's hard to keep your eyes on the road rather than watch its fast-moving water and its peculiarly beautiful blue-green. The **Toad River Lodge** at Mile 422 is a favorite stopping place for pie and coffee when relatives of mine drive the road every summer. They do have other items on the menu, as well as rooms, cabins, and camping amenities. Another attractive business a few more miles down the road is the **Poplars Campground & Café**, with cabins, RV sites, gifts, and plenty of baked goods to entice you.

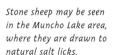

Stone sheep may be seen in the Muncho Lake area, where they are drawn to natural salt licks.

Muncho Lake

From Fort Nelson: 153 miles (246 km)
To Watson Lake: 177 miles (285 km)

With the crown of the Rocky Mountains towering above, and the jewel-colored waters of Muncho Lake at roadside, the highway here lies at an elevation of 2,680 feet. The province has developed campgrounds right along the lake, allowing you a wake-up view that will be indelible in your vacation memories. Copper oxide leaching into the lake is what creates these dramatic deep greens and blues. Anglers pull in Dolly Varden, rainbows, whitefish, lake trout, and the occasional grayling.

Muncho means "big lake" in Tagish, the aboriginal language. At 7.5 miles (12 km) long, it is one of the largest natural lakes in the Canadian Rockies. To the west lies the Terminal Range. "Terminal" refers to geographic position of the range—the northernmost section of the Rocky Mountains. Total length of the Rockies is almost 1,850 miles, from here to Santa Fe, New Mexico.

At **Double G Service** at the south end of Muncho Lake, you can book a guided, narrated tour on the lake aboard the MV *Sandpiper*. Call 250-776-3411 for information. Fishing, rafting, and flightseeing trips are available at various businesses in this stretch of the road, too. See below for details.

Lodging/Campgrounds/Meals

Muncho Lake is 437 miles (699 km) from Dawson Creek, but its Historical Milepost number is 456. For the locations of the following three businesses, we provide the actual distances from Dawson Creek. However, some of them prefer to use their Historical Milepost distances in advertising. Just be aware that all of these places lie along a 7-mile stretch of road on the eastern shore of the lake.

Double G Service
Mile 436.5 Alaska Highway
250-776-3411
Motel rooms, store, café. Narrated tours
on the lake.

J & H Wilderness Resort
Mile 444 Alaska Highway
250-776-3453
8 units with double and twin beds, free continental breakfast, store, gift shop, restaurant. 73 RV sites, lakeside, with full hookups, pull-throughs. Dump station, showers, laundry, fire pits, and firewood. Service station, fishing tackle, floatplane dock, boat tours. Other tour packages available.

Northern Rockies Lodge Ltd.
Mile 462 Alaska Highway
1-800-663-5269 or 250-776-3481
www.northern-rockies-lodge.com
45 units in modern log lodge, some wilderness cabins. 35 lakeshore RV sites with full or partial hookups. Laundry, restaurant, bakery, service station. Guided fly-in fishing, photo safari, floatplane service, flightseeing.

Liard River Hotsprings Provincial Park

Consider making time for a visit to Liard River Hotsprings Provincial Park, some 42 miles beyond Muncho Lake. If you're planning to spend the night, check in early. The 53 campsites are on a first-come, first-served basis, and they fill up quickly. Interpretive programs about area wildlife and the Liard (pronounced LEE-ard) hot springs attract large numbers of campers each night.

The big attraction here: the wondrous hot springs, which lie at the end of a boardwalk that crosses a superheated marsh. On either side of the walk, you can see the slow bubbling action of the mud beneath a clear layer of warm water. At the swimming hole, there's a changing room with benches and hooks. Outside, more benches and a wooden deck overlook naturally heated pools. Take care on the slippery steps leading into the water. Depending on how hot you like it, you move around to different levels of the pool until you are sufficiently cooked. The experience was heavenly after a day on the road.

Road Notes

The Trout River follows the road beyond Muncho Lake, with swift, clear water that foams over the rapids. For several miles, this part of the highway seems to echo the old days: It's paved, but it's curvy. Left, right, left, right. And then, for a while, the route is unpaved. On a rainy day, the wet mud sounds like gushy soup under the tires.

Just north of Coal River at Mile 514 (823 km), the road narrows and loses its shoulders, and the legal speed is reduced dramatically. This is an old section of the highway, with no shoulders, and blind hills and corners. I feel for anybody on a bicycle. Within a few miles, a couple of rest areas provide good views of rapids along the **Liard River** and of surrounding vistas. In the miles that follow, note several sections of the old Alcan where the former roadbed is buckled, broken, and overgrown with weeds.

At Mile 567 (909 km), or Historical Mile 588, is **Contact Creek**, with a plaque that remembers September 24, 1942, a key day in construction of the Alaska Highway. On that day, soldiers from two regiments, one working from the north and one working from the south, met here. The southern segment of the highway was completed. In 1942, this place was 588 miles (946 km) from Dawson Creek; road improvements now put it 568 miles (914 km) from Dawson Creek. Nearby Contact Creek Lodge sells fuel, coffee, souvenirs, fishing licenses, and groceries; 867-536-2262.

You may encounter extensive roadwork in these far-north reaches of British Columbia. A large realignment project has been ongoing for several summers. Get ready for a little flying mud and occasional delays while flaggers hold back traffic for heavy equipment. Farther ahead a solid, gravel roadbed is maintained with graders.

Muncho Lake is among the loveliest places on the Alaska Highway.

Unlike the early days of the highway, outposts such as Walker's Continental Divide can be found at regular intervals. There's no need to worry about running out of fuel or food.

Liard Hotsprings is a favorite rest stop for road-weary travelers. Minimal improvements have been made to keep the springs a natural wonder.

If you see large piles of brush alongside the road, that is where land has been cleared for more work. Evidence of a long-ago forest fire and regrowth is visible in the distance.

Pavement picks up again around Mile 576 (922 km), at **Iron Creek Lodge**. A motel, RV campground, and café are tucked away in these north woods. Call 867-536-2266. The trees are shorter, with pine and shrubby deciduous trees. Their uniform height suggests regrowth from a fire. Construction work at the Hyland River Bridge was in progress in 2004; normally pullouts on the north side would lead to the river's edge. Locals say there's good fishing here for rainbow trout, Dolly Varden, and arctic grayling.

WATSON LAKE, Yukon Territory

From Fort Nelson: 330 miles (531 km)
From Muncho Lake: 177 miles (285 km)
To Teslin: 163 miles (262 km)
To Whitehorse: 274 miles (441 km)

Welcome to Canada's Gateway to the Yukon. Driving through Watson Lake, you'll see the Stars and Stripes and the Maple Leaf paired on light-posts down the main drag. That may be a surprising sight to some, but it is reflective of the spirit of cooperation between Canada and the United States, not only in building the Alaska Highway, but also in using it for the last half century. Watson Lake, population 1,600, also is the junction city for the Alaska Highway and Campbell Highway 4, a north-bound unpaved highway.

Stop by the **Alaska Highway Interpretive Centre** at the heart of the **Watson Lake Signpost Forest** (see sidebar) for information about the birth of the signpost forest and to see a small exhibit that details the building of the Alcan in pictures and artifacts. You'll find free coffee, use of rest rooms, and lots of printed material on towns and attractions still ahead.

Across the highway, check out the **Northern Lights Space and Science Centre**, decorated outside with banners that simulate the aurora borealis. Inside, learn about the myth and science behind the phenomenon. Electric sky theater shows daily until early September. Contact 403-536-7827 or *www.northernlightscentre.ca.*

The town's recreation department maintains 18 multiuse trails in and around Watson Lake. They are color-coded with green, for the beginner level, to blue for intermediate, and black for advanced. Call 867-536-2246 with your questions.

Truck and RV service and repairs are available in Watson Lake. You can also arrange to go fishing, take a helicopter ride, or play a round of golf at Greenway's Greens, Yukon's first golf course to support grass greens. Full rentals are available, and a tee time is not required. Call 867-536-2477. Watson Lake's local shops sell art and jewelry pieces in gold, jade, and ivory.

Lodging

Air Force Lodge
Adela Trail at south end of town
867-536-2890
Comfortable, quiet rooms in restored
  historic building.

Belvedere Motor Hotel
On the Alaska Highway
867-536-7712
www.watsonlakehotels.com
48 rooms, suites, cable TV,
  whirlpools, in-room coffee.
  Cocktail lounge, coffee shop,
  dining room.

Big Horn Hotel
On Frank Trail, 1 block south of
  Alaska Highway in Watson Lake
867-536-2020
www.yukonweb.com/tourism/bighorn
29 rooms, wheelchair-accessible suite,
  kitchenettes, jacuzzi rooms. Cable TV,
  phones, coffee.

Cedar Lodge Motel
Junction of Adela Trail and
  Stubenberg Boulevard
867-536-7406
www.cedarlodge.yk.net
12 rooms, suites, kitchenettes,
  in-room coffee.

Watson Lake Hotel
Next to Signpost Forest
867-536-7781
www.watsonlakehotels.com
48 rooms, suites in historic building,
  nonsmoking available. Satellite TV,
  sauna. Coffee shop, dining room.
  Senior discount.

Campgrounds

Baby Nugget RV Park
Nugget City
Historic Mile 650, west of Watson Lake
867-536-2307
Pull-throughs, 15-, 30-, and 50-amp
  service. Room for big rigs. Modem
  access, laundry, RV wash. Restaurant,
  bakery, gift shop. Gold-panning,
  hiking, fishing.

Campground Services
Mile 632 Alaska Highway
867-536-7448
140 full and partial hookups. Laundry,
  food mart, RV wash, RV repairs, fuel.

Downtown RV Park
Lakeview Avenue and 8th Street north, at
  center of town
867-536-2646
Full hookups, pull-throughs, showers,
  laundry, RV wash. Walking distance
  to shopping, restaurants, visitor
  information.

Green Valley RV Park
Just south of the Liard River bridge
867-536-2276
Full or partial hookups, riverside camping
  in the shade, tenting area. Showers,
  laundry, groceries, souvenirs, boat ramp,
  and fishing

Junction 37 RV Park
Mile 659 Alaska Highway
867-536-2794
All RV sites have 30-amp service, some
  pull-throughs, showers, laundry.
  Restaurant, gift shop, store, saloon,
  gas, diesel, propane.

Watson Lake Recreation Park
2.5 miles (4 km) west of town center via
  Alaska Highway
55 RV and tent campsites, hang-pump water,
  camp kitchen, boat launch. Shelters,
  playground, trails, swimming, fishing.

Leaving One's Mark

The **Watson Lake Signpost Forest** began with a single sign placed by Carl K. Lindley, a homesick Illinois soldier, during construction of the Alaska Highway. By 1978, when I first came by this place, the addition of signs through the years had expanded to cover a row of telephone poles at a pullout along the road. Each pole was studded with signs from all corners of the world.

In 1999 I was astonished to walk along the many trails of a true forest of poles covered with more than 42,000 signs. A thousand had been added in the previous year alone. There was so much to see that it was hard to take in all of the colors, words, and messages that were meaningful to somebody, somewhere, at some time in this road's history.

An Alaska license plate caught my eye, but it was nailed sideways and low to the ground. Someone had dated it and posted it just a week earlier. "Going back to Alaska," somebody had written around the plate's letters and numbers with a thick black marker. "Samantha, Sandi and Roger, Scooby Doo, Hobbes, Patches. Never to leave again!" It was a declaration that nearly brought tears to my eyes, representing not one trip but two, a leaving home and a going home.

The Signpost Forest covers many acres representing visitors from around the world.

It made me think about the realm of human emotion represented by all of these signs—the grief, sorrow, anger, and gladness that this road has known since the 1940s when young soldiers were missing home, worrying about the battlefront, and wondering if the labor would ever end. Through the years, the highway has seen the bright anticipation of new life in a new land, the tears of a bride who fears what lies ahead, and the joy of this unknown family returning to the place they call home. The signpost forest, as garish as some may think it is, has become a testament to the living, a guest book for people who want to tell the world: I WAS HERE.

Restaurants

Bee Jay's Café
Adela Trail near 3rd Avenue
867-536-2335
Full menu, lunch and dinner specials.
Pastries, bread, ice cream.

Belvedere Motor Hotel
On the Alaska Highway
867-536-7712
www.watsonlakehotels.com
Hotel restaurant with full service dining
room and coffee shop.

Klondike Pattie's Burger Bar
Next to Signpost Forest,
in Watson Lake Hotel
867-536-7781
Eat-in or take-out burgers and more.

Wolf It Down Restaurant
Nugget City
Historic Mile 650 Alaska Highway
867-536-2307
Breakfast, lunch, dinner, baked goods.
Dine in or take out.

Road Notes

Just past Watson Lake, we spotted a "dog truck," a dog-mushing term for a vehicle that transports sled dogs. The trucks are capped with a row of dog boxes, each with an individual door, on each side of the truck bed. You'll see these vehicles all over the northland, usually with a dogsled strapped on top of it all. The musher driving this dog truck had his sled on top, and he was towing a trailer loaded with an all-terrain vehicle. Here was the classic setup for exercising dogs in the summer: running them in front of a four-wheeler. We were looking forward to heading back into the north country, and this was a welcome, familiar sight.

West of Watson Lake on the Alaska Highway is the junction with Canada Highway 37, which leads southbound to Dease Lake and the Cassiar Highway. This is the way to the coastal communities of Stuart, B.C., and Hyder, Alaska. (See the section on the Yellowhead-Cassiar Highways in Chapter 7, "Western Canada's Northbound Byways.")

As you journey north, you'll see another form of the signpost forest idea on the slopes along the highway, at a point about 630 miles (1,014 km) from Dawson Creek. For the last decade, "natural" graffiti artists have been writing messages using lines of small rocks.

You'll find several day-use or recreation sites and viewpoints in the beautiful miles between Watson Lake and Teslin. **Rancheria Falls Recreation Site** at Mile 695 (1,118.5 km) is a park-and-rest area with a boardwalk trail that leads to a waterfall.

About 3 miles farther along is the **Continental Divide**, and as you approach this point, the peaks become sharper, more visibly mountainous. At the crossing, a pullout includes signs with points of interest, maps, and outhouses. There are several lodges and visitor services through this section of the road. On the way to Teslin, the highway moves in gentle, winding curves through forest. Just before Teslin, you'll cross the longest bridge on the Alaska Highway, the **Nisutlin Bay Bridge**, which spans the Nisutlin River where it enters Teslin Lake. This is a gorgeous body of water—narrow, but long: 86 miles (138 km).

TESLIN

From Watson Lake: 163 miles (262 km)
To Whitehorse: 111 miles (179 km)

Teslin is an inland Tlingit village of fewer than 500 people, many of whom are related to members of the Alaskan coastal Tlingit tribes. Although it is a small town, it offers much in the way of visitor services. You'll find a couple of major motels with in-house restaurants and lounges, groceries and general merchandise, RV parks, gift shops, a trading post, and the George Johnston Museum, named for a resourceful Tlingit man who lived from 1884 to 1972. Find out more about Johnston, Teslin, and the area's natural and cultural history in the museum, operated by the Teslin Historical Museum Society. Call 867-390-2550.

Lodging/Campgrounds/ Restaurants

Dawson Peaks Resort & RV Park
Mile 770 Alaska Highway
867-390-2310
www.yukonweb.com/tourism/dawsonpeaks
Lakefront cabins with private baths and decks. Campsites with pull-throughs, water, dump station, fire pits, showers. Tenting area. Free firewood. Restaurant, gift shop, fishing charters, boat rentals.

Teslin Lake Provincial Campground
Mile 783 Alaska Highway
Km 1,309 Alaska Highway
27 RV and tent sites, hand-pump water, shelter, boat launch, fishing.

Yukon Motel and RV Park
Mile 804 Alaska Highway
867-390-2443, office; 867-390-2575, restaurant
Rooms with satellite TV. 40 pull-through RV sites with full hookups, RV wash, fuel. Restaurant, lounge, gift shop, liquor store. Fishing charters. Wildlife gallery of mounted animals.

Road Notes

A longtime landmark business 9 miles (14.5 km) north of Teslin, **Mukluk Annie's Salmon Bake**, offers all-you-can-eat meals, motel rooms, cabins, free camping, and free RV wash. Call 867-667-1200 or 867-390-2600.

A mile later, you'll cross the **Teslin River Bridge**, which is 1,770 feet (539.5 m) long and high enough to accommodate the steamers that once navigated the river between Whitehorse and Teslin. At the north end of the bridge, **Johnson's Crossing** offers camping opportunities, as well as souvenir shopping, fishing, canoeing, and wildlife-watching. Johnson's Crossing Campground Services, across from the Teslin River bridge, claims that its cinnamon buns are world famous. They also offer deli items, camping, laundry, fuel, and fishing licenses. Foot-long grayling run in the river here from spring to late fall. Call 867-390-2607.

We decided to put in a few more miles before choosing our campsite and ended up at **Squanga Lake,** a Yukon government campground at Mile 821 (1,366 km). It's said to have good fishing for northern pike, grayling, burbot, rainbow trout, and whitefish (which are called *squanga* in the local Native language). The setting sun cast a brilliant pink across the sky and the lake's surface, silhouetting the spruce trees in black. That late-August night was dark, superbly quiet, and cool—a great combination for sleepy Alaskans. The next morning we saw (and heard) loons out on the lake in the rain.

Farther up the highway comes an opportunity for an exciting side trip to the historic Alaska community of **Skagway.** To drive there, leave the Alaska Highway at Jake's Corner (Mile 874.5) and go west on Yukon Highway 8 for 34 miles (55 km) to Carcross and Klondike Highway 2. Skagway is then a scenic 66 miles (106 km) to the south. For details on the highway and on the history, attractions, lodging, and restaurants of Skagway, see the section on Klondike Highway 2 in Chapter 8, "Alaska's State Highways."

Just before Contact Creek, the Alaska Highway begins a zigzag westerly route, crossing the British Columbia–Yukon border seven times before it finally plunges fully into that immense northern territory—home to some 50,000 moose, 160,000 caribou, 10,000 black bears, 4,500 wolves, and 223 species of birds.

The Yukon was made famous by writers such as Jack London and Robert Service, each of whom had firsthand knowledge of this land's stark, gripping beauty in winter, and how its people, flora, and wildlife flourish under the midnight sun in summers. Tourism, mining, forestry, trapping, and fishing remain leading industries. The Yukon River, with its headwaters in British Columbia, courses through the territory for 1,979 miles (3,185 km), the second-longest river in Canada.

Yukon Territory at a Glance

Size: *186,661 square miles or 483,450 square km*

Population: *31,300*

Capital: *Whitehorse*

Tourism and Lodging: *Tourism Yukon and Culture, 1-800-661-0494 or touryukon.com*

Fishing and Hunting: *Yukon Department of the Environment, www.environmentyukon.gov.yk.ca.*

Government Campgrounds: *www.gov.yk.ca or check at any Tourism Yukon visitor information center*

Canada Customs: *1-800-461-9999 or 867-667-3943, www.ccra-adrc.gc.ca*

WHITEHORSE

From Watson Lake, Yukon: 274 miles (441 km)
From Teslin, Yukon: 111 miles (179 km)
To Haines Junction, Yukon: 98 miles (158 km)
To Alaska–Yukon border: 303 miles (488 km)

The beautiful capital of the Yukon Territory is situated on the banks of the Yukon River, along the route of the stampeders who were headed for the gold-fields more than a century ago. One of city's landmarks is a lovely giant: the 210-foot SS *Klondike*, a restored paddlewheeler that is dry-docked on the west bank of the Yukon. Named a National Historic Site, the *Klondike* is a tangible reminder of this region's history—a retired workhorse left from a fleet of more than 250 riverboats that reigned in transportation until construction of the highway. Restored to its 1937–1940 appearance, the *Klondike* remains a figure of elegance and grace. Come aboard for a tour of the decks, cargo holds, and passenger accommodations; RV parking, a gift shop, and a visitor center are located nearby.

More than 20,000 people live in Whitehorse year-round, and it also serves as the economic base for outlying communities. This is an economy that was built on mining and transportation services, and those industries remain important, along with tourism and government. Major airlines connect Whitehorse to the rest of the world, and the Alaska Highway brings thousands of visitors to its doorstep, mostly during the summer.

As is the case in other far north cities, living in Whitehorse sometimes means sharing the streets with wildlife. As we drove through a Whitehorse neighborhood, we spotted a small family of coyotes trotting across mowed lawns. One of the local constables said he'd seen them often, that they were part of the urban landscape. Almost every morning, he said, they were out and about at the same early hour. You could almost set your clock by them.

The **Visitor Reception Centre**, at 100 Hanson Street, offers advice and printed materials on attractions throughout the area, as well as films, maps, and displays. There's easy access for RV parking, and it's a good place to plan your day. Call 867-667-3084. For the active set, you'll find golfing, fishing, nature hikes, trail rides, swimming, biking, canoeing, kayaking, and more.

Downtown Whitehorse retains much of its old-time charm, with log structures and false-front buildings sharing city blocks with more modern stores and offices. Park your vehicle and join a **Historical Walking Tour**, which leaves Donnenworth House on 3rd Avenue, next to Lepage Park, on a regular basis. Learn about local characters and the city's history, and view architectural marvels such as the Old Log Church, built in 1900, and the Log Skyscraper. For information, call 867-667-4704.

A hydroelectric dam built in 1958 created **Schwatka Lake,** which is now a floatplane base. Beneath this stretch of deep water, there still exists the boulder-strewn river bottom once known as **Whitehorse Rapids.** The town was named after those rapids—the plumes of foamy water were as white as the mane of a white horse. For gold seekers on the trail to the Klondike, this was the most perilous stretch of the Yukon River. Ill-prepared stampeders had to maneuver through the rapids, often aboard homemade boats that shattered against the rocks. Those who were successful were next met with the Devil's Punchbowl, a swirling mess of confused current, then the roaring water and hundred-foot sheer rock walls of Miles Canyon. After such a frightening river run, shaken and no doubt relieved, the miners often pulled ashore to dry out their goods and rest.

Entrepreneurs arrived with the miners, eager to find ways to make money without digging in the ground. In 1897 two men devised a way around the natural obstacles by building tramways on either side of the rapids and canyon. During a short-lived boom, a tent city called **Canyon City** sprang up, with businesses such as a saloon and roadhouse to further mine the pockets of the thousands who passed through. North-West Mounted Police arrived to maintain order as more than 20,000 stampeders used this gateway to the Klondike.

The Yukon River stern-wheeler Klondike *in Whitehorse has been lovingly restored.*

The historic site of Canyon City is accessible by walking trail, and interpretive signs mark the way. To get there, take Miles Canyon Road from Mile 910 (146.5 km) of the Alaska Highway. At the lookout, enjoy a spectacular view, then drive down to the suspended footbridge and walk over the bridge to the site where Canyon City once stood.

With completion of the **White Pass & Yukon Route railway** in 1900, miners could travel in comfort to a point beyond the rapids. However, by then, all claims had been staked and the rush was in decline. Whitehorse is still connected by bus service to the railway, which offers service to Skagway, Alaska, between May and September. The historic depot stands near the river in downtown Whitehorse. The White Pass & Yukon Route remains the only operating narrow-gauge railroad in North America, and riding in the restored railcars is a rare treat. For tickets and reservations for daily departures, call 1-800-343-7373 or 867-668-RAIL. See *www.wpyr.com.*

MacBride Museum, at 1st Avenue and Wood Street, provides mining displays, natural history, First Nations culture, artifacts from the gold rush, and geology of the area. Exhibits teach about different kinds of gold deposits, where they are found, and how they are taken from the ground. You can pan for gold here, too. Call 867-667-2709.

Yukon Beringia Interpretive Centre, at Mile 915 (1,473 km) on the Alaska Highway, features prehistory displays that offer insight into a time when this land belonged to mastodons, saber-toothed cats, and lions. Call 867-667-8855. The **Yukon Transportation Museum**, next to the Beringia Centre, features displays on the various modes of transportation used on the Trail of '98, then and now. Murals painted by Yukon artists serve as backdrops. Call 867-668-4792.

"**The Frantic Follies**" has entertained audiences for nearly 40 years, so we expected a corny, tired stage show. Instead we discovered a first-class vaudeville show by talented performers. On the bill: ragtime piano, can-can girls, red-hot-mama singing, banjo extravaganzas, magic, family-oriented comedy—and some wild Robert Service poetry. You've never heard "The Cremation of Sam McGee" quite like this. The revue shows nightly from mid-May through mid-September. The box office is in the Westmark Whitehorse, 2nd Avenue and Steele Street. Call 867-668-2042.

The **Whitehorse Fishway** features the world's longest wooden fish ladder and three underwater viewing windows. Watch the migration of the Yukon River chinook salmon and other species, including trout and arctic grayling. The aquarium and fishway is open from June through August, and admission is free. Take 2nd Avenue from downtown, cross the bridge over the Yukon River to Lewes Boulevard, then follow the signs to Nisutlin Drive and the fish ladder. Call 867-633-5965.

One of the most popular river excursions is aboard the MV *Schwatka*, which offers a 2-hour cruise that begins at Schwatka Lake. The dock is 5 minutes from the city center via Miles Canyon Road on the north side of town. Just follow the signs. The lake serves as a floatplane base, so you'll see lots of traffic in the air and on the water. The route takes you through Devil's Punchbowl and into Miles Canyon. You can wave to the foot traffic above you on the Robert Lowe Suspension Bridge. Points of interest include an old fox farm and the historic site of Canyon City. An evening dinner cruise is available as well. The trip is popular, so advance tickets are recommended. Call 867-668-4716.

Takhini Hot Springs, with its naturally heated outdoor swimming pool, is a star attraction any time of year, but it's especially popular when the temperature drops below freezing. To get there, drive several miles north of Whitehorse, turn right onto the North Klondike Highway (Highway 2), and follow it for about 4 miles to the turnoff to the hot springs; follow the 6-mile spur road to the west. Out of the ground, the source water is 117°F, so it is mixed with cool water to maintain a temperature around 100°F for the swimming pool. While it is rich in minerals such as calcium, magnesium, and iron, no sulfur is present to foul the air or your swimsuit. A café, campground, climbing wall, and horseback riding are also on the rounds. Call 867-633-2706.

Local shopping is an adventure unto itself. Customized gold-nugget jewelry is a regional specialty, and several shops will sell you raw nuggets or fashion a piece just for you. Check along Main Street as you prospect for your own gold.

Yukon Gallery is the shopping outlet for original art, prints, pottery, and crafts, as well as fine jewelry. The gallery is at the corner of Lambert and 2nd Avenue downtown, across from the Visitor Reception Centre. Or stop by **North End Gallery,** at 1st Avenue and Steele Street, for scrimshaw, Inuit sculpture, and other original art. Your art purchases may be shipped anywhere in the world. The **Yukon Trappers Association** operates a retail outlet at 4194A Fourth Avenue. Aside from tanned furs, they offer finished items, such as beaded moosehide slippers, fur hats, old-style snowshoes, and smaller gift items. Many of their items are handmade by First Nations people.

Whitehorse is either the starting or finish line every February during the annual running of the **Yukon Quest International Sled Dog Race,** one of two major long-distance races in the Far North that attracts competitors from all over the world. At the other end of the race's grueling 1,000 miles is Fairbanks, Alaska. Visit the **Yukon Quest Store** at 205 Main Street, for race information and memorabilia. Call 867-393-8203 or visit *www.yukonqueststore.com.*

Services and parts for autos and RVs are available in Whitehorse. Twenty-four-hour cash machines may be found at the Bank of Montreal, the CIBC, or the Royal Bank of Canada, all on Main Street. The Thomas Cook Foreign Exchange, 2101A 2nd Avenue, is open 7 days a week during summer.

For information on city attractions and services, write the City of Whitehorse, 2121 2nd Avenue, Whitehorse, Yukon, Canada Y1A 1C2, or call 867-668-TOUR. Their Web site can be found at *www.city.whitehorse.yk.ca.*

Lodging

Airline Inn Hotel
16 Burns Road (across from the airport)
867-668-4400
30 rooms, some kitchenettes, laundry,
lounge, restaurant. Adjacent to
convenience store and gas station.

Airport Chalet
91634 Alaska Highway
867-668-2166
29 units, offering gas, diesel, RV dump,
and self-service laundry for guests.
Restaurant and lounge.

Best Western Gold Rush Inn
411 Main Street
867-668-4500
www.goldrushinn.com
106 deluxe rooms, suites, spas, barber shop,
beauty salon, laundry and dry-cleaning
services. Restaurant and lounge.

Bonanza Inn
4109 4th Avenue
867-668-4545
www.bonanzainn.com
52 rooms, some kitchenettes, TV, wheelchair
accessible. Dining facility.

Casa Loma Motel
1802 Centennial, Mile 921 Alaska Highway
867-633-2266
28 rooms, some kitchenettes, phone, TV,
wheelchair access. Dining.

Chilkoot Trail Inn
4190 4th Avenue
867-668-4190
32 rooms, some kitchenettes.

The Edgewater Hotel
101 Main Street
1-877-484-3334 or 867-667-2572
www.edgewaterhotel.yk.ca
30 deluxe rooms and suites, restaurant.
Cable TV, dataports, coffee, hair dryers.
Downtown location.

High Country Inn
4051 4th Avenue
1-800-554-4471 or 867-667-4471
www.highcountryinn.yk.ca
Jacuzzi or executive suites and kitchenettes
with view. Cable TV, free coffee, hair
dryer, irons and boards, laundry.
Downtown location.

River View Hotel
102 Wood Street
867-667-7801
www.riverviewhotel.ca
Comfortable rooms, cable TV, free coffee,
hair dryers. Indoor parking for bicycles
and motorcycles. English, German,
French spoken. Walking distance to
shopping, attractions.

*The mini-resort of
Takhini Hot Springs
offers swimming,
camping, and
horseback riding.*

The red tunics of the RCMP, Royal Canadian Mounted Police, symbolize law and order.

Westmark Whitehorse Hotel & Conference Centre
201 Wood Street
1-800-544-0970 or 867-393-9700
www.westmarkhotels.com
180 deluxe rooms, suites. Gift shop, restaurant, lounge, box office of The Frantic Follies.

The Yukon Inn
4220 4th Avenue
1-800-661-0454 or 867-667-2527
www.yukoninn.yk.ca
92 luxury guest rooms, suites, kitchenettes.Laundry, dry cleaning, hair salon, office services, winter plug-ins. Gift shop, exercise facilities. Café, two lounges, big-screen TVs. Walking distance to local attractions.

Roadhouse Inn
2163 Second Avenue
867-667-2594
Budget rooms in downtown location, hostel rooms, kitchen, laundry, saloon.

Stratford Motel
401 Jarvis Street
867-667-4243
www.yukoninfo.com/stratford
50 budget units, some kitchenettes, wheelchair access, laundry

Town & Mountain Hotel
401 Main Street
1-800-661-0522 or 867-668-7644
www.townmountain.com
30 executive-style suites, fridges, microwaves, irons and boards. Cable TV, parking, restaurant.

Westmark Klondike Inn
2288 2nd Avenue
1-800-544-0970 or 867-668-4747
www.westmarkhotels.com
99 deluxe rooms, suites. Gift shop, restaurant, lounge.

Area Campgrounds
Whitehorse:
Hi Country RV Park
91374 Alaska Highway
1-877-458-3806 or 867-667-7445
130 roomy sites with power. Showers, self-service laundry, cable TV, store, gift shop. Close to downtown.

Robert Service Campground
120 Robert Service Way
867-668-3721
68 treed sites along the Yukon River with showers, water, store, barbecue, playground. Close to downtown.

Trail of '98 RV Park
117 Jasper Street, just off Two Mile Hill at Industrial Road
1-800-377-2142 or 867-668-3768
150 sites with full or partial hookups, tent camping, self-service laundry, gift shop. Desk can set up city tours, tickets to attractions.

North of Whitehorse:
Takhini Hot Springs
Mile 6 (Km 10) Hotsprings Road
867-633-2706
www.whitehorsechamber.com
88 treed sites, with 15- and 30-amp
service, full and partial hookups.
Sani-dump, showers, water, store,
café. Horseback riding, swimming,
hiking, sauna.

West of Whitehorse:
Caribou RV Park
Mile 904 Alaska Highway
867-668-2961
www.sourdough.yk.ca
47 sites with power, satellite TV, car wash,
tent camping available.

MacKenzie's RV Park
18 Azure Road, junction of Alaska Highway
and Azure
867-633-2337
79 spacious sites with full or partial
hookups; 22 tent sites. Cable hookup,
modem, showers, laundry, store.
Playground, horseshoe pit, free gold
panning. Wheelchair access. Vehicle
wash. On city bus route.

Pioneer RV Park
Mile 911 Alaska Highway
1-866-626-7383 or 867-668-5944
www.pioneer-rv-park.com
150 sites, including full and partial
hookup, some pull-throughs.
Showers, laundry, rest rooms, store,
gift shop. Car and RV wash, some
automotive services, windshield
chip repairs. Tickets and reservations
for local attractions.

**Wolf Creek Provincial Campground and
Recreation Site**
Mile 875 (Km 1,459) Alaska Highway
40 RV and tent sites, 11 tent only sites.
Hand-pump water, shelters,
playground, trails.

Restaurants

Angelo's Vineyard
202 Strickland Street
867-668-6266
Classic Italian and Greek dining.

The Cellar Dining Room
101 Main Street, in Edgewater Hotel
1-877-484-3334 or 867-667-2572
Fine dining, specializing in salmon, crab,
halibut, arctic char, prime rib.

Cheechako's Sourdough Steakhouse
204B Main Street
867-393-2555
www.cheechakos.com
Steaks, seafood, salads, and more.

China Garden
309 Jarvis Street
867-668-2899
Chinese and western menus; lunch buffet,
dinners, takeout.

The Chocolate Claim
305 Strickland Street
867-667-2202
Soups, salads, sandwiches, coffee bar.

G & P Steak House & Pizza
Mile 918 Alaska Highway
867-668-4708
Greek and Italian specialties,
seafood, pasta.

Iron Horse Grill
151 Industrial Road, Unit 3
867-668-7871
Casual dining

Klondike Rib & Salmon BBQ
2116 2nd Avenue,
across from Westmark Whitehorse
867-667-7554
Fresh local fish, Yukon-style BBQ ribs,
caribou and musk ox Stroganoff.

Pandas
212 Main Street
867-667-2632
European fine dining, without the dress
code. Northern seafood specialties,
steaks, schnitzels, pasta.

Sam 'n' Andy's Tex Mex Bar & Grill
506 Main Street
867-668-6994
Mexican and Canadian food;
outdoor patio.

Steele Street Ale & Roast House
201 Wood Street,
in the Westmark Whitehorse
867-393-9747
Arctic char, cedar plank salmon, locally
brewed ales and beers.

Tim Hortons
Two locations:
2101B 2nd Avenue
(6 A.M.–11 P.M., no smoking)
2210 2nd Avenue
(open 24 hours, smoking allowed)
Eat in or take out; soups and sandwiches;
donuts and other pastries.

Tung Lock Chinese Restaurant
404 Wood Street
867-668-3298
Casual dining, specializing in seafood,
daily lunch and weekend dinner buffets.

Yukon Mining Company
4051 4th Avenue,
in the High Country Inn
867-667-4471
Salmon, halibut, wild game. Barbecue on
the deck, local beer specialties.

Road Notes

Just north of Whitehorse, the Alaska Highway connects with the North Klondike Highway (Highway 2), which heads north to Dawson City. (See the section on the North Klondike Highway in Chapter 7, "Western Canada's Northbound Byways.")

It's 98 miles (158 km) between Whitehorse and Haines Junction. In 1958, more than 1.5 million acres of forest burned in this region, and you can still see evidence of that fire in the landscape around you.

More homes along the roadside are decorated with caribou antlers and moose horns. You'll see more log cabins, more outbuildings, and places where homeowners have something of a collection on their property. While some might call this "junk," people of the North call it "storage" that's defended with: "You never know when I might need this." The blue tarp—more essential here, it seems, than many points south—often covers broken appliances, or a woodpile, or inoperable equipment that truly is of value to its owner.

About halfway to Haines Junction, the road used to pass through the First Nations village of **Champagne**. The highway was rerouted in recent years, and that surely brought traffic relief for this tiny community. A turnoff leads to the town now. Travelers are asked to be respectful of the villagers' private property and of their cemetery, which is not open to visitors. If you'd like to learn more about the Champagne-Aishihik Indian Band, you are welcome to visit the **Kwaday Dan Kenji** traditional camp at Mile 939.5 (1,512 km). Native interpreters will discuss what life was like for their ancestors, and you will visit a replica of a First Nations campsite. Dry camping is available for RV travelers who wish to overnight at Champagne.

A Japanese cyclist pauses for a photo at the top of the White Pass. It's hard to tell, but there actually is a bicycle under all of his gear.

Pay close attention to the junction at Haines Junction, at Mile 985 (1,585 km). To continue on the Alaska Highway, you must make a right turn, the first in many miles. Hundreds of wayward travelers have ignored the turn and ended up instead on Highway 3, heading south toward Haines, Alaska, instead of Fairbanks, Alaska. In the last decade, Canadian customs officials at the border before Haines reported more than 1,000 irate wrong-turners, even though signs at the intersection have gotten bigger. (See the section on the Haines Highway in Chapter 8, "Alaska's State Highways.")

After Haines Junction, the Alaska Highway crosses **Bear Creek Summit**, elevation 3,294 feet (1,004 m), and Boutillier Summit, elevation 3,293 feet (1,003 m), en route to the memorable **Kluane Lake**. The Alaska Highway skirts this vast and beautiful body of water for more than 60 miles (96.5 km), making this drive worthy of a few extra lines in your travel journal. On the way to the communities of Destruction Bay and Burwash Landing (where all services are available), take a few minutes to pull over at Mile 1,061 (1,707.5 km), the historical wayside for **Soldiers Summit**. A trail from the parking lot leads to the site of the Alaska Highway's official opening ceremonies, on November 20, 1942. Depending on whether road work is in progress, signage may or may not be present. However, at this location, officers in full-dress uniforms (with inadequate footwear) endured deep cold and snow while officials made grand speeches and cut the ribbon. Another ceremony here in 1992 celebrated the highway's 50th anniversary.

Unlike the Alcan's early years, today it's easy to find motels, lodges, campgrounds, and restaurants from Haines Junction to Beaver Creek, which lies ahead. Gas and other services are available, too. While many miles through the Yukon may appear wild and unsettled, help is never far away. Small communities along these miles can meet most of your service and shopping needs.

A forest fire in 1999 blackened the landscape near **Burwash Landing** and beyond it for several miles. Stop by the **Kluane Museum of Natural History**, along the highway, and you'll see how close the fire came to burning down this structure and

The World's Largest Gold Pan resides outside the Kluane Museum of Natural History.

These bizarre creations were drawn from burl wood and "Scully" Gordon's unusual sense of humor.

many others in the town. The fire line came within 30 feet of the museum's back door. For unexplained reasons, the winds changed direction and the town was spared. Get your picture by the "World's Largest Gold Pan" next to the museum.

The northernmost town on the Alaska Highway in the Yukon Territory is **Beaver Creek**. As at Contact Creek, this was a place where construction crews in 1942, working from opposite directions, met and completed a stretch of the Alaska Highway.

ALASKA–YUKON BORDER

From Whitehorse: 303 miles (488 km)
From Haines Junction: 205 miles (330 km)
To Tok: 92 miles (148 km)
To Fairbanks: 298 miles (480 km)

Crossing into Alaska is an achievement, and you're due for another round of photos. There's a wonderful place to pull over and record this moment, right at the demarcation line that separates the United States and Canada. Alaska and the Yukon Territory have each erected impressive welcome signs, massive wooden affairs that are beautifully painted. Between them is a parking area with a gazebo-like structure over the international border marker. Stand here and look north, then south, and you'll see the border as a brushed-out band in the scrubby trees, signifying the 141st meridian. At this wayside, most people like to pose with a foot in each country or sit on the nearby bench that's divided by a carved line with the word Yukon on one side, Alaska on the other.

Just ahead is the U.S. **Customs and Immigration station**, which is open 24 hours a day. Turn your watch back an hour to reflect the Alaska Time Zone.

Gas, RV camping, and tire services are available at the border, and just beyond it.

Road Notes

For the first 65 miles (104.5 km) into Alaska, the highway follows the border of 730,000-acre **Tetlin National Wildlife Refuge**, a sparsely treed region of marshes and lakes that attract thousands of nesting waterfowl and migrating sandhill cranes. Watch for other birds, too, including ptarmigan, trumpeter swans, loons, and some species of raptors. Mammals include black and brown bears, moose, caribou, and smaller furbearers such as lynx, red foxes, and coyotes. The Forest Service maintains two campgrounds, **Lakeview** and **Deadman Lake**, along the Alaska Highway, both before Northway Junction.

Eighty miles (129 km) from the border, at Tetlin Junction (not to be confused with Tetlin, Yukon), you'll find the northbound turnoff to Alaska Highway 5 (the Taylor Highway), an unpaved road that's closed in winter. This route leads to the Alaska villages of Chicken and Eagle, and connects with the Yukon's Top of the World

Highway, the northern route to Dawson City. (See the section on the Taylor Highway in Chapter 8, "Alaska's State Highways." Also see the section on the Top of the World Highway in Chapter 7, "Western Canada's Northbound Byways.")

Twelve miles (19 km) beyond Tetlin Junction is Tok, which was a construction camp during construction of the Alaska Highway.

Tok

From Alaska/Yukon border: 92 miles (148 km)
To Delta Junction: 108 miles (174 km)
To Fairbanks: 206 miles (331 km)

Surrounded by stands of spruce trees, Tok (TOKE) is a junction city. Motorists can continue northwest on the Alaska Highway toward Fairbanks, or veer southwest onto the Glenn Highway (known by Alaskans as the Tok Cutoff). This panoramic shortcut for southbound drivers leads to Glennallen or Valdez on the Richardson Highway, or to Anchorage at the end of the Glenn Highway. In November 2002, the Tok Cutoff was temporarily closed when east-central Alaska was rocked by a magnitude 7.9 earthquake that damaged roads, homes, and businesses. Portions of the Richardson and Parks Highways were also shut down until repairs could be made.

With a population of about 1,400, Tok is geared toward travelers' services and stays, and is especially busy in the summer months. Alaska's **Mainstreet Visitor Center** is housed in a massive log structure at the junction of the two highways. Cultivated flower beds around the center and elsewhere in town flourish in the long, sunny days of Alaska's Interior. At the center, you can learn about Tok's strategic role during the building of the Alaska Highway and about area wildlife, events, and attractions. Today it is known as Alaska's Dog Mushing Capital.

Take the kiddies to **Mukluk Land** at Mile 1317 of the Alaska Highway, just 2 miles (3 km) west of the highway junction. You'll find a lovely Alaska garden (mixing cabbages and flowers), videos on the trans-Alaska pipeline and the northern lights, golf, and a chance to do some gold panning (Mukluk Land guarantees the gold). Call 907-883-2571.

Tok is a great place to rest and restock. You'll find many choices here for comfortable accommodations, meals, gifts, groceries, and filling up the gas tank. Some campgrounds even offer a free breakfast for their guests.

Lodging

Golden Bear Hotel
Just south on the Tok Cutoff
907-883-2561
60 rooms, private baths. Cable TV, gift shop, coffee bar, Alaska displays, restaurant. Senior discount.

Snowshoe Motel
Mile 1314 Alaska Highway
1-800-478-4511 or 907-883-4511
www.alaskaoutdoors.com/eagle
24 units, satellite TV, phones. Continental breakfast, picnic area.

Tetlin National Wildlife Refuge lies to the south of the Alaska Highway as you enter the state.

Tok's visitor center features this impressive mount of an Alaska brown bear.

PLEASE DO NOT TOUCH THE BEAR

Tok Lodge
Near junction of Alaska and Glenn Highways
1-800-883-3007 or 907-883-2851
www.alaskan.com/toklodge
10 rooms in historic building; 38 motel units.
    Gift shop, café, lounge.

Westmark Tok
Junction of Alaska and Glenn Highways
1-800-544-0970 or 907-883-5174
92 deluxe rooms, nonsmoking available.
    Dining room, lounge. Adjacent to
    visitor center.

Young's Motel
Mile 1313 Alaska Highway
907-883-5023
43 rooms, private baths, nonsmoking
    available. Satellite TV, phones.
    Restaurant.

Campgrounds

Gateway Salmon Bake & RV Park
Mile 1313 Alaska Highway
907-883-5555
Space for big rigs to tenting campers.
    Water, electric, showers, rest rooms.
    Lunch and dinner.

Golden Bear Motel & RV Park
Just south on the Tok Cutoff
907-883-2561
Full and partial hookups, pull-throughs,
    tent sites. Showers, laundry, restaurant,
    gift shop, phone. Free sourdough
    pancake breakfast.

Sourdough Campground
1.5 miles (2.5 km) south on Tok Cutoff
907-883-5543
Full hookups, shaded area, dump
    station, laundry, showers, car wash,
    vacuum. Sourdough pancakes and
    reindeer sausage breakfast. Live
    music nightly. Gift shop, outdoor
    museum.

Tok RV Village
Mile 1313.5 Alaska Highway
907-883-5877
95 sites, full and partial hookups,
    pull-throughs. Showers, laundry,
    dump station, vehicle wash.
    Connection to check e-mail.
    Fishing licenses.

Tundra Lodge & RV Park
Mile 1316 Alaska Highway
907-883-7875
78 sites with full or partial hookups,
    pull-throughs, tent sites, dump station,
    laundry, RV wash. E-mail access.
    Cocktail lounge.

Restaurants

Fast Eddy's Restaurant
Mile 1313 Alaska Highway
Next to Young's Motel
907-883-4411
Steaks, seafood, pasta, burgers, pie.

Golden Bear Restaurant
Just south on the Tok Cutoff, adjacent to
    motel and RV park.
907-883-2561
Luncheon and dinner specials.

Tok Gateway Salmon Bake
Mile 1313 Alaska Highway
907-883-5555
King salmon, halibut, reindeer sausage,
    buffalo burgers. Shuttle pick-up
    available.

Tok Lodge & Café
Near junction of Alaska and Glenn Highways
1-800-883-3007 or 907-883-2851
Breakfast, lunch, dinner: prime rib, salmon,
    halibut, daily specials.

Young's Café
At highway junction
907-883-2233
Breakfast all day. Lunch specials, dinner,
    beer and wine, baked goods.

Road Notes

From Tok to Delta Junction is 108 miles (174 km) of almost unpopulated wilderness. The road follows or crosses several streams, the biggest of which is the Tanana River. Many of these streams were formed by runoff from glaciers in the Alaska Range. That's why the water tends to be a cloudy gray; in it are particles of suspended rock, called rock flour, carried by glaciers. The forest here is largely of spruce. Watch for moose and caribou.

*D*ELTA JUNCTION

From Dawson Creek: 1,422 miles (2,288.5 km)
From Alaska–Yukon border: 200 miles (322 km)
From Tok: 108 miles (174 km)
To North Pole: 83 miles (134 km)
To Fairbanks: 98 miles (157 km)

At Delta Junction, the Alaska Highway joins the Richardson Highway—marking the official end of the Alcan. Stop by the End of the Road milepost near the visitor center for a photo to add to your travel scrapbook. (This may be the official end, but for most travelers, Fairbanks is still the destination that marks completion of their journey up the Alaska Highway.) A nearby log structure is the old Sullivan Roadhouse, which houses historical exhibits. It was moved here from its former location along the old Valdez-to-Fairbanks Trail, the route of the present-day Richardson Highway.

Addresses for Delta Junction are Mile 1422 Alaska Highway or Mile 266 Richardson Highway. This crossroads town is an agricultural community where hardy strains of barley flourish in the short growing season and long hours of sunshine. Other crops include oats, wheat, grass seed, canola, and potatoes. Local farmers raise dairy cows, Tibetan yaks, elk, and reindeer. Nearby Fort Greely is a national missile defense site.

In Alaska, Delta Junction may be best known for its buffalo herd. Twenty-three plains bison, or buffalo, were transplanted to the area in 1928, and they flourished. A 90,000-acre bison range was established in 1978, with enough habitat to support between 400 and 500 animals. An annual hunt by permit keeps the population in line and helps feed families. New calves arrive in spring. In early summer you're most likely to see the herd browsing on the west side of the Delta River, but they move back over to the bison range in August. The Alaska Department of Fish and Game plants barley, oats, and hay on the range to keep the animals there and out of private fields. (Fences, as you can imagine, do not work when a headstrong herd wants to cross to the other side, especially if a meal is waiting.)

A historic roadhouse along the Tanana River has been restored by the Bureau of Land Management and put to good use, along with the adjacent BLM campground and picnic areas. **Rika's Roadhouse** is a favorite community gathering spot and houses museum displays, a gift shop, restaurant, and bakery. Call 907-895-4938 or visit *www.rikas.com*. Annual events in town include the Buffalo Wallow Square Dance in late May, the Buffalo Barbecue in July, and the Deltana Fair in late July and early August. A quirky mid-July event is the Mud Bog Races, when Alaskans pull out their snowmobiles in midsummer and race them through the mud.

Sample smoked reindeer, buffalo, elk, and yak sausage at **Delta Meat & Sausage Co.** at Mile 1413 Alaska Highway; 907-895-4006. See *www.deltameat.com*. Or try fishing in one of the more than 40 stocked lakes in the area. Local rivers hold trout and grayling, too. Outfitters are available to guide you on land and by air on your outdoor adventure.

Check in at the **Delta Junction Visitor Information Center** at the junction of the Alaska and Richardson Highways for more on what to see and do. While you're there, don't forget to ask for your end-of-the-road certificate. You can call the center at 1-877-895-5068 or 907-895-5068 or visit *www.deltachamber.org*.

Lodging

Alaska 7 Motel
Mile 270 Richardson Highway
907-895-4848
Rooms, kitchenettes available. TV, full baths. Daily and weekly rates.

Alaskan Steak House & Motel
Mile 265 Richardson Highway
907-895-5175

Buffalo Lodge
1575 Richardson Highway
907-895-9913

Cherokee Two Lodge
Mile 1425 Alaska Highway
907-895-4814

Clearwater Lodge
7028 Remington Road
907-895-5152
Comfortable rooms. Restaurant, campground.

Kelly's Alaska Country Inn
1616 Richardson Highway
907-895-4667
Rooms with private bath, phone, TV, kitchenettes.

Trophy Lodge
1420 Alaska Highway
907-895-4685

Campgrounds

Clearwater Lodge
7028 Remington Road
907-895-5152
RV and tent camping, cabins, restaurant open for dinner 7 days a week.

Mountain House Lodge
Mile 1412.5 Alaska Highway
907-895-5160
Campsites, rooms, restaurant, lounge.

Smith's Green Acres RV Park & Campground
Mile 268 Richardson Highway
1-800-895-4369 or 907-895-4110
Full and partial hookups, pull-throughs, tent sites. Showers, self-service laundry, rest rooms, phone, vehicle wash. Can arrange here for a pipeline pump station tour.

Alaska State Parks system maintains three nearby campgrounds on the Richardson Highway. They are:

Delta State Campground
1 mile past visitor center, with 24 campsites, water, picnic tables, and toilets.

Clearwater State Campground
2 miles past visitor center, turn right on Jack Warren Road for 10.5 miles. Offers riverside campsites, picnic tables, water, and a boat launch.

Quartz Lake Recreation Area includes two campgrounds (Lost Lake and Quartz Lake). 12 miles past visitor center, turn right on Quartz Lake Road for 2.5 miles.

Restaurants

Adam's Rib BBQ Restaurant
Mile 1412.5 Alaska Highway
907-895-5160
Ribs, chicken, brisket, seafood.

Alaskan Steak House & Motel
Mile 265 Richardson Highway
907-895-5175
Breakfast, lunch, dinner. Specializing in all-you-can-eat barbecue rib dinners.

Buffalo Center Diner
Across from IGA
907-895-5089
Family dining: breakfast, lunch, dinner.

Leaphy's Restaurant
7028 Remington Road
907-895-5152
Open for dinner 7 days a week; live music on weekends.

Pizza Bella
Across from visitor center
907-895-4841
Pizza, pasta, sandwiches, salads.

Rika's Roadhouse & Landing
Big Delta State Historical Park
907-895-4938
Baked goods and meals.

Trophy Lodge
1420 Alaska Highway
907-895-4685
Fine dining, cocktails.

Road Notes

The Richardson Highway between Delta Junction and Fairbanks is a four-lane route, but it remains a challenging road because much of it was built over permafrost. With Interior Alaska's extreme seasonal cycles of hot and cold damaging the road, you've got a roller-coaster ride in places. About 10 miles northwest of Delta Junction, you'll cross the Tanana River where the Big Delta Bridge parallels the suspension bridge supporting the trans-Alaska pipeline at this crossing. The bridge was built to withstand an earthquake measuring up to a magnitude of 7.5 and temperatures as low as $-60°F$.

About 7 miles (11 km) before you reach the town of North Pole, you'll pass by **Eielson Air Force Base,** home to 6,000 people in a major military installation named for Carl Ben Eielson, an early day Fairbanks pilot. A few miles later, note the eastbound turnoff for **Chena Lakes Recreation Area.** This popular park includes 80 campsites and dozens of picnic sites. Swimmers enjoy the sandy beach at Chena Lake; canoeists can navigate the lake or the Chena River, which flows through at one end. Boat rentals are available, and there's fishing, biking, hiking, and nature walks for outdoor fun. The Fairbanks North Star Borough charges a nominal use fee.

NORTH POLE

From Delta Junction: 83 miles (134 km)
To Fairbanks: 15 miles (24 km)

It's Christmas all year long in North Pole. That's because Santa doesn't disappear after Christmas Eve. On December 26, you can track him to his house and tell him what you want for next Christmas. This small community was founded in the 1950s, when several homesteading families sold their property for town lots. One far-thinking woman among them decided that a North Pole theme would likely help sell more lots, and maybe attract industry to their fledgling town.

The cheerful, candy-striped exterior of **Santa Claus House** is an invitation to any age, and the king-size likeness of Santa is a great photo opportunity. Mail your letters from here for that impressive North Pole cancellation. Inside the gift shop is a kiddie toyland. You can buy Christmas ornaments and order up a personalized Christmas letter for your favorite little ones. Santa makes regular appearances (with Mondays and Tuesdays off!) and greets children in his throne room. To order a Christmas letter, mail $7.50 along with the child's address to Santa Claus House, 101 St. Nicholas Drive, North Pole, AK 99705. Call 1-800-588-4078 or 907-488-2200. The jolly old elf is up-to-date on technology, too. He accepts e-mail. Write him at santa@santaclaushouse.com or browse his Web site at *www. santaclaushouse.com*. Visit Santa's reindeer next door at **Santaland RV Park,** a park with so many services, they even offer pet-sitting while you take a tour. Call 907-488-9132 or see *www.santalandrv.com*.

Several motels and campgrounds are nearby, and other North Pole businesses invite you to drive around town and enjoy all that the city of 1,600 people has to offer. Stop by the **Visitor Center Log Cabin** at 2550 Mistletoe Drive, or call 907-488-2242. See *www.northpolechamber.org*.

Santa's ready to receive little visitors
year-round in North Pole, Alaska.

Looking for the End of the Alaska Highway

No confusion exists about where the Alaska Highway begins: Mile 0, Dawson Creek, British Columbia. But far away in Alaska, two cities claim the distinction of being the end of the Alaska Highway: Delta Junction and Fairbanks. And in a way, they're both right. The former is the official end; the latter is the practical end.

Military convoys that used the Alcan in the 1940s were destined for installations in Fairbanks. But in constructing the highway, builders didn't have to lay new road all the way to the city limits. The new Alaska Highway simply joined the already existing Richardson Highway at Delta, 1,422 miles (2,288.5 km) from Dawson Creek, and almost 100 miles short of Fairbanks. That made Delta the official end of the Alaska Highway.

Delta was originally a construction camp for builders of the north-south Richardson Highway in 1919, and the town took its name from the nearby Delta River. As the joining place of two major highways, however, the name was changed to Delta Junction.

Now here's where it gets confusing: The State of Alaska did not assign the same route number to the entire length of the Richardson Highway. It is Route 4 from Valdez to Delta Junction, and it is Route 2 (same as the Alaska Highway) for those last hundred or so miles from Delta Junction to Fairbanks, thus implying, on road maps at least, that the Alaska Highway ends at Fairbanks.

Today you can have your picture taken at Delta Junction next to a monument inscribed with the words "Crossroads of Alaska" and "End of the Alaska Highway." The monument is flanked by flags of the United States, Canada, Alaska, and the Yukon Territory.

Fairbanks has a nearly identical monument, which also proclaims "The End of the Alaska Highway." It's just a few steps outside the front door of the Fairbanks Convention and Visitors Bureau log cabin, along the Chena River, where tourists by the thousands stroll each summer. Not surprising that a majority of them have their pictures taken here, too, adding to the belief that this is the end of the Alaska Highway.

The reality is that the end of the road is where you set your sights. It's wherever you stop, turn around, and head back. If you come as far as Delta Junction, you'll probably have your picture taken, and then continue on to Fairbanks—where you'll have your picture taken again. Then, back home, you'll be able to say without hesitation: "Yes, I've been to the end of the Alaska Highway. Wanna see my pictures?" ▬

Road Notes

It's a short hop from North Pole to Fairbanks, and the Richardson Highway continues as a four-lane route bordered by spruce, aspen, and birch trees as it heads toward town. Then it ends without fanfare, joining the Steese Highway near the entry to **Fort Wainwright**, which lies on the eastern edge of town. An army post today, Fort Wainwright was Ladd Air Field during World War II. Military spending has often stabilized or boosted the Fairbanks economy during the past 60-plus years.

FAIRBANKS

From Delta Junction: 98 miles (157 km)
From Alaska–Yukon border: 298 miles (480 km)
From Dawson Creek, British Columbia: 1,488 miles (2,395 km)

Welcome to another end of the road! You are standing at 64.8° north latitude. The Arctic Circle is only 66 air miles north.

Fairbanks was founded in 1901 by a trader named E. T. Barnette, who really didn't want to settle here. As a passenger aboard a stern-wheel riverboat, he had intended to set up shop in a place that was more accessible to the gold miners in the area. But following the tip of a local Native, he directed the captain up the Chena River, which he thought was a shortcut to his destination. The Chena was too shallow, and the summer was ending. In a hurry to return without his argumentative passenger, the captain ordered Barnette and his party, and his trade goods, off the ship. They landed at a spot that's marked today with a low rock monument, by the Fairbanks Convention and Visitors Bureau log cabin on 1st Avenue near the Cushman Street Bridge.

Luck was with Barnette. Within hours, he and his group had their first paying customers in the form of a couple of miners who had spotted the ship's plume of steam. One of the miners was **Felix Pedro**, an Italian immigrant who struck gold less than a year later. His find ignited a rush to Alaska's Interior, drawing miners from the goldfields of Fortymile country and the Klondike.

The long-term health of this fledgling community was cinched when Barnette struck a deal with federal district judge **James Wickersham**, who was stationed in Eagle, Alaska, a gold-mining town northeast of Fairbanks. Wickersham wanted to feed the ego of a political friend by naming a town after him. **Charles W. Fairbanks** was then a U.S. senator from Indiana; later he would be vice president under Theodore Roosevelt. In exchange for naming the town after Fairbanks, Wickersham promised Barnette that he would move the judicial seat from Eagle to Fairbanks—which he did, ensuring that the town was firmly rooted.

The people of Fairbanks today commemorate Felix Pedro's gold discovery with a weeklong festival called **Golden Days**. Held in mid-July, the festival includes sourdough pancake feeds, gold-panning demonstrations and mining lectures, dances, historical

The "end of the road" milepost, on the banks of the Chena River in Fairbanks, feels like the finish line for Alaska Highway travelers.

exhibits, and an old-fashioned community parade. The winner of the Pedro look-alike contest leads the parade, and he walks the downtown route with his gold poke full of nuggets.

Fairbanks has grown from the days of E. T. Barnette to a hub city for all of Alaska's Interior communities. It's also a major jumping-off point for flights into the bush. Overnight tours are available by air, and in fly/drive packages, to Barrow, the Arctic Circle, Nome, Kotzebue, and Anuktuvuk Pass. Another Alaska crossroads city, Fairbanks is the hub for the Elliott, Dalton (via Elliott), Steese, Richardson, and Parks Highways. Before you leave town for any of these highway trips, you can call or go on-line for road conditions, traffic hazards, closures, etc., by dialing 5-1-1 or by visiting *www.511.alaska.gov*. From out of state, dial toll-free 1-866-282-7577.

Other annual events include a **summer solstice celebration** in late June. That's when the Fairbanks semipro baseball team, the Goldpanners, hosts the Midnight Sun Baseball Game beginning at 10:30 P.M., without artificial lights. The **World Eskimo-Indian Olympics** are held in late July. Call 907-452-6646 or *www.weio.org*. In winter, mushing fans gather by the thousands for the start or finish of the **Yukon Quest International Sled Dog Race**, which follows a 1,000-mile route between Whitehorse, in the Yukon, and Fairbanks. Around town, you'll find movie theaters, shopping opportunities, art galleries, and outdoor adventures.

While you're in Fairbanks, visit some of these local attractions:

The University of Alaska Museum of the North. Newly expanded in 2005, this museum is at once an architectural beauty and a rich depository of more than 1.4 million artifacts. Gallery exhibits include dinosaur fossils, ivory carvings, historical photos, totem poles, natural history dioramas, and lots of gold. Be sure to visit Babe the Blue Bison, a 36,000-year-old bison mummy that was excavated by a Fairbanks scientist. Videos on the northern lights explain the scientific reason for the phenomenon. The museum store offers books, gifts, clothing, and Native art. The Museum of the North is on the University of Alaska Fairbanks campus, at College Road and University Avenue. Call 907-474-7505 for 24-hour information.

Creamer's Field Waterfowl Refuge. What was once the northernmost dairy farm in the country was converted to a waterfowl refuge many years ago, but the old

Fun-loving locals play rowdy gold rush gals during the annual Golden Days Parade in Fairbanks.

buildings remain. Anna and Charlie Creamer's farmhouse is now a visitor center, and signs along refuge trails describe the migratory birds that feed in great numbers here each spring and fall. Most are Canada geese and sandhill cranes. The Sandhill Crane Festival is the last week of August. Call 907-452-5162 or see *www.creamersfield.org.*

Historical walking tour. Meet at the Fairbanks Convention and Visitors Bureau log cabin on 1st Avenue near the Cushman Street Bridge. Guided or unguided walking tours of notable historic sites begin there. Call 907-456-5774 for information. Next door is Golden Heart Park, with its dramatic sculpture titled "The Unknown First Family." Plaques around the statue include names of people who helped build this town during its first century. This is a place for relaxing by the fountain or enjoying outdoor concerts on summer afternoons. Just a block away is the Alaska Public Lands Information Center, in the lower level of the old courthouse on 3rd and Cushman Streets. Operated by the National Park Service, and featuring films, books, gifts, and guest speakers, this is a terrific place to learn about Alaska's various cultures and ecosystems. Knowledgeable staffers are extremely helpful. Call 907-456-0527 or visit *www.nps.gov/aplic.*

World Ice Art Championships. March is the best time to visit Fairbanks if winter is your favorite season. On the bill: the annual Winter Carnival, sled-dog races, and Ice Art, the international ice-carving competition. You can walk through the Ice Park, which is filled with giant ice statuary, all of it lit with colored lights that sparkle through the nearly clear ice. See more at *www.icealaska.com.*

Pioneer Park. This 44-acre theme park, at Airport Way and Peger Road, was built in 1967 to commemorate the centennial of Alaska's purchase from Russia. The Centennial Exposition grounds were divided into themes that echoed Alaska history.

Activity was high along the Chena River in the early 1900s, when the town was born of a gold rush boom.

In one section, replicas of Native villages were constructed. In another, a gold rush town was re-created by relocating some of the oldest cabins and businesses of Fairbanks. The **Palace Saloon** is still operating as a bar and dance hall. Call the Palace to reserve tickets to its popular "Golden Heart Revue," which shows nightly during summer months. Call 907-452-7274. It's just a short walk from the **Alaska Salmon Bake,** which serves delicious northern fare from 5 P.M. to 9 P.M. nightly. The Salmon Bake is near the gold-mining "valley," which was created to demonstrate various ways that gold was extracted from the ground. And one of the region's hard-working stern-wheelers, the riverboat *Nenana,* was dry-docked here after retirement. It has since been beautifully restored. Come aboard for a tour.

Cruise the river on a modern stern-wheeler: the *Tanana Chief* and the *Riverboat Discovery* are two popular tours for panoramic views and a dose of local history. Prime rib dinner and sightseeing cruises are available every evening on the *Tanana Chief,* an authentic stern-wheeler that plies these waters. Call 1-866-452-TOUR or 907-452-8687. Browse *www.greatlandrivertours.com* for more information. The riverboat *Discovery* is operated by the Binkley family, whose members have been cruising Alaska rivers for five generations. The *Discovery* offers two tours daily and follows the Chena and Tanana Rivers on a narrated cruise that includes stops at a replica of an Athabascan Indian fish site and the sled-dog kennel of Iditarod champion Susan Butcher. Reservations are a must. Call 907-479-6673 or browse *www.riverboatdiscovery.com.*

For more information about local attractions and events, day trips, history, fishing, and hunting, contact the Fairbanks Convention and Visitors Bureau at 1-800-327-5774 or 907-456-5774. Visit their Web site at *www.explorefairbanks.com.*

Lodging

*If you're interested in B&B accommo-
dations, contact the Fairbanks
Association of Bed & Breakfasts at*
www.ptialaska.net/fabb/.

Alaska Motel
1546 Cushman Street
907-456-6393
www.ak-motel.com
36 rooms, kitchenettes. Cable TV, laundry.
  Senior discount; weekly rates.

Aspen Hotel
4580 Old Airport Road
1-866-GUEST4U
www.aspenhotelsak.com
97 rooms, refrigerator, microwave,
  iron, hair dryer, laundry. Exercise
  facility, pool, spa. Continental
  breakfast.

Best Western
1521 South Cushman Street
907-456-6602
www.bestwestern.com
102 rooms, fitness center, coffee
  bar, restaurant, lounge. Airport
  shuttle.

Bridgewater Hotel
723 1st Avenue
1-800-528-4916 or 907-452-6661
www.fountainheadhotels.com
94 units, dining, cocktails. Downtown
  location. Airport/train shuttle.

The Captain Bartlett Inn
1411 Airport Way
1-800-544-7528 (Outside) or
  1-800-478-7900 (Alaska)
www.captainbartlettinn.com
197 units, laundry, restaurant, saloon.
  Airport/train shuttle. Near shopping.

College Inn
700 Fairbanks Street
1-800-770-2177 or 907-474-3666
www.college-inn.com
100 units, laundry, pets allowed.

Fairbanks Golden Nugget Hotel
900 Noble Street
907-452-5141
www.golden-nuggethotel.com
36 air-conditioned units, cable TV, restaurant, lounge. Downtown location.

Fairbanks Princess Riverside Lodge
4477 Pikes Landing Road
1-800-426-0500 or 907-455-4477
www.princesslodges.com
200 deluxe units on the Chena River. Gift
  shop, health club, restaurant, lounge.
  Airport/train shuttle. Tour tickets.

Fairbanks SpringHill Suites by Marriott
575 1st Ave
1-877-729-0197 or 907-451-6552
www.springhillsuites.com
Spacious studio accommodations with
  dataports, microwaves, fridges,
  coffeemakers. Business center,
  continental breakfast.

Fairbanks Super 8 Motel
1909 Airport Way
1-800-800-8000 or 907-451-8888
www.super8.com
77 units, laundry, pets allowed. Walking
  distance to shopping.

Golden North Motel
4888 Old Airport Way
1-800-447-1910 or 907-479-6201
www.goldennorthmotel.com
62 units, free continental breakfast. Pets
  allowed. Shuttle service.

Pike's Waterfront Lodge
1850 Hoselton Rd
1-877-774-2400
www.pikeslodge.com
Guest rooms and deluxe cabins along the
  Chena River, restaurant, saloon.

Ranch Motel
2223 South Cushman Street
1-888-452-4783 or 907-452-4783
31 units, cable TV, coffee. Pets allowed.
  Restaurant.

Going for the Gold

Here are some golden opportunities for fun:

Eldorado Gold Mine. This family attraction is located about 12 miles (19 km) north of Fairbanks, just past Fox on the Elliott Highway. You can ride the narrow-gauge rails of the old Tanana Valley Railroad through a permafrost tunnel to the cook shack. Afterward, look on as two local miners, a husband-and-wife team, demonstrate modern mining. Then it's your turn to grab a gold pan and get some gold for yourself. You get to keep what you find. For reservations, call 907-479-7613. See www.eldoradogoldmine.com.

Ester Gold Camp. Just west of Fairbanks off the Parks Highway, the Ester Gold Camp was once a gold-mining community with a saloon, roadhouse, and other support businesses. The camp is still a hot spot with dinner and a show every evening from late May to early September. Dig into a buffet-style dinner featuring baked halibut, reindeer stew, and country chicken. Then enjoy a fun-filled evening at the Malemute Saloon, with melodrama, Robert Service poetry, honky-tonk piano, and free-flowing beverages for any age. Ester Gold Camp is on the National Register of Historic Places. Call 1-800-354-7274 or visit www.akvisit.com/ester.html.

Gold Dredge No. 8. In the 1930s and 1940s, great gold-processing dredges moved many tons of soil in this area. And while most of them are gone or broken-down, Gold Dredge No. 8 has been renovated for public touring. Located just north of Fairbanks, off the Steese Highway near Fox, Dredge No. 8 is a multi-story giant operated by Gray Line of Alaska. Learn about this amazing operation, and pan for gold. Food service is available, too. For reservations or information, call 1-800-544-2206.

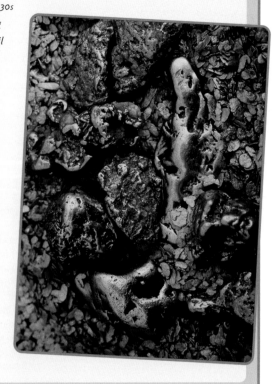

The great motivator—gold—attracted thousands to the Northland in the last century. Only a fraction got rich.

Regency Fairbanks Hotel
95 10th Avenue
1-800-348-1340 or 907-452-3200
www.regencyfairbankshotel.com
130 rooms, suites, nonsmoking available.
Laundry, whirlpools, dining, cocktails.
Car and room packages. Shuttle.

River's Edge Resort
4200 Boat Street
1-800-770-3343 or 907-474-0286
www.riversedge.net
Private cottages along the Chena River in
the heart of town. Restaurant, tours.

Sophie Station Hotel
1717 University Avenue
1-800-528-4916 or 907-479-3650
www.fountainheadhotels.com
147 suites, kitchens, laundry. Dining,
cocktails. Airport/train shuttle.

Tamarac Inn Motel
252 Minnie Street
1-800-693-6406 or 907-456-4606
Rooms, some with kitchens. Laundry.
Walking distance to city center.

Wedgewood Resort
212 Wedgewood Drive
1-800-528-4916 or 907-452-1442
www.fountainheadhotels.com
Elegant suites and guestrooms on
beautifully landscaped grounds.

Westmark Fairbanks Hotel
813 Noble Street
1-800-544-0970 or 907-456-7722
www.westmarkhotels.com
244 well-appointed rooms, laundry.
Restaurant, cocktails, coffee bar,
gift shop. Airport/train shuttle.

For more information about local bed-
and-breakfasts, contact the Fairbanks
Convention and Visitors Bureau,
1-800-327-5774 or 907-456-5774.

Campgrounds
Chena Marina RV Park
1145 Shypoke Drive
907-479-4653
www.chenarvpark.com
40 grassy sites with hookups and pull-
throughs on active Bush plane pond.
Showers, water, dump station. Phone
hookups, sleeping rooms, gift shop,
store, free showers. Tour tickets, free RV
wash. Reservations recommended.

Norlite Campground & RV Park
1160 Peger Road
907-474-0206
www.norlite.com
Roomy campsites, full and partial hookups,
pull-throughs, close to shopping, parks,
and transportation.

River's Edge RV Park & Campground
4140 Boat Street
1-800-770-3343 or 907-474-0286
www.riversedge.net
190 sites with hookups and pull-throughs,
tent camping. Showers, water,
laundry, dump station. Free shuttle
to attractions. Close to shopping.

Tanana Valley Campground
1800 College Road, on Tanana Valley State
Fairgrounds
907-456-7956
www.tananavalleyfair.org
32 RV units with hookups and
pull-throughs, tent camping. Showers,
laundry, fireplace/grills, dump station.

Restaurants
Ah Sa Wan Restaurant
600 Old Steese Highway
907-451-7788
A local favorite for Chinese lunch buffet
and dinner.

Alaska Salmon Bake
3175 College Road,
in Alaskaland's Mining Valley
1-800-354-7274 or 907-452-7274
Salmon, halibut, ribs, steaks over a fire.

Asiana Teriyaki Restaurant
2001 Airport Way
907-457-3333
Oriental favorites for lunch or dinner.

Bear 'n Seal Grill & Bar
813 Noble Street
In Westmark Fairbanks
1-800-544-0970 or 907-456-7722
Pacific Rim cuisine; open for breakfast,
lunch, dinner.

Bushati's Pizzaria & Restaurant
511 Gaffney Rd
907-457-1317
Pizza, sandwiches, salads.

Café Alex Wine Bar
310 1st Avenue
907-452-2539
Dining and piano bar.

The Castle
4510 Airport Way
907-474-2165
Steaks, Alaska seafood, live entertainment.

El Mariachi
541 3rd Avenue
907-457-2698
Mexican specialties.

Gambardella's Pasta Bella
706 2nd Avenue
907-456-3417
Italian cuisine for lunch, dinner.
Outdoor seating available.

Geraldo's Restaurant
701 College Rd
907-452-2299
American and Italian specialties, steaks,
seafood. Hand-tossed pizza.

Ivory Jack's
Mile 1.5 Goldstream Road
907-455-6666
Alaska dinner specialties: king crab,
Nome reindeer.

Lavelle's Bistro
575 1st Avenue
907-450-0555
www.lavellesbistro.com

Los Amigos
636 28th Avenue
907-452-3684
Authentic Mexican dishes.

Myong's Teriyaki
402 5th Avenue, downtown
907-452-5560
Japanese specialties. Homemade salad
dressing and teriyaki sauces.

Oriental House
1101 Noble St
907-456-1172
Chinese fare.

Pike's Landing Restaurant & Lounge
4438 Airport Way
907-479-7113
Brunch, lunch, dinner along the Chena
River. Outdoor seating available.

The Pump House Restaurant and Saloon
796 Chena Pump Road
907-479-8452
www.pumphouse.com
Alaskan specialties, steak, seafood.
Historic site with outdoor seating
along Chena River.

Souvlaki
310 1st Avenue
907-452-5393
Souvlaki and other Greek and East
Mediterranean dishes. Closed on Sunday.

The Turtle Club
10 Mile Old Steese Highway, in Fox
907-457-3883
Prime rib, prawns, lobster, ribs.
Reservations recommended.

The Vallata
2.5 Mile Goldstream Road
907-455-6600
Italian cuisine; open for dinner.
Reservations recommended.

Chapter 7

Western Canada's Northbound Byways

*P*ERHAPS you are one of those people who resist following the most-traveled path. You want a customized itinerary. In western Canada, you have plenty of options for exploring even more backcountry than where the Alaska Highway roams. From the well-developed, high-speed trans-Canada route to the narrow gravel byways that reach into the Yukon's northernmost regions, choose which route suits your sense of adventure. Spur roads and loops lead through pastureland or tundra, across mountains, or down to the sea. Along them lie ghost towns, industrious small towns, farms, and glittering cities. Use this chapter to discover what lies along the bends of western Canada's beautiful byways.

*N*ORTH KLONDIKE HIGHWAY

Part of the Klondike Loop
Alaska Highway (near Whitehorse) to Dawson City: 327 miles (526 km)

The Alaska Highway skirts along the southern reaches of the Yukon Territory from Watson Lake to Whitehorse to Haines Junction, then crosses the international border and moves on to Tok, Alaska. But there's another way to reach Tok—a way that gives you more time in the Yukon.

From Whitehorse, you can drive north to Dawson City (via the North Klondike Highway), west to cross the Alaska border (via the Top of the World Highway), and then back south to Tok (via the Taylor Highway). Together, these three northerly highways are called the Klondike Loop.

If you have the yearning to see some of the Yukon Territory's most scenic vistas and experience even more gold-rush charm, take the Klondike Loop. Better yet, on the way to Alaska, take the Klondike Loop, and on the way back, take the Alaska Highway. You'll get the best of both.

Travelers will find the beginning of the Klondike Loop several miles north of Whitehorse, where the Alaska Highway (Highway 1) continues west and the North Klondike Highway (Highway 2) heads north. Highway 2 is paved for all of its 327 miles (526 km) to Dawson.

On the Silver Trail

*At Stewart Crossing, 45 miles (72 km) north of Pelly Crossing, you can begin a side trip along Yukon Highway 11 to visit the historic silver- and gold-mining communities of **Mayo**, **Keno**, and **Elsa** on the Silver Trail. In the early 20th century, Mayo was a major settlement and river port. You will also pass through the traditional territory of the Na-Cho Nyak Dun people.*

The Silver Trail is partially paved and leads to areas for swimming, camping, and hiking, and stunning views of glaciated mountains. Government campgrounds, as well as privately owned motels, are available in Mayo and in Keno, which is 69 miles (111 km) east of Stewart Crossing. Investigate the placer gold-mine operation at Duncan Creek Golddusters in Mayo, and be sure to see the Keno City Mining Museum, which documents an era through artifacts, photographs, and written histories. Call 867-995-2792.

About 4 miles north of the highway junction, watch for the left turn to Takhini Hot Springs, 6 miles west on a spur road. There you can bask in a naturally heated outdoor pool, winter or summer. Hiking and trail rides are other summertime options. Unlike most hot springs, Takhini's water does not contain sulfur, so it doesn't have that lingering, unpleasant odor. Meals and overnight accommodations are available.

Continuing north on Highway 2, you'll soon spot Lake Laberge, made famous in "The Cremation of Sam McGee," by Yukon poet Robert Service. The lake is among the bodies of water, big and small, that make up the headwaters of the Yukon River. On the west, the road soon begins paralleling long, narrow Fox Lake, its pristine waters sparkling in the long summer days. While it appears to be an autonomous body, the lake is connected to Lake Laberge by Fox Creek. Watch for signs that indicate where you can go fishing or find a campsite in one of the Yukon's government-operated campgrounds. They are clean and modestly priced.

The entire North Klondike Highway is a pleasure to drive, but one of the greatest pleasures may be found at Mile 55 (88.5 km) in the kitchen of the Braeburn Lodge: their world-famous giant cinnamon rolls. These folks even named their landing strip after the dinner plate-size delicacy: Cinnamon Bun Airstrip. There are other items on the menu, believe it or not, and the lodge also offers necessities such as fuel, souvenirs, and tips on local fishing holes. Canoe rentals and campsites are available here, too. Braeburn Lodge is open year-round; its most famous winter guests are the mushers and the doggie athletes competing in the 1,000-mile (1,609-km) Yukon Quest International Sled Dog Race.

The historic Montague House, one of the earliest roadhouse stops on the old stagecoach line, lies along this route, about 80 miles (128 km) north of the Alaska Highway junction.

Up ahead, Carmacks and Pelly Crossing are towns of fewer than 500 people. Each year the villages host throngs of mushers and their dog teams, who stop at these checkpoints along the trail of the Yukon Quest. The race starts or finishes in Whitehorse, alternating with Fairbanks on the other end of the route. Carmacks and Pelly Crossing both feature a First Nations interpretive center, where you can learn more about the area's archaeology and cultural history.

Fuel, groceries, and campsites are available in **Carmacks**, 103 miles (165 km) from the junction, where the road crosses the Yukon River. This riverside town has long served as an important stopping point for steamboats on the Yukon.

Fifteen miles (24 km) north of Carmacks is an interpretive sign and viewing area for **Five Finger Rapids**—among the most treacherous places for stampeders to pass during the gold rush of 1898.

Pelly Crossing marks the halfway point of the North Klondike Highway—about equal in distance from the Alaska Highway junction and Dawson City. Pelly Crossing is a community of First Nations people. Basic services for your vehicle, as well as its occupants (bank, groceries, overnight accommodations) are all available here, and you are welcome to take a self-guided tour beginning at the **Selkirk Heritage Centre**, next to the Selkirk Gas Bar.

In the final 158 miles (254 km) to Dawson City, the road parallels or intersects numerous creeks and rivers, such as Crooked Creek, Moose River, McQuesten River, and Clear Creek. The streams of this gold-mining region continue to pique the interest of placer miners for their proximity to the great discovery by George Carmacks. His find on Bonanza Creek, just outside of Dawson City, incited the Klondike gold rush of 1898.

Apart from Stewart Crossing, you will find few settlements along the remainder of the road. A handful of businesses offer accommodations, sundries, and fuel. Rest areas and pullouts provide the basics of a level surface and a garbage can.

Midnight Dome, above Dawson, is an excellent place to view the confluence of the Yukon and Klondike Rivers.

Dawson City

From Whitehorse: 335 miles (539 km)
To Alaska/Canada border via Top of the World Highway: 66 miles (106 km)

In 1897, when news of a great gold discovery in the Klondike reached the outside world, more than 100,000 people resolved to pack up and head north, the mayor of Seattle among them. Only about 40,000 actually made it to the Klondike, and of those, a mere fraction made it rich, but the get-rich-quick compulsion was too great to ignore. Tens of thousands made uninformed decisions, not realizing that the way was hazardous, the cold could break a person's body and spirit, and the work was murderously difficult. Some men literally worked themselves to death, never enjoying the fruits of their labor. What remained was the romance—stories of men drinking champagne from ladies' slippers while gold nuggets spilled from their pockets. Most of it was bunk.

The gold rush still lingers in Dawson City, along with the refurbished and modernized historic buildings that are so attractive. But in little niches off the main streets are the derelict structures that have seen human dramas we can only imagine. Dawson was nearly falling down several decades ago when, in a drive to save historic buildings, city leaders began fund-raising in earnest. Today Dawson is an imaginative slice out of time. One of its favorite sons, Pierre Berton, is a trusted storyteller who uses books and videos to share the true story of Dawson's riotous beginning, its years of quiet retirement, and its rebirth as a major visitor attraction. Berton's books and videos are available in gift stores throughout Dawson City, including the Dawson City Museum gift shop (or through your favorite on-line source).

Gold is still king in Dawson, and you can pan for some yourself. Or buy a hunk of the yellow metal at one of several jewelry stores. You can have your nuggets made into a special piece of jewelry at the Gift Box, at 1041 A 2nd Avenue, at Fortymile Gold, located at 3rd and York, or at the Klondike Nugget and Ivory Shop, at the corner of Front and Queen Streets, which has been in business since 1904. At the Nugget, gold samples from more than 70 creeks are on display.

Unlike refined gold, nuggets are slightly dull, dimpled, and irregular. They possess a compressed, raw beauty that still strikes a note of discovery in your chest. The metal and its shape remind you of the powerful forces that made it centuries ago under this very ground.

From the vantage point of **Midnight Dome** above the city, you can look out over this countryside that miners have tried to strip of its gold. Across the confluence of the **Yukon** and **Klondike Rivers**, the land below looks as if giant earthworms had burrowed beneath the surface. These peculiar marks are telltale signs of gold dredges, which operated like mechanical soil-eaters. These multistory gold-processing ships floated on small ponds and worked efficiently. Using a conveyor belt of steel buckets, a dredge would eat at the earth in front of it, sort out the gold from the useless rock and soil, then dump these tailings out the back. The dredges slowly moved forward, opening up the pond in front and filling it in behind the dredge. The machines followed the veins of gold, operating until the early 1960s and leaving behind these unique signs that are still visible today. Visit **Gold Dredge No. 4** on Bonanza Creek for a tour of the largest wood-hull dredge in the world, built in 1912. Call 867-993-7200.

Mining remains the most important industry in the Yukon Territory, and tourists are invited to try their hand at gold panning, or digging with a shovel and pick ax, at **Gold Claim No. 6** above Discovery Claim on Bonanza Creek. This venture is operated by the Klondike Visitors Association, and there is no charge. Bring your own gold pan or rent one in town. From Dawson Creek, take the North Klondike Highway 2 east to Bonanza Road for 13 miles (21 km). You'll drive past Dredge No. 4 and Discovery Claim. Signs will lead the way from there.

Many of Dawson's historic buildings saw their 100th birthday in 2001, among them the old Territorial Administration Building, the Commissioner's Residence, the Territorial Courthouse, and the Arctic Brotherhood Hall. And 2002 marked Dawson City's centennial, a formal designation, recognizing Dawson's incorporation as a Canadian city, even though it existed as a wild-and-woolly boomtown prior to that.

Dawson attractions include:

George Black Ferry. This ferry across the Yukon River is a free service offered by the Yukon government, at work 24 hours a day, except between 5 and 7 on Wednesday mornings, when the vessel is serviced. Commercial businesses hold special passes for priority boarding, so make sure you enter the correct lane for boarding your vehicle. Rush hours for tourists are as predictable as those for a big-city workforce. Between 7 A.M. and 11 A.M., most drivers are outbound tourists. Peak times for those headed into Dawson are between 2 P.M. and 8 P.M. Work around those rush hours and you'll have a shorter wait.

Dawson City Museum. The features of this museum on 5th Avenue in the Old Territorial Administration Building include goldfield exhibits, a First Nations Collection, films, a Klondike history library, and steam locomotives. A gift shop and coffee shop are on site. Open Victoria Day to Labour Day. Call 867-993-5291.

Robert Service Cabin. One block south of Mission Street and 8th Avenue is the site of the Robert Service cabin, a Klondike National Historic Site. It was here that Service wrote such classics as "The Cremation of Sam McGee" and "The Shooting of Dan McGrew." At 3 P.M. daily from mid-May to September, the Westmark Hotel features actor Tom Byrne presenting stirring recitals of Service's works. The Westmark Hotel is located at 5th Avenue and Harper Street.

Just one block south of the Robert Service Cabin, you'll find the **Jack London Cabin and Interpretive Centre.** The former Dawson City bank teller who became a famous author lived in this cabin when he first made his way to the Yukon. (The cabin has been moved to this site from its original location in the backcountry.) Among London's most famous books are *White Fang* and *The Call of the Wild.*

Like other visitor offerings in Dawson, the Interpretive Centre is open from late spring to early fall.

Palace Grande Theatre. Another Klondike National Historic Site, the Palace Grande continues to host top-flight entertainment such as the Gaslight Follies. Nightly family shows are performed throughout the summer. Call 867-993-5575. The theater was constructed in 1901 using wood salvaged from stern-wheelers that once plied the Yukon River. It has been restored to its original splendor by Parks Canada.

Gold City Tours. See Dawson City aboard an antique car, visit the goldfields, or take in the view from atop Midnight Dome. Call 867-993-5175 or browse *www.goldcitytours.info.*

Ancient Voices Wilderness Camp. Come along for an evening barbecue, or take a day trip and learn about First Nations traditions from local interpreters. For tickets or information: 867-993-5605.

Diamond Tooth Gerties Casino. The casino at 4th Avenue and Queen Street offers three different shows every night. A cover charge gets you in the door for can-can entertainment and gambling until 2 A.M. Call 867-993-5575.

Top of the World Golf Course. This is Canada's northernmost golf course, with grass greens, nine holes, a driving range, and a pro shop. Take the Top of the World Highway for 5 miles (8 km) out of Dawson City and follow the signs. Shuttle service from Dawson City is available; golfers arriving by RV are permitted to dry camp overnight. Call 867-993-5888 during the summer months or browse *www.topoftheworldgolf.com.*

Take a cruise. Dinner cruise on the *Yukon Lou.* Travel the Dawson City waterfront and along the Klondike River on the *Yukon Lou,* a cruise that includes all-you-can-eat barbecued salmon, steak, or chicken, at **Pleasure Island Restaurant.** Get information and tickets from **Birch Cabin Gift Shop,** on Front Street, 867-993-5482. Another favorite is a longer trip—follow the historic route of the old stern-wheelers on a

Ice sculptors created this statue at the door of Diamond Tooth Gertie's one winter.

cruise from Dawson City to Eagle, Alaska, aboard the MV *Yukon Queen II.* Fare includes a meal. Call 867-993-5599. And yet another option is to book passage on the *River Dancer,* operated by Ancient Voices Wilderness Camp. Guests visit a First Nations camp on the river and learn more about the traditions and customs of the local Natives.

Two highways extend beyond Dawson: the Dempster Highway, which heads north, and the Top of the World Highway, which goes west to Alaska. See the sections on these two highways in this chapter.

In Whitehorse, a favorite family-oriented show is "The Frantic Follies," which combines Klondike history with singing, fiddling, can-can dancing, and some great Robert Service poetry.

Lodging

Bonanza Gold Motel
1 mile (1.6 km) from downtown,
   just past Bonanza Road
1-888-993-6789
www.bonanzagold.ca
45 rooms, suites, nonsmoking available,
   wheelchair-accessible suites. Cable TV,
   fax, high-speed Internet access,
   whirlpool. Restaurant.

Downtown Hotel
2nd Avenue and Queen Street
1-800-661-0514 or 867-993-5346
59 modernized rooms in a historic
   building. Cable TV, whirlpool, winter
   plug-ins. Gift shop, restaurant, saloon.
   Airport shuttle.

The El Dorado Hotel
3rd Avenue and Princess Street
1-800-764-3536 or 867-993-5451
www.eldoradohotel.ca
Modern rooms in a historic building,
   suites, kitchenettes. Laundry, winter
   plug-ins. Dining room, lounge.
   Open year-round.

Klondike Kate's Cabins, Rooms & Restaurant
1102 3rd Avenue
867-993-6527
www.klondikekates.ca
Modern cabins with private baths,
   cable TV, phone, Internet hookup.
   Family restaurant, gift shop,
   wheelchair accessible.

Midnight Sun Hotel
3rd Avenue and Queen Street
867-993-5495
www.midnightsunhotel.com
Historic property in downtown
   Dawson City location.
   Restaurant, lounge.

Triple J Hotel
5th Avenue and Queen Street
1-800-764-3555 or 867-993-5323
Rooms, executive suite, kitchenette cabins.
   Restaurant, lounge. Free airport limo.

Westmark Inn
5th Avenue and Harper Street
1-800-544-0970 or 403-993-5542
www.westmarkhotels.com
Nicely appointed rooms, restaurant,
   lounge. Gift shop, guest laundry.

Whitehouse Motel
1626 Front Street, north end
867-993-5576
www.whitehousecabins.com
Units with kitchenettes, overlooking Yukon
River. Cable TV, private bathrooms.
Walking distance to town attractions.

Campgrounds
Bonanza Gold RV Park
1 mile (1.6 km) from downtown Dawson City
1-800-993-6789
Full hookups, dry camping, tenting,
laundry, showers, RV wash. Restaurant,
gold panning.

Dawson City RV Park and Campground
1 mile (1.6 km) south of town,
across Klondike River
867-993-5142
Full and partial hookups, tent campsites,
showers, phone. Cable TV. Dining, gold
panning, gift shop. Adjacent to gas
and diesel station.

Gold Rush Campground / RV Park
5th Avenue and York Street
867-993-5247
www.goldrushcampground.com
Full hookups, downtown, close to attractions.

GuggieVille
On Bonanza Road
1-800-860-6535 or 867-993-5008
Full hookups available along Bonanza Creek.
Showers, self-service laundry, gift shop,
car wash. Gold panning.

The Yukon Territory government operates
two campgrounds near Dawson City:

Klondike River Territorial Campground
Near the airport, southeast of Dawson City
38 campsites for RV or tent camping.
Partial hookups.

Yukon River Territorial Campground
From downtown Dawson City, take the ferry
across the Yukon River to reach this campground next to the ferry access road.
98 campsites for RV or tent camping.
Partial hookups.

Restaurants
Black Bird Bistro
Corner Klondike Highway South and
Bonanza Creek Road
867-993-5032
Mexican food. Free minigolf.

Bonanza Dining Room
3rd Avenue and Princess Street,
in the El Dorado Hotel
867-993-5451
Steaks, ribs, chicken, northern specialities.

The Grub Stake
1054 2nd Avenue
867-993-6706

Jack London Grill and Sourdough Saloon
2nd Avenue and Queen Street, in the
Downtown Hotel
867-993-5346
Barbecue, steaks, seafood.

Klondike Kate's Restaurant & Cabins
3rd Avenue and King Street
867-993-6527
www.klondikekates.ca
Breakfast, lunch, and dinner featuring
Canadian and ethnic foods.

Mama Cita's Ristorante
2nd Avenue between Queen and Princess
Street
867-993-2370
Lunch and dinner specials.

Pleasure Island Restaurant
Tickets: Birch Cabin Gift Shop, Front Street
867-993-5482
Lunch or dinner restaurant cruises on
the *Yukon Lou* with Yukon River
Cruises feature all-you-can-eat
king salmon buffet; steak or chicken
by request.

Ruby's Shady Lady's
882 5th Avenue
867-993-5721

TOP OF THE WORLD HIGHWAY

Part of the Klondike Loop
Dawson City to Alaska–Yukon border:
66 miles (106 km)

From Dawson to the Alaska–Yukon border, the Klondike Loop continues west on Highway 9 (the Top of the World Highway) for 66 miles (106 km). Before you leave Dawson, check on current road conditions by calling 867-456-7623 or see *www.gov.yk.ca/roadreport*.

The Top of the World cuts into mountainsides and crosses peaks, dipping and rising hundreds of feet, while just beyond the edge of the road, a beautiful valley beckons. Above tree line, the view is so broad and inspiring that you suppress a loud "Wow!" (or maybe you don't). Seal-coated in some sections, dusty and gravelly in others, the road is less inspiring when you are traveling behind a truck or slow-moving RV. But take heart, the next pullout may offer a view that's too great to pass up.

This region is known as Fortymile country, for the Fortymile River that wends its way nearby. It was a place of uncertain possession when American miners thought they were mining U.S. soil. With the arrival of the North-West Mounted Police and officials who certified the international demarcation line, some of the miners left for more golden opportunities. Others settled in to live as Canadians.

This highway is unplowed in winter months, leaving it to snowmobilers who gladly use this major road as their trail. Each year in late February and early March, hundreds of snowmobilers travel this highway and Alaska's Taylor Highway for their Trek Over the Top event, a dash between Tok, Alaska, and Dawson City, Yukon.

The winter that I traveled in the pack of Trekkers, we were headed east from Alaska to the Yukon when, shortly after crossing the border, we spied a large hump in the deep snow. Mounties had placed sticks and pink flagging around the unusual rise on the side of the road. It was a car, completely snowed over, with only a few windows still slightly visible.

I remembered the story: Just a couple of months earlier, a man had tried to drive from Alaska to the Lower 48 via this closed road and had become stuck in the snow. He tried walking out for help. A few weeks later, snowmobilers found his body. The car would stay there until late spring, when the snow released its grip and the road reopened.

Between Dawson City and the border, there is little man-made clutter—just miles and miles of awe-striking scenery. The handful of buildings at the border are for customs officials only. There are no facilities, no rest rooms, no currency exchange. And the customs station is open summers only, from 9 A.M. to 9 P.M. Yukon Time (or 8 A.M. to 8 P.M. Alaska Time).

From the border, the road continues into Alaska for a dozen miles before reaching the Taylor Highway.

Throughout the Yukon and Alaska road systems, the broad swaths between the road and the forest edge provide a secondary highway for four-wheelers in summer and snowmachines in winter.

Taylor Highway

Part of the Klondike Loop

For details on this section of the Klondike Loop, see the section on the Taylor Highway in Chapter 8, "Alaska's State Highways."

Dempster Highway

North Klondike Highway
(near Dawson City) to Inuvik:
460 miles (740 km)

Meant for only the most dogged motorists, this undeveloped highway wends north from the Dawson City area to the upper reaches of the Yukon, across untamed wilderness and into the Northwest Territories. Completed in 1979, the route begins from the North Klondike Highway at a point 25 miles (40 km) east of Dawson and ends in the village of Inuvik, 460 miles (740 km) later.

This gravel road was named for Cpl. W. J. Dempster, a member of the North-West Mounted Police, who led the search for the famous Lost Patrol. The party had become lost near Fort McPherson in the winter of 1911 and froze to death.

This is wilderness at its finest, with humans few and far between as you drive over mountains and onto vast river floodplains. The only service stations are at Eagle Plains, Fort McPherson, and Inuvik. You'll cross the **Arctic Circle** at Mile 250 (402 km), at latitude 66° 33' N. Free ferry service is available at two crossings: the Peel River and the Mackenzie River.

If you're looking for outdoor adventure throughout the Yukon, you can book rafting, fishing, dog-sledding, hiking, horseback riding, and more through *www.wildyukon.com*, an association of 24 tour operators in association with Yukon Tourism and Culture.

Hotel accommodations, fuel, dining, camping, and other services are available at Eagle Plains Hotel, Mile 231 (371.7 km). Yukon government campgrounds may be found at Tombstone Mountain, Mile 45 (72.5 km); Engineer Creek, Mile 120.5 (194 km); and Rock River, Mile 278 (447 km). The Dempster Highway Interpretive Centre, at the Tombstone Mountain campground, is open from mid-June to early September.

In the Northwest Territories, you can camp at Mile 340 (547 km) at the **Nitainlaii Campground and Information Centre**, operated by the territory government.

For Inuvik-area travel information, contact the town of Inuvik at 867-777-8618. For more on the Dempster Highway, visit *www.explorenwt.com*.

CAMPBELL HIGHWAY

Watson Lake to North Klondike Highway
(near Carmacks): 363 miles (584 km)

Motorists on their way to Dawson City can shorten their drive by taking the alternate route around Whitehorse: the Campbell Highway (Highway 4). The road heads northwest from Watson Lake and, after 373 miles, connects with the North Klondike Highway (Highway 2) just north of Carmacks.

You accomplish three things by taking this route to Dawson City: You save 20 miles on your odometer; you miss out on all the fun that's waiting in Whitehorse; and you eat a lot of dust. On the other hand, you also see some beautiful land as you follow the route of early day fur traders who worked for the Hudson's Bay Company. Robert Campbell himself was sent here in the 1840s to explore on behalf of the company.

Completed in 1968, the Campbell is mostly unpaved, and this road less traveled wends through the communities of Ross River and Faro, where you can buy gas, food, and groceries, as well as find a place to stay with or without an RV.

YELLOWHEAD-CASSIAR HIGHWAYS

Prince George to Alaska Highway
(near Watson Lake): 744 miles (1,197 km)

Alaskabound travelers can shave some 100 miles (161 km) off the drive between Prince George and Watson Lake by taking westbound Yellowhead Highway 16 and then northbound Cassiar Highway 37. Some motorists are less concerned about time, but still take the Yellowhead-Cassiar route for a change of scenery through British Columbia's outstanding Skeena Mountains. Most portions of this route are paved, but drivers should stay alert for sections of washboard in gravel stretches of the Cassiar.

Yellowhead Highway 16 is a trans-Canada route that extends from southern Manitoba and trends westward and north across Saskatchewan, Alberta, and British Columbia. In western Canada, it is a primary east-west route linking Edmonton with Prince George. Through mountain passes, along glacial lakes, and into canyons, the Yellowhead promises stunning vistas and plenty of wildlife-watching.

The Yellowhead continues west to the coastal city of **Prince Rupert, B.C.** From there, travelers may connect with the British Columbia ferry system and the Alaska Marine Highway System. (See Appendix 1, Alaska Marine Highway System.)

The junction of the Yellowhead and Cassiar Highways is 298 miles (480 km) west of Prince George near the village of Kitwanga. From here, the Cassiar trends north for 446 miles (718 km) to its junction with the Alaska Highway 13 miles (21 km) west of Watson Lake.

From the Cassiar Highway, motorists can access the coastal communities of Stewart, B.C., and Hyder, Alaska. The turnoff to these towns is at Mile 96 (155 km) on the Cassiar Highway, at Meziadin Junction. Stewart and Hyder straddle the international border 41 miles (66 km) west of the junction.

The Yellowhead Highway got its name from the story of an Iroquois-Caucasian trapper who was called Tête Jaune, or Yellowhead, for the blond cast to his hair. He led fur traders through the Rocky Mountains and opened the way for a trade route across western Canada.

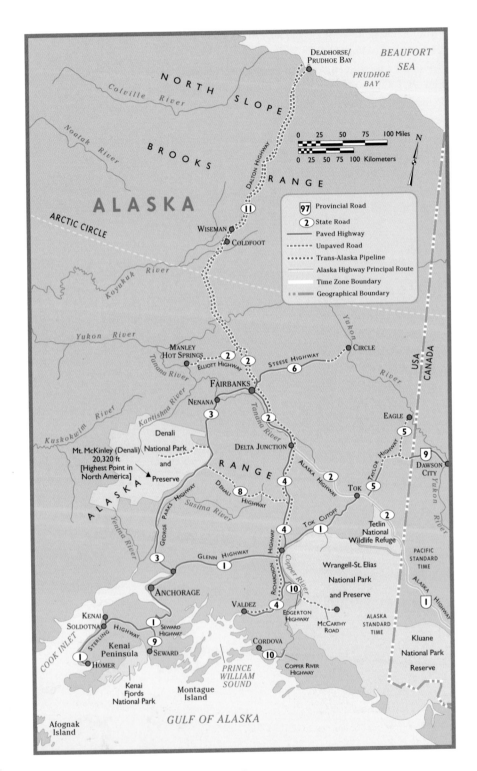

DEADHORSE/
PRUDHOE BAY

BEAUFORT
SEA

PRUDHOE
BAY

NORTH SLOPE

Colville River

Noatak River

BROOKS RANGE

DALTON HIGHWAY

ALASKA

ARCTIC CIRCLE

WISEMAN

COLDFOOT

⑪

Koyukuk River

97	Provincial Road
②	State Road
——	Paved Highway
-----	Unpaved Road
••••	Trans-Alaska Pipeline
‖	Alaska Highway Principal Route
	Time Zone Boundary
‖	Geographical Boundary

0 25 50 75 100 Miles N

0 25 50 75 100 Kilometers

Yukon River

MANLEY
HOT SPRINGS

② ②

ELLIOTT HIGHWAY

STEESE HIGHWAY

⑥

CIRCLE

Tanana River

FAIRBANKS

NENANA

③

②

Yukon River

USA
CANADA

Kuskokwim River

Kantishna River

Denali
National Park
and
Preserve

DELTA JUNCTION

②

EAGLE

⑤

⑨

DAWSON
CITY

Mt. McKinley (Denali)
20,320 ft
[Highest Point in
North America]

RANGE

ALASKA RANGE

TAYLOR HIGHWAY

GEORGE PARKS HIGHWAY

Susitna River

DENALI HIGHWAY

⑧

④

②

TOK ⑤

Yukon River

④

TOK CUTOFF

①

②

Tetlin
National
Wildlife Refuge

Yentna River

③

GLENN HIGHWAY

①

RICHARDSON HIGHWAY

Copper River

Wrangell-St. Elias

National Park

and Preserve

PACIFIC
STANDARD
TIME

ALASKA HIGHWAY

ANCHORAGE

VALDEZ

④

EDGERTON
HIGHWAY

McCARTHY
ROAD

ALASKA
STANDARD
TIME

①

KENAI

SOLDOTNA

STERLING HIGHWAY

①

SEWARD
HIGHWAY

⑨

CORDOVA

⑩

Kluane

Kenai
Peninsula

SEWARD

COPPER RIVER
HIGHWAY

National Park

COOK INLET

HOMER

①

Kenai
Fjords
National Park

Montague
Island

PRINCE
WILLIAM
SOUND

Reserve

Afognak
Island

GULF OF ALASKA

Chapter 8

Alaska's State Highways

DRIVING ALASKA. Most visitors to Alaska are accustomed to choosing from a vast menu of roads, reading and following maps, and watching for their exits. When they ask directions, they commonly refer to route numbers. So when they arrive in Alaska, they might ask, "Where is the exit for Route 9?" The puzzled Alaskan will answer with another question, "Where do you want to go?" Choices are so few that decision-making is made easy. Name your destination and there's usually only one way to get there.

Portage Glacier is such a place. Located about 45 minutes south of Anchorage off the Seward Highway, the glacier is counted among Alaska's top tourist attractions, along with the Inside Passage and Mount McKinley. Its popularity is due in part to its accessibility by road. Each summer, thousands of people take a 1-hour cruise to the glacier's face on a custom-built icebreaker named the MV *Ptarmigan*. I was selling tickets there one summer when a man stopped by after his cruise, an Alaska map in his hand. "We came down here on Route 1 in our rental car," he said as he

South of Anchorage, the Sterling and Seward Highways of the Kenai Peninsula provide access to coastal communities, outstanding fishing, and unforgettable views.

Highway Name	Length	Number	Route Description
Copper River Highway	48 miles 77 km	10	Disconnected from highway system. Connects Cordova, on Prince William Sound, with the derelict Million Dollar Bridge to nowhere; mostly unpaved.
Dalton Highway	414 miles 666 km	11	Splits northbound from Elliott Highway (north of Fox) to Deadhorse, where it dead-ends at the Arctic Ocean; mostly unpaved; almost no services.
Denali Highway	136 miles 219 km	8	Road between Richardson Highway and Parks Highway; connects Paxson and Cantwell; unpaved; few services.
Edgerton Highway	33 miles 53 km	10	Connects Richardson Highway (south of Glennallen) to Chitina, 33 miles (53 km) east on paved road; from there, unpaved McCarthy Road travels east for 60 miles (96.5 km) almost to McCarthy; few services; not maintained in winter.
Elliott Highway	152 miles 245 km	2	From Fox (north of Fairbanks) to Manley Hot Springs, where it dead-ends at the Tanana River; partially paved; few services.
Glenn Highway	328 miles 528 km	1	Connects Anchorage with Glennallen and the Richardson Highway, and connects Gakona Junction with Tok via the Tok Cutoff; paved, sections often under repair; services at regular intervals. *(continued)*

smoothed his creased map on the counter, "but we'd like to go back to Anchorage another way and see some different country. What do you recommend?"

"Well, sir," I told him, "the Seward Highway out there is your only road, and it runs north-south. You're south right now, so just turn the car around and keep driving until you bump into Anchorage." He could hardly believe it until I showed him on his own map. He was driving in the country's biggest state, with fewer roads per square mile than Rhode Island. I knew the trip back wouldn't disappoint him, though. The fabulous Seward Highway is among only a few dozen roads in the United States chosen for the federally designated title of National Scenic Bypass.

A separate issue entirely is the Alaskan preference of calling highways by name, not route number: the Steese, the Parks, the Seward. You'll hear the names regularly, the route numbers rarely. Most of the highways dead-end at small towns along a major body of water. Consequently, the term "end of the road" applies to several communities around the state, although one, in particular, was made famous by author/humorist Tom Bodett. He put his hometown of Homer, Alaska, on the map with his books and national radio program *The End of the Road Show.*

Highway Name	Length	Number	Route Description
Haines Highway (Via Yukon Route 3 and B.C. Route 4)	152 miles 245 km	7	Connects Alaska Highway at Haines Junction, Yukon, with Haines, Alaska, where it dead-ends on Lynn Canal; paved.
Klondike Highway 2 (Yukon road)	99 miles 159 km	2	Connects Alaska Highway just south of Whitehorse, Yukon, with Skagway, Alaska, where it dead-ends on Lynn Canal; paved.
Parks Highway	358 miles 576 km	3	Connects Anchorage with Fairbanks via the Glenn Highway. Completely paved; services at regular intervals.
Richardson Highway	364 miles 586 km	4 & 2	Connects Valdez with Fairbanks. Paved; services at regular intervals.
Seward Highway	127 miles 261 km	1 & 9	Connects Anchorage with Seward, where it dead-ends on Resurrection Bay off the Gulf of Alaska; paved; services at regular intervals.
Steese Highway	162 miles 261 km	6	Connects Fairbanks with Circle City, where it dead-ends on the Yukon River; mostly unpaved; few services.
Sterling Highway	143 miles 230 km	1	Branches off the Seward Highway for south-bound travelers to Homer, where it dead-ends on Cook Inlet; paved; services at regular intervals.
Taylor Highway	160 miles 257 km	5	Connects Alaska Highway at Tetlin Junction (southeast of Tok) with Eagle, where it dead-ends on the Yukon River; unpaved; few services. Not maintained in winter.

If you want to drive northwest, west, or southwest from this narrow, north-south cluster of blacktop, you can forget it. Most of Alaska remains accessible only by air or, along Alaska's Panhandle (Southeast Alaska), by marine highway (see Chapter 9, "Alaska Marine Highway System").

In 1942, when the Alaska Highway was built and attached to the existing Richardson Highway at Delta Junction, there were even fewer roads. Alaska's busiest highway between Anchorage and Fairbanks, the Parks, didn't even exist. Travelers had to use the longer, roundabout way via the Richardson and Glenn Highways. The pipeline was still 30 years in the future, so the Dalton Highway (also known as the Haul Road for pipeline construction) hadn't been conceived. Nor had the Sterling Highway, which wends down the Kenai Peninsula. If you wanted to go to Homer, you took a ferry.

What are now considered major transportation routes (by Alaska standards) weren't much more than improved trails that had been used by early day settlers, traders, and miners. A century ago and more, the pioneering Europeans simply traveled along the ancient trading routes of Alaska's first people, who were familiar with the passes through the mountains, and who graciously showed the newcomers the way.

Today, although Alaska's roads are called highways, a few remain rustic and unpaved; in winter, four of them (the Copper River, Edgerton, Taylor, and Denali Highways) are not plowed, so they are impassable except to snowmobilers. Even if a road is regularly plowed, wise winter travelers will check the local phone book and call the Department of Transportation's recorded information line to obtain road conditions before setting out. (See the section on Driving in Winter in Chapter 1, "Getting Ready.")

Generally speaking, most of Alaska's major roads are in great shape. The paved roads are well-marked, two-lane routes (sometimes even four lanes) with ample shoulders. Unpaved sections are graded regularly, and sometimes serve better than the broken-down parts of paved roads. Small towns, gas stations, and other services appear at regular intervals, and restaurants and lodging aren't hard to find, either. That can't be said for all of Alaska's "highways," though, so read up on your route before you embark.

Road maintenance workers have a particular challenge in Alaska, considering what they have for a subsurface. In many parts of the state, they contend with an underground enemy called permafrost: permanently frozen sections of soil that are riddled with ice. When the insulating overgrowth is scraped away to create a road, the ground begins to melt and sink. Adding a layer of weighty, heat-conductive blacktop creates more subsurface problems. With the freeze and thaw of seasonal change, some roadbeds suffer, and an army of maintenance workers sets out to make repairs each year in the short summer construction season. As a motorist, plan for one or two delays, because flaggers, pilot cars, dust, and lumbering trucks are virtual guarantees. Please be patient. If they weren't out there doing their jobs, you wouldn't be willing (or able) to set out on these passageways into some of America's most magnificent places.

Of course, one must include gawking time in any Alaska road trip. When the evening light turns the sky pink-orange above a mountain range, the view can be distracting. Glacier-fed rivers merge and divide across a broad floodplain, and low clouds drag across the vivid, white mountain peaks. Wild animals step out onto the pavement ahead, or pause to feed along the shoulder, and your camera is at the ready. In the midst of such beauty, "making good time" loses its appeal.

Since 1995, the Alaska Department of Transportation and Public Facilities has named 11 transportation routes as Alaska Scenic Byways. Since 1998, three were designated a National Scenic Byway. To qualify for the state designation, a byway must possess some or all of these intrinsic qualities: scenic or natural beauty, cultural importance, recreational value, or archaeological or historic significance. Not all 11 are paved roadways, however—the Alaska Railroad and the Alaska Marine Highway System are among the names on the list. And the Marine Highway was "promoted" to a National Scenic Byway in September 2004. Others in the state list are the Dalton Highway, Haines Highway, Parks Highway (from Denali State Park to Healy), Richardson Highway (from Glennallen to Valdez), Seward Highway, Steese Highway, Sterling Highway (from Wye to Skilak, and Anchor Point to Homer), and the combination of the Taylor and Top of the World Highways. For more information and photos of Alaska's Scenic Byways, visit the following Web site: *www.dot.state.ak.us/*.

This chapter features Alaska's highways, in alphabetical order, and includes the cities, services, access, recreational opportunities, and attractions that you'll find along this exceptionally scenic road system.

An innovative public service recently introduced by the Alaska Department of Transportation and Public Facilities allows motorists to use any phone or the Internet to obtain the latest information about road conditions, traffic hazards, closures, and roadwork—even near times for state ferry arrivals—by dialing 5-1-1 or by visiting *www.511.alaska.gov*. If you're calling from out of state, dial toll-free 1-866-282-7577.

COPPER RIVER HIGHWAY

Cordova to Million Dollar Bridge: 48 miles (77 km)
Travel Opportunities: *Scenic fishing village; flightseeing over Wrangell–St. Elias National Park; Prince William Sound cruises; rafting on the Copper River; chartered fishing for salmon or halibut; Childs Glacier; Million Dollar Bridge; bird-watching.*

Among Alaska's unique roads, the Copper River Highway is a standout—a mere fragment of a highway that's disconnected from the rest of the highway system, but still official enough to merit a route number: Alaska Highway 10. To drive this road, you'll need to fly in and rent a car at Cordova on Prince William Sound. Or bring your vehicle along on the Alaska Marine Highway System and disembark at Cordova (see Chapter 9, "Alaska Marine Highway System"). Pay heed to the return schedule if you choose to cruise, or you may stay longer than you had planned.

For centuries, Native Alaskans have lived in this region, moving with the seasons to fish and hunt as they drew life from the land. The ways of the early Native people are not just in museum displays today. In this area, you'll find many Athabascan, Eyak, and Alutiiq people who still follow the cultural practices of their ancestors in dance, song, and art, as well as through a subsistence lifestyle of hunting and fishing for food. Throughout the small Native villages of Southcentral Alaska, people live in log or wood-frame houses, drive cars, go to work, and follow the same television "soaps" as anybody else in the country. Some of them, however, have great-grandmas who remember the moment they saw a white person for the first time.

Explorers, gold seekers, and traders brought the stamp of the Western world to the Copper River Delta, especially during the 19th century. In 1902 geologists made the first major oil discovery in Alaska—at Katalla, southwest of Cordova. In 1907 entrepreneur Michael J. Heney began building the Copper River & Northwestern Railway to transport the ore mined from the Kennecott Copper Mine, to the north. The mine and railroad flourished for more than 20 years, closing in the late 1930s. In the mid-1940s, builders of the Copper River Highway chose to follow the railway's bed and planned to join Cordova with Chitina and the Richardson Highway. In 1964, a natural disaster thwarted the project, and the work stalled out. That year, the Good Friday Earthquake devastated Cordova and many Southcentral coastal communities. The earthquake originally was measured at a magnitude of 8.6 and later was upgraded to an unbelievable 9.2.

The state's Department of Transportation is still interested in completing the road from Cordova, but protests from residents and others have further delayed the project. It turns out that a majority of the Cordovans like their insulation and don't want more road traffic. There are several USFS trailheads and recreational opportunities along this route.

The first 12 miles (19 km) are paved, followed by a gravel surface that threads for another 36 miles (58 km) through awesome beauty to the **Million Dollar Bridge,** which crosses the Copper River, and was added to the National Register of Historic Places in 2000. One section of the bridge collapsed in the 1964 earthquake. Even though the structure looks damaged, it is still usable, but at your own risk. A crude road extends another 10 miles (16 km) beyond the bridge, but only four-wheel-drive vehicles should give it a go. Near the bridge, you'll get a panoramic view of **Childs Glacier.** Plan a picnic here amid unforgettable surroundings.

In the course of its 48 miles (77 km), the highway crosses a number of glacially fed streams and the multifingered Copper River Delta. Magnificent glaciers are visible on the north side of the road as you drive east. And all around you, for miles and miles, is **Chugach National Forest,** close to 6 million acres of it. On this drive, you'll find viewpoint turnouts with informational plaques, trailheads, and developed recreation areas at **Cabin Lake** and **Alaganik Slough.** Fishing, wildlife-watching, hiking, biking, and camping are popular activities around here, and the Copper River is famed for its annual runs of salmon. Freshwater and saltwater fishing takes place in an angler's paradise. Learn about local regulations and closures when you obtain your fishing license at any number of retail outlets in Cordova.

Cordova is a photogenic town with a population of about 2,400 people. Because its economy is largely based on fishing, commercial fishing vessels outnumber pleasure boats in the harbor, and a U.S. Coast Guard vessel is moored just outside the small-boat harbor. It's fun to walk the docks and read the names of the vessels and to watch the fishermen gear up or down from a trip. The catch may be salmon, halibut, or herring, depending on season. In town, nearly everything you need lies within walking distance. North of Cordova, the Alaska Marine Highway ferry terminal offers scheduled service aboard the MV *Aurora* or the MV *Matanuska* on the Southcentral/Southwest Alaska ferry route (see Chapter 9, "Alaska Marine Highway System").

The region is a stopover on the largest shorebird migration in the world. Located on a major flyway for 2 million waterfowl and 5 million shorebirds, Cordova hosts the **Copper River Delta Shorebird Festival** in early May each year. Birders come from all over the world to view the millions of birds that nest and feed in the delta. So vital to the birds' survival, this portion of the Chugach National Forest gained added protection in 1978 when it was named a Critical Habitat Area.

The favorite party of the winter season is the Cordova Iceworm Festival, set each year on the first weekend of February. Events include a parade, entertainment, an arts and crafts show, skiing events, a best-beard contest, and selection of a king and queen. Call 907-424-5756 for more information.

Cordova Museum and Library on First Street offers exhibits on the rich Native cultures of this region, as well as its exploration in 1778 by Captain James Cook, the gold rush, and more recent copper-mining history. Also inside are art displays, a fishing diorama, gift shop, and a modest bookstore. At the U.S. Forest Service office, in a historic 1925 building at 612 2nd Street, you can learn about the Chugach National Forest and local natural history. The USFS offers 17 cabins in the area, available for a fee and by reservation. Call 1-877-444-5777 or see *www.reserveusa.com*.

Other options from Cordova include rafting the Copper River, a fly-in fishing trip, a cruise on Prince William Sound, or a flightseeing excursion above the fabulous Wrangell–St. Elias Range. For more information on what to see and do in Cordova, contact the Chamber of Commerce at 907-424-7260, or visit *www.cordovachamber.com*.

Lodging

Cordova Lighthouse Inn
P.O. Box 1495
1-888-424-7080
www.cordovalighthouseinn.com
Comfortable guest rooms.
    Gift shop, café.

Cordova Rose Lodge
1315 Whitshed Road
907-424-7673
www.cordovarose.com
Historic setting of landlocked
    barge offers rooms with a view.
Tour arrangements. Breakfast
and dinner.

The Northern Nights Inn
P.O. Box 1564
907-424-5356
Rooms with a view of the inlet; kitchens,
    laundry, freezer for your fish.

Prince William Motel
2nd and Council Streets
1-888-796-6835 or 907-424-3201
16 rooms and kitchenettes. TV, microwaves,
    refrigerators, laundry, store.

Campgrounds

Odiak Camper Park
Whitshed Road off Copper River Highway
907-424-6200
24 sites, tenting area, showers;
    operated by the city.

U.S. Forest Service
1-877-444-6777
www.reserveusa.com
17 cabins available in this district;
    most accessible only by boat or plane.
    Three are on the trail system.

Restaurants

Cordova Lighthouse Inn
P.O. Box 1495
1-888-424-7080
www.cordovalighthouseinn.com
Café and bakery.

Cordova Rose Lodge
1315 Whitshed Road
907-424-7673
www.cordovarose.com
Sourdough pancakes, seafood specialties.

Powder House Bar and Restaurant
Mile 2 Copper River Highway
907-424-3529
Soups, sandwiches, seafood. Eat in or take out.

DALTON HIGHWAY (Haul Road)

From Elliott Highway to Deadhorse: 414 miles (666 km)
Travel Opportunities: *Trans-Alaska pipeline views; Coldfoot; Wiseman gold-mining village; Brooks Range continental divide; Arctic Circle crossing; guided tours to Prudhoe Bay oil operations.*

The Dalton Highway originally was called the Haul Road because it was built for one purpose: to haul goods and supplies for the building of the trans-Alaska pipeline. The road was named for James William Dalton, a principal player in North Slope oil development. Although experimental ice roads, seasonal at best, had been built in the Arctic, the Dalton was the first planned and engineered roadway into the farthest north reaches of the state. Even though the Dalton was finished in 1974, its entire length wasn't opened to the public until 1995.

You will share the road mostly with truckers headed to or from Deadhorse and Prudhoe Bay at the top of the state, a small number of hardy souls like yourself, and a handful of tourism operations. As far as services go, this route remains largely undeveloped. With a few exceptions—such as businesses at the Yukon River Bridge, Coldfoot, Wiseman, Deadhorse, and a couple of wayside stops—you'll encounter long stretches of no towns, no gas stations, few outhouses, and few other travelers. Emergency and medical services also are limited. Officials suggest contacting one of the highway maintenance camps to relay a call for assistance. Or, reach the Alaska State Troopers by CB on Channel 19.

The Dalton Highway is the northernmost state road in the country.

The trans-Alaska pipeline parallels the Dalton Highway for the entire length of the route to Deadhorse.

As you head north, the terrain changes in degrees of beauty: from sparsely treed rolling hills, to lofty mountains, to limitless undulating tundra. Your most constant companion is the nearby pipeline, visible only in the stretches where the permafrost in the soil was so bad that builders put it up on supports and ran it above ground. The 48-inch-diameter pipeline was built between 1974 and 1977. Its 800-mile (1,287.5-km) length stretches from Mile 0 at Prudhoe Bay to its terminus at Valdez on Prince William Sound. South of Fairbanks, most of the pipeline route parallels the Richardson Highway.

A wide, unpaved wilderness road with a good roadbed, the Dalton extends from Mile 73 of the Elliott Highway, north of Fox, all the way to Deadhorse and the working oil fields of Prudhoe Bay. Don't expect to waltz in anywhere at will. Most of these places are off-limits to the traveler. In Deadhorse you'll find an airport, general store, filling station, and a couple of hotels, which are the best places to line up a guided tour of the area. With a guide, you may dip your toes in the frigid Arctic Ocean, view Mile 0 of the pipeline, and learn about how the vast oil reservoir beneath Alaska's North Slope was discovered and developed.

Consider the following option for less wear-and-tear on your vehicle and your sensibilities: rent a vehicle that's equipped for the Dalton from a specialty operator, or if you'd rather not drive, take a fly-drive combo tour. I did this once and found the trip very worthwhile. Even though you begin the trip with strangers, within hours you'll find fast friends in the group. A shuttle bus will pick you up from your Fairbanks campground or hotel. Pack an overnight bag, but don't worry about food.

You'll be well fed throughout the trip. Look on the Bureau of Land Management's Northern District Office Web site to get a list of approved businesses operating on the Dalton: *www.aurora.ak.blm.gov* or call 1-800-437-7021.

After a 45-minute flight from Fairbanks to **Deadhorse**, we boarded an 18-passenger van and cruised around the oil fields, with permitted access to places where we would not have been allowed as independent visitors. Naturally this is a high-security area, and tourism is only a recent development. The population of Deadhorse is officially 25— plus 2,500 transient workers. Most work a fluctuating schedule of two-weeks-on, two-weeks-off, or something similar. You won't see many people, actually. Most work indoors.

Around the low buildings and ground-level maze of pipes, the road meanders among the oil-company installations and enclosed drilling rigs. We saw numerous caribou, waterfowl, and wildflowers in what I considered unexpected places. In one spot, we saw a group of caribou resting under a raised part of the pipeline. Without trees to block the view, they were easy to spot. At the **Arctic Ocean**, I handed off my camera to a fellow traveler and asked him to take my picture standing ankle deep in the water. (I threw my arms in the air and said "Hurry!" through a clenched smile. The water was piercing cold.)

Our driver had packed lots of good food in coolers, and we had plenty of water, coffee, and soft drinks. Driving south that day, he told us all about the unique forces of nature here, the climate, the geology, and the wildlife. We learned how to pronounce "Sagavanirktok River," and understood instantly why everybody calls it the Sag.

Farther south we spied a hunter who had bagged a caribou with bow and arrow, and some of us tried walking out to him over the tundra. It was like trying to walk on and between underinflated basketballs that are covered with mossy, leafy growth.

We stopped again to share our drinking water with a British couple on a bicycle journey from Fairbanks to Prudhoe Bay, then visited the century-old mining town of Wiseman. A woman behind the counter in the general store told us that in the last couple of days, a local miner had uncovered a record-size gold nugget: flat and big enough to eclipse a saucer.

After an overnight at Coldfoot, in buildings that once housed pipeline construction workers, we continued our southbound trip and later came upon the only structure around for a hundred miles: the tour company's private, off-road outhouse, placed there just for our comfort. Next stop was the Arctic Circle, marked by a sturdy sign showing your place on the globe. Our driver asked us to wait a moment, then literally rolled out a red carpet and shook our hands, welcoming us across the invisible line. That evening, we pulled in to Fairbanks, tired but thrilled to have seen such rare sights.

My advice is to go with a tour guide if you want the best experience and the least worry. It was a privilege to have someone drive, especially when a good-size piece of gravel damaged the tour van's windshield (and not mine).

Places of note along the Dalton Highway, from south to north:

E. L. Patton. The highway crosses the river at Mile 56 (90 km), where many travelers are happy to encounter the businesses of Yukon River Camp: motel rooms, gas station, tire repairs, gift shop, and restaurant. You may launch your boat on the Yukon River. There are good views of the pipeline from here, too. In summer months, the Bureau of Land Management staffs the Yukon Crossing Visitor Contact Station, a rest stop with outhouses, information, and viewing platform. Just a few miles ahead, the BLM maintains a site for RV dumping and water fill-ups. Nearby, another popular business, the Hot Spot, offers food and lodging.

This area lies within the Yukon Flats National Wildlife Refuge, which supports moose, caribou, bears, millions of migrating birds, and small furbearers such as lynx, snowshoe hares, foxes, and beavers.

Arctic Circle. At Mile 115 (185 km), an expansive wayside with viewing platform, outhouses, and great signs is worth a stop to record your momentous crossing of the Arctic Circle—that invisible boundary that encircles the globe at the southernmost latitude where the sun never sets on the day of the summer solstice (June 21 or 22). Likewise, at this latitude the sun does not rise on the day of the winter solstice (December 21 or 22). Nearby, the Bureau of Land Management offers undeveloped camping with tables, grills, and outhouses.

Coldfoot. This former pipeline construction camp was given this name for obvious reasons. Winter temperatures plunge well below zero all along the Dalton Highway. The farther north you go, the deeper the plunge. I once visited Coldfoot with a television crew in January, and I still remember the heartbreaking sound of an expensive and important part of the camera when it went *crraack!* in the –50°F air. In summer, Coldfoot is pleasantly warm, but be advised that mosquitoes and other biting insects are a nuisance. There is no town here, but rather a welcome stop in the road at Mile 175 (282 km), where truckers and tourists refresh and refill at Coldfoot Camp. A post office, 24-hour fuel, tire repair, restaurant, and overnight

A cow moose crosses the Dalton north of the Brooks Range.

accommodations in a former pipeline camp facility are available. Call 907-474-3500 or *www.coldfootcamp.com*.

Wiseman. Gold miners gather where there's gold to be found. Towns are created by the people who follow: the scores who offer services and supplies for those miners. That's how Wiseman came to be, nearly a century ago here in the Koyukuk Mining District. Disconnected from the rest of the world as it was, the town nearly died out before the Haul Road was built. Now located about 3 miles (5 km) off the Dalton Highway (at Mile 188) and populated by a scant 21 people, it has managed to cling to life as gold and tourism now feed the town.

Pay mind to private property as you walk among the log homes—it's easy to imagine this as a Disney set, but people do live and work here! Visit the **Wiseman Historical Museum** to learn more about local and regional mining history. It's located in the historic Carl Frank cabin in north Wiseman. On the south end of town, cross the river to reach the two cabin-and-breakfast businesses: Arctic Getaway (907-678-4456) and Boreal Lodging (907-678-4566). Ask permission and directions to the old cemetery on a beautiful hillside above town, where many area pioneers have gone to rest.

Continental Divide. Drive through the majestic Brooks Range and cross the northernmost Continental Divide in the United States, at Mile 245. Atigun Pass, at 4,739 feet, is the highest point on the 800-mile north-south route of the pipeline.

The North Slope. To oil company workers, this name—or its abbreviated version, the Slope—is synonymous with Prudhoe Bay. It is derived from a geographical feature. On the north side of the Brooks Range, this country takes its time returning to sea level. It is that slow, almost unrecognizable slope toward the Arctic Ocean that is referred to in "North Slope."

Deadhorse. End of the line. Stop at the Prudhoe Bay General Store (and U.S. post office) to send a postcard from the top of the world. The store features its own little museum, too, along with sales of souvenirs, sweatshirts, outdoor gear, hats, and more. Call 907-659-2412. Accommodations, meals, and fuel can be found in town.

Lodging/Meals

Coldfoot:
The Inn at Coldfoot
Mile 175 Dalton Highway
907-474-3500
www.coldfootcamp.com
80 rooms, plus service station, post office, gift shop, Trucker's Café, Frozen Foot Saloon. RV hookups and dump station.

Deadhorse:
Arctic Caribou Inn
Near airport
907-659-2368
75 rooms with private or shared baths. Near restaurant, gift shop, airport. Tours available: oil field; Mile 0 of the pipeline; Arctic Ocean walk.

Arctic Oilfield Hotel
Corner of Sag River Road and Spine Road
907-659-2614
Rooms, showers, laundry, buffet-style meals. Tire repair, towing, welding.

Wiseman:
Arctic Getaway Cabin and Breakfast
Mile 189 Dalton Highway
907-678-4456
www.arcticgetaway.com
Located in a historic building: Pioneer Hall, Igloo No. 8.

Boreal Lodging
South end of Wiseman
907-678-4566
Cabins, rooms, showers, phone, TV. Aurora-viewing, sled-dog rides in winter.

At or near Yukon River Bridge:
Yukon River Camp
Mile 56 Dalton Highway
907-474-3557
www.yukonrivercamp.com.
40 rooms, plus service station, tire repair, boat launch, gift shop, restaurant.

The Hot Spot Café
Mile 60 Dalton Highway
907-451-7543
Rooms, burgers, pies, barbecue.

Campgrounds
Coldfoot:
Coldfoot Camp
Mile 175 Dalton Highway
907-474-3500
www.coldfootcamp.com
RV hookups and dump station. Service station, post office, gift shop, Trucker's Café, Frozen Foot Saloon.

Deadhorse:
Arctic Caribou Inn
907-659-2368
RV parking is available adjacent to this hotel.

Arctic Oilfield Hotel
Corner of Sag River Road and Spine Road
907-659-2614
RV parking, showers, laundry, buffet-style meals. Tire repair, towing, welding.

Deadhorse–Prudhoe Bay Tesoro
907-659-3198
This service station permits overnight parking. Phone, rest rooms, and free area maps. Fuel available 24 hours a day.

The Bureau of Land Management oversees four camping areas along the Dalton Highway. For more information, contact the Northern Field Office in Fairbanks at 1-800-437-7021 or visit the bureau's Web site at www.aurora.ak.blm.gov. The camping areas are:

Sixty Mile Site
Mile 60 Dalton Highway
Undeveloped 5 acres with dump station, water, outhouse.

Arctic Circle Site
Mile 115 Dalton Highway
Undeveloped 5 acres above wayside, outhouse.

Marion Creek Campground
Mile 180 Dalton Highway
Developed 1.5 acres with 28 campsites, 11 pull-through sites, fire pits, water, toilets, campground hosts.

Galbraith Lake Site
Mile 275 Dalton Highway
Undeveloped 5 acres, outhouse.

A tour driver literally rolled out the red carpet for his guests as he welcomed them across the Arctic Circle. Each was issued a certificate signifying this important event.

*D*ENALI HIGHWAY

From Richardson Highway to Parks Highway: 136 miles (219 km)
Travel Opportunities: *No towns, just fabulous mountain vistas; hiking,*
biking, berry picking; fishing at lakes and stream crossings;
wildlife-watching and bird-watching.

The Denali Highway first opened in 1957 as the only road access to what
was then called Mount McKinley National Park. The George Parks Highway,
finished in 1972, made the park even more accessible. Using a grand scale,
visualize the Richardson Highway and George Parks Highway as parallel
uprights in the letter H. Then the Denali Highway is the crossbar that joins
them. Connecting **Paxson** on the Richardson Highway to **Cantwell** on the Parks
Highway, this mostly unpaved wilderness road is a 136-mile shortcut through
an awesome landscape.

Three major peaks dominate the skyline in this section of the Alaska Range: **Mount
Deborah**, at 12,339 feet; **Mount Hess**, at 11,940 feet; and **Mount Hayes**, at 13,892 feet.

In 1980 the national park's name was changed to reflect local use of the name
for the highest peak in the continent: Denali. In the Athabascan language, the word
means "the high one." The park became **Denali National Park and Preserve**, though
the official name for the peak remains **Mount McKinley.**

The park attracts thousands of visitors who most often arrive via the Alaska
Railroad or with major tour operators, such as Gray Line of Alaska and Princess
Tours. But the road travelers are many as well. From June through early August,
RV and tent campers often fill up every available spot in the park's camping areas.
(See the section on the Parks Highway, in this chapter, for tips on securing a camp-
site reservation.)

The **Tangle Lakes, Tangle River,** and a dozen other lakes and streams along
the Denali Highway are popular destinations for anglers. Typical in these waters
are grayling, whitefish, burbot, and lake trout. Inquire in Paxson or Cantwell for
licensing and tips on what is biting. Consider hiring a guide for a more fulfilling
experience.

The Denali Highway is a wonderful drive, particularly during sunny days that offer
boundless views of the Alaska Range. RV travelers take heed that while the road out
of Paxson is paved and broad, after 20 miles (32 km) it is a gravel road that gradually
narrows as it journeys west. The maximum recommended speed, even when no one
is around, is 30 mph.

There are few services along its length, but plenty at each end. Milepost addresses
are measured from Paxson, on the Richardson Highway. And, of course, keep your
eye out for moose and caribou. This is their kind of country.

Lodging/Meals

Tangle River Inn
Mile 20 Denali Highway
907-822-7304 or 907-822-3970
www.tangleriverinn.com
Rooms, cabins, liquor store, bar, restaurant
overlooking Tangle Lakes. Canoe rentals.

Tangle Lakes Lodge
Mile 22 Denali Highway
907-822-4202 or 907-688-9173
www.tanglelakeslodge.com
Rooms, log cabins, fine dining and
cocktails. Guided fishing, canoe rentals,
birding and wildlife-watching.

Gracious House Lodge & Flying Service
Mile 82 Denali Highway
907-333-3148 or 907-259-1111
www.alaskaone.com/gracious
Rooms, with or without private bath.
Fuel, café, bar.

Campgrounds

*The Bureau of Land Management
oversees two campgrounds along
the Denali Highway. For information,
call the Glennallen Field Office at
907-822-3217 or visit the bureau's
Web site at www.glennallen.ak.blm.gov.
The campgrounds are:*

Tangle Lakes Campground
Mile 21.5 (from Paxson)
60 acres for RV or tent campsites with
water, wheelchair-accessible toilets,
boat launch, fishing.

Brushkana Campground
Mile 104.5 (from Paxson)
20 sites for RV or tent campsites with
water, toilets, picnic shelter.

EDGERTON HIGHWAY

From Richardson Highway to Chitina: 33 miles (53 km)
From Chitina to McCarthy (on McCarthy Road): 60 miles (97 km)
Travel Opportunities: *Athabascan Indian culture in Tonsina and Chitina; fishing
or rafting the Copper River; salmon dip-netting in the Chitina River; McCarthy,
historic copper-mining town; derelict Kennecott Copper Mine.*

Named for a former member of the Alaska Territorial Road Commission, U.S.
Army Major Glenn Edgerton, the Edgerton Highway is an eastbound spur road off
the Richardson Highway at a point 32 miles (51.5 km) south of Glennallen, or 83
miles (133.5 km) north of Valdez. You're on pavement for 35 miles (56 km)—to the
village of Chitina—and there the Edgerton officially ends.

This village lies at the edge of Wrangell–St. Elias National Park and Preserve,
13.2 million acres of some of the most beautiful, glaciated mountain wilderness
you've ever seen from ground level. From a plane, its mountain peaks and hanging
valleys are even more incredible.

This region is the traditional homeland of the Athabascan Indians, and along the
Edgerton Highway or in Chitina, take advantage of opportunities to purchase locally
made Native art, as well as to visit with descendants of the first Alaskans. Roam
around Chitina (CHIT-na) to view evidence of a boomtown grown old. A few buildings have been restored and placed on the National Register of Historic Sites.

In the early part of the 20th century, when the Kennecott Copper Mine was in its heyday, Chitina was a busy center of commerce, with hotels, restaurants, saloons, and even a movie theater. Today's Chitina, population 120, is no longer essential to the defunct copper mine, but neither is it a ghost town. As the gateway to Wrangell–St. Elias National Park, the village sees hundreds of visitors annually.

In summer, the tiny population really swells when the salmon are running in the **Copper River** and the Alaska Department of Fish and Game declares a "subsistence opener." This is a great time to come and watch the fishing action. Monitoring fish numbers throughout each run, the state opens the river to Alaska residents who depend on fish to feed themselves and their families. They hold a special permit for subsistence fishing. Dip-netting is the fast and preferred method of harvesting the fish. It's a partylike atmosphere as men and women don waders and walk into the river with billowy nets attached to a frame with a long handle. The fishing is as simple as dipping into the water and walking back to shore with the fish. It's that easy, or hard. These are weighty fish, ranging from 15 to 35 pounds or better.

You may see places along the river where local Athabascan Indians have set up a fish wheel to capture fish using the river current to turn the net-covered arms of the contraption. Beneath the surface, a fish is swept up and out of the water by the net and, as the wheel turns, the fish then drops into a holding box.

Stop at the National Park Service visitor information office, housed in one of Chitina's historic cabins, for publications, videos, and slide shows about Wrangell–St. Elias Park. The office also is a good place to ask about weather and road conditions in the park, as well as questions on land ownership, as much of the land is privately owned. Call 907-823-5234.

From Chitina, the unpaved, 60-mile (96.5-km) McCarthy Road leads to the village of **McCarthy** within the park. From there you may take a van or bus ride to visit the old Kennicott town site and the remains of a once-great copper operation: the **Kennecott Mine.** (The spelling of both place-names is correct. The mine and town names don't match due to a century-old spelling error!)

The McCarthy Road is so rugged, however, that big-rig RVs would be advised to think twice about making this adventure drive. Even family-car drivers have to stay under 25 mph to keep their hubcaps on! And flat tires are not unusual. Because the road follows the stripped railbed of the defunct Copper River & Northwestern Railway, drivers should watch out for old railroad spikes, along with potholes, washboard, or slippery sections in the rain. This isn't to say don't go—just know that it will be slow going.

So think about letting someone else do the driving. **Backcountry Connection** at 907-822-5292 offers scheduled van service between Glennallen and McCarthy, and on to Kennicott. Or you can arrange a fly-in day trip between Chitina and Kennicott with **Wrangell Mountain Air,** based in McCarthy. Call 1-800-478-1160 or visit their Web site at *www.wrangellmountainair.com.* Other charter air services may be arranged out of Gulkana, Glennallen, or Valdez.

The payoff for putting up with the McCarthy Road is getting to the village of McCarthy, population 42, in a striking, mountain-rimmed setting. But bear in mind that you can't just drive into the town itself. The McCarthy Road ends in a parking area on the west side of the Kennicott River. Overnight parking is permitted for RV travelers. To reach McCarthy, you still must cross the river via two footbridges and travel another mile on land (shuttle service is available). The footbridges here are still a fairly new development. For some, they are a most welcome replacement for the hand-operated cable tram that once spanned the river. Others believe that losing the tram was a blow to what makes McCarthy so charming. You decide.

This little village was founded in 1910 at the height of the copper rush. Several historic buildings are still standing and still doing business. In summer, the little community buzzes with activity as wilderness guides, bush pilots, anglers, photographers, mountain climbers, and tourists drift in and out of town.

Arrange for a rafting excursion on the Kennicott River with the Copper Oar; call Wrangell Mountain Air for a flightseeing expedition; book a shuttle ride to the ghost town of Kennicott and wander amid the ruins of a once-great copper mine. All businesses are within walking distance, and the locals will have answers to your questions.

Lodging/Camping/Meals

Chitina:
Chitina Cabins
907-823-2223
Overnight rentals or longer, cookstove, kitchens. Full-service RV park with dump station.

Silver Lake Campground
Mile 11 McCarthy Road
RV and tent sites along Silver Lake. Fishing; boat and canoe rentals.

Swift Creek Cabins
Mile 57 McCarthy Road
907-554-1234
www.swiftcreekalaska.com
Rustic cabins, nicely appointed.

Kennicott:
Kennicott Glacier Lodge
Kennicott's main street
1-800-582-5128
www.kennicottlodge.com
25 rooms, dining room, spacious porch, overlooking Kennicott Glacier and Chugach Mountains.

Kenny Lake:
Kenny Lake RV & Mercantile
Mile 7 Edgerton Highway
907-822-3313
Rooms with shared baths. Store, fuel, fishing licenses, RV parking for dry or partial hookups. Tent sites, dump station, self-service laundry, showers, pay phone, café.

Wrangell St. Elias Lodging & Tours
Mile 7.5 Edgerton Highway
907-822-5978
www.alaskayukontravel.com
Arrangements for lodges, cabins, flights, day trips.

McCarthy:
McCarthy Lodge
Ma Johnson's Hotel
Downtown McCarthy
907-554-4402
www.mccarthylodge.com
All-Alaskan decor in 1916 hotel with modern fixtures, lodge, saloon, dining room.

ELLIOTT HIGHWAY

Fox to Manley Hot Springs: 152 miles (245 km)
Travel Opportunities: *Gold panning at Eldorado Gold Mine; viewing the pipeline; views of Minto Flats; hiking BLM trails; fishing the Tolovana River; wildlife-watching; soaking in Manley Hot Springs.*

The Elliott Highway begins a short 11 miles (18 km) north of Fairbanks, at the town of Fox. At the only intersection in Fox, continue driving straight ahead and you'll be on the Elliott. Travelers who want to stay on the Steese Highway and head toward Chatanika, Central, or Circle have to take a sharp right. About half of the Elliott is paved, and in these early miles, the surface is lumpy-bumpy from the damaging work of freeze-thaw action.

Just a mile from the intersection, on the left, is one of the most popular attractions in the Fairbanks area: the **Eldorado Gold Mine.** Featured on an NBC broadcast, the two-hour Eldorado tour begins and ends with a ride on a narrow-gauge railroad, on tracks that were recycled from a railway that once operated among the gold-rich fields of this area. The train's engineer is a fiddler, too, and his entertainment and narration make for an enjoyable ride as you pass an old sourdough's cabin, enter a permafrost tunnel, and watch antique mining equipment at work once again. Round a bend to an expansive, old-time cookshack, where you are greeted by Yukon Yonda and Dexter Clark, a husband-and-wife mining team that has been extracting gold from Interior streams and valleys for more than 20 years. Through their demonstration and banter, you learn about modern mining practices. Next, everybody gets to pan, then have their gold weighed in the cookshack/gift shop. Call 1-866-479-6673 or 907-479-6673. See them online at *www.eldoradogoldmine.com.*

Mile 5.5 is a must-stop if pie is one of your major food groups. The **Hilltop Truckstop** feeds the truckers and fills their rigs, and visitors are welcome to dine and fuel up as well. There's an ATM, ice, groceries, propane, and showers, as well as a menu of hearty selections. The cream and fruit pies come to the table in slabs, not slices. Try the Fat Man.

For Fairbanks-area hikers, the 20-mile trail up **Wickersham Dome** is a favorite. The trailhead is at Mile 28, providing access to other trails in the White Mountains National Recreation Area.

The **Arctic Circle Trading Post** at Mile 49 is more that just a gift shop. They issue certificates to those who cross the circle and maintain the "Official Arctic Circle Registry," as well as sell Arctic Circle memorabilia. They also stay abreast of Dalton Highway road conditions, so go ahead and ask. Call 907-474-3507 or see *www.arcticcircletradingpost.com.*

At Mile 66 (106 km), the turnoff leads to the old mining camp known as **Livengood.** Although you may want to read that as "livin' GOOD," this place-name

A pair of bicyclists from Great Britain found plenty of northern hospitality
on the Elliott Highway. Motorists shared sunscreen and water.

is actually pronounced "LIVE-en-good" for one of the two men who discovered gold near here in 1914. With a population of 32, there are no visitor services. While the old town hints at the millions in gold that was taken out of the Livengood-Tolovana Mining District, large-scale gold-mining operations have ceased.

The Elliott Highway parallels the trans-Alaska pipeline for part of its path through the paper birch and spruce forests. You'll catch views of the above-ground stretches of the pipeline flashing silver through the trees. At Mile 73 (117.5 km), watch for the fork in the road. Here is Mile 0 of the Dalton Highway, which trends north while the Elliott veers west toward the Tanana River.

The Elliott's unpaved sections rise above tree line and grant vistas of grand valleys on either side of this ridge. Beyond them lie the White Mountains. At Mile 110 (177 km), a spur road leads to the Athabascan Indian village of **Minto**. Here you can refuel your car, and buy some snacks. This village is centrally located in Minto Flats, through which flows the Tolovana River. The area is exceptionally rich in fish, waterfowl, big game, and small furbearers. It is only natural that Alaska Natives would choose this location for its abundant resources. As were their ancestors, residents of Minto are dependent upon hunting and fishing to feed their families. Natives of contemporary times supplement their diets with store-bought groceries. You may be able to buy locally made Athabascan crafts, such as a birch-bark basket or beaded moosehide slippers.

Even though the Elliott is unpaved and dusty, up and down, the exceptional views and the prize at the end of the road make it all worthwhile. The highway dead-ends at Manley Hot Springs, a modest, mini–resort town that has offered comfort to miners and travelers for more than a century. It's even more historically significant if you consider that the Athabascans of the Interior knew and loved these springs long before the first Europeans showed up on the scene.

Manley Hot Springs calls to visitors and Fairbanks residents, winter and summer. A quiet town along the Tanana River, its buildings include a trading post and a roadhouse dating from the early 1900s. Follow the road past the old Northern Commerical Co. store to reach the Tanana River and salmon fishing throughout the summer. Today there is no formal hot springs resort; however, owners of the greenhouse, fed by the springs, allow visitors to soak in one of three concrete tubs for a fee.

Winter travelers to Manley are rewarded with exceptional views of the northern lights, dogsled tours, and the opportunity to converse with local mining and dog-mushing folks. Gas and groceries are available at the Manley Trading Post. Roads are spare in town, so it's easy to find your way around.

Lodging/Meals

Manley Hot Springs:
Manley Roadhouse
End of the road
907-672-3161
Rooms, cabins, dining room, bar. The roadhouse is a historic gem dating from the early 1900s, with historical artifacts on display.

Campgrounds

RV travelers are permitted to dry camp in gravel pullouts along the Elliott Highway.

Olnes Pond Campground
Mile 10.5 Elliott Highway
Campsites, toilets, picnic areas, boat ramp, fishing. In the Lower Chatanika State Recreation Area.

Whitefish Campground
Mile 11 Elliott Highway
Campsites, toilets, picnic areas, boat ramp, fishing. Also in the Lower Chatanika State Recreation Area.

Manley Hot Springs:
Manley Roadhouse
End of the road
Park with campground, playground, picnic area.

GLENN HIGHWAY including the Tok Cutoff

Tok to Anchorage: 328 miles (528 km)
Travel Opportunities: *Glennallen; Matanuska Glacier and River; Musk Ox Farm; Independence Mine; Palmer Visitor Center and Garden; Eklutna; Anchorage-area attractions.*

The Glenn Highway is a well-traveled route because it connects the Anchorage area (where nearly half the state population lives) to the towns and wilderness areas along the Glenn and Richardson Highways. Further, this is the way to Tok, the Alaska Highway, and the most-used route to the Lower 48. Likewise, if you're headed into Alaska from Canada, and Anchorage is your destination, the Glenn is your highway. The Glenn is the single most important east-west road in the state highway grid.

The Glenn's official start is at Tok, at Mile 1314 (2114.5 km) Alaska Highway, where the Glenn branches south and west toward Anchorage, 328 miles (528 km) away. The first 125 miles (201 km) of the Glenn is widely known as the **Tok Cutoff**—a shortcut between the Alaska Highway and the Richardson Highway. In fact, it may come as a surprise to many Alaskans that this section actually is a part of the Glenn.

After leaving Tok, don't expect to find much development or services along this subtly beautiful stretch of road. An exception is the area of the **Eagle Trail State Recreation Site**, about 16 miles (26 km) from Tok, which offers a campground with picnic shelter, water, toilets, and trailhead access. A handful of B&Bs, lodges, and gas stations are tucked into the woods, so watch for their signs. This may seem like a lonely stretch of highway, but you're not alone.

The road crosses **Mentasta Summit** (2,434 feet/742 m) about 45 miles (72 km) from Tok. From here, most of the Tok Cutoff follows the boundary of **Wrangell–St. Elias**

Index Lake in the Talkeetna Mountains lies about halfway between Glennallen and Anchorage on the Glenn Highway.

National Park and Preserve. These northern lowlands of the park are inhabited by caribou, moose, black and brown bears, coyotes, and numerous other creatures.

The Cutoff connects with the Richardson Highway near the village of **Gulkana**, about 15 miles (24 km) north of Glennallen. The most-traveled portion of the Glenn begins at Glennallen, 139 miles (224 km) from Tok at the busy junction of the east-west Glenn Highway and the north-south Richardson Highway. For decades, a gas station on this corner has called itself, in large letters, "The Hub of Alaska." It's an active intersection with more than just fuel and snacks for travelers on either road. A spacious visitor center at this intersection is staffed with informative people, along with the usual brochures and newsletters. For more information about local history, businesses, and attractions, call 907-822-5555 or see *www.traveltoalaska.com.*

Glennallen is the unofficial capital of this region, situated on the western edge of Wrangell–St. Elias Park and 189 miles (304 km) from Anchorage. As a highway junction city, this town caters to travelers. You'll find campgrounds, restaurants, lodges, and visitor attractions. This region is the traditional homeland of the Athabascan Indians, who have lived in the Copper River Basin for centuries. When a U.S. military party of explorers came through here in 1885, they were amazed at the accuracy of the hand-drawn maps they received from Natives who assisted them. (Glennallen is named for two of those explorers: Capt. Edwin F. Glenn and Lt. Henry T. Allen.)

Athabascans continue to fish and hunt for food (as do many people of other ethnic backgrounds who have arrived during the past century). Some people trap for furs; others work at local businesses. Sales of locally made craft items such as birch-bark baskets and beaded combs, slippers, and earrings help support a small cottage industry. Watch for parking-lot craft fairs, where you can learn more about local culture as well as pick up some wonderful gifts.

The Copper River Basin is especially popular for winter recreation, such as snowmobiling,

Identifying themselves only as the Mendeltna Snowman, Smitty, and Jesse, this trio of Alaskans was working on a cabin when we met them along the Glenn. Smitty had declared, "This is the only way to build a cabin!" To which the Snowman said, "Or you could go to Spenard Builders Supply and get a kit with numbers on the logs . . . " The response: "Yeah. There's that."

skiing, and snowshoeing. Flightseeing, mountaineering, hiking, biking, fishing, and rafting are favorite summertime activities. Numerous creeks and lakes are suitable for a fine day of fishing. For fishing regulations and openers, check with the Alaska Department of Fish and Game office in Glennallen, downtown at Mile 186 (299 km) Glenn Highway. Call 907-822-3309. Licenses are available at most retail outlets.

From Glennallen, the westward way begins flat and fairly straight, while to the east, the peaks of the Wrangell Mountains are standouts on clear days. On either side of the road, you'll see occasional boggy lowlands and sad, spindly-looking spruce trees that tell a story about survival against the odds. These "used pipe cleaners" are black spruce trees, tenaciously growing in poorly drained soil where permafrost is present. Their root systems are so shallow that they sometimes tip over into each other, hence the name **Drunken Forest**. Because of the seasonal freeze and thaw of permafrost, this road can be wavy or sunken in places. Watch for flagged signs that warn "Dip in Road." They really mean it.

The state maintains recreation sites with camping, water, and toilets in the stretch between Glennallen and Palmer. They include Little Nelchina, at Mile 137.5 (221 km); Matanuska Glacier, at Mile 101 (162.5 km); Long Lake, at Mile 85 (137 km); and King Mountain, at Mile 76 (122 km). All distances are from Anchorage.

The land changes as you travel west through dry, treeless uplands and farther still into dazzling mountainous beauty. The road bends, rises, and falls as you follow the **Matanuska River Valley**, which flows between rocky mountains that turn purple in a certain light. This silty, braided river is a head-turner. You'll see it from various angles and elevations along the way, and its beauty is enhanced by the changes in light and weather.

Views of the **Matanuska Glacier** only get better and better. Stop at the marked waysides that offer photo opportunities, or you'll always regret that you didn't. In broad daylight, the glacier is brilliant white with hints of blue, but overcast days are best, when the blue of the glacier seems to glow from within. The **Matanuska River**, which flows from beneath the glacier, is a milky gray color due to the ground "rock flour" that is suspended in its water. Float trips or whitewater adventures can be arranged at sites along the highway (watch for signs) or in Palmer, 42 miles (67.5 km) north of Anchorage.

About 74 miles from Anchorage, watch for a distinctive rock formation called Lion Head that looks like it's blocking the road. This striking feature is a mini-mountain shaped by the Matanuska Glacier as it retreated from the area.

Between Glennallen and Palmer, you can stop at remote, family-operated roadhouses and restaurants, such as Sheep Mountain Lodge (Mile 113 from Anchorage) or Long Rifle Lodge (Mile 102) to bring even more color to your trip. Hicks Creek Roadhouse (Mile 96) offers food, camping, cabins, and trail rides. Their portable sign along the road reads, "Stop and Eat or We'll Both Starve." A classic old log place, King Mountain Lodge (Mile 76), boasts of a resident ghost.

As you approach Palmer from the east, you'll see signs and a right turnoff at Mile 50 (80.5 km) for the **Musk Ox Farm**, a don't-miss attraction. A herd of musk oxen here is the core of a small industry that centers on the gathering, spinning, and knitting of the animals' underwool, called qiviut (KIV-ee-oot). The gift shop features the handiwork of Native women who knit the garments in their home villages and mail them to this cooperative headquarters. Tours introduce you to these unique animals and the wonderfully warm garments made from their qiviut. For information, call 907-745-4151 or see 907-745-4151.

Palmer is 42 miles (67.5 km) northeast of Anchorage, or 147 miles (236.5 km) west of Glennallen. During the Great Depression of the 1930s, the federal government offered Midwest farmers the opportunity to move to this valley for a fresh start in a new land, in a program known as the **Matanuska-Susitna Colony Project.** Whole families arrived to find that their free land first needed clearing of trees and rocks, and many spent their first cruel winter in a canvas tent with wood floors and a hungry woodstove. Through their hard work and perseverance, the community took root and thrived.

The colony project was the settlement seed for what is now the community of Palmer, with a population of just over 4,500. Many descendants of those settlers still live in the Matanuska-Susitna (or Mat-Su) Valley. As you drive along the Glenn Highway, you'll see farmhouses and barns built in a style reminiscent of the Midwest. Wheat, hay, potatoes, lettuce, tomatoes, carrots, cabbages—the land keeps providing, and the abundance of grain and produce continues to support valley farmers.

Palmer is the seat of the **Alaska State Fair,** where the stiffest agricultural competition is seen in the giant-vegetables category. Under a blessed 22 hours of

Over the Top on Hatcher Pass Road

If you're interested in the area's gold-mining history, turn north off the Glenn Highway at Mile 49.5 (79.6 km) onto Hatcher Pass Road (also known as Fishhook–Willow Road). This is a gorgeous drive where in places you follow the course of a boulder-strewn, fast-moving stream. Watch for pullouts to let faster drivers pass by, or stop for a picnic and stick your toes in these chilly waters. At Mile 14, the Motherload Lodge offers rooms, dining, and a saloon. Call 907-745-6171 or see www.motherlodelodge.com.

Independence Mine Historical Park is just over 31 miles (50 km) up the road, at Hatcher Pass (elevation 3,886 feet). Getting there is slow driving for big-rig RVs at times, since it is paved for only the first 14 miles leading to the mine, and the last 10 miles beyond it, to where it connects with the Parks Highway. The rest is gravel and dirt—with potholes and washboard that slows you down in a hurry. Walking trails lead throughout this extensive mine site, which includes buildings under restoration. Borrow a gold pan from the visitor center and try your hand at panning the stream. Nearby, overnight accommodations and meals are available at Hatcher Pass Lodge. Call 907-745-5897 or visit the lodge's Web site at www.hatcherpasslodge.com. ◾

summer sunlight, Palmer farmers grow cabbages that balloon to between 40 and 60 pounds. Squash, carrots, and other vegetables thrive in the cool soil and long doses of sunlight. If you're in Alaska in late August and early September, stop by the Palmer fairgrounds to see the giants for yourself, and enjoy the midway rides, food booths, and equestrian competitions. Although it's an Alaska state fair, it feels as cozy as a Kansas county fair, until you lift your eyes and take in the peaks of the Chugach Range, which seems to be just a field away.

Streams and lakes in this valley yield world-class fishing in picturesque settings. Anglers routinely land prized king salmon weighing an average of 20 to 30 pounds, but these fish can reach 70 pounds. Other salmon runs include reds, chums, pinks, and silvers. Trout, Dolly Varden, northern pike, arctic grayling, and other species also are found in local waters. Pick up your required license at any number of retail outlets, from grocery stores to sporting goods stores.

In Palmer, turn east off the Glenn Highway and drive four blocks to the railroad tracks. Near the old railroad depot, you'll see the Palmer Visitor Center, a log building where a history of the colony can be found in photos and artifacts, and a gift shop is stocked with Alaska souvenirs. Ask about a walking tour of Palmer's historic buildings. Call 907-745-2880.

Next door to the visitor center is the **Matanuska Valley Agricultural Showcase,** where local gardeners have done a magnificent job of showing what happens when skilled hands sow seed under the midnight sun. Walk around the garden paths for a peaceful break from traveling.

Just a few miles south of Palmer, the Glenn Highway is joined by the Parks Highway from Fairbanks. The Glenn is in excellent shape from here all the way to Anchorage, with four lanes of traffic and a legal speed of 65 mph. The lay of the land changes as you follow the Glenn around this side of the Chugach Range. The divided highway passes through a broad expanse of wild grasses dotted with tall trees that look like they died a long time ago—which they did. This is the **Palmer**

The Matanuska River is fed by glacial runoff from a massive glacier of the same name.

Hay Flats State Game Refuge, which supports a diversity of wildlife, from big game to eagles to waterfowl and more. This entire region dropped several feet during the 1964 Good Friday Earthquake that damaged so much of the Anchorage coastline. Seawater flooded in, killing mature trees and creating wetlands where once there had been hayfields.

Up ahead, two four-lane bridges cross the **Knik** (kuh-NIK) **River,** a popular staging area for local duck hunters. Because Cook Inlet experiences such extreme tides (up to 30 feet), the tidal zone of the Knik River likewise fluctuates dramatically.

Twenty-six miles (42 km) from Anchorage, an exit leads to **Eklutna Historical Park,** which includes a historic Russian Orthodox church and nearby graveyard. Developed by the Athabascan residents of Eklutna village, population 45, this park offers tours and cultural interpretation. The tradition of placing brightly colored "houses" over the graves is neither completely Orthodox nor completely Athabascan. As in other areas of the state, western religions have been integrated into the Native culture, and some practices reflect a unique third culture. Although the residents of Eklutna live close to Alaska's biggest city, many continue in a largely subsistence-based life, hunting and fishing for much of their diet. Grocery stores supply the rest.

Inside the city limits of Anchorage, the Glenn Highway peters out, unmarked, somewhere along the small-plane airport called Merrill Field. Stay on the same road and it becomes 5th Avenue, which leads you into the downtown core.

Anchorage

Born of necessity, as many Alaska towns were, Anchorage was once a tent city along the muddy banks of Ship Creek. The people who gathered here in 1915 were builders of the Alaska Railroad, their families, hoteliers, restaurateurs, laundry operators, freight haulers, and others who supplied services.

When conditions at the tent city became dangerously overcrowded, threatening disease, Alaska Railroad officials took charge and cleared building lots on the bluff overlooking the creek. In July 1915, town-site lots were auctioned off, and building began immediately. Today, few original homes or businesses exist, mainly because they were wooden and therefore fairly expendable as the town matured. Notable survivors include two side-by-side buildings on the 5th Avenue and E Street corner of Town Square.

Anchorage is Alaska's biggest city, with 274,000 people, almost half of the state's population. It is an international crossroads in passenger and air cargo, as well as headquarters for the biggest names in the oil industry. This modern community is bordered on the north by military installations, on the east by the **Chugach Range,** on the south by **Chugach National Forest,** and on the west by **Cook Inlet.** Options for city sprawl are limited. Its proximity to wilderness means that moose often wander into the streets, making the "Anchorage bowl" a unique urban habitat. Car-moose encounters are causing city officials to ponder the question of what to do as moose numbers continue to multiply.

The Log Cabin Visitor Information Center on the corner of 4th Avenue and F Street is operated by the Anchorage Convention and Visitor Bureau. Staffers can answer questions and direct you to a self-guided historical walking tour throughout downtown. Call 907-276-4118 or see *www.anchorage.net.*

In summer, Anchorage is a tourism hub. Its downtown streets are filled with color and the contagious enthusiasm of people on vacation. Gift shops, restaurants, street vendors, and musicians lend a partylike atmosphere to every summer day. Dining experiences can range from a stop at a fast-food outlet, hot dog stand, grocery-store deli, or burger joint, to elegant dining above Cook Inlet.

As Alaska's biggest city and hub of two major highways, this is an ideal spot to consider renting an RV if you didn't arrive in one. You may contact any number of local businesses for daily or weekly rentals (check the local phone listings). If you are traveling in your own RV, this is a good place to take care of any mechanical or windshield repairs or have your oil changed.

Walking 4th and 5th Avenues on foot, you can stop in and book a glacier day cruise on Prince William Sound or on Resurrection Bay, south of Anchorage. Tour operators usually offer shuttle transportation to harbor cities. Down the street, you can book a flightseeing trip to fly over Mount McKinley and even land on a glacier to walk a bit. Large coaches provide day trips around town, north to the Matanuska-Susitna Valley, south to Portage Glacier, and beyond. Many adventure travelers book fly-in fishing or visits to remote, luxury lodges, such as those operated by celebrity chef Kirsten Dixon. See more at www.withinthewild.com.

If shopping for Alaska Native-made art is part of your plan—or a pure impulse—learn to read labels. A label with a silver hand indicates a guarantee that the item was made by a Native Alaskan artisan. A label with a mom-and-baby-bear silhouette is an official "Made in Alaska" indicator, but the maker may be an Alaskan company or a state resident, not necessarily a Native Alaskan.

Soak up local color as you stroll around downtown. Especially popular is 4th Avenue, where in summer every lamppost bears two huge flower baskets of lobelia and marigold, representing Alaska's state colors, blue and gold. In Anchorage's mild temperatures and prolonged light, the flowers are extraordinarily bright and fresh, here and in gardens throughout the city. Due to the low angle of the sun, there is no heat of midday to wilt them. A few years ago, the mayor of Anchorage instituted a program to recognize the exceptional gardening all over town by designating Anchorage the City of Flowers. If you can't get your fill of flowers, visit the Alaska Botanical Garden for a self-guided tour through their spectacular gardens. Call 907-770-3692 for more information.

All winter long, as dusk comes earlier and daybreak comes later, the seasonal theme is Anchorage, City of Lights. Millions of tiny white lights decorate trees, homes, and businesses, further illuminating the snow and creating a true winter wonderland.

Follow the crowds to the outdoor markets in Anchorage. These mini-fairs include entertainment, food booths, crafts, and sales of Mat-Su Valley vegetables. Each

Wednesday through the summer, you'll find an open-air market at the Northway Mall. Get more details at 907-272-5364. On Saturdays, you'll find markets in downtown Anchorage (907-272-5634) and in the *Anchorage Daily News* parking lot (907-745-6656).

Other attractions of the Anchorage area include:

Anchorage Fur Rendezvous. This is the country's biggest winter carnival, celebrated in Anchorage at the end of February. Events include snowshoe softball, the Outhouse Classic (the race entries are outhouses equipped with skis), and a waiter/waitress competition in which contestants run an obstacle course while carrying a tray of drinks. Craft fairs, a fur auction, carnival rides, snow sculpture competitions, and an Eskimo blanket toss are other highlights. The World Championship Sled Dog Races are another main Rondy event, with dogs and drivers lining up to start the race on 4th Avenue.

Iditarod Trail Sled Dog Race. For more than a quarter century, Anchorage has been the official starting line for the men, women, and dogs of the 1,000-mile Iditarod Trail Sled Dog Race. Thousands of people jam the sidewalks of 4th Avenue and connecting streets as these champion athletes—human and canine—leave the chute for the trail that leads to Nome. The Iditarod (eye-DIT-uh-rod) begins on the first Saturday of March. The Iditarod headquarters and museum is in Wasilla, north of Anchorage off the Parks Highway. Call 907-376-5155 or visit their Web site at *www.iditarod.com*.

Alaska Railroad. Daily north-south rail service between Anchorage, Denali National Park and Preserve, and Fairbanks is available through the Alaska Railroad or through tourism companies that operate specialty railcars on the train. Southbound passengers between Anchorage and Seward can do the same: book a seat with the Alaska Railroad or travel in a luxury railcar operated by a tour operator. The luxury railcars offer a great way to take in the scenery, enjoy bar service and an excellent meal, and stretch your legs regularly while crossing the state in style. Contact the Alaska Railroad at 907-265-2494 or *www.alaskarailroad.com*. For special railcar travel information, call Gray Line of Alaska at 907-277-5581, browse *www.graylineofalaska.com*, or contact Princess Tours Rail Operations at 1-800-PRINCESS.

Chugach State Park. Serving as a spectacular backdrop for Alaska's biggest city, the Chugach (CHOO-gatch) Range lies along the eastern edge of Anchorage. Here too is Chugach State Park, nearly a half-million acres, an extremely popular getaway for hikers, bikers, picnickers, or those who simply want to drive uphill and get a great view of the city and the twin bodies of water around it, Knik Arm and Turnagain Arm.

A hike up the sawed-off mountain known as Flattop is invigorating, yet suitable for families. Groomed trails lead the way from the Glenn Alps parking area. On clear days, you can see Mount McKinley from here. Park headquarters is in the Potter Section House, just south of Anchorage on the Seward Highway, but the park is accessible from Anchorage's Hillside area as well as from Eagle River. For directions and information, call park headquarters at 907-345-5014. See *www.anchorage.net/hike* for details on other hikes.

Alaska Native Heritage Center. One of Anchorage's most popular attractions focuses on the wonders and diversity of Alaska's Native cultures. Located near the

The view from the Glenn Alps affords a sweeping panorama of Anchorage and the distinctive Mount Susitna, known locally as "The Sleeping Lady."

Anchorage's Town Square Park is a popular gathering place for downtown business people and shoppers as well as visitors.

intersection of the Glenn Highway and Muldoon Road, the Heritage Center features art, music, photography, and a variety of exhibits. The spacious Welcome House at the center offers programs of dancing and singing in the theater, photography and artifact exhibits, and a chance to watch an artist at work. From there, paths lead to five village settings that show traditional home-building methods and tools. Interpreters from each culture are on site too. Call 1-800-315-6608 or 907-330-8000.

Anchorage Museum of History and Art. The museum, at 121 West 7th Avenue, is an architectural beauty that shows Alaska art treasures as well as visiting exhibits. The Alaska Gallery includes exquisite displays from Alaska's Native, Russian, and U.S. history. Other features include a children's gallery, gift shop, café, and special theater programs that entertain visitors year-round. For more information, call 907-343-4326.

Other popular museums include the Alaska Aviation Museum, near the airport (907-248-5325), the Alaska State Trooper Museum (907-279-5050), and the Anchorage Fire Department Museum (907-267-4936). Each one offers rare insight into Alaska's early days.

Town Square Park. An army of gardeners takes exquisite care of this floral showcase. Split by curving paths, with a simple fountain at the center, Town Square Park is frequented by business people, travelers, walkers, and people-watchers. In places, inscribed sidewalk bricks pay homage to people and businesses that have helped make Anchorage great. The adjoining Alaska Center for the Performing Arts is a venue for national and international talent, further evidence that Anchorage has come a long way since its days as a tent city.

Lodging

If you're interested in bed-and-breakfast accommodations in Anchorage, call the Anchorage Alaska Bed & Breakfast Association at 1-888-584-5147 or 907-272-5909, or browse the Web site at www.anchorage-bnb.com.

The Mat-Su Bed and Breakfast Association has information on rooms, apartments, and cabins from Glennallen to Anchorage to Denali. Visit the association's Web site at www.alaskabnbhosts.com.

Anchorage:
Alaska's Tudor Motel
4423 Lake Otis Parkway
1-800-550-2234 or 907-561-2234
Kitchenettes, one-bedroom apartments, cable TV. Close to self-service laundry. Senior discounts.

Anchorage Grand Hotel
505 West 2nd Avenue
1-888-800-0640 or 907-929-8888
www.anchoragegrandhotel.com
31 luxury suites, kitchen, cable TV, high-speed Internet, free continental breakfast. Downtown location.

Anchorage Mariott Downtown
820 West 7th Avenue
1-800-228-9290 or 907-279-8000
392 rooms in full-service hotel. Pool, exercise facility.

Aspen Hotel
108 East 8th Avenue
1-888-506-7848 or 907-868-1605
www.aspenhotelsak.com
Rooms with fridges, microwaves, coffeemakers. Pool, spa, and exercise room. Free airport and train shuttle. Downtown location.

Captain Cook Hotel
4th Avenue and K Street
1-800-483-1950 or 907-276-6000
www.captaincook.com
Rooms and suites, plus health club, travel
agency, gift stores, café, lounge.
Penthouse-level restaurant with view.
Central downtown location.

Clarion Suites
325 West 8th Avenue
1-888-389-6575 or 907-274-1000
Suites with fridges, microwaves, phones,
two TVs. Free continental breakfast.
Pool, spa. Free 24-hour airport and
train shuttle.

Coast International Inn
3333 West International Airport Road
1-800-544-0986 or 907-243-2233
www.coasthotels.com
141 rooms with coffeemakers, hair dryers.
Sauna, fitness center, restaurant,
lounge. Free airport shuttle.

Comfort Inn
111 West Ship Creek
1-800-228-5150 or 907-277-6887
100 rooms and suites, free continental
breakfast. Indoor pool, spa. Along Ship
Creek, downtown. Airport shuttle.

Courtyard by Marriott
4901 Spenard Road
1-800-729-0197 or 907-245-0322
Rooms, pool, restaurant, lounge.

Creekwood Inn
2150 Gambell
1-800-478-6008 or 907-258-6006
www.hillside-alaska.com
Rooms with private bath, kitchenettes.
Coffee, cable TV, data ports, bicycle
rentals.

Dimond Center Hotel
700 East Dimond Boulevard
866-770-5002 or 907-770-5000
www.dimondcenterhotel.com
Boutique hotel next to major shopping
mall. Free breakfast, free shuttle.

Fairfield Inns & Suites
5060 A Street
1-800-228-2800 or 907-249-2503
www.marriott.com/fairfieldinn
Spacious units in full-service facility.
Midtown location.

Hampton Inn
4301 Credit Union Drive
1-800-HAMPTON or 907-550-7000
www.hamptoninn.com
Rooms with deluxe breakfast.
Indoor pool, fitness facility.
Midtown location. Free shuttle.

Hilton Anchorage
500 West 3rd Avenue
1-800-245-2527 or 907-272-7411
Deluxe accommodations, fitness room,
gift shops, three restaurants. Walking
distance to downtown attractions.

Hilton Garden Inn
100 West Tudor Road
1-800-HILTONS or 907-729-7000
Rooms include free high-speed Internet
access. Pool, fitness facility. Free shuttle.

Historic Anchorage Hotel
330 E Street
1-800-544-0988 or 907-272-4553
www.historicanchoragehotel.com
Boutique hotel in central downtown
location. Free breakfast, newspaper,
high-speed Internet. On National
Register of Historic Places.

Holiday Inn Downtown
239 West 4th Avenue
1-800-545-7665 or 907-793-5500
250 rooms, restaurant, pool, in downtown
location. Walking distance to shopping,
dining, attractions.

Holiday Inn Express
4411 Spenard Road
907-248-8848
Rooms with pool, spa, fitness facility,
free continental breakfast, shuttle.
Near airport.

Homewood Suites by Hilton
140 West Tudor Road
1-800-225-5466 or 907-762-7000
Studios, 1- and 2-bedroom suites.

Inlet Tower Hotel & Suites
1200 L Street
1-800-544-0786 or 907-276-0110
www.inlettower.com
Boutique hotels offers free parking, free
airport shuttle. Restaurant on premises.

Lake Hood Inn
4702 Spenard Road
907-258-9321
Rooms with private decks overlooking
floatplane lake. Near airport. Free
continental breakfast, airport shuttle.

Long House Alaskan Hotel
4335 Wisconsin Street
1-888-243-2133 or 907-243-6060
54 rooms, free continental breakfast.
Close to airport; shuttle service.

Microtel Inn & Suites
5205 Northwood Drive
1-888-771-7171 or 907-245-5002
Rooms, suites, free continental breakfast,
laundry facility. Close to airport;
shuttle service.

Millennium Alaskan Hotel
4800 Spenard Road
1-800-544-0553 or 907-243-2300
248 deluxe guest rooms, some lakeside
rooms with views of floatplanes. Wildlife
displays, historical photos decorate
lobby. Gift shop, restaurant, lounge.

Motel 6
5000 A Street
1-800-4MOTEL6 or 907-249-2503
Newer hotel in midtown location.

Ramada Inn Anchorage Downtown
115 East 3rd Avenue
866-726-2327 or 907-272-7561
www.ramada.com
Full-service hotel with business center.
Downtown location.

Ramada Limited
207 Muldoon Road
907-929-7000
Rooms and suites, free breakfast buffet,
coffee. Cable TV, data ports, voice mail.
Restaurant, lounge. Shuttle to downtown or airport.

Sheraton Anchorage Hotel
401 East 6th Avenue
1-800-478-8700 or 907-276-8700
Well-appointed rooms and suites, cable TV,
room and laundry service, fitness room.
Gift store, lounge, penthouse restaurant
with view.

Super 8 Motel of Anchorage
3501 Minnesota Drive
1-800-800-8000 or 907-276-8884
Rooms with cable TV, 24-hour shuttle.

Glennallen:
Brown Bear Rhodehouse
Mile 183.5 Glenn Highway
907-822-3663
Motel, cabins, campsites. Restaurant,
lounge. Grizzly bear photo display.

Caribou Hotel
Mile 187 Glenn Highway
907-822-3302
Rooms, suites, kitchenettes, wheelchair
access. Satellite TV, whirlpool. Caribou
Café family restaurant, gift shop, fuel,
propane, tires.

The Sports Page
Mile 187 Glenn Highway
907-822-5833
Cabin rentals, tent camping, 22 RV spaces
with full hookups, laundry, showers.
Restaurant, sporting goods, clothing.

Palmer:
Colony Inn
325 Elmwood Street
907-745-3330
Located in historic Teachers' Dorm from
the Mat-Su Colony.

Gold Miner's Hotel
918 South Colony Way
1-800-7ALASKA or 907-745-6160
Large rooms, restaurant, lounge.
Downtown location.

Pioneer Motel
124 West Arctic Avenue
907-745-3425
28 units with cable TV. Daily or
weekly rentals.

Valley Hotel
606 South Alaska Street
1-800-478-7666 or 907-745-3330
Rooms with private bath, cable TV. 24-hour
coffee shop. Lounge, liquor store.

Tok:
See listings in the section on Tok in
Chapter 6, "The Alaska Highway."

Campgrounds
Anchorage:
Anchorage RV Park
1200 North Muldoon Road
1-800-400-7275 or 907-338-7275
196 sites with full hookups, pull-throughs.
Showers, laundry, water, dump station.
Quiet wooded setting just outside city.

Creekwood Inn
2150 Gambell Street
1-800-478-6008 or 907-258-6006
www.hillside-alaska.com
RV hookups, cabin rentals with fridges,
coffeemakers, hair dryers, cable TV.
Walking distance to restaurants,
shopping.

Golden Nugget Camper Park
4100 Debarr Road
1-800-449-2012 or 907-333-2012
Full and partial RV hookups.

John's Motel & RV Park
3543 Mountain View Drive
1-800-478-4332
www.johnsmotel.com
Full hookups, rooms, cabins, cable TV.
Close to downtown.

Glennallen:
Brown Bear Rhodehouse
Mile 183.5 Glenn Highway
907-822-3663
Camping, cabins, motel with restaurant,
lounge. Display of grizzly bear photo
collection.

Northern Lights Campground & RV Park
Mile 189 Glenn Highway
907-822-3199
Campsites with partial hookups, pull-throughs, tent sites. Rest rooms, hot
showers, phone, wooded setting, close
to visitor center and shopping.

The Sports Page
Mile 187 Glenn Highway
907-822-5833
22 RV spaces with full hookups, cabin
rentals, tent camping, laundry, showers.
Restaurant, sporting goods, clothing.

Tolsona Wilderness Campground
Mile 173 Glenn Highway
907-822-3865
80 campsites with full or partial hookups,
tenting, creekside location. Showers,
laundry, dump station, Internet
access, store.

Palmer:
Fox Run RV Park & Campground
Mile 36 Glenn Highway, on Matanuska Lake
1-877-745-6120 or 907-745-6120
www.foxrun.freeservers.com
Full hookups, rest rooms, showers, tables,
playground, e-mail access. Tenting
area, boat rental, tackle.

The Homestead RV Park
5 miles south of Palmer on Glenn Highway
1-800-478-3570 or 907-745-6005
Campsites with a view. Partial hookups,
tent sites, dump station, showers,
laundry, walking trails.

Mountain View RV Park
Off Old Glenn Highway on Smith Road
1-800-264-4582 or 907-745-5747
83 sites with full hookups, most pull-
throughs, laundry, rest rooms, pay
phone.

Town & Country RV Park
Mile 39.5 Glenn Highway
907-746-6642
Full hookups, pull-throughs, laundry,
showers, dump station. Close to golf,
stocked lakes, fairgrounds.

Tok:
*See listings in the section on Tok in
Chapter 6, "The Alaska Highway."*

Restaurants
Anchorage:
Alaska Salmon Chowder House
443 West 4th Avenue
907-278-6901
Casual dining featuring crab, halibut,
salmon.

Arctic Roadrunner
5300 Old Seward Highway
907-561-4016
Burgers, fries, shakes.

Club Paris
417 West 5th Avenue
907-277-6332
Popular downtown steakhouse since 1957.

Corsair Restaurant
944 West 5th Avenue
907-278-4502
Fine dining, Alaska seafood specialties.

Country Kitchen
346 East 5th Avenue
907-677-2122
Family restaurant in downtown core.

Crow's Nest
939 West 5th Avenue, in Hotel Captain Cook
907-276-6000
Fine dining with panoramic views from
atop hotel.

Dianne's Restaurant
550 West 7th Avenue, in Atwood Building
907-279-7243
Soups, salads, sandwiches, lunch specials.

Downtown Deli & Café
525 West 4th Avenue
907-276-7116
From sourdough pancakes to reindeer stew,
and more.

Fancy Moose
4800 Spenard Road, in Millennium Alaskan
Hotel
907-243-2300
Light meals, sandwiches; overlooking floatplane lake.

Glacier Brewhouse
Corner of 5th Avenue and H Street
907-274-BREW
www.glacierbrewhouse.com
Brew pub featuring wood-grilled seafood,
pizzas, grilled meats.

Gwennie's Old Alaska Restaurant
4333 Spenard Road
907-243-2909
Alaska decor, Alaska-size meals.

Hogg Brothers Café
1049 West Northern Lights Boulevard
907-276-9649
Inventive breakfasts, "hogg-size" meals.

Humpy's Great Alaskan Alehouse
610 West 6th Avenue
907-276-2337
43 brews on tap, live music nightly.
Downtown.

Jens' Restaurant
701 West 36th Avenue
907-561-5367
Fine dining, featuring pepper steak,
seafood, lamb, veal.

Josephine's
401 East 6th Avenue,
    in Sheraton Anchorage
907-343-3160
Fine dining on the 15th floor. Dinner and
    Sunday brunch, excellent views.

Kincaid Grill
6700 Jewel Lake Road
907-243-0507
www.kincaidgrill.com
Fine dining specializing in seafood,
    quality meats.

La Mex
900 West 6th Avenue
907-274-7511
Mexican, barbecue, prime rib, seafood.

Lucky Wishbone
1033 East 5th Avenue
907-272-3454
A local favorite for chicken and burgers.

Marx Brothers Café
627 West 3 rd Avenue
907-278-2133
www.marxcafe.com
Fine dining, award-winning wines,
    memorable desserts.

Moose's Tooth Pub & Pizzaria
3300 Old Seward Highway
907-258-2537
Ales, sodas, gourmet, hand-tossed pizzas.

ORSO
737 West 5th Avenue
907-222-3232
www.orsoalaska.com
Alaska seafood, wood-grilled meats, pasta,
    desserts, cocktails.

Phyllis's Café and Salmon Bake
Corner of 5th Avenue and D Street
907-274-6576
Specializing in seafood. Downtown location.

Ptarmigan Bar and Grill
401 East 6th Avenue,
    in Sheraton Anchorage Hotel
907-276-8700
Alaska cuisine, casual dining.

Simon & Seafort's Saloon & Grill
420 L Street
907-274-3502
Seafood, prime rib, desserts; great view of
    Cook Inlet.

**Snow Goose Restaurant
    & Sleeping Lady Brewing Co.**
3401 Denali Street
907-277-7727
www.alaskabeers.com
Brew, burgers, pizza, views, live music.

Sourdough Mining Company
5200 Juneau Street
907-563-2272
Seafood, ribs, sourdough bread. Family
    dining. Free evening show.

Villa Nova
5121 Arctic Boulevard
907-561-1660
Fine Italian dining.

Glennallen:
Brown Bear Rhodehouse
Mile 183.5 Glenn Highway
907-822-FOOD
Steaks, broasted chicken, seafood, pizza.

Caribou Café Family Restaurant
Downtown Glennallen
907-822-3656
Open daily; homemade soups, pies,
    baked goods.

Park's Place
Mile 187.5 Glenn Highway
9097-822-3334
Hot foods, espresso, sandwiches.

Palmer:
Colony Kitchen
Mile 40.5 Glenn Highway
Across from fairgrounds
907-746-4600
Breakfast all day; steaks, burgers, salad, pie.

Gold Miner's Restaurant
918 South Colony Way, in Gold Miner's Hotel
1-800-7ALASKA or 907-745-6160
Steaks, seafood, burgers, sandwiches,
   salad bar.

The Inn Café
326 Elmwood Avenue
907-746-6118
Fine dining in historic Colony Inn.

Open Café
606 South Alaska Street, in Valley Hotel
907-745-3330
Gourmet pizza, full menu, take-out
available. Open 24 hours.

Palmer Bar
828 S. Colony Way, downtown
907-745-3041
Bar food and special grill-your-own-steak
   nights.

Slack's Sugar Shack Bakery
340 West Evergreen Avenue
907-745-4777
Breads, pastries, cookies, donuts.

Vagabond Blues
Downtown Palmer
907-745-2233
Homemade soups, wraps, quiche, pastries.
Coffee and live music.

Tok:
*See listings in the section on Tok in
Chapter 6, "The Alaska Highway."*

HAINES HIGHWAY

Haines Junction, Yukon, to Haines, Alaska: 152 miles (245 km)
Travel Opportunities: *Chilkat Bald Eagle Preserve;
Tlingit culture; Fort Seward.*

Haines is an all-Alaska town, but it's disconnected from the rest of the state highway system by miles and miles of water on one side, and miles and miles of Canada on the other. Alaskans on the highway system literally have to leave the country for the roundabout drive to this Alaska town. And international cooperation makes it possible. Built in 1943, just after principal construction of the Alaska Highway, this single spur road crosses land belonging to a state and two provinces.

The paved 152-mile Haines Highway is a southbound road off the Alaska Highway at Haines Junction (985 miles, or 1,585 km, north of Dawson Creek). The highway cuts through the Canadian and Alaska wilderness as Yukon Route 3, B.C. Route 4, and Alaska Route 7. It borders sparkling lakes and rivers, and crosses mountain passes, portions of a historic trade route used by First Nations people for centuries.

Haines also is accessible via the Alaska Marine Highway System, which connects the town of 2,800 people with other Southeast and Southcentral Alaska coastal communities by ferry. Some travelers choose the mostly water route to get to Alaska, boarding their vehicles onto the ferry system at Bellingham, Washington, the southernmost port, and disembarking at Haines, thus skipping the 1,000 miles or more of driving through Canada. (See Chapter 9, "Alaska Marine Highway System.") You can also book a day trip to Skagway on Chilkat Cruises' MV *Fairweather Express*, which operates daily in summers. Call 907-766-2100.

Set beneath an alpine range that includes impressive peaks such as 3,610-foot **Mount Rapinsky** and 1,760-foot **Mount Riley**, Haines was settled in the early 1900s and incorporated in 1910. Presbyterian missionaries arrived, hoping to convert, serve, and educate the Native population. Like other towns on the route to the goldfields, Haines grew wild in the atmosphere of greed and hurry.

Evidence of Alaska's first permanent military post is still present at **Fort Seward**, which has long since been decommissioned. Still, its clean-cut parade grounds are encircled by former officer's quarters, now private homes and businesses.

Long before the arrival of any military or gold miners, this beautiful coastal region supported people for thousands of years. Nearly all of today's Southeast Alaska was traditional land for the **Tlingit Indian people**. In the Haines area, local tribes include the **Chilkat** and **Chilkoot**, which may be best known for intricately woven blankets and raven's tail robes, as well as carvings in totems and masks.

Salmon and the small, greasy fish known as hooligan have traditionally been important to the Native diet, as have goat, sheep, and deer, which are hunted for meat and hide. And centuries-old stories are still passed from one generation to the next. In Haines, you can be part of the hearing. A workshop in the old hospital of Fort Seward is home to the **Alaska Indian Arts** carvers and weavers. Drop by to watch them at work, and visit their Web site at *www.alaskaindianarts.com*. You're also invited to watch dance demonstrations, or enjoy the salmon dinner held on Wednesday and Thursday nights at the **Totem Village Tribal House** on the Fort Seward parade grounds. For reservations, call 907-766-2000.

The **Sheldon Museum and Cultural Center**, on Main Street near Beach Road, exhibits typical offices and living quarters from early day Haines. You can also learn there about the valley's natural history, the Tlingit people and their traditions, the founding of Fort Seward, and the influences of early missionaries and gold miners. Call 907-766-2366.

Just outside town, at the **Southeast Alaska Fairgrounds**, visit the set used in the filming of the Disney movie *White Fang*, based on the Jack London novel. Many locals were enlisted for the production. These days, shops, a restaurant, and a micro-brewery have taken up residence.

Along the Haines Highway, the 48,000-acre **Chilkat Bald Eagle Preserve** attracts thousands of visitors each year who arrive in late fall to observe the great numbers of eagles. Their rendezvous is determined by the salmon—a late-season run of chum makes the Chilkat River one of the last places where the eagles can easily feed before the water freezes. So they congregate here—sometimes 3,500 and more—and roost in the cottonwood trees along the riverbank. The birds engage in unique social behavior, fighting for a single scrap of fish when thousands more fish are within reach.

Depending on when you visit the preserve, the highest concentration of eagles usually is found between 18 and 22 miles (29–35.5 km) northwest of Haines on the Haines Highway. Make sure your camera batteries don't fail you now. Don't expect to see large groups of eagles in spring or summer, but you should see some individuals or pairs because the preserve is the year-round home to several hundred birds. Learn all about the birds, their behavior, and their favorite habitat at the American Bald Eagle Foundation interpretive center in Haines at 2nd Avenue and the Haines Highway. Knowledgeable staffers can answer your questions, and they offer videos, books, and other printed materials. Call 907-766-3094 or see *www.baldeagles.org*.

If you've come to fish, you'll find plenty in these rich waters. Book a charter for halibut or salmon fishing. Lakes and streams also support hooligan, trout, and Dolly Varden. Keep your license current, and check in with the Alaska Department of Fish and Game for regulations at 907-766-2625. Other recreation includes flightseeing, biking, rafting, canoeing, and hiking. There are several tour operators and guiding businesses in town. Contact the Haines Chamber of Commerce at 907-766-2202 or see *www.haineschamber.org*.

A must-stop is the visitor center at 2nd Avenue and Willard Street. Call the Haines Convention & Visitors Bureau at 1-800-458-3579 or 907-766-2234, or visit their Web site at *www.visithaines.com*.

Lodging

Bear Creek Cabins
1.5 Mile Small Tracts Road
907-766-2259
Cabins for the family; bunks for solo travelers. Kitchen and bath facilities. Camping, laundry.

Cabin Fever
8 Mile Mud Bay Road
907-766-2390
Cabins on the beach. Private baths, kitchenettes.

Captain's Choice Motel
108 2nd Avenue North
907-766-3111
39 rooms with view of Lynn Canal. Room service, tour booking, car rentals. Walking distance to restaurants. Shuttle service.

Eagle's Nest Motel
Mile 1 Haines Highway
907-766-2891
13 rooms, kitchenettes. Tours, car rentals, courtesy van.

Fort Seward Condos
On historic fort grounds
907-766-2425
1- and 2-bedroom suites with kitchens, two-night minimum. Historic building with view of Lynn Canal.

Fort Seward Lodge
On historic fort grounds
1-800-478-7772 or 907-766-2009
10 rooms with private or shared bath, ocean-view kitchenettes. Restaurant, lounge. Courtesy van.

Hotel Halsingland
On Fort Seward grounds
1-800-478-5556 or 907-766-2000
www.hotelhalsingland.com
60 rooms, private bath, cable TV, phones, car rental. Seafood restaurant, lounge. Historic building with canal views.

Mountain View Motel
2nd Avenue and Mud Bay Road, near Fort Seward grounds
1-800-478-2902 or 907-766-2900
9 rooms, kitchenettes, views. Walking distance to restaurants.

Thunderbird Motel
2nd Avenue and Dalton Street
1-800-327-2556 or 907-766-2131
www.thunderbird-motel.com
20 rooms, kitchenettes. Walking distance to
restaurants, shops.

Campgrounds
Haines:
Haines Hitch-up RV Park
Haines Highway and Main Street
907-766-2882
www.hitchuprv.com
92 sites with full and partial hookups, dry
camping. Wireless Internet, laundry,
gift shop.Tour tickets available.

Oceanside RV Park
Front and Main Streets
907-766-2437
Full hookups overlooking Lynn Canal.
Walking distance to showers, shopping,
laundry, dining.

Port Chilkoot Camper Park
Next to Fort Seward
1-800-542-6363 or 907-766-2000
Full and partial hookups, showers,
laundry, dump station. Close to town.

Salmon Run RV Campground
Almost 2 miles (3 km) north of ferry
on Lutak Road
907-766-3240 or 907-723-4229
Forested campsites with fire rings, tables,
showers, trails, boat launch. Inlet
and mountain views.

Northeast of Haines:
Swan's Rest RV Park
On Mosquito Lake Road,
off Mile 27 Haines Highway
907-767-5662
12 sites with full hookups, cabin
available. Borders the Bald Eagle
Preserve. Showers, laundry, rest
rooms, fishing and boat rental.

Chilkat Charlie's RV & Tent Park
Mile 33 Haines Highway
907-767-5510
8 sites with full and partial hookups, some
pull-throughs, dry camping, showers.
Next to 33 Mile Roadhouse.

*The state maintains three campgrounds
near Haines, offered on a first-come,
first-served basis:*

Portage Cove State Recreation Site
About 1 mile (1.6 km) south of Haines on
Beach Road
Tent camping for backpackers and
bicyclists, no overnight parking.
Water pump, tables, fire rings, toilets.

Chilkat State Park
8 miles (13 km) south of Haines on Mud Bay
Road
32 pull-through sites, 3 beachfront tent
sites. Water, toilets, fishing, boat
launch, hiking, log cabin interpretive
center.

Chilkoot Lake State Recreation Area
10 miles (16 km) north of Haines,
off Lutak Road
32 spaces, lake views, water, toilets,
fishing, boat launch, log cabin
interpretive center.

Restaurants
Bamboo Room Restaurant
2nd Avenue and Dalton Street
907-766-2800
Breakfast, lunch, dinner; espresso,
halibut fish and chips. Seniors'
and children's menus. Sports bar.

Chilkat Restaurant & Bakery
5th Avenue and Dalton Street
907-766-2920
Breakfast, lunch, dinner; pastries.

Fort Seward Restaurant & Saloon
Mile 0 Haines Highway
1-800-478-7772 or 907-766-2009
Three meals a day. Prime rib, crab, steaks,
salad bar.

Haines Salmon Bake
Parade grounds, next to Tribal House
907-766-2000
Salmon bake on Wednesday and
 Thursday evenings in summer. Call
 for reservations.

Hotel Halsingland Restaurant
On Fort Seward grounds
907-766-2000
Seafood and other Alaska specialties;
 historic building.

Klondike Restaurant
Dalton City
On the grounds of Southeast Alaska State Fair
907-766-2477
Open summers only.

33 Mile Roadhouse
Mile 33 Haines Highway
907-767-5510
Breakfast, lunch, dinner.

*K*LONDIKE HIGHWAY 2

From Alaska Highway to Skagway: 99 miles (159 km)
Travel Opportunities: *White Pass & Yukon Route railway; Skagway;*
Gold Rush Cemetery; Slide Cemetery; Arctic Brotherhood Hall;
Dyea and trailhead to Chilkoot Pass.

Klondike Highway 2 is a fairly new road (built in 1978) that covers very old ground. This route over White Pass is an ancient one used by the coastal Tlingit who traveled to trade with inland tribes. During the 1898 Klondike Gold Rush, White Pass and nearby Chilkoot Pass were the two major overland routes to the goldfields.

Klondike Highway 2 heads south to Skagway from the Alaska Highway at Mile 874 (1,407 km), about a dozen miles south of Whitehorse. The high-elevation lakes and rocky cliffs along this highway rank it among the most impressive topographically. At White Pass, the wind is fast and chilly, even in the middle of summer.

You will cross from the Yukon into Alaska at the international border about 7 miles (11 km) before you reach Skagway, so be prepared for U.S. Customs and Immigration. Remember to turn your watch back an hour—you'll be in the Alaska Time Zone.

A historical photo depicts the summit of the White Pass during the Gold Rush of 1898. Stampeders were not allowed to cross without a year's worth of supplies.

Skagway

Skagway is one of two Alaska communities on the northern end of the Inside Passage that are served by the Alaska Marine Highway System. Haines is the other. It's possible to board your vehicle in Bellingham, Washington, and take the ferry all the way along the protected waters of Southeast Alaska, then rejoin the road system at Haines or Skagway. (See Chapter 9, "Alaska Marine Highway System.")

Walking through Skagway is like stepping into a colorized postcard from 1898, when businesses like these also lined the streets and served the gold seekers who were headed to Dyea and over Chilkoot Pass. This northernmost town on the Inside Passage was the gateway to the Klondike, and in the two years between 1897 and 1899, the primary reason to be here was to get rich quick—by either mining the ground or mining the pockets of the miners. Skagway boomed into a city of 20,000 in a few months' time.

The Chilkoot Trail was a steep and treacherous route over Chilkoot Pass to the goldfields. Photos often depict a dark line of men (and a few women) hiking an arm's length from each other as they climbed the snowy steps to the pass. Today the 33-mile (53 km) route remains a challenge, even to hikers dressed in the latest outdoor gear. If you're planning to try the Chilkoot, check first with the **Klondike Gold Rush National Historical Park** visitor center at 2nd and Broadway in Skagway. The center is housed in the restored White Pass & Yukon Route railway depot. Ask about guided tours of the historic downtown, or programs in the auditorium. Call 907-983-2921.

The **White Pass & Yukon Route** narrow-gauge (36-inch) railway offers trips in railcars pulled by a steam locomotive, letting full- and half-day-trippers retrace the

steps of gold-rush stampeders. Call 1-800-343-7373 or 907-983-2217 to arrange a ride.

The **Arctic Brotherhood Hall** on Broadway between 2nd and 3rd, its false front decorated with 10,000 pieces of driftwood, looks the same today as it did a century ago. The Visitor Center is inside. 1-888-786-1898 or 907-983-2854, or browse *www.skagway.org*.

The **Skagway Museum and Archives**, loaded with Gold Rush artifacts, records, and photos, can

Having scaled the Chilkoot Pass, these hikers were ready to celebrate in Skagway. (Note the duct tape on the right man's boots!)

Many thousands of pieces of driftwood adorn the exterior of the Arctic Brotherhood Hall, a Skagway original still standing from the Gold Rush.

be found at 7th Avenue and Spring Street. The collection also includes personal artifacts from the late 1800s, donated by local people since 1961. Call 907-983-2420.

The saloons, restaurants, gift shops, and soda fountains of Skagway are all wrapped in historical storefronts. A horse-and-buggy tour operator is dressed in the garb of old. The storefront windows along Main Street are trimmed with the hats, gloves, and doodads that would have pleased your grandma. The big difference between then and now, besides the plumbing and telephone lines, lies in the harbor: Enormous cruise ships bring their passengers to Skagway to soak up a little atmosphere of the Days of '98.

A century ago, outlaw **Soapy Smith** reigned here, along with his gang of con artists and thugs who took advantage of the weak, the innocent, and even the dead. One story tells of the terrible avalanche that killed dozens of men on the Chilkoot Trail. Soapy set up a "morgue" near the site, and he and his men dug up bodies, took them into his morgue, and stripped them of their valuables before the real authorities arrived. His reign ended when he was confronted by a man named **Frank Reid**, who shot Soapy several times and was mortally wounded himself.

The graves of both men, in the **Gold Rush Cemetery**, are visited by thousands of people every year. To get to the cemetery, go north on State Street, then follow the signs. Reid's grave bears these words: "He gave his life for the honor of Skagway." Every July 4, the city remembers those days with an event called Soapy Smith's Wake. Another cemetery holds the remains of victims from that Chilkoot avalanche.

You can drive to what used to be Dyea, a town of thousands, where nothing but a derelict dock remains. From the parking area, you can walk to the Chilkoot Pass trailhead.

Lodging

Chilkoot Trail Outpost
Dyea Valley
907-983-3799
www.chilkoottrailoutpost.com
Modern luxury log cabins nestled in
the woods, free breakfast.

Gold Rush Lodge
6th Avenue and Alaska Street
907-983-2831
www.goldrushlodge.com
Smoke-free rooms, private bathrooms.
Cable TV and Showtime. Free
continental breakfast. Walking
distance to downtown Skagway
historic district, courtesy van.

Sgt. Preston's Lodge
6th Avenue and State Street
907-983-2521
30 rooms on street level. Cable TV
and phones. Courtesy van. Close
to bank and post office.

Skagway Bungalows
Near town
907-983-3986
Log cabins furnished with microwaves,
fridges, king- or queen-sized beds.

Skagway Inn
7th Avenue and Broadway Street
1-800-752-4929 or 907-983-2289
12 rooms in historic district.
Breakfast, van service. Reservations
for White Pass & Yukon Route,
shows, tours.

Westmark Inn Skagway
3rd Avenue and Spring Street
1-800-544-0970 or 907-983-6000
www.westmarkhotels.com
195 deluxe rooms, nonsmoking
available. Cable TV, dining room,
lounge. Close to shopping and
entertainment.

The White House
8th and Main Streets, near downtown
907-983-9000
www.atthewhitehouse.com
Rooms with private baths in 1902 family-
run inn. Complimentary breakfast.

Campgrounds

Garden City RV Park
State Street between 15th and 17th Avenues
907-983-2378
Level sites with full and partial hookups,
pull-throughs. Laundry, rest rooms,
coin-operated showers.

Pullen Creek RV Park
2nd Avenue near Alaska State Ferry dock
1-800-936-3731
Partial hookups. Showers, dump station.
Walking distance to shopping and
attractions.

Skagway Mountain View RV Park
12th Avenue and Broadway Street
1-888-778-7700
Wooded sites with partial hookups,
pull-throughs, cable TV access. Picnic
tables, firewood. Showers, laundry,
rest rooms, dump station. RV wash
facilities. Tour reservations. Near
downtown historic district.

Restaurants

Alaska Garden Gourmet
7th and Broadway, in Skagway Inn
907-983-2289
Dinners, box lunches, tours of working
kitchen garden, seafood cooking
demonstration.

Alaska Gourmet Express
5th Avenue between Broadway and State
907-983-2448
Home-cooking from local seafood
and produce.

Bonanza Bar & Grill
On Broadway, between 3rd and 4th Avenues
907-983-6214
Seafood, pizza, drink specials,
entertainment.

The Corner Café
4th Avenue and State Street
907-983-2155
Three meals a day, specializing in pizza.
Free delivery.

Haven Café Espresso & Light Fare
9th Avenue and State Street
907-983-353
Breakfast, soups, sandwiches, salads,
desserts, espresso.

Ofelia's Restaurant
4th Avenue, behind the hardware store
907-983-3325
Chinese and American, seafood, crab,
halibut. Breakfast, lunch, dinner.

The Red Onion Saloon
2nd Avenue & Broadway Street
907-983-2222
Food and libations in 1898 saloon,
entertainment.

Skagway's Pizza Station
444 4th Avenue
907-983-2200
Dine in or take out. Delivery.

Sweet Tooth Café
315 Broadway Street
907-983-2405
Breakfast, lunch, dinner. H
omemade donuts, soups, bread,
fries. Takeout available.

Parks Highway

Anchorage to Fairbanks: 358 miles (576 km)
Travel Opportunities: Iditarod Trail Sled Dog Race Headquarters, Wasilla;
Independence Mine; Talkeetna; Denali State Park; Denali National Park
and Preserve; Fairbanks.

The (George) Parks Highway connects the state's largest and second-largest cities, Anchorage and Fairbanks, in a 358-mile south-to-north trek from the Southcentral coast into Alaska's great Interior. It is among the newest of the highways (completed in 1972) and sees heavy summer use, often by motorists on their way to Denali National Park and Preserve.

To reach the Parks Highway from Anchorage, take the Glenn Highway north for 35 miles (56 km). At a major interchange near Wasilla, the Glenn continues east, while the northbound Parks is marked with clear roadside signs directing drivers to Fairbanks and Denali Park. Even though this place is the official start of the Parks Highway, roadside mileposts will reflect total mileage from Anchorage. (For details on Anchorage-area attractions, lodging, campgrounds, and restaurants, see the section on the Glenn Highway, in this chapter.)

Just north of the Glenn Highway and Parks Highway junction is **Wasilla**. Once a sleepy little stop along a two-lane road, Wasilla has experienced a population boom in the past two decades, and the two-lane Parks Highway widens into four lanes as it passes through town. Wasilla is a good last-chance, full-service shopping stop before you begin your lengthy road trip north. Although many small, family-operated stores and service stations lie ahead, Wasilla offers a variety of goods, services, fast-food restaurants, grocery stores, and so forth. Almost the entire shopping district lies at roadside.

To learn more about local history, visit the **Dorothy Page Museum & Historical Townsite**, 323 Main Street, in Wasilla. Exhibits focus on the development of the Iditarod Trail Sled Dog Race, area homesteading, and settlement in the Mat-Su Valley. Admission is charged. For information, call 907-373-9071. Visit the Farmers Market there on Wednesday afternoons.

At the Knik-Goose Bay Road traffic light in Wasilla, you can turn west and follow the road for a little more than 2 miles (3 km) to the impressive log building that is **Iditarod Trail Sled Dog Race Headquarters**. Inside are the administrative offices of the famous 1,000-mile race across Alaska, as well as a free museum, video theater, and gift shop. Admission is free. A mount of a champion sled dog named Andy is on display here, too. A leader for five-time Iditarod champion Rick Swenson, Andy is a testimonial to the athletic ability of Alaska sled dogs. For a nominal fee, you can take a dogsled ride in summer with a member of the Redington family, descendents of "Father of the Iditarod," Joe Redington Sr. The teams pull wheeled carts instead of sleds. At a replica of a checkpoint cabin, learn more about this phenomenal race. Call 907-376-5155 or visit the Iditarod Web site at *www.iditarod.com*.

Transportation buffs will enjoy a visit to a museum north of Wasilla off the Parks Highway at Mile 47 (75.6 km). Follow the signs for another mile to the **Museum of Alaska Transportation & Industry**. Here you'll see early day snowmobiles, vehicles, airplanes, trains, and more. Call 907-376-1211.

As you drive the Parks Highway, you'll occasionally pass through little enclaves where people choose to live far away from big cities. **Willow** is such a town. It has its own post office, library, convenience store, gas station, café, lodge, and dozens of little homes sprinkled throughout the surrounding forests and around lakes. Roadside fishing opportunities exist all along this stretch of the Parks Highway. Even if you don't fish, it's fun to pull over and watch the anglers.

A popular attraction for campers and fishers is **Nancy Lake State Recreation Area**, at Mile 66.5 (107 km) Parks Highway, developed with 30 campsites, water, toilets, a trail, and a boat launch. Just past Willow at Mile 71 (114.5 km) is the westbound turn for Willow Creek State Recreation Area, located at the end of the **Willow Creek Parkway**, about 5 miles (8 km) from the highway. The area is nicely developed with RV parking, water, outhouses, tent camping, trails, and river access.

Just north past the entrance to Willow Creek Parkway is the eastbound turnoff for Hatcher Pass Road and access to **Independence Mine**. (See details in the section on the Glenn Highway, in this chapter.)

Take a side trip to **Talkeetna** for a taste of old Alaska. Almost 99 miles (159 km) north of Anchorage, make the right turn onto a spur road that leads to Talkeetna. This is an excellent drive along a paved 14-mile (22.5-km) road that dead-ends in a historic gold-mining town. On clear days, views of Mount McKinley practically fill up the windshield. And at certain times of the year, Talkeetna is overrun with mountain

On clear days, North America's tallest mountain, Mount McKinley—or Denali, as it's also known—
is visible from a paved pullout at Mile 135 on the Parks Highway.

climbers who have journeyed here from all over the world. Local Bush pilots fly the climbers and their gear to the base camp of Mount McKinley for ascents up North America's tallest peak.

Park on Main Street and poke around Talkeetna on foot. A car only gets in the way. At one end of the street, you'll find tent camping or RV sites for dry camping. Outhouses are nearby. Several of Talkeetna's buildings are on the National Register of Historic Places. Although it's small, the town features museums, two roadhouses, a modern National Park Service ranger station, a post office, motels, a country store, and several gift shops.

Each summer, Talkeetna hosts the Mountain Mama Contest, where women can prove their mettle by chopping wood and hauling water while packing a baby doll in a carrier on their backs. The town also hosts the infamous Moose Dropping Festival on the second weekend of July. Come for the parade, the food, the entertainment, and games with moose droppings. (Yes, droppings, as in scat.)

Here you can arrange a jet-boating adventure, a flightseeing trip, a float trip, a day or more on the water fishing for big salmon. In Talkeetna, you'll find a number of outfitters, some of them with storefronts along Main Street. Ask for directions at the visitor information cabin by the sign that says "Welcome to Beautiful Downtown Talkeetna."

On clear days, a crowd gathers at the Mile 135 (217 km) wayside on the Parks Highway. From here, you'll gain an incredible view of 20,320-foot **Mount McKinley** and the lesser surrounding mountains, which would receive more notice were they not flanking McKinley. Neighboring peaks include Mount Foraker, rising to 13,395 feet (4,082 m); Mount Hunter, at 14,580 feet (4,444 m); and Mount Silverthrone, at 13,220 feet (4,029 m); plus three others with summits that exceed 12,000 feet (3,658 m). Portable toilets and litter barrels, plus interpretive signs and the chance to see The High One, make this a popular stop along the Parks.

The boundary of **Denali State Park** lies about 132 miles (212 km) north of Anchorage. This park straddles the highway and offers 325,460 acres filled with recreational opportunities: fishing, hiking, biking, camping, canoeing, floating. Three state-operated campgrounds are in the park: Byers Lake, Lower Troublesome Creek, and Denali View North. Thirty-seven miles (59 km) of developed trails thread above and below tree line in a panoramic landscape. For more information, call the Alaska Division of Parks and Outdoor Recreation in Wasilla at 907-745-3975, or visit the Web site at *www.dnr.state.ak.us/parks/index.htm.*

A popular landmark at Mile 188.5 (303 km) is a private business that has long been a curiosity as well as a milepost: a three-story igloo. The giant geodesic structure originally was built as a hotel but never served that purpose. Ask about its history when you stop at **Igloo City Resort** for gas or gifts. The igloo marks roughly the halfway point between Anchorage and Fairbanks.

At Mile 210 (338 km), near Cantwell, an eastbound turnoff leads to the Denali Highway, which connects the Parks Highway with the Richardson Highway. (See the section on the Denali Highway, in this chapter.)

The crown jewel of North America, Mount McKinley rises within the 6-million-acre **Denali National Park and Preserve**. And while views of The Mountain tease motorists during their northbound drive, the park entrance doesn't arrive until Mile 237 Parks Highway (381 km), about 4.5 hours north of Anchorage.

An extended visit to Denali National Park takes some advance planning, because reservations are necessary for campsites, for hotel rooms, and for seats on the shuttle buses that travel on the only road that penetrates the park. You can easily drop in and check out the visitor center, walk around the local trails, enjoy a picnic, and take off. But overnight stays are more complicated. The nationwide reservation phone number is 1-800-622-7275; in Anchorage, call 907-272-7275.

Most visitors to the park stay in hotels along the Parks Highway just a few miles farther north, where development of restaurants, gas stations, hotels, gift shops, and tour operators has clustered in what is known as **McKinley Village**, outside the park's boundaries. In the park, a modern visitor center serves as the operation center as people come and go on hikes, catch rides to sled-dog demonstrations, head out on guided nature walks, or leave for the bus ride to the end of the 87-mile (140-km) park road. Private vehicles are not allowed beyond Mile 30 (48 km) on that road, so if you want the best chance to see wildlife, you have to take the shuttle bus. Wildlife-watching (and mountain-watching) remain the top draw. Chances are you might see a bear, caribou, moose, ptarmigan, fox, Dall sheep, or snowshoe hare.

The **Alaska Railroad** depot lies within the park, too, and shuttle buses transport passengers to their waiting hotels. The place is abuzz with activity—and the scenery, close and far away, is awesome. Out on the Parks Highway, the Nenana River races below the road's edge. Look for whitewater rafters down there any time of day. Overhead, small airplanes and helicopters engage in viewing Denali from the top down.

About a half hour farther north on the Parks Highway, the coal-mining town of Healy lies in the northern foothills of the Alaska Range. This is the next place along the road to find a meal, accommodations, and fuel. A small community, Healy is growing as more visitors to Denali National Park want to leave the crowds behind when they find a hotel room.

From here, the Parks Highway continues north through the boreal forests of Alaska's Interior. Set between the Alaska Range and the Brooks Range, this vast region charts the coldest colds and the hottest hots in the state. From Healy to Nenana, you'll find occasional services, gift shops, and gas stations, but little other development.

The section of the Parks between Nenana and Fairbanks wends through the Tanana uplands, round-topped tall hills (they would be called mountains elsewhere) that border the Tanana Valley. As you cross these hills, passing lanes are available for faster traffic. Be sure to stay to the right if your vehicle pulls hills slowly. Every few miles, pullouts offer clear views, from the top down, of the braided Tanana River and its tributaries. Local forests are mostly spruce and birch and aspen.

About 5 miles (8 km) before entering Fairbanks on the Parks Highway, you'll note signs that lead west to **Ester Gold Camp**. Ester was once a vibrant gold-mining community; today it's a historic site where a handful of people live. But every evening in the summer, Ester Gold Camp is filled with more visitors than residents. After a buffet dinner of Alaska specialties at the camp, the old Malemute Saloon fires up with melodrama, readings of Robert Service poetry, music, and other live entertainment. The floor is sawdust, and the peanut shells can fall where they may. A hotel and RV parking are available on the grounds, too. Call 1-800-676-6925 or 907-479-2500, or visit *www.akvisit.com.*

For information on Fairbanks history, attractions, events, lodging, campgrounds, and restaurants, see the section on Fairbanks in Chapter 6, "The Alaska Highway."

The famed 1,049-mile sled dog race is headquartered near Wasilla, off the Parks Highway.

Lodging

The Mat-Su Bed & Breakfast Association has information on rooms, apartments, and cabins from Glennallen to Anchorage to Denali. Visit the association's Web site at www.alaskabnbhosts.com.

Denali Park:
Denali Backcountry Lodge
Kantishna
1-800-841-0692 or 907-783-1342
www.denalilodge.com
30 units, dining, cocktails. Inside the park. Private wildlife-viewing bus. Train shuttle service.

Denali Bluffs Hotel
Mile 238.5 Parks Highway
866-683-8500 or 907-683-8500
www.denalialaska.com
112 rooms with views, private baths, coffee service, fridges, phone. Restaurant, tour desk, gift shop. Shuttle service.

Denali Cabins
Mile 229 Parks Highway
1-800-450-2489 or 907-683-2642
43 cedar cabins with private bath. Hot tubs, dining. South of park entrance, train shuttle service.

Denali Crow's Nest Log Cabins
Mile 238.5 Parks Highway
1-888-917-8130 or 907-683-2723
www.denalicrowsnest.com
39 units with view. Hot tub, restaurant, lounge. Train/airport shuttle service.

Denali Grizzly Bear Cabins and Campground
Mile 231 Parks Highway
907-683-2696
21 kitchenette units, laundry. Pets allowed.

Bush pilots out of Talkeetna land on Ruth Glacier daily, allowing visitors to step out of the plane and onto a glacier.

The Alaska Railroad wends through the Alaska Range, traveling daily in summers between Anchorage and Fairbanks.

Denali Lodging
Mile 238 Parks Highway
1-866-683-8500 or 907-683-8500
www.denalialaska.com
Fine accommodations and views at
Grande Denali Lodge.

Denali Park Hotel
Mile 247 Parks Highway
1-866-683-1800 or 907-683-1800
www.denaliparkhotel.com
King or two full beds. Satellite TV,
phone. Located in Healy.

Denali Perch Resort
Mile 224 Parks Highway
1-800-322-2523 or 907-683-2523
www.denaliperchresort.com
Cabins with free breakfast. Mountain views;
restaurant features Alaskan specialties.

Denali Princess Wilderness Lodge
Mile 238.5 Parks Highway
1-800-426-0500 or 907-683-2800
www.princesslodges.com
280-unit deluxe hotel overlooking
Nenana River with mountain views.
TV, phones, hot tubs, tour desk,
theater. Restaurants, lounges. Train
shuttle service.

Denali River Cabins
Mile 231 Parks Highway
1-800-230-PARK or 907-683-2500
www.denalirivercabins.com
Newer cabins at Denali Park
river boundary.

Denali Sourdough Cabins
1 mile from Denali Park entrance
1-800-544-0970 or 907-683-1500
www.westmarkhotels.com
Comfortable, well-appointed cabins,
close to park entrance.

McKinley Chalet Resort
Mile 238 Parks Highway
1-800-276-7234 or 907-279-2653
www.denalinationalpark.com
345 units, restaurant, cocktails.
Train shuttle service.

McKinley Creekside Cabins
Mile 224 Parks Highway
907-683-2277
www.mckinleycabins.com
Lodge, cabins, café near the Park.

McKinley Village Lodge
Mile 231 Parks Highway
1-800-276-7234 or 907-276-7234
www.denalinationalpark.com
150 units, dining, cocktails.
Overlooks Nenana River. Train
shuttle service.

Mount McKinley Princess Wilderness Lodge
Mile 133 Parks Highway,
in Denali State Park on Chulitna River
1-800-426-0500
www.princesslodges.com
Luxury accommodations with views of the
mountain. TV, phones, hot tub, tour
desk, theater, gift shop. Restaurants,
lounges. Shuttle service.

Fairbanks:
See listings in the section on Fairbanks
in Chapter 6, "The Alaska Highway."

Healy:
Denali North Star Inn
Mile 249 Parks Highway
907-488-1505
100 rooms, plus gift shop, salon services,
sauna, exercise room, tour desk,
lounge. Train shuttle service.

Denali Suites
15 minutes north of Park entrance
on Healy Spur Road
907-683-2848
www.denalisuites.com
Units include 2- or 3-bedroom suites,
kitchens, TV, VCR, private bath,
laundry facility.

Motel Nord Haven
15 minutes north of Park entrance on
Parks Highway
1-800-683-4501
www.motelnordhaven.com
28 rooms with queen beds, RVs,
phones, private baths.

Park's Edge
Off Mile 247 Parks Highway
on Hilltop Road
907-683-4343
www.parks-edge.com
Log cabins in quiet, convenient location.

Totem Inn
Mile 249 Parks Highway
1-800-478-2384 or 907-683-2420
50 units, plus laundry, dining, cocktails.
Train shuttle service.

Wasilla:
Alaskan View Motel
2650 East Parks Highway
907-376-6787
26 rooms, Alaska decor in log building.
Cable TV, mountain and inlet views.

Lake Lucille Inn
1300 West Lake Lucille Drive
907-373-1776
54 deluxe rooms, suites. Athletic facility,
whirlpool, gift shop. Floatplane and
boat docks, boat rentals.

Mat-Su Resort
1850 Bogard Road
907-376-3228
Deluxe rooms, cabins with view, cable TV,
refrigerators. Restaurant, lounge.
Floatplane dock, paddleboats.

The Windbreak
Mile 40.5 Parks Highway
907-376-4209
Rooms, plus café serving breakfast, lunch,
dinner.

Campgrounds
Denali Park:
**Denali Grizzly Bear Cabins
and Campground**
Mile 231 Parks Highway
907-683-2696
40 RV sites with full hookups and pull-
throughs, tent sites. Showers, laundry,
water, dump station.

Denali RV Park and Motel
Mile 245 Parks Highway
1-800-478-1501 or 907-683-1500
90 RV sites with hookups and pull-
throughs, cable TV. Showers, water,
dump station.

Denali Rainbow Village RV Park
1 mile north of Denali Park entrance
907-683-7777
www.denalirvrvpark.com
77 sites with full or partial hookups,
satellite TV, close to park and activities.

McKinley RV and Campground
Mile 248.5 Parks Highway
1-800-478-2562 or 907-683-2379
77 RV sites with full hookups and
pull-throughs, tent sites.
Fireplace/grills. Showers, water,
dump station.

Ester:
Ester Gold Camp
3660 Main Street
1-800-676-6925 or 907-479-2500
www.akvisit.com
16 RV sites, 3 tent sites, showers,
dump station.

Fairbanks:
See listings in the section on Fairbanks
in Chapter 6, "The Alaska Highway."

Wasilla:
Best View RV Park
Mile 35.5 Parks Highway
1-800-478-6600 or 907-745-7400
64 sites with full hookups, pull-
throughs, tenting area. Mountain
views. Free showers; laundry,
dump station.

Big Bear RV Park
Mile 37 Parks Highway
907-373-4049
Campsites with pull-throughs available.

Iceworm RV Park
Mile 50 Parks Highway
1-888-484-9088 or 907-892-8200
www.icewormrvp.com
Sites with full hookups, some pull-throughs,
   tent sites, showers, laundry, propane,
   dump station.

Lake Lucille Park
Operated by Matanuska-Susitna Borough
Follow signs from 2.5 Mile Knik-Goose
   Bay Road
64 sites in treed area, covered picnic
   area, firewood, rest rooms. Walking
   distance to lake and fishing.
   On-site host.

Restaurants

Denali Park:
*Also check the Denali Park lodging
listings, above, for hotels with
restaurants and lounges.*

Alaska Cabin Nite Dinner Theater
Mile 238 Parks Highway
1-800-276-7234 or 907-276-7734
Dinner and a popular show.

Alpenglow Restaurant
Mile 238 Parks Highway
907-683-8720
www.denalialaska.com
Fine dining, views, shows
   every evening.

Denali Perch Resort
Mile 224 Parks Highway
1-800-322-2523 or 907-683-2523
Breakfast, lunch, and dinner featuring
   steak, seafood, Alaska specialties.
   Outdoor seating available.

Ester:
Ester Gold Camp
3660 Main Street
1-800-676-6925 or 907-479-2500
Dinner buffet and entrees featuring
   Alaska specialties.

Fairbanks:
*See listings in the section on Fairbanks
in Chapter 6, "The Alaska Highway."*

Wasilla:
Great Bear Brewing Co.
238 North Boundary Street
907-373-4782
www.greatbearbrewing.com
Brews, sandwiches, soups, salads.

Mat-Su Resort
1850 Bogard Road
907-376-3228
Restaurant, lounge open daily for lunch
   and dinner; weekend breakfasts.

The Windbreak
Mile 40 Parks Highway,
   in Windbreak Hotel
907-376-4484
Breakfast, lunch, dinner.

The Worthington Glacier is accessible for those who wish to hike alongside its path. A visitor information wayside instructs readers about glaciers and local history.

RICHARDSON HIGHWAY

Valdez to Fairbanks: 364 miles (585 km)
Travel Opportunities: Valdez; glacier cruises, pipeline terminus on Prince William Sound; Thompson Pass; Worthington Glacier; pipeline pump stations; Delta Junction; North Pole; Fairbanks.

The original name for this historic route was the Valdez to Fairbanks Trail. Work on the road began in 1903, after the Tanana Valley gold strike near Fairbanks. In 1904 the government pushed development along by requiring every man along the road to work two days per year on the project or pay a tax of $8.

You are forgiven if you pronounce **Valdez** as val-DEZ, because everywhere else in the world, that's how you'd say it. But in Alaska, a mispronunciation has stuck and it's called val-DEEZ. The massive 1964 earthquake virtually destroyed the original townsite, and the current location was chosen when the townspeople rebuilt. This is an ice-free, deepwater port on an arm of Prince William Sound in an area that's also known as Alaska's "Little Switzerland," as it is surrounded by the Chugach Mountains, the tallest coastal range in North America. Here, too, is the terminus of the 800-mile trans-Alaska pipeline. From town, you can see the terminal and massive tanker ships.

With a population of about 4,100, Valdez lies along the Alaska Marine Highway System, with the ferry terminal located near Hazelet Avenue and Fidalgo Drive. For outdoor adventures, arrange for a fishing charter, rent a kayak, book a glacier-viewing cruise, go whale-watching, or sign up for whitewater rafting. There's hiking, tours of the salmon hatchery, gold-panning, or taking in all that the Museum has to offer. Begin at the Valdez Convention & Visitors Bureau at 200 Fairbanks Street. Phone 907-835-4636 or browse their Web site at *www.valdezalaska.org*.

This little city gets more snow than anywhere else in Alaska. In the winter of 1999–2000, some 380 inches of snow fell on the town. A paralyzing 596.9 inches fell in the winter of 1994–1995. That's almost 50 feet of snow—enough to bury a house, or at least cave in its roof during many months when there is rare chance of any snow melting. Snow, and what to do with it, is the reason Valdez is laid out as it is. Side streets end in cul-de-sacs with rights-of-way for snowplows to push snow out of the streets and into a dump area behind the homes. Note that most roofs are metal, and angled so that snow slides off into yards, not onto walkways or driveways.

The **Valdez Museum**, at 217 Egan Drive, features rotating exhibits as well as displays and photos on town history, the gold rush, cultural history, and the *Exxon Valdez* oil spill that tainted Prince William Sound in 1989. Call 907-835-2764. A host of restaurants and gift shops and a couple of grocery stores are easy to find on the simple street grid of Valdez.

Each year Valdez hosts the **Prince William Sound Community College/Edward Albee Theater Conference**, which attracts top writers and actors, and continues to gain in national prominence.

Traveling north from Valdez on the Richardson Highway, you'll encounter awe-inspiring canyons and waterfalls, and the looming **Worthington Glacier**, named a National Natural Landmark. A wayside at Thompson Pass, elevation 2,678 feet (816 m), provides information about the nearby glacier. The route to the Pass remains daunting, even in modern vehicles, but a century ago and more, the trail included numerous switchbacks to make it easier for the horse-drawn double-ender sleighs that traveled in winter and the wagons that crossed the pass in summer.

Record snowfall on the pass in the winter of 1952–1953 measured 974.5 inches. And yet Thompson Pass is not the highest on the Richardson Highway. That honor goes to Isabel Pass, at 3,000 feet. It was named for the wife of Fairbanks founder E. T. Barnette, who traveled with his wife, Isabelle (yes, it's spelled differently than the pass), over this route several times, summer and winter.

Eighty-three miles (134 km) north of Valdez, the Edgerton Highway splits off to the east, leading to Chitina. From Chitina, the McCarthy Road continues to the town of McCarthy, and access to the former mining town of Kennicott. (See the section on the Edgerton Highway, in this chapter.)

Watch for views of the trans-Alaska pipeline along the Richardson Highway, and pullouts for pump stations with signs that explain the operation of these sites.

Plan to stop farther north, about 106 miles (170 km) north of Valdez, where the staff at Wrangell–St. Elias Visitor Center can answer questions, direct you to nearby campgrounds and attractions, and name the mountains you've been admiring. Informational displays, rest rooms, and a gift shop can be found here, too.

Some 115 miles (185 km) from Valdez, Glennallen marks the junction of the Richardson and Glenn Highways. (See the section on the Glenn Highway, in this chapter.) For 14 miles, the Richardson and Glenn Highways now share the same route—until Mile 129 (207.6 km) on the Richardson, at Gakona Junction, where the Glenn veers northeast toward Tok, a road section referred to as the Tok Cutoff.

From Gulkana to Paxson, you'll be driving on the Richardson toward the Alaska Range and great picture-taking possibilities. The Gulkana River near Sourdough, Mile 147.5 (237 km), is popular with anglers, canoeists, and river rafters. Gulkana River paddlers usually put in at Paxson, almost 30 road-miles ahead, and then float the 50 river-miles down to Sourdough Creek for takeout. Managed by the Bureau of Land Management, the Gulkana was designated a Wild and Scenic River in 1980. A BLM campground at Sourdough Creek offers 60 campsites near the boat launch.

Farther north at **Paxson** is the turn onto the Denali Highway, which travels west to meet the Parks Highway near Denali National Park. Here in the foothills of the Alaska Range, the views are broad and mountainous, and plenty of camping opportunities exist, either in developed campgrounds or simply along a broad road wayside, where it is permissible to dry camp overnight. Paxson is home to 43 people. Services include lodging, meals, fuel, and fishing guides.

At **Delta Junction**—266 miles (428 km) north of Valdez and 98 miles (158 km) south of Fairbanks—the Alaska Highway joins the Richardson Highway. The two highways share the ride for the rest of the way into Fairbanks, passing by the community of North Pole on the way. For details on attractions, lodging, and restaurants in Delta Junction, North Pole, and Fairbanks, see the last portion of Chapter 6, "The Alaska Highway."

Lodging

Delta Junction, North Pole, and
Fairbanks:
See listings under the respective town
names in Chapter 6, "The Alaska Highway."

Valdez:
Numerous bed-and-breakfast businesses
operate in Valdez. For more information,
call the Valdez Convention & Visitors
Bureau at 907-835-4636 or browse
www.valdezalaska.org.

Aspen Hotel
100 Meals Avenue
1-800-478-4445 or 907-835-4445
www.aspenhotelsak.com
104 rooms in newer, downtown hotel. Cable TV, modems, microwaves, coffeemakers. Pool, spa, exercise room, free continental breakfast.

Occasionally the trans-Alaska pipeline is visible from the Richardson on its route from Prudhoe Bay to Valdez.

Best Western—Valdez Harbor Inn
100 Fidalgo
1-888-222-3440 or 907-835-3434
www.valdezharborinn.com
Renovated hotel on harbor with view of the port and small boat harbor. Barbershop, airport and ferry shuttle.

Downtown Inn
113 Galena Drive
1-800-478-2791 or 907-835-2791
31 rooms with private or shared baths, free continental breakfast.

Glacier Sound Inn
210 Egan Drive
1-888-835-4485 or 907-835-4485
www.glaciersoundinn.com
40 rooms, microwaves, fridges, coffeemakers. Restaurant, lounge, free continental breakfast. Downtown location.

Keystone Hotel
401 Egan Drive
1-888-835-0665 or 907-835-3851
www.alaska.com/keystonehotel
107 rooms with free continental breakfast. Close to ferry.

Pipeline Inn
112 Egan Drive
907-835-4444
15 rooms, cable TV, restaurant, lounge.

Totem Inn
144 East Egan Drive
1-888-808-4431 or 907-835-4443
www.toteminn.com
70 units including suites, standard rooms, cottages. Restaurant, gift shop. Central location.

Campgrounds

Delta Junction, North Pole, and
Fairbanks:
See listings under the respective town
names in Chapter 6, "The Alaska Highway."

Valdez:

Bayside RV Park
230 Richardson Highway
1-888-835-4425 or 907-835-4425
www.baysidervpark.com
95 RV sites with full and partial hookups,
   cable TV. Bookings for cruises and
   charter fishing trips.

Bear Paw Camper Park
3181 Richardson Highway
907-835-2530
Log cabins and 25 RV sites on
   landscaped property by stream.
   Shower house, laundry, dump
   station, picnic area.

Eagle's Rest RV Park & Cabins
131 East Pioneer Drive
1-800-553-7275 or 907-835-2373
www.eaglesrestrv.com
Campsites with full or partial hookups,
   pull-throughs, tent camping.
   Showers, laundry, dump station.
   Freezer space and fish-cleaning
   table. Tickets for local tours. Private
   cabins available.

Sea Otter RV Park
South Harbor Drive
907-835-2787
Full service RV park on the water. Fishing,
   wildlife watching.

Restaurants

Delta Junction, North Pole, and
Fairbanks:
See listings under the respective town
names in Chapter 6, "The Alaska Highway."

Valdez:

Alaska Halibut House
208 Meals Avenue
907-835-2788
Breakfast, lunch, and dinner,
   seven days a week.

Alaskan Restaurant
144 East Egan Drive,
   in the Totem Inn
907-835-4443
Family dining. Hearty breakfast, lunch,
   and dinner, Alaskan seafood, steaks.

Alaska's Bistro
100 Fidalgo Drive, in Best Western
907-835-5688
Fine dining, seafood, steaks, extensive
   wine list. View of the water.

Fu Kung Chinese Restaurant
207 Kobuk Street
907-835-5255
Chinese food, sushi; beer and wine.
   Lunch and dinner.

Latte Dah
100 Meals, in Harbor Court
907-835-3720
Snacks, espresso, smoothies.

Pipeline Club
112 Egan Drive
907-835-4332
Steaks, Alaska seafood. Lounge,
   entertainment.

SEWARD HIGHWAY

Anchorage to Seward: 127 miles (204 km)
Travel Opportunities: *Potter Marsh; Turnagain Arm; Alyeska Ski Resort at Girdwood; Portage Glacier and Exit Glacier; Seward and Resurrection Bay.*

The Seward Highway was named for Secretary of the Interior Frederick Seward, a key figure in the purchase of Alaska from Russia in 1867. Looking at a map of Alaska, you'll see that the Seward name gets around. The Seward Highway is on the **Kenai Peninsula**; the Seward Peninsula is in Northwest Alaska; and then there's Fort Seward in Southeast Alaska.

The views along this highway are so stunning that the road has been designated a National Scenic Byway. From Anchorage heading south, it cuts into the foot of the mountains along the edge of Cook Inlet's Turnagain Arm. Wending between the mountains and the water, motorists may see Dall sheep, whales, eagles, and running salmon. Rest stops and recreation areas are abundant. Most of what you're driving through is public land, either **Chugach State Park** or **Chugach National Forest**. Only a handful of small communities existed before development of the parks.

Just south of Anchorage, the road borders **Potter Marsh**, a portion of the Anchorage Coastal Waterfowl Refuge. A boardwalk trail winds above the wetlands, with interpretive signs. Here, and in other places along the Seward Highway, you'll see some unusual areas of sunken land where the ground dropped by several feet during the huge 1964 earthquake. In these coastal areas, still-standing dead trees were killed when the land dropped and their roots were flooded with saltwater from Turnagain Arm.

Continuing south on the Seward, Turnagain Arm flanks the right side of the road. The water is not the cerulean blue that one might imagine at oceanside, but rather a flat gray from the many tons of glacial silt that is carried in streams pouring from the mountains. The silt buildup has created a mudflat all around Anchorage's coastal areas, and the extreme tide at this point (sometimes surpassing 30 feet) means that for part of every day, the view is of gray mudflats. At other times, it's a vision—especially when the returning water creates a bore tide, sometimes a foot high or more, which floods the arms of Cook Inlet on either side of Anchorage. In Turnagain Arm, sightings of the bore tide often cause motorists to pull over and watch in awe. In a bore tide, the volume of returning water is so great that a low wall of water forms the leading edge of the incoming tide. Signs warn about the dangers of walking on the mudflats. Even though the surface looks firm, it's possible to become trapped in the silty mud—a perilous spot when the tide is about to turn.

Turnagain Arm was given its name by Captain James Cook. In his search for the Northwest Passage, Cook ventured down this body of water, mistakenly believing it was a river. When Cook saw the retreating tide taking the water out from beneath his ship, he realized his error and advised his men to hurriedly "turn again." Take your time and stop at the waysides, where often you can spy Dall sheep close to the road, or beluga whales chasing eulachon up the Arm.

Most drivers slow down at bridges to check on the progress of salmon fishermen. Keep your eye out for Indian Creek, Bird Creek, and Twentymile Creek. Hiking trails are well marked, too, with parking at trailheads.

Thirty-seven miles (59.5 km) south of Anchorage, turn left at the spur road into Girdwood for world-class skiing at Alyeska Ski Resort. This picturesque little town beneath 3,939-foot (1,200.6-m) Mount Alyeska has been on the map since a minor gold rush in the early part of the 20th century. It was only in the last half of the century that Girdwood discovered its economic potential as a ski resort.

Although known internationally, Girdwood and Alyeska Resort retain a small-town feel. Among the area's amenities is luxurious **Alyeska Prince Resort**, as well as an enclosed tram that travels up the mountain to the Seven Glaciers Restaurant. The views are spectacular. At ground level, take Crow Creek Road to Crow Creek Mine, where you can pan for gold or enjoy a picnic among the old buildings and artifacts. **Crow Creek Mine** is a national historic site. Dry camping is available here. See *www.crowcreekgoldmine.com.*

Further down the highway, view the remains of Portage, a small town that was ravaged in the 1964 earthquake. You can still see remnants of homes and business structures in the abundant fireweed along the road. Dead trees in this area are a testament to that terrible event, too.

Near Portage, 48 miles (77 km) south of Anchorage, the Whittier/Portage Glacier Access Road connects the Seward Highway with **Whittier**, a port on **Prince William Sound.** A toll is charged to pass through the 2.5-mile-long Anton Anderson Memorial Tunnel for eastbound travelers; there is no fee for westbound drivers. The travel direction in the tunnel alternates every 15 minutes, as it is a one-lane road. The Alaska Railroad also offers passage from Portage to Whittier.

Whittier was originally a military post, valued for its ice-free, deepwater location on Prince William Sound. Today the harbor is home port for dozens of pleasure vessels and several cruise operations. If you book your cruise in Anchorage, operators often make the arrangements for travel by bus to Portage, where the bus is loaded onto a railroad flatcar bound for Whittier. Whittier is a port on the Alaska Marine Highway System, connected with Valdez and Cordova by ferry.

Travelers wishing to see **Portage Glacier** should veer right on the Whittier/Portage Glacier Access Road when the road forks. Portage Lake lies within Chugach National Forest. At lakeside you'll find food and gift shopping at Portage Glacier Lodge and natural history information and displays at the Begich-Boggs Visitor Center. Kids will have fun touching fur samples and bones from various animals and learning more about them. Photos tell the story of a gold rush that boomed here a century ago.

The Seward Highway, wending south from Anchorage to the ice-free port of Seward, is on the list of National Scenic Byways.

Because Portage Glacier has been in retreat for decades, it's difficult to see it from the visitor center. But you can travel near the face of the glacier by tour boat, operated by Gray Line of Alaska; call 907-277-5581.

Back on the Seward Highway, near the turnoff to Portage Glacier, look for the **Alaska Wildlife Conservation Center**, where you can view bison, elk, eagles, moose, caribou, and musk oxen in a natural setting. This drive-through park is open 7 days a week. Call 907-783-2025.

The Seward Highway rounds the end of Turnagain Arm, which is fed here by the Placer River. Sometimes, especially during late winter and early spring, a dozen or more moose may be seen resting here among the sparse trees.

A "Welcome" sign greets drivers at the gateway to the Kenai Peninsula, and the road now rises and falls as it wends its way through the pristine Kenai Mountains above and below tree line. At the fork in the road 89 miles (143 km) south of Anchorage, continue straight. The town of **Seward** lies another 38 miles (61 km) ahead. (The right-hand fork marks the start of the Sterling Highway, which leads to Soldotna, Kenai, and Homer. See the section on the Sterling Highway, in this chapter.)

About 4 miles (6.5 km) north of Seward, you can follow the signs and turn west for several miles to reach **Exit Glacier**. Trails lead the way to this very accessible glacier. You can even walk up to its face, but be wary—multiple signs warn of the danger.

The Alaska Railroad train is headed south from Anchorage as visitors walk the Potter Marsh boardwalk, which is marked with interpretive signs about the birds and fish that inhabit this protected wetland.

Bird Creek's jadelike color is caused by the suspended sediment in the water, often a sign that the water is fed by glacial runoff.

The oceanside community of **Seward** lies at the end of the Seward Highway, 2.5 hours south of Anchorage. Settled in 1903, Seward was founded as a shipping port and in 1915 became the southernmost terminal on the Alaska Railroad. Seward is a port along the Alaska Marine Highway System (see Appendix 1).

At the edge of **Resurrection Bay**, protected waters off the Gulf of Alaska, Seward is the home of the **Alaska SeaLife Center**, located along the waterfront. Educational exhibits bring viewers close to seabirds and to marine mammals such as sea lions, seals, and otters. The center also serves as a research laboratory, designed so biologists can work as visitors look on. Call 907-224-6300 for ticket information, or visit *www.alaskasealife.org*.

As the gateway to **Kenai Fjords National Park**, Seward has a small-boat harbor that is filled with pleasure craft as well as commercial fishing vessels and tour boats. The **Kenai Fjords National Park Visitor Center** at the harbor has information on the birds and animals that inhabit the park; call 907-224-3175. Cruise operators offer full-day or half-day tours for wildlife-watching or glacier-viewing or both. Usually a meal is served on board. At the harbor, you can also find fishing charters. Seward's Silver Salmon Derby and Jackpot Halibut Tournament are hot competitions. The Silver Salmon Derby alone offers more than $250,000 in prizes.

Seward's visitor information center is at 2001 Seward Highway. Stop by and learn more about how to make the most of your time here. Call 907-224-8051. Staffers can also direct you on a 1- or 2-hour walking tour of the town's historic area. Seward was among the coastal communities severely damaged in the 1964 earthquake. See the Seward Museum at Jefferson Street and 3rd Avenue. The collection includes historical and cultural artifacts, photos from the 1964 earthquake, World War II, and other pieces of local history. The Community Library, at 5th Avenue and Adams Street, presents a program about the earthquake at 2 P.M. daily, except Sundays, throughout the summer.

Each July 4, scores of runners assault Mount Marathon, the peak just at the town's back. It's a grueling race to the top and back down, and city streets are choked with spectators.

Check at the Chugach National Forest district office at 334 4th Avenue for information on hiking and biking. Call 907-224-3374.

Lodging

Anchorage:
See information at the end of the section on the Glenn Highway, in this chapter.

Girdwood:
You may book Girdwood accommodations through Alyeska/Girdwood Accommodations Association at 907-222-3226 or www.agaa.biz.

Alyeska Prince Resort
1000 Arlberg Avenue
1-800-880-3880 or 907-754-1111
www.alyeskaresort.com
307 deluxe rooms, suites in AAA 4-Diamond hotel. Fitness center, shops, tour desk, tramway sight-seeing. Lounges, cafés.

Indian:
Bird Ridge Motel
Mile 101 Seward Highway
907-653-0100
Rooms near excellent fishing. RV parking, café and bakery.

Brown Bear Saloon-Hotel
Mile 103 Seward Highway
907-653-7000
www.brownbearmotel.com
Rooms and cabins with private baths, kitchens. Near salmon fishing, hiking, wildlife watching.

Moose Pass:
Summit Lake Lodge
Mile 46 Seward Highway
907-244-2031
Rooms, plus gift shop, restaurant, lounge.

Seward:
A Creekside RV Park & Motel
6.5 miles (10.5 km) north of Seward
on Bear Lake Road
907-224-3647
Streamside RV sites with full or partial hookups. Free shower, courtesy van, tour booking service.

Breeze Inn
At Small Boat Harbor
1-888-224-5237 or 907-224-5238
86 rooms, nonsmoking available. Gift shop, coffee and espresso bar, restaurant, lounge.

Camelot Cottages
Mile 3.2 Seward Highway
1-800-739-3039 or 907-224-3039
Cabins, kitchenettes, hot tub, laundry.

Harborview Inn
804 3rd Avenue
1-888-324-3217 or 907-224-3217
Rooms with view, wheelchair access. Cable TV, phone/data ports. Walking distance to tours, train, downtown.

Hotel Edgewater
200 5th Avenue
1-888-793-6800 or 907-224-2700
Well-appointed rooms with cable TV, nonsmoking available. Overlooks Resurrection Bay.

Hotel Seward
221 5th Avenue
1-800-656-2723 or 907-224-2378
Rooms and executive suites, nonsmoking available, cable TV, movies. Half block to Alaska SeaLife Center.

Marina Motel
Near Train Station
907-224-5518
www.sewardmotel.com
Two double beds, private baths, fridges, coffeemakers, cable TV, free movies.

Miller's Landing
On Resurrection Bay
1-866-541-5739 or 907-224-5739
Oceanfront cabins. Laundry, showers, toilets. Tours, fishing, kayaking, transportation. Country store.

Murphy's Motel
911 4th Avenue
907-224-8090
Rooms with a view.

River Valley Cabins
Mile 1, Old Exit Glacier Road
907-224-5740
Log cabins: family cabin for four to six people; six cabins for two to three people. Baths, phones, continental breakfast.

Seward Military Resort
1-800-770-1858 or 907-224-5559
www.sewardresort.com
Motel rooms, cabins, RV sites. Fishing charters. Exclusive use by current and retired military personnel, their guests, and families, as well as federal employees, their guests, and families.

Seward Windsong Lodge
0.5 Mile, Exit Glacier Road
1-800-208-0200 or 907-265-4501
Rooms with cable TV, VCRs, phones.
  Forested setting. Dining, lounge.

The Taroka Inn Motel
3rd Avenue and Adams Street
907-224-8975
Rooms with private baths, kitchens, cable
  TV, data ports. Downtown.

The Van Gilder Hotel
308 Adams Street
1-800-204-6835 or 907-224-3079
Accommodations in a National Historic Site.

Campgrounds

Anchorage:
See information at the end of the section
on the Glenn Highway, in this chapter.

Bird Creek:
Bird Creek State Recreation Site
26 miles (42 km) south of Anchorage
28 campsites, picnic tables, water, toilets.
  Close to salmon fishing, bike trails.

Girdwood:
Crow Creek Mine
3 miles (5 km) up Crow Creek Road
907-278-8060
Historic gold mine offers sites for dry
  camping and tenting.

Portage:
Portage Valley Cabins & RV Park
Mile 1.7 Portage Glacier Road
907-783-3111
www.portagevalleycabins.com
Cabins, RV park, campground. Hiking trails,
  stocked fishing ponds.

Williwaw Creek Campground
Mile 4 Portage Glacier Road
1-877-444-6777 for reservations
60 campsites, picnic tables, water, toilets.
  Deck for viewing spawning salmon,
  late July to mid-September. Nature
  trails. Campground operated by U.S.
  Forest Service.

Seward:
A Creekside RV Park & Motel
6.5 miles (10.5 km) north of Seward
  on Bear Lake Road
907-224-3647
Streamside RV sites with full or partial
  hookups. Free shower, courtesy van,
  tour booking service.

Bear Creek RV Park
6.5 miles (10.5 km) north of Seward
  on Bear Lake Road
907-224-5724
Full and partial hookups. Showers, laundry,
  rest rooms, dump station, store. Fishing
  and glacier tours, courtesy van.

Miller's Landing
On Resurrection Bay
1-866-541-5739 or 907-224-5739
Oceanfront cabins, RV and tent camping.
  Laundry, showers, toilets. Tours, fishing,
  kayaking, transportation. Country store.

Stoney Creek RV Park
From 6.3 Mile Seward Highway,
  off Stoney Creek Avenue
907-224-6465
www.stoneycreekrvpark.com
81 creekside campsites, full and partial
  hookup, some pull-throughs. Satellite
  TV, showers, laundry.

Restaurants

Anchorage:
See information at the end of the section
on the Glenn Highway, in this chapter.

Girdwood:
Alyeska Prince Resort
1000 Arlberg Avenue
1-800-880-3880 or 907-754-1111
www.alyeskaresort.com
Choose from several restaurants for the
  dining experience of your choice; casual
  to fine dining.

The Bake Shop
At Alyeska Ski Resort
907-783-2831
Homemade soups, sourdough pancakes,
  breads, pizza.

McHugh Creek Park is a beautifully developed mini-park overlooking Turnagain Arm off the Seward Highway. The Seward has been designated a National Scenic Byway.

Chair 5 Restaurant
5 Linblad Avenue, off Hightower Road
907-783-2500
www.chair5.com
Seafood, pizza, microbrews.

Coast Pizza
Mile 90 Seward Highway,
   at turnoff to Girdwood
907-783-0122
Pizza by the slice.

Double Musky Inn
On Crow Creek Road
907-783-2822
Cajun specialties, Alaska seafood;
   funky Alaska decor.

Indian:
Bird Ridge Café & Bakery
26 miles (42 km) south of Anchorage
907-653-7302
Home-style cooking, pastries, beer, wine.

Moose Pass:
Summit Lake Lodge
Mile 46 Seward Highway
907-244-2031
Restaurant, lodge, lounge, gift shop.

Portage:
Portage Glacier Lodge
Across from visitor center
907-783-3117
Soups, sandwiches. Eat in or take out.

Seward:
Breeze Inn
At Small Boat Harbor
1-888-224-5237 or 907-224-5238
Dining with a view. Seafood specialties.

Camelot Cottages
Mile 3.2 Seward Highway
1-800-739-3039 or 907-346-3039
www.alaska.net/akcabins
Cabins, kitchenettes, hot tub, laundry.

Christo's Palace
133 4th Avenue, downtown
907-224-5255
Pizza, steak, seafood, Mexican, cocktails.

Exit Glacier Salmon Bake
.25 Glacier Exit Road
907-224-2204
Full-service restaurant. Salmon, halibut,
   steaks, burgers.

Harbor Dinner Club
220 5th Avenue
907-224-3012
Steaks, seafood, lounge, outdoor seating.

Ray's Waterfront
Overlooking Seward Boat Harbor
907-224-5606
Seafood specialties.

Resurrection Roadhouse
0.5 Mile, Exit Glacier Road
1-800-208-0200
Good food, casual atmosphere with a
   view, microbrews.

STEESE HIGHWAY

Fairbanks to Circle City: 162 miles (261 km)
Travel Opportunities: *Chena Hot Springs; Gold Dredge No. 8; Fox;*
Eagle Summit; Central, Circle Hot Springs, and Circle City.

If the Steese Highway were ever renamed, it should be the Gold Road, for this is the historic transportation corridor between some of the state's richest gold-fields near Central and Circle City, and Fairbanks, the boomtown that was built on the discovery of gold. In fact, the road edges Pedro Creek, near the very place where Italian immigrant Felix Pedro discovered gold in 1902, launching yet another gold rush.

The Steese Highway is at the intersection of Airport Way and Gaffney Boulevard in Fairbanks. Quickly, it splits into the Old Steese and, a block away, the New Steese. The older road is retired from heavy-duty service and now merely meanders through residential areas. But the New Steese is a four-lane highway that tends toward a gentle roller-coaster ride with the occasional missing two feet of track. Just remember that the insidious permafrost works against the road builders' best efforts.

These early miles of the Steese are heavily used by Fairbanks residents who live in the surrounding hills or along Chena Hot Springs Road. Take this 56-mile spur road east to its dead end and you'll land at **Chena Hot Springs Resort**. Winter or summer, you can soak in 100-degree pools of mineral water that seem to suck the tension out of every pore. The resort offers nicely appointed rooms or rustic cabins. Swim in an enclosed pool area, or soak in outdoor hot tubs. You can go horseback riding, pick blueberries, and in winter, view the aurora. Call 907-451-8104 or visit *www.chenahotsprings.com*.

Back on the Steese Highway, press on past Chena Hot Springs Road to experience some of the area's best tourism sites, as well as unparalleled views of the Tanana Valley and beyond.

View Fairbanks from atop Engineer Hill, 6.5 miles (10.5 km) north of town. At the top, turn west on Hagelbarger Road to the pull-out parking area immediately on your right. This is the place to get the best bird's-eye view of Fairbanks. On clear days, the Tanana Valley is spread at your feet and, beyond it to the south, the Alaska Range.

Return to the Steese Highway and travel north (left) off Hagelbarger. During your descent down Engineer Hill, portions of the **trans-Alaska pipeline** will be visible on your right. At Mile 8.5 (13.6 km), a spacious parking area with interpretive signs allows visitors to roam around and walk up to the pipeline. A visitor information center there is usually staffed, and free brochures are available. A sign cautions, "Please do not climb on the pipeline." Near here, the Steese Highway reduces from four lanes to two, but remains paved for many more miles.

A mile later, turn left to access **Gold Dredge No. 8**, a piece of mining history that has been restored for visitors. Operated by Gray Line of Alaska, the attraction includes tours aboard this floating gold-processing ship. You can pan for gold yourself, and eat hearty at a miners' buffet lunch. For ticket information, call 907-451-6835.

If you plan to stay on the Steese Highway, the upcoming intersection, at Mile 11 (18 km), may be confusing. The Steese makes a sharp right. If you go straight, you'll be on the Elliott Highway and bound for the Brooks Range.

One other option at this intersection is well worth your time, particularly if you're hungry or thirsty. Turn left and you'll be driving through the "main street" of beautiful downtown Fox, where few people live, but many come to eat and drink. The Fox General Store and gas station on this corner is the last place to fuel up for many miles, so top off here if you haven't done so in Fairbanks.

Other notable businesses include **The Howling Dog Saloon**, your classic funky Alaska bar. Pizza and other bar grub are available, as well as a full bar selection of beverages. There's live music on weekends, too. **The Fox Roadhouse** may not look like a historic building from the outside, but step inside and you'll discover that the original roadhouse has been completely encased by the newer exterior. The roadhouse offers lunches, dinners, and bar selections. Farther down the road, The Turtle Club is a Fairbanks-area favorite for casual dining and large portions of prime rib. Reservations are suggested.

A pullout north of Fairbanks brings you up close and personal to the trans-Alaska pipeline. Informational signs tell more about this monumental building project as well as critters of the Interior.

The Howling Dog Saloon in Fox isn't a tourist attraction in the classic sense, but it's a good place to meet local folks.

Twenty miles (32 km) from Fairbanks, from the Cleary Summit Scenic Viewpoint, outstanding valley views are marred by evidence of wildfires that plagued this area in the summer of 2004. Thirty-eight miles (61 km) from Fairbanks is the site of an old gold-mining town that's long gone. Left behind is a monster gold dredge, just over a hill from the highway, and a historic lodging, dining, and drinking establishment named **Chatanika Lodge.** Call 907-389-2164 for a room reservation. They'll tell you more about the days when this was a bona fide community, with a postmaster and plenty of people, and that derelict gold dredge across the way was hard at work.

Just around the bend, the University of Alaska Fairbanks conducts research on the aurora borealis from **Poker Flat Rocket Range,** a remote site marked by a mounted rocket at the entrance. As you can imagine, it's not open for drop-in visitors, but you can arrange a tour through the university's Geophysical Institute at 907-474-7558.

Up ahead, a series of summits and interesting switchbacks makes driving the Steese an on-your-toes proposition. For one, you run out of pavement. However, the gravel surface is well graded in summer, and the snowy surface is plowed often in winter. Views of the river valleys from above are breathtaking, and as you drive over the mountain range, above tree line, with few guardrails along the road, you can experience something like vertigo.

The road leads over Cleary Summit and Twelve-Mile Summit with access to the **Pinnell Mountain National Recreation Trail**, managed by the Bureau of Land Management. For maps of this trail and others in the area, contact the BLM's Northern Field Office at 1-800-437-7021 or visit *aurora.ak.blm.gov*.

At Mile 107.5 (173 km), you'll cross **Eagle Summit**, the tallest of them all at 3,685 feet (1,123 m) above sea level. For those accustomed to trees and roadside businesses, the trek up and over Eagle Summit will come as a surprise in its nakedness. The road threads over rolling mountains and above tree line with nothing between you and the distant valley floor except fresh air. At the top, the view is nearly dizzying, with nothing but undulating country on all sides. Here is where dozens of people drive on June 20 or 21, summer solstice, to observe and photograph an unobstructed view of the midnight sun. Their photographs, taken over several hours with timed exposures, will show an orange orb gently touching down to the horizon line before beginning its slow ascent.

In the village of **Central**, 127 miles (204 km) northeast of Fairbanks, most of the folks are gold miners, or have been miners, or at least know miners. This little town of log cabins includes a couple of restaurants and some roadside lodging.

The people of Central raised money to open the town's mining museum, which has limited hours due to a volunteer staff. It's worth a stop if you're in town between noon and 5 P.M.

At the end of an 8-mile, unpaved spur road that leads southeast out of Central is **Circle Hot Springs**. You'll find a delightful old wooden hotel surrounded by log structures of every size and age. But the centerpiece of it all is the Olympic-size, naturally heated outdoor swimming pool. Summer or winter, the pool attracts people who come to warm their bones in water that emerges from the ground so hot, it has to be mixed to cool it for swimmers. People were coming here long before gold miners discovered the hot springs in the late 1800s. Native Alaskans already knew about the soothing warmth of the water.

In winter, the below-zero air above the pool turns the steam into ice fog that settles on everything near it, turning the pool area into a fairyland of frosted outdoor furniture. Swimmers can float in inner tubes, and the parts of them that are above water likewise become frost-covered, down to the smallest hairs on their arms, until they slip underwater again. You can even hold your wet hair straight up or sideways, and it will freeze that way. Winter guests often have the privilege of seeing the aurora borealis color the skies overhead.

Circle Hot Springs Resort includes a restaurant and saloon, and rooms range from deluxe accommodations on the first floor to dormitory-style hostel quarters in the attic. RV parking is available, too. Almost a century ago, pioneers Frank and Emma Leach worked this ground, and watered their superb gardens with hot-springs water. Their graves are on a nearby hill, and it is said that they still haunt the place. In the game room, we even dealt an extra hand of poker for Emma, in case she showed up.

Beyond Central, the Steese Highway consists of nearly 34 unpaved miles (54 km) of winding road through the boreal forest. At the end of the road, you'll find Circle City. The claim to be the Paris of the North seems to have been overused during the gold rushes of the late 1800s. That was the claim for Dawson City, but Circle City came up with it first, based on all the theaters and other signs of refinement that accompanied the boom here.

Located along the Yukon River, Circle was misnamed by miners more than a century ago when they mistakenly thought they were on or near the Arctic Circle. They figured out their mistake soon enough, but the name stuck. Before the 1898 gold rush to the Klondike, Circle was the center of mining activity, and the town boomed to 10,000 people in a matter of months. There were saloons and dance halls, theaters, two-story hotels, and streets filled with people.

Looking at Circle now, it's hard to believe. A smattering of cabins has collected along the waterfront, more homes have been built away from the water, and several businesses supply the needs of local folks and the visitors who are intent on driving to the Yukon River. But the Paris of the North? Today it takes a great stretch of the imagination.

A sign at the river with another end-of-the-road message is among the most-photographed images in the area.

Lodging/Campgrounds/Meals

Central:
Mills Junction
Mile 127.5 Steese Highway
907-520-5599
Motel rooms, laundry facility. Restaurant, bar, gas, diesel, propane, store.

Circle City:
H.C. Company Store
End of the Steese Highway
907-773-1222
Gas, groceries, snacks, tire repair.

Circle Hot Springs:
Arctic Circle Hot Springs Resort
Mile 8 Circle Hot Springs Road
907-520-5113
Hotel rooms, cabins, restaurant, saloon, shops, year-round outdoor pool.

Russian Orthodox missionaries were among the earliest outsiders to influence the Native cultures on the Kenai Peninsula, and Russian place-names linger on. This church overlooks Cook Inlet at Ninilchik.

STERLING HIGHWAY

From Seward Highway to Homer: 143 miles (230 km)
Travel Opportunities: *Kenai Lake at Cooper Landing; fishing the Kenai and Russian Rivers; deep-sea charter fishing at Anchor Point or Homer; day trips to Seldovia and Halibut Cove.*

The Sterling Highway leaves the Seward Highway at a fork 90 miles (145 km) south of Anchorage. It wends west and south through a sparsely populated wilderness area and passes through a handful of small towns on the way to its dead end in another small town, Homer. Lofty mountains shoulder the two paved lanes, and nearby lakes and streams run clean and cold. Most of the land is included in the 1.9-million-acre **Kenai National Wildlife Refuge**. Moose and bear numbers are strong, and you might see Dall sheep, caribou, loons, eagles, and trumpeter swans. Offshore, watch for sea otters, seals, puffins, and numerous birds.

Flightseeing operations offer bird's-eye views of unbelievable beauty. Hiking, canoeing, and rafting are other recreation offerings on the Kenai Peninsula. Nature photography ranks high on the list as well. Beautifully adorned subjects lie all around you. Distant glaciers flow from the **Harding Ice Field**, and along the road the gem-green **Kenai Lake** flows into a magnificent river of the same color and name.

The biggest towns along the Sterling Highway are **Cooper Landing**, Mile 11 (17.7 km); Sterling Highway, 101 miles (162.5 km) south of Anchorage; **Sterling**, at Mile 44 (71 km); **Soldotna**, at Mile 58 (93 km); and the end of the road at **Homer**, Mile 142.5 (229 km). In each town, you'll find gas, food, campgrounds, services, fishing licenses, hotels, and opportunities to line up a guide or gather some local knowledge.

What the Kenai Peninsula may be best known for worldwide is its prime fishing. Sportfishers travel great distances to fish the **Kenai River**, to wade into turquoise-colored waters in the hope of wrestling with a king, the salmon that can grow into the size and weight of a 7-year-old child. (The world-record king salmon of 97.4 pounds was taken from the Kenai River in 1985.) Equally attractive is another world-class, roadside sportfishing stream, the **Russian River**. On this river, the prized fish is the red salmon.

Every day of every summer, campgrounds near these rivers are jammed with RVs and cars as anglers head for the water. This is a camping experience like none other. Don't expect peace and solitude when the salmon are running. Anglers stand shoulder to shoulder and work in cooperation to flip out their lines to drift with the current without tangling with those of their neighbors. The cry "Fish on!" is the signal to reel in your line and get out of the way until a lucky angler nets his or her fish.

Charter fishing operations at Anchor Point, Deep Creek, Ninilchik, and Homer lead clients to unforgettable deep-sea halibut fishing. Getting a 100-pound lunker off the bottom and over the side of the boat takes more than finesse. It's just sheer muscle-fishing. The biggest halibut caught in Cook Inlet weighed about 465 pounds.

Six peninsula towns offer prizes for the biggest salmon or halibut in annual fishing derbies (combined, the prizes equal about $100,000). For recorded sportfishing information, call the Alaska Department of Fish and Game in Soldotna at 907-262-2737. The Soldotna Visitor Information Center is across the bridge in Soldotna, and offers information on wildlife viewing, fishing, and other outdoor recreation. Call 907-262-9814 or visit *www.soldotnachamber.com*.

Fishing in a new region always carries with it a hefty learning curve, so consider whether you want to devote the time necessary to learning how these fish behave. Hiring a guide is often the best option. They know the best holes, the best time of day, and the regulations. It's likely, too, that a guide will haul you away from the crowds in a boat or floatplane. Most places can arrange to have your fish smoked or frozen and shipped home when you're ready to receive it.

The biggest town on the Kenai Peninsula lies on the shores of Cook Inlet and shares the same name as the peninsula: **Kenai**. Located on the Kenai Spur Highway, westbound from Soldotna, the city is home to fishing and oil industry workers, tourism operators, and other people in support services.

A visitor information log cabin is at the corner of Kenai Spur Highway and Main Street Loop. Pick up a walking map for Old Town Kenai, and learn about its early Kenaitze Indian and Russian residents. The Holy Assumption of the Virgin Mary Russian Orthodox Church has stood here since 1894. The Dena'ina Athabascans have lived and hunted in this region for thousands of years. Get information about the area at 907-283-1991 or see *www.visitkenai.com.*

From Kenai and its neighboring town, Nikiski, the view across Cook Inlet is panoramic: Mount Spurr, Mount Redoubt, and Mount Iliamna are the cone-shaped volcanoes on the horizon—and they are *not* dormant. Two of these beauties have erupted in the last 15 years, spewing fine ash that rained down on Southcentral Alaska for hundreds of miles.

Private campgrounds may be found near or in the towns that dot the length of the Sterling Highway and the Kenai Spur Highway. The state maintains several recreation areas and sites along these roads, too, and campsites are plentiful at Clam Gulch, Deep Creek, Ninilchik, Kenai, Nikiski, and Johnson Lake, and in Homer at Kachemak Bay State Park. Another dozen less-developed grounds also offer campsites, rest rooms, and water. For full details, call the Division of Parks and Outdoor Recreation's Soldotna office at 907-262-5581.

The Kenai is steeped in the ancient Kenaitze Indian culture and in that of the Russians whose two centuries of influence are still visible in the blue-domed churches at Kenai and Ninilchik. Native surnames often possess an echo of Russia, as do place-names such as Kalifornsky, Nikiski, Kasilof, and Ninilchik. At the village of Ninilchik, the Russian Orthodox church majestically overlooks Cook Inlet from atop a bluff. Visitors are welcome to photograph the church, but remember that this is a place of worship. The local people ask that you do not enter the cemetery. Throughout the Kenai, shops offer handmade Native crafts and Russian gift items, as well as the more typical Alaska souvenirs.

The Sterling Highway ends at the sea at Homer, a town that's a wonderful mix of artist colony, commercial fishing seaport, small-town Alaska, and tourist destination. Homer is a port of call on the Alaska Marine Highway System; for information, call 1-800-382-9229 or visit *www.ferryalaska.com.*

The Alaska Islands and Oceans Visitors Center, headquarters for the Alaska Maritime National Wildlife Refuge is right at the entrance to town at 50 Sterling Highway. The 4.4-million-acre refuge extends along much of the Alaska coastline. Allow lots of time to explore this beautiful building and the free exhibits. Call 907-235-6961.

More than 100,000 shorebirds migrate through this part of the state annually. Each May the city hosts the Kachemak Bay Shorebird Festival, drawing hundreds of birders to witness thousands of sandpipers, turnstones, dowitchers, and dunlins. Eagles are year-round residents.

You can learn more about the natural and cultural history of this area at the Pratt Museum in Homer, on Bartlett Street off Pioneer Avenue. Artifacts from prehistory to homesteaders, information on marine mammals, and guided ecology tours are among the offerings. The items for sale at the art gallery and gift shop include Alaska-made crafts and collectibles. Call 907-235-8635 or see *www.prattmuseum.org.*

Fine art galleries featuring the work of local and guest artists may be found throughout town and on the Homer Spit, a 4.5-mile finger of land that extends into Kachemak Bay. Homer is a creative place, so take a gallery trek. Along the Homer Spit, you can walk along an elevated boardwalk and watch happy anglers posing with the day's catch of halibut. You can book a salmon or halibut charter, or arrange a day boat trip across the bay to visit the tiny villages of Seldovia and Halibut Cove. Look into the options at the Homer Chamber of Commerce at 907-235-7740 or *www.homeralaska.org.*

On the spit are RV and tent camping, hotel rooms, gift shops, art galleries, pleasure boats, and commercial fishing vessels. Have a cold drink at the Salty Dog Saloon; enjoy a meal with an amazing view at Land's End; walk the beach with your kids and examine what high tide has delivered. The spit, with its festival-like atmosphere, is a gathering place for revving up or winding down. Rest your eyes on the horizon. You've reached the end of the road.

Lodging

Cooper Landing:
Gwin's Lodge
Mile 52 Sterling Highway
907-595-1266
Cabins, rooms, full RV hookups, restaurant, bar. Tours, charters, outdoor clothing, licenses, souvenirs. Fish processing and shipping drop site.

Homer:
To learn more about Homer-area bed-and-breakfasts, call 1-800-764-3211 or 907-235-4983 or visit the Web site at www.homeraccommodations.com.

Anchor River Inn
Just north of Homer at Anchor Point
1-800-435-8531 or 907-235-8531
20 rooms, fitness facility, pool tables, dance floor, store, gift shop, restaurant, lounge.

Best Western Bidarka Inn
575 Sterling Highway
907-235-8148
Full-service hotel, restaurant, sports bar, charters.

Driftwood Inn & RV Park
135 West Bunnell Avenue
1-800-478-8019 or 907-235-8019
Historic beachfront inn with full hookup campsites.

Land's End Resort
4789 Homer Spit Road
907-235-0400
Beachfront rooms, mountain and bay vistas, Chart Room Restaurant.

Ocean Shores Motel
3500 Crittenden Drive
1-800-770-7775 or 907-235-7775
www.akoceanshores.com
Seaside rooms, private beach, walking distance to town.

Kenai:
Beluga Lookout Lodge & RV Park
929 Mission Avenue, in historic Old Town
907-283-4939
www.belugalookout.com
Lodge rooms. 75 full-hookup spaces, pull-throughs, grills, picnic tables, rest rooms, showers, laundry, Internet. Gift shop, bike rentals.

Kenai Merit Inn
260 Willow Street
907-283-6131
Rooms with cable TV, phones, free continental breakfast. Fishing packages. Downtown location.

Soldotna:
Best Western King Salmon Motel, RV Park & Restaurant
Downtown Soldotna
1-888-262-5857 or 907-262-5857
www.bestwestern.com
Large rooms, kitchenettes, cable TV, coffee. Restaurant. 39 RV sites, most pull-throughs. Full hookups, rest rooms, showers, laundry.

Eagle's Roost Lodge
35555 Spur Highway
1-877-262-9900 or 907-262-4050
Log cabins, RV and tent camping. Sauna, tackle and gift shop, salmon bake, smokehouse. Fishing charters, boat rentals.

The Riverside House
44611 Sterling Highway
1-877-262-0500 or 907-262-0500
www.riverside-house.com
Rooms, RV parking, restaurant, lounge, nightclub.

Soldotna B&B Lodge
399 Lovers Lane
1-877-262-4779 or 907-262-4779
www.soldotnalodge.com
16-unit European-style lodge on banks of Kenai River. Multilingual hosts. Full breakfast, fishing packages, guides, private bank fishing, and other charters.

Sterling:
Naptowne Inn & Café
Mile 84.5 Sterling Highway
907-260-2005
www.naptowneinn.com
15 rooms with queen-sized beds, restaurant serving three meals a day.

Campgrounds
Anchor River:
Kyllonen's RV Park
1 Mile Anchor River Beach Road
Full and partial hookups, fish-cleaning station, free firewood, showers, rest rooms, laundry. Gift shop, espresso bar. Licenses and charters. Close to Cook Inlet and Anchor River.

Cooper Landing:
Kenai Princess RV Park
Mile 47.5 Sterling Highway
907-595-1425
35 sites, power, tables. Shower, laundry, water, dump station. Groceries. Next to Kenai Princess Lodge. Turn at Mile 47.5 (76.5 km), then drive 2 miles (3 km) on Bear Creek Road.

Kenai Riverside Campground & RV Park
Mile 50 Cooper Landing
1-888-536-2478
25 partial hookups, dump station, rest rooms, showers. Fishing and licenses on site.

The U.S. Forest Service manages the following campgrounds near Cooper Landing:

Quartz Creek Recreation Area
Turn off at Mile 45 Sterling Highway and follow Quartz Creek Road
RV parking and tent sites. Water, toilets, fishing.

Cooper Creek Campground
Mile 50.5 Sterling Highway
RV parking and tent sites. Water, toilets. On south bank of upper Kenai River.

The Homer Spit attracts campers, anglers, shoppers, and sightseers by the score. The finger of land juts out into Kachemak Bay for several miles.

Russian River Campground
Mile 52.5 Sterling Highway
RV parking and tent sites. Water, toilets, dump station. Excellent salmon fishing in season. Fish-cleaning stations.

The Kenaitze Indian Tribe operates a traditional/cultural campground within the Seward Ranger District of the Chugach National Forest:

K'Beq Footprints
Mile 52.5 Sterling Highway
907-283-3633
Camping, guided tours, traditional plane lore, legends, stories. Gift shop.

The U.S. Fish and Wildlife Service has developed several campgrounds between Cooper Landing and Sterling:

Skilak Lake
21 miles (33.8 km) west from the junction of Sterling and Seward Highways is the first turnoff for Skilak Lake Road, a loop along which there are three campgrounds. Two developed campgrounds are on Skilak Lake; a third lies nearby on Hidden Lake. All three have fire pits, toilets, water, and boat ramps. Hidden Lake campers enjoy campfire programs on Friday and Saturday evenings in an outdoor theater. Campground hosts.

Kenai-Russian River Campground
Mile 55 Sterling Highway, near boundary of Kenai National Wildlife Refuge
Developed campsites, with water, and toilets. Near excellent fishing.

Homer:
Driftwood Inn & RV Park
135 West Bunnell Avenue
907-235-8019
Full hookups on beachfront sites.

Heritage RV Park
3550 Homer Spit Road, by the Fishing Hole
907-226-4500
www.alaskaheritagervpark.com
Bayview sites with 20-, 30-, or 50-amp
power, sewer, water, satellite TV.
On-site gift shop, coffee shop, showers,
rest rooms, laundry. Walking distance to
fishing, beach, shopping, restaurants.

Homer Spit Campground
At the end of the road
907-235-8206
Oceanfront camping for RVs, with partial
hookups, tent camping, showers, dump
station. Gift shop, charter bookings,
trailer rentals.

Hornaday Hillside Park
Operated by City of Home
Bartlett and Fairview Avenues,
follow signs
Dry camping for smaller RVs. 31 campsites,
water, picnic tables, dumpster,
playground.

Oceanview RV Park
173 Sterling Highway
907-235-3951
Full and partial hookups, pull-throughs,
tent camping. Panoramic views.
Showers, rest rooms, gift shop.
Special charter rates.

*Alaska State Parks manages the
following campgrounds between
Ninilchik and Homer:*

Ninilchik River Campground
North end of Ninilchik
Mile 134.5 Sterling Highway
RV parking and tent sites. Water, toilets,
dump station. Fishing.

Ninilchik Beach Campground
Beach access road
35 campsites, toilets, water.

Ninilchik View Campground
Mile 135 Sterling Highway,
east side of highway
12 campsites, water, toilets, fishing.

Deep Creek State Recreation Area
Mile 137 Sterling Highway
164 sites near excellent fishing.

Stariski State Recreation Site
Mile 152 Sterling Highway
Partial hookups, tent camping.
Water, picnic shelter, wheelchair-
accessible toilets.

Anchor River State Recreation Area
Mile 157.5 turnoff to Anchor River Beach
Road
5 campgrounds with more than
150 campsites.

Kenai:
Beluga Lookout Lodge & RV Park
929 Mission Avenue,
in historic Old Town
907-283-4939
www.belugalookout.com
Lodge rooms. 75 full-hookup spaces,
pull-throughs, grills, picnic tables,
rest rooms, showers, laundry, Internet.
Gift shop, bike rentals.

Captain Cook State Recreation Area
Miles 36—29 Kenai Spur Highway
Campsites, fishing, hiking, picnic shelter,
boating.

Kenai Riverfront RV Park
2 Mile Big Eddy Road
907-262-1717
www.kenairiverfront.com
10 RV sites with electric, gravel sites,
riverfront views. Boat launch,
bank fishing.

Kenai RV Park
Corner of Highland and Upland Streets
907-398-3382
18 sites with hookups, tent camping,
showers, laundry, rest rooms.
One block from Kenai visitor center.

Soldotna:
**Best Western King Salmon Motel,
RV Park & Restaurant**
Downtown Soldotna
1-888-262-5857 or 907-262-5857
www.bestwestern.com
Large rooms, kitchenettes, cable TV,
coffee. Restaurant. 39 RV sites,
most pull-throughs. Full hookups,
rest rooms, showers, laundry.

Centennial Park Municipal Campground
On Funny River Road near Mile 96 Sterling
Highway
126 campsites, some along river,
tables, fire pits, firewood, water,
dump station. Boat launch and
on-site fishing.

Discovery Campground
Near intersection Kenai Spur and
Sterling Highways
53 campsites, hiking trail, water,
fireside programs.

Edgewater RV Park
44770 Funny River Road
907-262-7733
www.sunriseresorts.com
40 full hookups and pull-through sites,
18 partial hookups, showers, laundry.
Bank fishing on the river, guide services,
fish-cleaning station.

The Riverside House
44611 Sterling Highway
1-877-262-0500 or 907-262-0500
www.riverside-house.com
RV park, hotel, riverview dining, lounge,
nightclub.

Sterling:
*Alaska State Parks manages the
following recreation sites and
campgrounds near Sterling:*

Bing's Landing
Mile 79 (127 km), 36 sites
Izaak Walton, Mile 81 (130 km), 25 sites
Morgan's Landing, Mile 85 (136.8 km),
42 sites

Real Alaskan Cabins and RV Park
Mile 80 near Bing's Landing
907-262-6077
www.realalaskan.com
33 sites with full hookups, cabins,
wooded setting, showers, laundry.
Park/fishing packages. Boat rentals.

Bing Brown's RV Park & Motel
Mile 81 Sterling Highway
907-262-4780
www.bingbrowns.com
Full RV hookups, dump station, showers,
laundry. Kitchenettes. Book guided
fishing and tours, tackle, licenses,
liquor, snacks.

Moose River Resort & Hot Tub
Overlooking river at Sterling
907-262-9777
www.mooseriverresort.com
Riverfront chalet & RV park.

Moose River RV Park
Mile 81.5 Sterling Highway
907-260-7829
www.stayalaska.com
Full hookups; some pull-throughs. Visitor
center, rest rooms, high-speed Internet,
satellite TV, showers, laundry. Café.
Local fishing.

Alaska Canoe & RV Park
Mile 84 Sterling Highway
907-262-2331
RV sites, laundry, showers. Canoe and
mountain bike rentals. Shuttle service.
Fishing licenses and gear.

Restaurants
Cooper Landing:
Gwin's Lodge
Mile 52 Sterling Highway
907-595-1266
Restaurant, bar, cabins, rooms,
RV hookups.

Homer:
Boardwalk Fish & Chips
Homer Spit Road
907-235-7749
Burgers, fresh halibut, and the works.

Don Jose's
127 Pioneer Avenue
907-235-7963
Authentic Mexican food.

Eric's BBQ
4025 Homer Spit Road
907-235-9197
Pit barbecue beef, pork, and chicken.

Fresh Sourdough Express
  Bakery & Café
1316 Ocean Drive
907-235-7571
Breakfast, lunch, dinner; box lunches,
  desserts, espresso, bakery.

Homestead Restaurant
Mile 8 East End Road
907-235-8723
Lunches and dinners; views of
  Kachemak Bay.

Two Sisters Bakery
233 E. Bunnell Street
907-235-2280
Soups, sandwiches, baked goods.

Kenai:
Charlotte's Restaurant
115 South Willow
907-283-2777
Home cooking and baking. Soups,
  desserts, and more.

Don Jose's
205 Willow Street
907-283-8181
Authentic Mexican food.

Louie's Steak & Seafood
Mile 47 Spur View Drive
Adjacent to Uptown Motel
907-283-3660
Fine Alaska seafood.

Veronica's Coffee House
604 Peterson Way
907-283-2725
Food, coffee, live music on weekends, in
  historic building in Old Town.

Soldotna:
Best Western King Salmon Motel,
  RV Park & Restaurant
Downtown Soldotna
1-888-262-5857 or 907-262-5857
www.bestwestern.com
Steaks, seafood, early breakfasts for
  fishermen. Salad bar, beer and wine.

China Sea Buffet Restaurant
Soldotna Mall, half a mile
  north of the bridge
907-262-5033
All-you-can-eat buffet, salad bar.

Coffee Concepts
35228 Kenai Spur Highway
907-260-3255
Sandwiches, soups, gourmet
  coffees, muffins.

Jersey Subs
44224 Sterling Highway
907-260-3393
Hot and cold submarine sandwiches.

The Riverside House
44611 Sterling Highway
1-877-262-0500 or 907-262-0500
Riverview dining, lunch and dinner;
  lounge, nightclub.

Sal's Klondike Diner
Mile 95.5 Sterling Highway
907-262-2220
Alaskan and Yukon burgers, breakfast
  anytime. Sack lunches to go.

Wild King Grill Restaurant
Mile 101.5 Sterling Highway
907-262-4606
Steaks, halibut, cedar-plank salmon,
  special desserts.

TAYLOR HIGHWAY

Part of the Klondike Loop
From Alaska Highway to Eagle: 160 miles (257 km)
Travel Opportunities: *Town of Chicken; Fortymile gold-mining country;*
Jack Wade No. 1 gold dredge; Eagle; Fort Egbert; Yukon River;
riverboat Yukon Queen II.

The Taylor is the highway for stouthearted drivers who promise to pay close attention to the road; let your navigator take the pictures for you to enjoy later. Unpaved and narrow, the Taylor climbs and descends, turns and doubles back, changing its mind multiple times in a matter of miles as it wends through and above some of the most spectacular country in east-central Alaska. For those who want a taste of what the Alaska Highway used to be like, this is the road.

The Taylor Highway takes off northward from Tetlin Junction on the Alaska Highway, about a dozen miles east of Tok. The Taylor is part of the **Klondike Loop**, the route over a series of three highways that connects Tok and Whitehorse via Dawson City. (See the sections on the North Klondike Highway and the Top of the World Highway in Chapter 7, "Western Canada's Northbound Byways.")

The Taylor provides access to two distinctive Alaska towns, Chicken and Eagle, both of which are steeped in gold-mining history. The towns are inaccessible by road in winter, however. The Taylor is one of the few Alaska highways that is not maintained throughout the winter, meaning that the state does not plow it, making it good for dog-mushing and snowmobile traffic, but not much more.

Chicken is the town that the late author Ann Purdy made famous in *Tisha,* her novel based on her own life. The book details the adventures of a young teacher who moves to Chicken, falls in love with the place and her Athabascan Indian students, and settles down to make it home. Chicken, she is told, was given this name because miners couldn't correctly spell the name of the local chickenlike bird, the ptarmigan.

It's easy to pass by the best parts of Chicken if your eyes look dead ahead. At about Mile 66 (106 km) from Tetlin Junction, follow the Airport Road turnoff to the historic Chicken business district. Chicken offers a couple of restaurants, a saloon, a gift shop and bookstore, and a gas station. The Goldpanner at the Chicken Center hosts RV parking and daily tours of Chicken, including a stop at Tisha's Schoolhouse.

At Mile 86 (138 km), you'll see the ruins of the old **Jack Wade No. 1** gold dredge, which sits right at roadside and makes for a wonderful photo opportunity.

At Mile 96 (154 km), you'll encounter the only fork in the highway. At this point, you may choose to continue north on the Taylor Highway to its dead end at the town of Eagle on the Yukon River. Or you may turn east and connect with the **Top of the World Highway** to continue along the Klondike Loop.

If you turn east, 12 miles (19 km) of travel will take you to the Alaska–Yukon border—and after another 66 miles (106 km) of driving adventure on a winding, unpaved road, you'll land in Dawson City, Yukon. Along the way, you'll catch a glimpse of why they named it the Top of the World Highway. At Dawson City, you can connect with the North Klondike Highway as you proceed along the Klondike Loop.

Each late February, over the course of three weekends, more than 700 snow-mobilers dominate the Taylor and Top of the World Highways during a fun run between Tok and Dawson City that's called the **Trek Over the Top**. Trekkers travel 200 miles (322 km) one way in a day, stopping to refuel in Chicken. They spend a couple of days seeing Dawson and visiting Diamond Tooth Gerties for entertainment and one-armed bandit fun, then jump back on their machines for the return trip. Since all of the traffic is headed in one direction, and there's no concern of meeting a car or RV on a nasty bend, the snowmobilers pull out all the stops and enjoy the ride.

The **Fortymile caribou herd** migrates across the Taylor Highway twice a year: from east to west during March and April, and from west to east during October and November. Watch for moose and bears, too.

At the end of the Taylor Highway is Eagle. Imagine this sleepy little town as the hustle-bustle community it was in 1897. The city was crawling with gold miners, traders, merchants, and soldiers; commerce often was conducted with gold. This was a regular stop for the fleet of steam paddleboats that traveled the Yukon, delivering passengers and supplies. Here, too, was **Fort Egbert**, a military installation that brought order to the gold boomtown.

A mature community when Fairbanks was still merely a forested bend on the Chena River, Eagle was then the seat of the Third Judicial District, with Judge James Wickersham on the bench. The judge would play a major role in Eagle's decline, however, when he made a deal with the founder of Fairbanks, E. T. Barnette, to move the judicial seat from Eagle to Fairbanks. The old courthouse has been restored to its days of yore, as have the old customs building and the adjacent Fort Egbert. Another Eagle landmark is the wind-powered water well that was dug in 1903 and continues to serve. From the waterfront, the stern-wheeler *Yukon Queen II* offers daily trips between Eagle and Dawson City.

At the river, you may see rafters preparing for a float trip from Eagle to Circle City, several days away by raft. Planning for this trip takes some extraordinary effort in shuttling vehicles and rafts, as Circle is hundreds of miles away by road at the end of the Steese Highway. But most say it's worth it for the experience of floating through this stretch of the **Yukon-Charley Rivers National Preserve**. The National Park Service offers informational talks, videos, publications, and books, along the river near Fort Egbert. Other rafters or canoeists may be arriving from a Dawson

City-to-Eagle excursion. (Having crossed an international border on the water, they need to check in with U.S. Customs at Eagle.)

Eagle is still a part of the active Fortymile Mining District, and gold-mining operations continue in this region. You may meet a gold miner or support crew member during your stay here, as the town is the nearest point of civilization for many of these folks. They'll come into town for mail, gossip, and a change of menu, as well as to stock up on supplies.

For more information on what Eagle has to offer, contact the Eagle Historical Society and Museums at 907-547-2325.

Lodging/Meals

Eagle Trading Co. Motel
Along the Yukon River, in Eagle
907-547-2220
Rooms, laundry, public showers. Store, fuel, café. Hunting and fishing licenses.

Falcon Inn
220 Front Street, Eagle
907-547-2254
Rooms with private baths, hot breakfast. Walking distance to museums. Along the Yukon River.

Campgrounds

The Bureau of Land Management oversees three camping areas along the Taylor Highway. They are open seasonally, mid-April to October, based on road openings. For more information, contact the Northern Field Office in Fairbanks at 907-474-2302 or visit the bureau's Web site at www.aurora.ak.blm.gov.

West Fork Campground
Mile 48.5 Taylor Highway
Developed campsites on 20 acres, with 7 pull-throughs, wheelchair-accessible toilets. Fishing.

Walker Fork Campground
Mile 82 Taylor Highway
21 developed campsites on 60 acres. Water, toilets, hiking trails, fishing, gold panning.

Eagle Campground
Mile 160 Taylor Highway
16 developed campsites on 80 acres, with toilets.

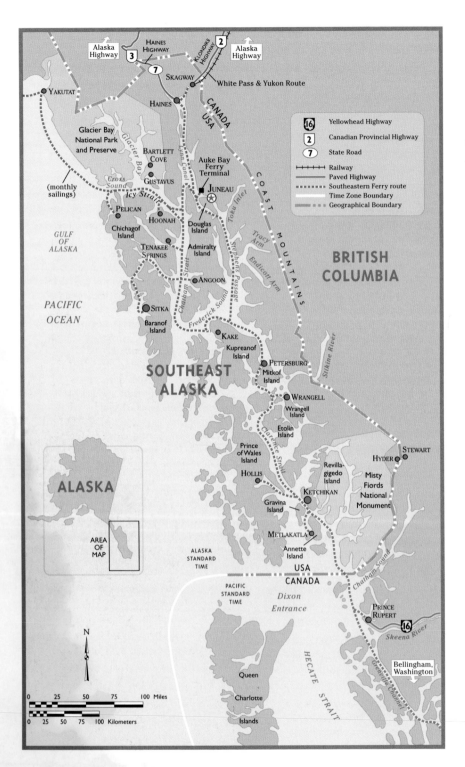

Alaska Highway [3]

HAINES HIGHWAY   Alaska Highway [2]

KLONDIKE HIGHWAY

[7] SKAGWAY

White Pass & Yukon Route

YAKUTAT

HAINES

CANADA
USA

Glacier Bay National Park and Preserve

BARTLETT COVE

Auke Bay Ferry Terminal

JUNEAU

COAST

[16] Yellowhead Highway
[2] Canadian Provincial Highway
[7] State Road
+++++ Railway
——— Paved Highway
••••• Southeastern Ferry route
Time Zone Boundary
▪ ▪ ▪ Geographical Boundary

Glacier Bay

(monthly sailings)

Cross Sound

GUSTAVUS

Icy Strait

PELICAN

HOONAH

Chichagof Island

Douglas Island

TENAKEE SPRINGS

Admiralty Island

Tracy Arm

Endicott Arm

Stephens Passage

Taku Inlet

Lynn Canal

BRITISH COLUMBIA

GULF OF ALASKA

PACIFIC OCEAN

ANGOON

SITKA

Baranof Island

Chatham Strait

Frederick Sound

KAKE

Kupreanof Island

MOUNTAINS

SOUTHEAST ALASKA

PETERSBURG

Mitkof Island

WRANGELL

Wrangell Island

Stikine River

Etolin Island

Prince of Wales Island

Clarence Strait

STEWART

HYDER

Revilla-gigedo Island

Misty Fiords National Monument

HOLLIS

KETCHIKAN

Gravina Island

ALASKA

AREA OF MAP

METLAKATLA

Annette Island

ALASKA STANDARD TIME

USA
CANADA

Chatham Sound

PACIFIC STANDARD TIME

Dixon Entrance

PRINCE RUPERT [16]

Skeena River

N

HECATE STRAIT

Greenville Channel

Bellingham, Washington

0   25   50   75   100 Miles

0   25   50   75   100 Kilometers

Queen

Charlotte

Islands

Chapter 9
Alaska Marine Highway System

*T*HE Inside Passage marine route from Washington to Alaska gained international fame in the late 1890s when Klondike miners and their gold arrived in Seattle and ignited a gold rush. The news spread quickly, and people came to believe that riches awaited in the north—and that all it took was to jump on a steamer headed up the Inside Passage.

The thrill of traveling by ship on the Inside Passage has taken on a new slant today. Even occasional dreary weather cannot suppress the extraordinary beauty of a trip on these protected waters between mainland and islands.

Three ferry systems operate in these waters. BC Ferries, an arm of British Columbia's transportation system, owns a fleet of more than 40 vessels of all sizes, which cruise among the islands and mainland ports of the province. From Victoria to Prince Rupert, with many stops between, BC Ferries connects with the Alaska Marine Highway System at Prince Rupert. The Inter-Island Ferry Authority operates between two Alaskan islands: Ketchikan on Rivillagegedo Island, and Hollis on Prince of Wales Island. Their Web site is *www.interislandferry.com*.

The Alaska Marine Highway System ferries, affectionately called the "blue canoes," stick to a routine schedule for picking up and dropping off passengers at coastal communities, almost like a vast city bus system. The vessels of the fleet also vary in size and in

The M/V Tustamena, *fondly known as "The Trusty Tusty," serves Homer and several other coastal communities in Southcentral Alaska.*

their specialized routes. Two new vessels joined the fleet in the summer of 2004: the M/V *Lituya,* on the Ketchikan-to-Metlakatla route, and the M/V *Fairweather,* a high-speed ferry that operates between Haines and Skagway on the Lynn Canal.

The southeastern portion of the Alaska system operates all the way from Bellingham, Washington, on the southern end, to Prince Rupert, B.C., then farther northward to the cities of Alaska's Inside Passage, up to Skagway.

The southcentral/southwestern portion of the Alaska system operates on a separate schedule with an entirely different fleet. That portion includes Cordova, Valdez, Whittier, Seward, Homer, Kodiak, Port Lions, and seven ports in the Aleutian Islands. The two parts of the Alaska system are connected in summers by the M/V *Kennicott,* the largest vessel in the fleet, which crosses the Gulf of Alaska twice each month.

People come aboard the Alaska state ferries on foot, sometimes for a day trip to a nearby town. Or they arrive in campers, ready to drive their rigs into the hold and then head upstairs to a stateroom and a warm bed. Others carry their belongings on their backs. Travelers without a stateroom are welcome to bunk under the stars on the vessel's top deck. This is freedom at its finest—come one, come all—and presents plenty of opportunity to make friends with someone from a local village or someone from the other side of the planet.

Major ports of call in Southeast Alaska are Ketchikan, Wrangell, Petersburg, Sitka, Juneau, Haines, and Skagway. Between them, shorter trips link Kake, Angoon, Tenakee, and Hoonah.

These ports each claim a unique personality: Petersburg, the fishing town with Norwegian roots; Sitka, the former capital of Russian America, as Alaska was known before its purchase by the United States; Native villages that welcome visitors eager to know more about Tlingit, Haida, and Tsimshian culture; Juneau, Alaska's capital—and, like most Southeast Alaska towns, inaccessible by road. Skagway and Haines, the northernmost ports in Southeast Alaska, are connected to the Alaska Highway by spur roads. (See the sections on the Haines Highway and Klondike Highway 2 in Chapter 8, "Alaska's State Highways.") Consider a southbound trip on the marine highway as a way to return home after your northbound drive up the Alaska Highway.

The cost for passage depends on distance between ports, whether a stateroom is reserved, length of your vehicle, and other factors. You can customize your trip so that you can disembark and tour the towns of your choice before continuing on your journey.

Here are some contacts for more information on marine travel in Alaska and along the Inside Passage:

Alaska Marine Highway System
1-800-642-0066 or 907-465-3941
www.ferryalaska.com

BC Ferries
1-800-448-7181
www.bcferries.com

Inter-island Ferry Authority
www.interislandferry.com

Further Reading

Canada

Berton, Pierre. *The Klondike Fever*. New York: Carroll & Graf, 1985.

———. *The Klondike Quest: A Photographic Essay 1897–1899*. North York, Ontario: Stoddart Publishing, 1997.

Bruhn, Karl. *Best of B.C.: Lake Fishing*. Vancouver, B.C.: Whitecap Books, 1998.

Coull, Cheryl. *A Traveller's Guide to Aboriginal B.C.* Vancouver, B.C.: Whitecap Books, 1996.

Madsen, Ken, and Graham Wilson. *Rivers of the Yukon: A Paddling Guide*. Whitehorse, Yukon: Primrose Publishing, 1990.

Neering, Rosemary. *A Traveller's Guide to Historic B.C.* Vancouver, B.C.: Whitecap Books, 1993.

Schofield, Janice J. *Discovering Wild Plants: Alaska, Western Canada, the Northwest*. Portland, Ore.: Alaska Northwest Books, 1989.

Short, Steve, and Bernie Palmer. *Best of B.C.: Exploring Canyons, Glaciers, Hotsprings, and Other Natural Highs*. Vancouver, B.C.: Whitecap Books, 1992.

Wolf Creek. *The Klondike Gold Rush: Photographs from 1896–1899*. Whitehorse, Yukon: Wolf Creek, 1997.

Zuehlke, Mark. *The Alberta Fact Book*. Vancouver, B.C.: Whitecap Books, 1997.

———. *The B.C. Fact Book*. Vancouver, B.C.: Whitecap Books, 1995.

———. *The Yukon Fact Book*. Vancouver, B.C.: Whitecap Books, 1998.

Alaska

Alaska Geographic. *Denali*. Portland, Ore.: Alaska Geographic Society, 1995.

———. *Kenai Peninsula*. Portland, Ore.: Alaska Geographic Society, 1997.

———. *Southeast Panhandle*. Portland, Ore.: Alaska Geographic Society, 1997.

Alaska Northwest Books. *The Alaska Almanac: Facts About Alaska, 28th ed*. Portland, Ore.: Alaska Northwest Books, 2000.

———. *The Alaska–Yukon Wild Flowers Guide*. Portland, Ore.: Alaska Northwest Books, 1990.

Armstrong, Robert. *Guide to the Birds of Alaska, 4th ed*. Portland, Ore.: Alaska Northwest Books, updated 2004.

Brown, Tricia, ed. *Alaskan Wilderness* (Discovery Travel Adventures). London: Discovery Channel Inc., 1999.

Brown, Tricia, and Roy Corral (photography). *Children of the Midnight Sun: Young Native Voices of Alaska*. Portland, Ore.: Alaska Northwest Books, 1998.

———. *Fairbanks: Alaska's Heart of Gold*. Portland, Ore.: Alaska Northwest Books, 2000.

Ewing, Susan. *The Great Alaska Nature Factbook*. Portland, Ore.: Alaska Northwest Books, 1996.

Hunt, William R. *North of 53°: The Wild Days of the Alaska–Yukon Mining Frontier, 1870–1914*. New York: Macmillan, 1974.

Jettmar, Karen. *The Alaska River Guide: Canoeing, Kayaking, and Rafting in the Last Frontier, 2nd ed*. Portland, Ore.: Alaska Northwest Books, 1998.

Kelley, Mark, and Sherry Simpson. *Alaska's Ocean Highways: A Travel Adventure Aboard Northern Ferries*. Seattle: Epicenter Press, 1995.

Littlepage, Dean. *Hiking Alaska*. Helena, Mont.: Falcon Publishing Co., 1997.

Morgan, Lael. *Good Time Girls of the Alaska–Yukon Gold Rush*. Seattle: Epicenter Press, 1998.

Murie, Margaret E. *Two in the Far North, 2nd ed*. Portland, Ore.: Alaska Northwest Books, 1997.

Murphy, Claire Rudolf, and Jane G. Haigh. *Gold Rush Women*. Portland, Ore.: Alaska Northwest Books, 1997.

Piper, Ernie. *Alaska Sportfishing*. Portland, Ore.: Alaska Geographic Guides, 1997.

Ritter, Harry. *Alaska's History: The People, Land, and Events of the North Country*. Portland, Ore.: Alaska Northwest Books, 1993.

Satterfield, Archie. *Chilkoot Pass: A Hiker's Historical Guide*. Portland, Ore.: Alaska Northwest Books, updated 2004.

Sherwonit, Bill. *Alaska's Bears: Grizzlies, Black Bears, and Polar Bears*. Portland, Ore.: Alaska Northwest Books, 1998.

Simmerman, Nancy (photography), Helen Nienhueser, and Johnson Wolfe. *55 Ways to the Wilderness of Southcentral Alaska, 4th ed*. Seattle: The Mountaineers Books, 1994.

———— and Tricia Brown. *Wild Alaska: The Complete Guide to Parks, Preserves, Wildlife Refuges, & Other Public Lands, 2nd ed*. Seattle: The Mountaineers Books, 1999.

Smith, Dave. *Backcountry Bear Basics: The Definitive Guide to Avoiding Unpleasant Encounters*. Seattle: The Mountaineers, 1997.

————. *Alaska's Mammals*. Portland, Ore.: Alaska Northwest Books, 1995.

Distance Charts

Distances in Western Canada and the U.S.

*In **Miles** and Kilometers*

Origin	Cache Creek, BC	Calgary, AB	Dawson City, YT	Dawson Creek, BC	Edmonton, AB	Fairbanks, AK	Fort Nelson, BC	Great Falls, MT	Prince George, BC	Seattle, WA	Watson Lake, YT	Whitehorse, YT
Anchorage, AK (mi)	2135	2160	515	1608	1975	363	1281	2473	1678	2435	967	724
(km)	3416	3456	824	2573	3160	581	2136	3960	2685	3896	1611	1158
Cache Creek, BC (mi)		438	1722	527	545	2013	800	753	277	294	1139	1411
(km)		701	2755	843	872	3221	1280	1205	443	470	1822	2258
Calgary, AB (mi)			1747	549	108	2037	835	315	635	738	1164	1436
(km)			2795	878	291	3259	1336	504	1016	1181	1862	2298
Dawson City, YT (mi)				1195	1562	393	900	2078	1390	2022	586	327
(km)				1912	2499	629	1501	3325	2318	3235	976	523
Dawson Creek, BC (mi)					367	1488	282	867	250	821	612	886
(km)					587	2395	451	1387	400	1314	979	1418
Edmonton, AB (mi)						1855	630	500	442	790	979	1253
(km)						2968	1050	800	737	1264	1566	2005
Fairbanks, AK (mi)							1206	2353	1728	2313	875	601
(km)							1930	3765	2781	3701	1400	962
Fort Nelson, BC (mi)								1335	532	1027	330	604
(km)								2225	851	1712	528	966
Great Falls, MT (mi)									790	681	1615	1731
(km)									1317	1090	2692	2731
Prince George, BC (mi)										571	737	983
(km)										914	1228	1639
Seattle, WA (mi)											1272	1707
(km)											2120	2781
Watson Lake, YT (mi)												274
(km)												438
Whitehorse, YT												

To read, choose a place-name at the bottom of a column and scan upward to meet the corresponding horizontal line.

Distances within Alaska

In **Miles** *and* Kilometers

	Circle	Delta Junction	Eagle	Fairbanks	Glennallen	Haines	Homer	Prudhoe Bay	Seward	Skagway	Tok	Valdez
Anchorage	520 / 832	338 / 541	501 / 802	363 / 581	187 / 299	775 / 1240	226 / 362	847 / 1355	127 / 204	832 / 1331	328 / 525	304 / 486
Circle		260 / 416	541 / 866	162 / 259	411 / 658	815 / 1304	746 / 1194	1972 / 3155	646 / 1034	872 / 1395	368 / 589	526 / 842
Delta Junction			281 / 450	98 / 157	151 / 242	805 / 1288	564 / 902	587 / 939	464 / 742	603 / 965	108 / 173	266 / 426
Eagle				379 / 606	324 / 518	620 / 992	727 / 1163	868 / 1389	627 / 1003	579 / 926	173 / 277	427 / 683
Fairbanks					249 / 398	653 / 1045	584 / 934	489 / 783	487 / 779	710 / 1136	206 / 330	364 / 582
Glennallen						589 / 942	413 / 661	738 / 1181	313 / 501	636 / 1018	141 / 226	115 / 184
Haines							1001 / 1602	1142 / 1827	901 / 1442	359 / 574	447 / 715	701 / 1122
Homer								1073 / 1717	173 / 277	1058 / 1693	554 / 886	530 / 848
Prudhoe Bay									973 / 1557	1199 / 1918	695 / 1112	853 / 1365
Seward										958 / 1533	454 / 726	430 / 688
Skagway											504 / 806	758 / 1213
Tok												254 / 406
Valdez												

Index

Page numbers in **bold italic** font indicate maps.

100 Mile House, 104

Abbotsford, 89; weather, 36
Access Canada, 36
air shows: Fort St. John, 125; Lethbridge, 48
airstrips, 127–28
Alaska: Department of Transportation and Public Facilities, 187; fishing licenses, 28; hunting licenses, 29–30; maps, *118*, *182*, *268*; record snowfalls, 238; Scenic Byways, 186; state campgrounds, 25; state fair, 208; state highways, 182–267; State Troopers, 23–24; Time Zone, 35, 152; vocabulary, 23; weather, 35; wheelchair access, 36
Alaska Aviation Museum, 213
Alaska Highway, *118*–68, 185; Alaska/Yukon border to Tok, 152; avoiding wildlife while driving, 131; building of, 38–41; cost, 39; Dawson Creek to Fort St. John, 123–24; Delta Junction to Fairbanks, 160; facts, 39; 50th anniversary, 41; Fort Nelson to Muncho Lake, 120–31; Fort St. John to Fort Nelson, 127–28; highest point, 131;

historic sites, 41; Interpretive Centre, 136; joined with Richardson Highway, 156, 160; junction, 149–50; length, 39; longest bridge, 139; lowest point, 128; map, *118*; mileposts, 127; Muncho Lake to Watson Lake, 133–36; official end, 156, 160; Teslin Lake to Whitehorse, 141; Tok to Delta Junction, 155; unofficial end, 160; Watson Lake to Teslin, 139; Whitehorse to Alaska-Yukon border, 149–50
Alaska Islands and Oceans Visitors Center, 258
Alaska Marine Highway System, 186, 188, 219–20, 224, 237, 243, 246, 258, *268*–70; information, 270; map, *268*; ports, 270
Alaska Maritime National Wildlife Refuge, 258
Alaska Native Heritage Center, 211, 213
Alaska Railroad, 186, 196, 211, 231
Alaska SeaLife Center, 246
Alaska state highways, *182*–267; information, 187; maintenance of, 186;

map, *182*; names/numbers/lengths/descriptions, 184–85; winter conditions, 186, 265. *See also individual entries*
Alaska Wildlife Conservation Center, 244
Alberta, 43–85; facts, 44; fishing license, 27; hunting license, 29; Legislature Building, 71; maps, 8, 42, 86; tourism, 44; weather, 36; wheelchair access in, 36
Alcan Highway. *See* Alaska Highway
alcohol, 24
Alyeska Ski Resort, 243
ammunition, 28–29
amusement parks: Calgary, 58; Chilliwack, 90; Edmonton, 79. *See also* family activities; water parks
Anchorage, 209–19; attractions/history, 209–13; campgrounds, 217; festivals/events, 210–11; Fur Rendezvous, 211; lodging, 214–16; Log Cabin Visitor Information Center, 210; Museum of History and Art, 213; restaurants, 217–19; Town Square Park, 213; weather, 35

Anchorage Coastal
Waterfowl Refuge, 242
Ancient Voices
Wilderness Camp, 175
Apple Farm, The, 90
Arctic Circle, 179, 193
Arctic Circle Trading
Post, 200
Ashcroft Manor & Tea
House, 100
Athabascan people,
171, 187, 197, 202, 205,
209, 258
Aurora, 188
aurora borealis.
See northern lights

Barkerville, 107
Barrowtown Pump
Station, 89
baseball, 162
BC Ferries, 269;
information, 270
bears, 128
Beaver Creek, 150
Beaverlodge, 84
Bellevue Mine, 53
Big Delta Bridge, 158
bird-watching:
Anchorage Coastal
Waterfowl Refuge, 242;
Calgary, 59;
Chilkat Bald Eagle
Preserve, 220–21;
Copper River Delta, 188;
Creamer's Field
Waterfowl Refuge, 162;
Fairbanks, 162; Grande
Prairie, 81; Homer, 258;
Inglewood Bird
Sanctuary, 59; Kenai
Fjords National Park,
246; Palmer Hay Flats
State Game Refuge,
209; Tetlin National
Wildlife Refuge, 152;
Williams Lake, 105;
Yukon Flats National
Wildlife Refuge, 193

bison:
Babe the Blue bison,
162. *See also* buffalo
Blackfoot Confederacy
tribes, 47, 57
border crossings, 24;
Alaska/Yukon border,
152, 177;
with children, 26–27;
with guns, 28–29;
Sumas (Washington/
British Columbia), 89;
Sweetgrass (Montana/
Alberta), 45
Braeburn Lodge, 170
Bridal Falls, 90
British Columbia, 87–117,
119–36; campground
reservations, 25; facts,
88; fishing license,
27–28; hunting license,
29; maps, *8, 42, 86, 118;*
weather, 36; wheel-
chair access in, 36.
See also BC Ferries
Buckinghorse, 127
buffalo, 54, 56, 156;
Head-Smashed-In
Buffalo Jump, 54
Burwash Landing,
weather, 35

cabins, Chugach
National Forest, 189.
See also campgrounds
Caboose Park, 101
Cache Creek, 101–4;
attractions/history,
101–2; campgrounds,
104; jade, 103; lodging,
103–4; restaurants, 104
Calaway Park, 58
Calgary, 57–64;
attractions/history,
57–59; campgrounds,
62–63; Exhibition
and Stampede, 58;
lodging, 59–62;
restaurants, 63–64;

Science Centre, 58;
weather, 36;
Zoo Botanical Garden
& Prehistoric Park, 58
cameras, 19–20
Campbell Highway,
Watson Lake to North
Klondike Highway, 180
campgrounds, 24–25;
115 Creek Provincial
Campsite, 130;
Anchorage, 217;
Cache Creek, 104;
Calgary, 62–63;
Central, 255; Chena
Lakes Recreation Area,
158; Chetwynd, 116;
Chilliwack, 91–92;
Circle City, 255;
Circle Hot Springs, 255;
Coldfoot, 195; Cordova,
189; Dawson City, 176;
Dawson Creek, 122;
Deadhorse, 195;
Delta Junction, 156–57;
Dempster Highway, 179;
Denali Highway, 197;
Denali National Park,
235–36; Denali State
Park, 230; Devon, 75;
Eagle, 267; Edmonton,
75; Elliott Highway, 203;
Ester, 236; Fairbanks,
167; Fort Macleod, 55;
Fort Nelson, 129–30;
Fort St. John, 126;
Girdwood, 248;
Glenn Highway, 206;
Glennallen, 216;
Grande Prairie, 83–84;
Haines/north of Haines,
222; Hells Gate, 98;
Homer, 261–62; Hope,
96; Johnson's Crossing,
141; Kenai, 259–60,
262–63; Kenai Spur
Highway, 259; Kenaitze
Indians, 260; Kenny
Lake, 199; Leduc, 75;

Lethbridge, 50–51;
Lytton, 100;
Manley Hot Springs,
203; Milk River, 45;
Muncho Lake, 132;
Northway Junction, 152;
Palmer, 216;
Portage, 248;
Prince George, 112–13;
Quesnel, 108; Red Deer/
Red Deer area, 67–68;
Seward, 248; Sherwood
Park, 76; Skagway, 226;
Soldotna, 262;
Spring Lake, 76;
Squanga Lake, 141;
Sterling, 261–62;
Sterling Highway, 258,
260–63; Stony Plain, 76;
Takhini Hot Springs,
147; Teslin Lake, 140;
Testa River Regional
Park, 130; Toad River,
131; Tok, 155; Valdez,
240; Valleyview, 80;
Wasilla, 235–36; Watson
Lake, 137; Whitecourt,
78–79; Whitehorse, 147;
Whitehorse, west of,
148; Williams Lake, 106
Canada: gun regulations,
28–29; Royal Canadian
Mounted Police, 33;
vocabulary, 25–26.
See also Alberta;
British Columbia;
Northwest Territories;
Yukon Territory
Canyon City, 143–44
Cariboo gold rush, 97,
100, 108
Cariboo Jade & Gifts, 103
Cariboo Trail, 97
Cariboo Wagon Road,
100, 102, 105
caribou, Fortymile herd,
266
Carmacks, 171
casinos, Dawson City, 174

Cassiar Highway, 139;
Yellowhead Highway to
Alaska Highway, 180–81
cats, traveling with, 32
cell phone service, 26
Central, 254;
lodging/campgrounds/
meals, 255
chainsaw sculpture:
Chetwynd, 115;
Hope, 93
Champagne, 149
charts:
distances, 273, 274;
metric conversion, 31;
temperature
conversion, 35
Chatanika Lodge, 253
Chena Hot Springs
Resort, 251
Chena Lakes Recreation
Area, 158
Chetwynd, 115–17;
attractions/history,
115–16; campgrounds,
116; Greenspace Trail
System, 115–16;
Leisure Wave Pool, 116;
lodging, 116;
restaurants, 116–17;
Visitor Information
Centre, 115
Chicken, 265;
attractions/history, 265
children,
traveling with, 26–27.
See also family activities
Chilkat Bald Eagle
Preserve, 220–21
Chilkat Indians, 220
Chilkoot Indians, 220
Chilkoot Trail, 224
Chilliwack, 89–92; attrac-
tions/history, 89–90;
campgrounds, 91–92;
festivals, 90; lodging, 91;
Museum, 90; restau-
rants, 92; Visitor
Information Centre, 90

Chinook Country Tourist
Association, 46, 48
Chitina, 197–98;
attractions/history,
197–98; lodging/
camping/meals, 199
Chugach National Forest,
188; cabins, 189
Chugach State Park,
211–13
Church of St. John the
Divine, 97
Church Street, 71
Circle City, 255;
lodging/campgrounds/
meals, 255
Circle Hot Springs, 254–55;
lodging/campgrounds/
meals, 255
Claresholm, 56;
Claresholm Museum,
56
Cleary Summit, 253, 254
clothing, 14
coal mining, 53
Coldfoot, 193;
campgrounds, 195;
lodging/meals, 194
Collicutt Centre, 66
Contact Creek, 133
Continental Divide,
139, 194
conversion charts:
metric, 31;
temperature, 35
Cooper Landing, 257;
lodging, 259;
restaurants, 263
Copper River Basin,
205–6
Copper River Delta,
187–89
Copper River Delta
Shorebird Festival, 188
Copper River Highway,
186; Cordova to Million
Dollar Bridge, 187–89;
length/number/
description, 184

Coquihalla Canyon Provincial Recreation Area, 94
Cordova, 187–89; attractions/history, 188–89; campgrounds, 189; Iceworm Festival, 188; lodging, 189; Museum and Library, 188; restaurants, 189
Country Living Festival, 90
Creamer's Field Waterfowl Refuge, 162
Crow Creek Mine, 243
Crowsnest Pass, 53
Cruise America, 18
cruising:
Dawson City, 174–75;
Delta Queen, 266;
Edmonton, 71;
Fairbanks, 164;
Haines to Skagway, 220;
Heritage Park, 60;
Kenai Fjords National Park, 246;
Muncho Lake, 132;
Portage Glacier, 183;
Whitehorse, 144–45
Crystal Lake Waterfowl Refuge, 81
Cultus Lake, 90

Dalton Highway, 185, 186; Elliott Highway to Deadhorse, 190–95; length/number/description, 184
dams, 114
Dawson City, 172–76, 266; attractions/history, 172–75; campgrounds, 176; Dawson City Museum, 173; lodging, 175–76; restaurants, 176; weather, 35
Dawson Creek, 120–23; attractions/history, 120–21;

campgrounds, 122; Exhibition & Stampede, 121; lodging, 121–22; Mile 0, 85, 120, 121; restaurants, 122–23; Visitor Information Centre, 121; weather, 36
daylight hours, 27
Deadhorse, 191–92, 194; campgrounds, 195; lodging/meals, 194–95
Dease Lake, 139
Delta Junction, 156–58, 160, 185, 239; attractions/history, 156–57; campgrounds, 156–57; lodging, 157; restaurants, 157–58; Visitor Information Center, 157
Dempster Highway, 175; Interpretive Centre, 179; North Klondike Highway to Inuvik, 179
Denali Highway, 186, 230, 239; campgrounds, 197; length/number/description, 184; lodging/meals, 197; Richardson Highway to Parks Highway, 196
Denali National Park and Preserve, 196, 230–31; campgrounds, 235–36; lodging, 230, 232–35; restaurants, 236; weather, 35
Denali State Park, 230
Department of Transportation and Public Facilities, Alaska, 187
Devil's Coulee Dinosaur Egg Interpretive Centre, 46
Devon, 68–69; campground, 75

Devonian Botanic Garden, 69
Devonian Gardens, 59
Dickson-Stevenson Stopping House, 64–65
dinosaurs, 46, 58, 73, 81, 114
distance charts:
towns in western Canada and U.S., 273;
towns within Alaska, 274
dogs, traveling with, 32
dog sledding, 171;
dog trucks, 139;
Iditarod Trail Sled Dog Race, 211, 228;
Yukon Quest International Sled Dog Race, 145, 162, 171
Dorothy Page Museum & Historical Townsite, 228
driving:
avoiding wildlife, 131;
road manners, 33;
in winter, 20–21. *See also* RV travel; vehicles
Drumheller, 73
Drunken Forest, 206
duty-free shopping, 27
Dyea, 225

E. L. Patton, 193
Eagle, 266–67; attractions/history, 266–67; lodging/meals/campgrounds, 267; weather, 35
Eagle Motorplex, 101
Eagle Plains, 179
Eagle River Outfitting, 78
eagles, Chilkat Bald Eagle Preserve, 220–21. *See also* bird-watching
Eagle Summit, 254
Eagle Trail State Recreation Site, 203
earthquake, Good Friday, 188, 209, 237, 243, 246

Eastern Route (Alberta
to Dawson Creek),
42–85; Calgary to
Red Deer, 64–65;
Edmonton to
Whitecourt, 77–78; Fort
Macleod to Calgary, 56;
Grande Prairie to
Dawson Creek, 84–85;
Lethbridge to Fort
Macleod, 52; map, *42;*
Montana border to
Lethbridge, 45–46;
Red Deer to Edmonton,
68–69; Whitecourt to
Grande Prairie, 80
Edgerton Highway, 186,
238; length/number/
description, 184;
Richardson Highway
to Chitina, 197–99
Edmonton, 69–77; attrac-
tions/history, 69–71;
campgrounds, 75;
festivals, 70; lodging,
71–75; restaurants,
76–77; shopping, 79;
Tourism, 71; weather, 36
Edmonton Queen, 71
Eielson Air Force Base, 158
Eklutna Historical Park,
209
Eldorado Gold Mine, 166,
200
Elliott Highway, 252;
campgrounds, 203;
Fox to Manley Hot
Springs, 200–203;
length/number/
description, 184;
restaurants, 200
Elsa, 170
Engineer Hill, 251
equipment. *See* supplies
Ester: campgrounds, 236;
restaurants, 236
Ester Gold Camp, 166, 231
events.
See festivals/events

Exit Glacier, 244

Fairbanks, 160, 161–68,
251, 252; attractions/
history, 161–64;
campgrounds, 167;
Convention and
Visitors Bureau, 164;
hiking/walking, 200;
lodging, 164–67;
restaurants, 167–68;
weather, 35
Fairweather Express, 220
family activities:
Calgary, 58, 59;
Chetwynd, 116;
Chilliwack, 90;
Edmonton, 79;
Fairbanks, 163;
Red Deer, 65–66;
Tok, 153
Faro, 180
ferries:
BC Ferries, 269, 270;
George Black Ferry, 173;
Inter-Island Ferry
Authority, 269, 270;
McKenzie River, 179;
Peel River, 179.
See also Alaska Marine
Highway System
festivals/events:
Chilliwack, 90;
Cordova, 188–89;
Delta Junction, 156;
Edmonton, 70;
Fairbanks, 161, 162;
Harrison Hot Springs,
93; Homer, 258;
Lethbridge, 47–48;
Lytton, 99; Quesnel, 108;
Talkeetna, 229;
Valdez, 238
first-aid kit, 20
First Nations people, 81,
100, 110, 149, 171, 175.
See also Native
culture and history;
individual entries

Fish Creek Community
Forest, 124
fishing: Chetwynd, 116;
Chitina, 198;
Delta Junction, 156;
Denali Highway, 196;
derbies, 257;
Fort St. John, 124;
Haines, 221;
Homer, 259; Hyland
River Bridge, 136;
information, 257;
Kenai Peninsula, 257;
Kenai River, 257;
Matanuska-Susitna
Valley, 208;
Muncho Lake, 132;
Parks Highway, 228;
Prince George, 109;
Quesnel, 108; Russian
River, 257; Seward, 246;
Squanga Lake, 141;
Whitecourt, 78
fishing licenses, 27–28
fish ladder, 144
fish wheels, 198
Five Finger Rapids, 171
Fort Calgary Historic
Park, 58
Fort Edmonton Park, 70–71
Fort George Park, 109
Fort Macleod, 52–55;
attractions/history,
52–53; campgrounds,
55; Empress Theatre,
52; lodging, 55;
restaurants, 55;
Tourism Information
Centre, 52
Fort McPherson, 179
Fort Nelson, 128–30;
attractions/history,
128–29; campgrounds,
129–30; Heritage
Museum, 129;
Information Centre, 129;
lodging, 129;
restaurants, 130;
weather, 36

Fort St. John, 124–26;
air show, 125;
campgrounds, 126;
lodging, 125–26;
restaurants, 126;
Visitor Information
Centre, 124
Fort Seward, 220
Fort Wainwright, 159
Fort Whoop-Up
Interpretive Centre, 47
Fortymile River, 177
Fox, 200, 252;
attractions/meals, 252
Fox Creek, 80
Fox Lake, 170
Fox Roadhouse, 252
Frank Slide, 53
"Frantic Follies, The," 144
Fraser Canyon, 97–98
Fraser-Fort George
Regional Museum, 109
fuel, 28
Fur Rendezvous, 211

Galaxyland Amusement
Park, 79
gardens:
Calgary, 59;
Chilliwack, 90;
Devon, 68–69;
Lethbridge, 48;
Tok, 153
gasoline, 28
geology, Lytton jellyroll,
101
George Black Ferry, 173
George Johnston
Museum, 140
George Parks Highway.
See Parks Highway
Girdwood, 243;
campgrounds, 248;
lodging, 246;
restaurants, 248, 250
Glacier National Park, 49
Glenbow Museum,
Art Gallery, Library
and Archives, 58

Glennallen, 205–6;
campgrounds, 216;
lodging, 215–16;
restaurants, 217
Glenn Highway, 153, 185,
227; campgrounds,
206; length/number/
description, 184; Tok
to Anchorage, 203–9.
See also Tok Cutoff
gold dredges:
Chatanika, 253;
Jack Wade No. 1, 265;
No. 4, 173; No. 8, 166,
251–52, 253
gold mining, 107, 251–52,
253; Chatanika, 253;
Crow Creek Mine, 243;
Dawson City, 172–73;
Eagle, 267;
Ester Gold Camp, 231;
Fairbanks, 164, 166, 200;
Fox, 200;
Independence Mine
Historical Park, 207;
Keno, 170; Livengood,
200–2; Mayo, 170;
Wiseman, 193–94
Goldpan Provincial Park,
100
gold rush: Cariboo, 97,
100, 107; Klondike, 142,
143, 161, 171, 172, 223;
Pedro Creek, 251
Gold Rush Cemetery, 225
golf: Calgary, 59;
Chetwynd, 116;
Chilliwack, 90; Dawson
City, 174; Edmonton, 70;
Fort Nelson, 129;
Fort St. John, 124;
Lethbridge, 48;
Watson Lake, 136–38;
Whitecourt, 77;
Williams Lake, 105
Graham Acre Golf and
Country Club, 77
Grande Prairie, 81–84;
attractions/history, 81–82;

campgrounds, 83–84;
lodging, 82–83;
Museum, 81;
restaurants, 84;
Stompede, 82; Visitor
Information Centre
2000, 81; weather, 36
Great Divide Waterfall, 70
Gulkana, 205
Gulkana River, 239
guns, 28–29

Haines, 219–23;
attractions/history,
219–21; campgrounds,
222; lodging, 221–22;
restaurants, 222–23;
weather, 35
Haines Highway, 186;
Haines Junction to
Haines, 219–23;
length/number/
description, 185
Haines Junction, 149–50
halibut, 257
Harrison Hot Springs, 93
Hatcher Pass Road, 207;
lodging/meals, 207
Hat Creek Ranch, 102
Haul Road.
See Dalton Highway
Head-Smashed-In Buffalo
Jump, 54
health insurance, 30
Healy, 231; lodging, 235
Helen Schuler Coulee
Centre, 47
Hells Gate, 97–98;
Airtram, 97–98
Henderson Lake Golf
Course, 48
Heritage Park, 60
Heritage Ranch, 61
Hicks Creek Roadhouse,
206
High Level Bridge, 46
High River, 56
hiking.
See walking/hiking

Homer, 184, 185, 256, 257, 258–59; attractions/history, 258–59; campgrounds, 261–62; lodging, 260; restaurants, 264; weather, 35
Homer Spit, 259
honey, 124
Hope, 93–97; attractions/history, 93–94; campgrounds, 96; lodging, 94–96; Memorial Park, 93; restaurants, 96–97; Visitor Information Centre, 94
hot springs: Chena Hot Springs Resort, 251; Circle Hot Springs, 254–55; Harrison Hot Springs, 93; Liard River Hotsprings Provincial Park, 133; Manley Hot Springs, 202–3; Takhini Hot Springs, 145, 170
Hudson's Hope Loop, 114, 125
hunting license, 29–30

ice carving, Fairbanks, 163
Iditarod Trail Sled Dog Race, 211; headquarters, 228
igloo, Parks Highway, 230
Independence Mine, 228; Historical Park, 207
Indian: lodging, 247; restaurants, 250
Indian Battle Park, 47
Inglewood Bird Sanctuary, 59
Inside Passage, 269
insurance, 30
Inter-Island Ferry Authority, 269; information, 270

Inuvik, 179
Iron Creek Lodge, 136
Isabel Pass, 238

Jack London Cabin and Interpretive Centre, 173–74
Jack Wade No. 1 gold dredge, 265
jade, 103
Johnson's Crossing, 141
Juneau, weather, 35

Kachemak Bay Shorebird Festival, 258
Kenai, 257–58; campgrounds, 259–60, 262–63; lodging, 260; restaurants, 264
Kenai Fjords National Park, 246
Kenai National Wildlife Refuge, 256
Kenai Peninsula, 256–59
Kenai Spur Highway, 258, 259
Kenaitze Indians, 258; campground, 260
Kennecott Mine, 199
Kennicott, 199; lodging/camping/meals, 199
Kenny Lake, lodging/camping/meals, 199
Keno, 170
Kerry Wood Nature Centre, 65
Ketchikan, weather, 35
kilometers, metric conversion, 31
King Mountain, 206
King Mountain Lodge, 206
Kleskun Hills, 81
Klondike, 142
Klondike gold rush, 142, 143, 171, 172, 223
Klondike Gold Rush National Historical Park, 224

Klondike Highway 2: Alaska Highway to Skagway, 223; length/number/description, 185
Klondike Loop, 169; Dempster Highway, 179; North Klondike Highway, 169–71; Taylor Highway, 265–66; Top of the World Highway, 177
Klondike Visitors Association, 173
Kluane Lake, 150
Kluane Museum of Natural History, 150
Knik River, 209
Kwaday Dan Kenji, 149

Ladd Air Field, 159
Lake Laberge, 170
Leduc: campground, 75; No. 1 Historic Site, 66–67
Leitch Collieries, 53
length of Alaska Highway, 39
Lethbridge, 46–51; attractions/history, 46–48; campgrounds, 50–51; Lethbridge & District Exhibition Park, 47; lodging, 49–50; Nikka Yuko Japanese Garden, 48; restaurants, 51; weather, 36
Liard River Hotsprings Provincial Park, 133
Links of GlenEagles, 59
Lion Head, 206
Lion's Heritage Park, 100
Little Nelchina, 206
Livengood, 200–2
lodging, 30; Anchorage, 214–16; Cache Creek, 103–4;

Calgary, 59–62; Central, 255; Chetwynd, 116; Chilliwack, 91; Chitina, 199; Circle City, 255; Circle Hot Springs, 255; Coldfoot, 194; Cooper Landing, 259; Cordova, 189; Dawson City, 175–76; Dawson Creek, 121–22; Deadhorse, 194; Delta Junction, 157; Denali Highway, 197; Denali National Park and Preserve, 230; Denali Park, 232–35; Eagle, 267; Eagle Plains, 179; Fairbanks, 164–67; Fort Macleod, 55; Fort Nelson, 129; Fort St. John, 125–26; Girdwood, 243, 246; Glennallen, 215–16; Grande Prairie, 82–83; Haines, 221–22; Hatcher Pass Road, 207; Healy, 235; Homer, 260; Hope, 94–96; Indian, 247; Kenai, 260; Kennicott, 199; Kenny Lake, 199; Lethbridge, 49–50; Manley Hot Springs, 203; McCarthy, 199; Moose Pass, 247; Muncho Lake, 132; Prince George, 111–12; Red Deer, 66–6; Seward, 247–48; Skagway, 226; Soldotna, 260; Sterling, 259; Teslin Lake, 140; Tok, 153–55; Valdez, 239–40; Wasilla, 232; Watson Lake, 137; Whitecourt, 78; Whitehorse, 145–47; Williams Lake, 106; Wiseman, 194; Yukon River Bridge, 194

London, Jack, Cabin and Interpretive Centre, 173–74
Long Lake, 206
Long Rifle Lodge, 206
Lytton, 98–100; attractions/history, 98–100, 101; weather, 36
Lytton jellyroll, 101

MacBride Museum, 144
Manley Hot Springs, 202; campgrounds, 203; lodging/meals, 203
maps: Alaska/Canada/ northwest U.S. state, provincial, and interstate highways, *8*; Alaska Highway, *118*; Alaska Marine Highway System, *268*; Alaska state highways, *182*; Eastern route, *42*; Western Route, *86*
Matanuska, 188
Matanuska Glacier, 206
Matanuska River Valley, 206
Matanuska-Susitna Colony Project, 207
Matanuska-Susitna Valley, 207–8
Mayo, 170
McCarthy, 199; attractions/history, 199; lodging/camping/ meals, 199
McCarthy Road, 198–99
McKenzie Meadows Golf Club, 59
McKenzie River ferry, 179
medical needs, 20
metric conversion, 31
Midnight Dome, 172
Midnight Sun Baseball Game, 162

mileposts, 127; Mile 0, 85, 120; Mile Zero Park, 121; numbering, 127
Milk River, 45
Million Dollar Bridge, 188
mining. *See* coal mining; gold mining
Minter Gardens, 90
Minto, 202
money, 31–32
Montague House, 170
Montana, interstate highway, 8
moose, encounters with, 37
Moose Dropping Festival, 229
Moose Pass: lodging, 247; restaurants, 250
mosquitoes, 32
Mountain Mama Contest, 229
Mounties. *See* Royal Canadian Mounted Police, 33
Mount McKinley, 196, 230. *See also* Denali National Park and Preserve
Mukluk Land, 153
Muncho Lake, 132; lodging/campgrounds/ meals, 132
Museum of Alaska Transportation & Industry, 228
Museum of the Cariboo Chilcotin, 105
Museum of the North-West Mounted Police, 52
museums: Anchorage, 213; Barkerville, 107; Beaverlodge, 84; Burwash Landing, 150; Calgary, 57–58, 60; Central, 254;

Chilliwack, 90;
Claresholm, 56;
Dawson City, 172, 173;
Drumheller and
vicinity, 73;
Edmonton, 70–71;
Fairbanks, 162;
Fort Macleod, 52–53;
Fort Nelson, 129;
Fort St. John, 125;
Grande Prairie, 81;
Homer, 258–59;
Keno, 170;
Lethbridge, 48;
Nanton, 56;
Pouce Coupe, 84;
Prince George, 109;
Quesnel, 108; Red
Deer, 65–66; Skagway,
224–25; Teslin Lake,
140; Valdez, 238;
Wasilla, 228;
Watson Lake, 136;
Westaskiwin, 69;
Whitehorse, 144;
Williams Lake, 105;
Wiseman, 194
Muskoseepi Park, 81
Musk Ox Farm, 206–7
Muskwa Bridge, 128

Nancy Lake State
Recreation Area, 228
Nanton, 56
Nanton Lancester
Society Air Museum, 56
Native culture and
history, 53, 54, 57, 81,
100, 162;
Alaska Native Heritage
Center, 213;
Anchorage, 210, 213;
Calgary, 57;
Carmacks, 171;
Champagne, 149;
Chilliwack, 90;
Chitina, 197; Copper
River Delta, 187;
Dawson City, 175;

Eklutna Historical
Park, 209; Fort
Macleod, 53, 54;
Glennallen, 205;
Haines, 220;
Head-Smashed-In
Buffalo Jump, 54;
Kenai, 258;
Lethbridge, 47;
Lytton, 100; Minto, 202;
Native-made art, 110,
202, 210, 258;
Pelly Crossing, 171;
Prince George, 110;
Teslin Lake, 140;
Williams Lake, 105
Niitsitapi people, 57
Nikiski, 258
Nikka Yuko Japanese
Garden, 48
Ninilchik, 258
Nisutlin Bay Bridge, 139
North Klondike Highway,
Alaska Highway to
Dawson City, 169–71
North Peace Museum, 125
North Pole, 158–59; attrac-
tions/history, 158–59
North Slope, 194
Northern Alberta
Railway Park, 120–21
northern lights, 254;
Fort Nelson, 129;
research, 253;
Watson Lake, 136
Northern Lights Space
and Science Centre, 136
Northway Junction, 152
Northwest Staging Route,
127–28
Northwest Territories, 179;
map, 8
Northwood Inc., 109

Odyssium, 71
oil, 68–69, 70; Copper
River Delta, 187;
pipeline, 191, 202, 237,
238, 251

Old Calgary Trail, 61
Oldman River, 52
Olympic Hall of Fame
and Museum, 58

Palace Grande Theatre,
174
Palmer, 207–8;
attractions/history, 208;
campgrounds, 216;
restaurants, 217
Palmer Hay Flats State
Game Refuge, 209
Paradise Canyon Golf
Resort, 48
parks.
See individual entries
Parks (George) Highway,
186, 196, 209; Anchorage
to Fairbanks, 227–31;
length/number/
description, 185
Patton, E. L., 193
Paxon, 239
Peace Canyon Dam, 114
Peace River, 80
Pedro Creek, 251
Peel River ferry, 179
Peigan Nation Annual
Celebration and
Powwow, 53
Peigan Reserve, 53
Pelly Crossing, 171
petroglyphs, 45–46, 105
pets, 32
photography, 19–20
pictographs, 45–56
Piikani Lodge
Interpretive Centre, 53
Pink Mountain, 127
Pinnell Mountain
National Recreation
Trail, 254
Pioneer Park, 163
pipeline, 191, 202, 237,
238, 251
Plains Indians, 54
Poker Flat Rocket Range,
253

police: Alaska State
Troopers, 23–24;
Royal Canadian
Mounted Police, 33
Poplar Hills Golf and
Country Club, 129
Portage, 243–44;
campgrounds, 248;
restaurants, 249
Portage Glacier, 183,
243–44
Portage Lake, 243
postage, 33
Pouce Coupe, 84
Pratt Museum, 258–59
Prince George, 109–13;
attractions/history,
109–10;
campgrounds, 112–13;
lodging, 111–12;
restaurants, 113;
weather, 36
Prince George Railway
and Forestry Museum,
109–10
Prophet River, 127
Provincial Museum of
Alberta, 70
Prudhoe Bay, 191–92, 194;
weather, 35.
See also Deadhorse
Ptarmigan, 183

qiviut, 207
Quesnel, 108;
Quesnel Museum, 108

rafting: Eagle, 266–67;
Lytton, 98–99;
Matanuska River, 206;
McCarthy, 199;
Yukon-Charley Rivers
National Preserve, 266
Rancheria Falls
Recreation Site, 139
recreational vehicles.
See RV travel
Red Deer, 65–68; attrac-
tions/history, 65–66;

campgrounds, 67–68;
lodging, 66–67;
restaurants, 68
restaurants, 33;
Anchorage, 217–19;
Cache Creek, 104;
Calgary, 63–64; Central,
255; Chetwynd, 116–17;
Chilliwack, 92; Circle
City, 255; Circle Hot
Springs, 255; Coldfoot,
194; Cooper Landing,
263; Cordova, 189;
Dawson City, 176;
Dawson Creek, 122–23;
Deadhorse, 194–95;
Delta Junction, 157–58;
Denali Highway, 197;
Denali Park, 236;
Eagle, 267; Edmonton,
76–77; Elliott Highway,
200; Ester, 236;
Fairbanks, 167–68;
Fort Macleod, 55;
Fort Nelson, 130;
Fort St. John, 126;
Fox, 252; Girdwood, 243,
248; Glennallen, 217;
Grande Prairie, 84;
Haines, 222–23;
Hatcher Pass Road, 207;
Hells Gate, 98; Homer,
264; Hope, 96–97;
Indian, 250; Kenai, 264;
Kennicott, 199; Kenny
Lake, 199; Lethbridge,
51; Manley Hot
Springs, 203; McCarthy,
199; Moose Pass, 250;
Muncho Lake, 132;
Palmer, 217; Portage,
250; Prince George,
113; Red Deer, 68;
Seward, 250; Skagway,
226–27; Soldotna,
263–64; Teslin Lake,
140, 141; Toad River,
131; Tok, 155; Valdez,
241; Wasilla, 236;

Watson Lake, 139;
Whitecourt, 80;
Whitehorse, 148–49;
Williams Lake, 106–8;
Wiseman, 194; Yukon
River Bridge, 194–95
Reynolds-Alberta
Museum, 67
Richardson Highway,
153, 156, 158, 185, 186,
196, 203, 205; Delta
Junction to North Pole,
158; highest pass, 238;
length/number/
description, 185;
North Pole to
Fairbanks, 159; Valdez
to Fairbanks, 237–39
Rika's Roadhouse, 156
riverboats:
Edmonton Queen, 71;
Klondike, 142;
Riverboat Discovery, 164;
River Dancer, 175;
Schwatka, 144;
Tanana Chief, 164;
Yukon Queen II, 175, 266
River Dancer, 175
roadhouses: Ashcroft
Manor & Tea House,
100; British Columbia,
100, 102; Chatanika
Lodge, 253; Delta
Junction, 156–57;
Dickson-Stevenson
Stopping House,
64–65; Fox Roadhouse,
252; Hicks Creek
Roadhouse, 206; King
Mountain Lodge, 206;
Long Rifle Lodge, 206;
Montague House, 170;
Rika's Roadhouse, 156;
Sheep Mountain
Lodge, 206; Sullivan
Roadhouse, 156.
See also lodgings;
restaurants
Robert Service Cabin, 173

rock flour, 156, 206
rock graffiti, 139
rodeos:
    Calgary, 57, 58;
    Dawson Creek, 121;
    Edmonton, 70;
    Grande Prairie, 82;
    High River, 56;
    Lethbridge, 50; museum,
    105; Quesnel, 108;
    Williams Lake, 105
Ross River, 180
Royal Canadian
    Mounted Police, 33
Royal Tyrell Museum of
    Paleontology, 73
Russian churches, 209, 258
RV travel, 16–19;
    Anchorage, 210;
    campgrounds, 25;
    Fort Nelson, 128;
    Grande Prairie, 81;
    North Pole, 159;
    road manners, 33;
    Watson Lake, 136;
    Whitehorse, 145.
    See also campgrounds

salmon, 257; Chitina, 198;
    Whitehorse, 144.
    See also fishing
Santa Claus House, 159
Schwatka, 144
Schwatka Lake, 142–43
Scout Island Nature
    Centre, 105
Selkirk Heritage Centre,
    171
Service, Robert, Cabin, 173
Seward, 244–45;
    attractions/history,
    244–46; campgrounds,
    248; lodging, 247–48;
    restaurants, 250;
    weather, 35
Seward Highway, 184, 186;
    Anchorage to Seward,
    242–46; length/num-
    ber/description, 185

Sheep Mountain Lodge,
    206
Sheldon Museum and
    Cultural Center, 220
Shepherd's Inn, 127
Sherwood Park,
    campgrounds, 76
shopping:
    duty-free, 27;
    gold, 172;
    jade, 103;
    Native-made art, 110,
    202, 210, 258
signpost forest, Watson
    Lake, 136, 138
Sikanni Chief, 127, 128
Silver Trail, 170
Sir Alexander Galt
    Museum & Archives, 48
Skagway, 141, 224–27;
    attractions/history,
    224–25; campgrounds,
    226; lodging, 226;
    Museum and Archives,
    224–25; restaurants,
    226–27; weather, 35
Skihist Provincial Park,
    100
skiing:
    100 Mile House, 104;
    Prince George, 109
sled dogs.
    See dog sledding
Smith, "Soapy," 225
snowfall:
    Thompson Pass, 238;
    Valdez, 238
snowmobiling, 266;
    Trek Over the Top,
    177, 266
Soldiers Summit, 150
Soldotna, 257;
    campgrounds, 262;
    lodging, 260;
    restaurants, 263–64
solstice, 27, 193, 254;
    celebrations, 162
South Peace Centennial
    Museum, 84

Spring Lake,
    campground, 76
Squanga Lake, 141
state fair, 208
State Troopers,
    Alaska, 23–24;
    museum, 213
Steese Highway, 159,
    186, 200; Fairbanks to
    Circle City, 251–55;
    length/number/
    description, 185
Sterling, 257;
    campgrounds, 261–62;
    lodging, 259
Sterling Highway, 185, 186;
    campgrounds, 258,
    260–63; length/number/
    description, 185;
    Seward Highway to
    Homer, 256–59
Sterling Highway (town),
    257
Sto:lo Native Interpretive
    Centre and
    Longhouse, 90
Stony Plain,
    campground, 76
Sullivan Roadhouse, 156
Sumas, 89
Sunnybrook Farm
    Museum and
    Agriculture Interpretive
    Centre, 65–66
supplies: clothing, 14;
    emergency, 15;
    medical, 20;
    miscellaneous, 14;
    RV, 18; vehicle, 15;
    winter, 21
Sweetgrass, 45
swimming: Chena Lakes
    Recreation Area, 158;
    Fort St. John, 124;
    Red Deer, 66.
    See also water parks
Sylvan Lake, 66
Takhini Hot Springs, 145,
    170; campgrounds, 147

Talkeetna, 228–30; attractions/history, 228–30
Tanana Valley, 251
Tangle Lakes, 196, 197
Taylor Highway, 152, 169, 186; Alaska Highway to Eagle, 265–66; length/number/description, 185; snowmobiling, 177
Teetering Rock, 131
telephones, cell phone service, 26
temperature conversion, 35
Ten Mile Lake Provincial Park, 108
Teslin Lake: attractions/history, 140; length, 139; lodging/campgrounds/restaurants, 140, 141
Teslin River Bridge, 141
Tetlin Junction, 152, 265
Tetlin National Wildlife Refuge, 152
theaters: Dawson City, 174; Fort Macleod, 52; Whitehorse, 144
Thompson Pass, 238
time zones, 35, 85; Alaska Time Zone, 152; Pacific Time Zone, 85
Tlingit Indians, 140, 220, 223
Toad River, 131
Tok, 153–55, 203; attractions/history, 153; campgrounds, 155; lodging, 153–55; restaurants, 155
Tok Cutoff, 153, 203–5, 239
Top of the World Golf Course, 174
Top of the World Highway, 152, 169, 186, 265–66;

Dawson City to Alaska/Yukon border, 175, 177; snowmobiling, 177
Totem Village Tribal House, 220
Town Square Park, 213
trains: Alaska Railroad, 186, 196, 211, 231; Northern Alberta Railway Park, 120–21; Prince George Railway and Forestry Museum, 109–10; White Pass & Yukon Route Railway, 144, 224
Trans-Canada Highway (Highway 1), 8, 42
Transportation and Public Facilities, Alaska Department of, 187
travel planning, 12–21. See also insurance; money; pets
Trek Over the Top, 177, 266
Tsuu Tina Culture Museum, 57
Turnagain Arm, 242–43
Twelve-Mile Summit, 254

University of Alaska: Fairbanks, 253; Museum of the North, 162

Valdez, 237–38; attractions/history, 237–38; campgrounds, 240; lodging, 239–40; Museum, 238; restaurants, 241
Valleyview, 80
vehicles: driving in winter, 20–21; emergency equipment, 15;

insurance, 30; road manners, 33; supplies, 15. See also driving vocabulary: Alaska, 23; Canada, 25–26
volcanoes, 258

W.A.C. Bennett Dam, 114
walking/hiking: Chetwynd, 115–16; Fairbanks, 200; Fort St. John, 124; Grande Prairie, 81; Hope, 94; Lethbridge, 47; Pinnell Mountain National Recreation Trail, 254
Warner, 45
Wasilla, 227–28; attractions/history, 227–28; campgrounds, 235; lodging, 232; restaurants, 236
water parks: Chetwynd, 116; Chilliwack, 90; Edmonton, 79; Red Deer, 66
Waterton Lakes National Park, 49
Watson Lake, 136–39; attractions/history, 136–37; campgrounds, 137; lodging, 137; restaurants, 139; Signpost Forest, 136, 138; weather, 35
weather: Alaska, 35; Alberta, 36; British Columbia, 36; Yukon Territory, 35
West Edmonton Mall, 70, 79
Westaskiwin, 69
Western Boot Factory, 71

Western Route (British Columbia to Dawson Creek), 86–117; Cache Creek to Williams Lake, 104; Chilliwack to Hope, 93; Hope to Lytton, 97–98; Lytton to Cache Creek, 100–101; map, *86;* Washington border to Chilliwack, 89; Washington to British Columbia border, 89; Williams Lake to Prince George, 108

Weyerhaeuser Canada, 82

wheelchair access, 36

Whitecourt, 77–80; attractions/history, 77–78; campgrounds, 78–79; lodging, 78; restaurants, 80; Tourist Information Centre, 77

White Mountains National Recreation Area, 200

White Pass & Yukon Route Railway, 144, 224

Whitehorse, 142–49; attractions/history, 142–45; campgrounds, 147; Fishway, 144; lodging, 145–47; restaurants, 148–49; Visitor Reception Centre, 142; weather, 35

Whittier, 243

Whoop-Up Days, 47–48

Wickersham Dome, 200

wildlife, 36–37; Alaska Maritime National Wildlife Refuge, 258; Alaska Wildlife Conservation Center, 243; avoiding while driving, 131; Calgary, 59; Denali National Park and Preserve, 231; Fort Macleod, 52; Kenai Fjords National Park, 246; Kenai National Wildlife Refuge, 256; Lethbridge, 47; Lytton, 99; Palmer Hay Flats State Game Refuge, 209; Seward Highway, 242, 243; Taylor Highway, 266; Tetlin National Wildlife Refuge, 152; Whitehorse, 142; Wrangell–St. Elias National Park and Preserve, 203–5; Yukon Flats National Wildlife Refuge, 193; Yukon Territory, 140. *See also* buffalo; moose; zoo

Williams Lake, 105–8; attractions/history, 105; campgrounds, 106; lodging, 106; restaurants, 106, 108; Stampede, 105; Visitor Information Centre, 105

Williamson Provincial Park, 80

Willow, 228

Willow Creek Parkway, 228

Willow Creek State Recreation Area, 228

winter driving, 20–21

Wiseman, 193–94; Historical Museum, 194; lodging/meals, 194–95

Wonowon, 127

World Ice Art Championships, 163

World War II, 40

World Waterpark, 79

Worthington Glacier, 238

Wrangell–St. Elias National Park and Preserve, 197, 198, 203–5; Visitor Center, 238–39

Writing-on-Stone Provincial Park, 45–46

Xats'ull Heritage Village, 105

Yale, 94, 97

Yellowhead Highway (Highway 16), 8, 42, 77, 110; name origin, 181; Prince George to Cassiar Highway, 180

Yukon Beringia Interpretive Centre, 144

Yukon-Charley Rivers National Preserve, 266

Yukon Crossing Visitor Contact Station, 193

Yukon Flats National Wildlife Refuge, 193

Yukon Lou, 174–75

Yukon Queen II, 175, 266

Yukon Quest International Sled Dog Race, 145, 162, 171

Yukon River, 141, 143; Devil's Punchbowl, 143; George Black Ferry, 173; Schwatka Lake, 142–43

Yukon River Bridge, lodging/meals, 194

Yukon Territory, 136–51; campgrounds, 25; facts, 141; fishing licenses, 28; hunting licenses, 29–30; map, *118;* North Klondike Highway, 169–71; provincial highways, 8; weather, 35; wheelchair access in, 36; wildlife, 140

Yukon Transportation Museum, 144

zoo, Calgary, 58

About the Author

Perry and Tricia Brown, with their traveling companion, Kvichak [QUEE-chak], who was named for a great river in southwestern Alaska.

TRICIA BROWN first traveled the then-unpaved Alcan in 1978, in a memorable 4,000-mile move from northern Illinois to Fairbanks. She has been writing articles and books on Alaska subjects for nearly twenty-five years. A former editor of *Alaska* magazine, Tricia has traveled extensively throughout the state, both on and off the road system. Her travel books include *Fairbanks: Alaska's Heart of Gold, Iditarod Country, Alaskan Wilderness*, and children's books: *Children of the Midnight Sun* and *Groucho's Eyebrows*. Tricia and Perry met in 1980 at the University of Alaska Fairbanks, where she was studying journalism and he was a geology graduate student (and an avid fisherman). Together they have explored many thousands of miles in Alaska and Canada. They currently make their home in Scappoose, Oregon, and frequently visit friends and family in Alaska.